P9-EDQ-833

FEMINISM
From Pressure to Politics

FEMINISM

From Pressure to Politics

edited by

Angela R. Miles
and
Geraldine Finn

Montréal - New York

Canadian Cataloguing in Publication Data

Main entry under title:
  Feminism: from pressure to politics

2nd rev. ed.
First published under title: Feminism in Canada.
Bibliography p.
IBSN 0-921689-23-3 (bound). –ISBN 0-921689-22-5 (pbk.).

I. Feminism. 1. Miles, Angela Rose II. Finn, Geraldine.

HQ1111.F45 1989   305.4′2   C88-090104-7

Cover design: Richard Parent

Black Rose Books

C.P. 1258   340 Nagel Drive
Succ. Place du Parc   Cheektowaga, New York
Montréal, Québec   14225 USA
H2W 2R3 Canada

Printed in Canada
A publication of the Institute of Policy Alternatives of Montréal (IPAM)

Table of Contents

PART ONE
Scholarship: Theory and Practice

PART TWO
Politics: Theory and Practice

Acknowledgements

Chapters One, Two, Six, Eight, and Fourteen of this book are based on presentations made in a day-long feminist inter-disciplinary session organized by the editors for the 1981 Annual Meeting of the Canadian Political Science Association. The editors wish to thank the Association for its very real material and logistical support in presenting the session.

Wendy Johnston wrote the Introduction to her translation of Madeleine Gagnon's work in 1978. Her political views have changed substantially since that time, but she nevertheless very kindly agreed to have it published here.

Karen Flikeid and Francine Sylvestre-Wallace contributed their time as translators as well as their encouragement. Their sisterly support turned what could have been nightmare difficulties with translation into fine feminist network-building.

This book reflects one aspect of the ongoing development of feminist praxis in Canada. It is the product of the activism and the thought, the cooperation and the dialogue of many women. We hope that some of the commitment, excitement, enthusiasm, and sisterhood of that practice has come through in the book. It certainly did in the long process of putting the book together, and for that we thank all the contributors, our editor at Black Rose, Jane Broderick, and our sisters in struggle everywhere. We hope they will find this volume a useful contribution to their continuing work.

Angela Miles and Geraldine Finn

Introduction
to the Second Edition

Angela Miles

Thirteen of these articles were originally published in 1983 as a collection entitled *Feminism in Canada: From Pressure to Politics*. Chapters Four, Five, Twelve, Thirteen, Fifteen, and Eighteen have been added to this retitled second edition to extend the coverage generally and to include areas that have become important more recently.

The first edition of this book was among the first to pose systematically, across a number of disciplines, a challenge to the false masculine universal in the name of an alternative female subject. The displacement of the male as norm and universal—in these articles and others—was, at that time, beginning to open the way for a feminist critique of the very structures of patriarchal knowledge and for the development of feminist alternatives. The book is meant to document and support this scholarly and political project in its early stages and to show its centrality to the creation of women as full subjects and the development of a feminist politics that goes beyond pressure to seek the transformation of man's world rather than only women's inclusion in it.

The difference between feminisms that claim a specific voice and vision for women and those that do not is the difference between pressure politics and transformational politics, between politics that addresses the woman question and politics that addresses the whole of society. This is the most important political division within feminism today, but it is masked by our tendency to use, in our analyses, categories like "liberal feminism," "socialist feminism," and "radical feminism," which cut across this divide. These categories are all built around feminism's relationship to other politics and emphasize differences among us that are rooted in these politics rather

11

than more significant differences in feminism itself. Although many of us use these labels for self-definition, our differences with feminists who use the same labels are often as great or greater than with others who use different ones. The labels do not actually correspond in any consistent way to the political realities we actually experience.

The term "integrative feminism," as defined in the Introduction to the first edition, was coined to distinguish, as broadly as possible, between feminism as a full politics and feminism as pressure. The aim of the book is to reveal transformative feminism as a tendency of the women's movement through the presentation of articles on diverse topics, in a variety of disciplines, by feminists with different self-definitions so as to highlight the principles and vision they share. The hope has been to strengthen this radical or "integrative" tendency of feminism by identifying and defining it more clearly and consciously than has hitherto been the case.

In general, the collection has been successful in this. Each of the original thirteen articles has been influential in its field in Canada. The shared themes are clear and consistent enough for the book to add up to much more than the sum of its parts. It has been widely used in feminist classrooms and by feminist groups and has provided a theoretical resource for feminists in graduate schools, professions, communities, women's projects and campaigns, in their jobs, and in their homes to resist the tyranny of the linear logic of equality. This is the essentially anti-feminist logic that defines any recognition of our specific needs and sensibilities as contradictory to our claim of equality and insists that we deny our femaleness in its name. It requires that we accept and excel at all the worst competitive and individualistic aspects of society and social relations if we want our demands for equality to be taken seriously; that we, for instance, deny our discomfort with negative male rituals, resist our need for reciprocal support networks, repudiate maternity leave as "special treatment"— in fact, emulate men in all things.

Today we have more resources from which to draw in our resistance to this political attack. The development of a specifically feminist epistemology is well advanced in all fields. It is much more widely accepted that we make feminist politics from our experience and our point of view as women than it was when the first edition of this book was published. We are stronger and firmer in our critique of the male world itself, and not just its exclusion of us. In the 1980s it has become

12

more obvious that in order to develop the autonomous, alternative voice required to make this general politics we have to reclaim and redefine *woman* as *our* person, not simply deny her as man's creation.

The last ten years have seen the development of explicitly feminist activism among increasing numbers of ever more diverse women in both the "developed" world and the Third World. As new groups of women gain the power to be heard and feminism becomes a greater presence all over the world, integrative feminism has become stronger. For farm women, peasant women, working-class women, single mothers, aboriginal women, Black women, immigrant women, disabled women, and old women, gender, class, race, and colonial forms of oppression cannot be separated; feminism must be an attack on all systems of domination and it must be a full politics that speaks to the whole of society and not only to certain selected aspects.

Many of these women, as well, are speaking and acting from a longer and more intact tradition of female culture and organization and from a more secure woman identification than we in liberal urban settings have been able to draw on. The liberal ideology of equality and sameness and progress has been used to mask the dependent and subordinate integration of women into men's world, and to hide our loss of each other (a point that is explored in Chapter Five in "Inherited Biases Within Feminism"). In the 1960s, young, urban North American feminists consciously and courageously (and joyfully) rediscovered a sense of shared oppression and identity as women that most rural and traditional women have never lost. North American feminism's hard-won recognition of women's specificity is strengthened and enriched by our exchanges with Third World and rural women whose lives and identity remain more firmly connected to other women; and integrative feminism's conscious affirmation of women's specificity as the necessary basis for a transformational politics provides a framework for those exchanges across our diversity.

As our international movement grows and our networks and understanding develop, women in the "modernized" world who have lived this process and learned to know its consequences for women even in the rich nations are connecting with women who are now experiencing the negative consequences of "development" for themselves and their communities in the Third World. We are joining forces to articulate a deeper critique and fuller alternatives than would be possible for either group of us alone. This shared process is reflected in Chapter Twelve, "A Feminist Perspective on Development."

Since the United Nations decade for women began in 1975, international and regional conferences, networks, and publications have provided the opportunity for general exchange and education and for focused strategizing and action on—to name just a few issues—female sexual slavery, antimilitarism/peace, women's studies, development, health, reproductive technology, clitoridectomy, economic equality, and violence against women. These issues, and the struggles around them, take different forms in Latin America, Asia, Africa, Europe, and North America, and for the various countries and groups of women within these regions. But at base they are all struggles against the same worldwide systems of domination. The emergence of feminism as a global politics both requires and ensures that we understand this. We are learning, sometimes not without difficulty and pain but often with celebration, that the diversity of our experiences of oppression and of struggle is a resource for our analysis and our vision. Because our unity must be consciously forged, and this can only be done at the deepest level of critique and transformation, our differences force us to extend ourselves and to go deeper in our understanding.

Theory and practice in the Third World have provided much of the energy for feminism's development in recent years, and integrative politics in North America has benefitted from this. However, political developments here have also been important. Feminists in Canada and the United States are operating in a right-wing climate. Free Trade's threat to cultural and economic sovereignty and survival in Canada, imperialist aggression and outlawry in the United States, and increasing inequality and poverty in both countries are driving home the need to fight on all fronts.

Yet, paradoxically, our relative success in achieving liberal reforms for women has revealed the limits of equality. "Equality with a vengeance" is giving divorced women smaller shares of family property, smaller support payments, and weaker custody claims, jailing women who refuse to testify against their batterers, and taking parental rights away from birth mothers with surrogacy agreements. Chapter Four, which deals with "Feminism and Law," documents all this as well as the new, specifically feminist critique of liberalism that is emerging in response, and the beginnings of an integrative strategy for feminist lawmaking.

14

Despite the fact that feminism has been much strengthened as a transformative politics since this book first appeared, the collection has not outlived its usefulness.

The same right-wing pressures that are forcing a broad and inclusive politics on feminists make it a possibility that we will lose our voice and identity and power in general liberal and left coalitions unless we consciously foster the autonomy and specificity that this collection keeps central.

The strident right-wing glorification of woman's difference in the interests of our subservience is making some feminists more hesitant to acknowledge that difference in the interests of our liberation. So the message of these articles—that truly radical feminist politics cannot be built on the denial of women—is still timely. The support this offers for feminists to resist the intimidation of the right, and the pressure of liberals and the left to do that, is still important.

The increasing diversity of our movement and the difficult but rewarding attention to that diversity in practice is fueling a deeper radicalism and a deeper understanding of our shared struggle among some feminists. But it is leading others to doubt the possibility of a shared analysis and struggle and to distrust claims of women's shared condition and concerns. Articles in this volume are an important testimony to the fact that recognizing women's commonality is the necessary condition for the exploration of women's diversity, and not the denial of diversity that it is sometimes presumed to be.

In recent years, deconstructionists—including some feminists—have extended feminism's important critique of patriarchy's false knowledge claims to criticize all knowledge claims, and have carried the unseating of men's false status as universal subject to the unseating of all subjects. The work collected here presents an important counter-viewpoint to this disabling relativism.

Feminist radicalism is under constant threat of recuperation, co-optation, destruction, and attack by conservatives, liberals, and the left; by both the establishment and the opposition. This volume is a record and celebration of the continuing development of feminism's radical vision. At the same time, the theoretical framework it supplies continues to be a much-needed resource in the struggle to maintain and strengthen that vision.

Introduction
to the First Edition

Angela Miles

Since the 1960s, the women's movement has grown from its origins in mainstream politics,[1] the civil rights movement, and the New Left to become the most widespread, varied, and sustained social movement in North America. A large part of both its reform and its radical activity consists of pressure for women to have access to the rights, activities, and responsibilities commonly available to men, and to be "let in" to full participation in all areas of society as it currently exists. For some, including some feminists, this adequately describes the totality of feminism's programme.

However, much women's-movement activism is based on a wider sense of feminism's project and significance. The authors in this volume, like many other feminists, speak and act from a large sense of historical purpose in which their concerns, their forms of practice, and their vision represent a major break with the existing male-defined world and politics. For these feminists, solidarity among women—defining the world from women's point of view, building women's autonomy as individuals and as a collective power—is not merely the addition of one more "constituency" to an existing radical politics nor only the articulation of the interests of yet one more special-interest group. It is, instead, a qualitatively new challenge to domination, by a group whose relatively recent arrival on the political stage marks a major departure for progressive struggle in general.

The domination of women by men precedes the emergence of class domination and is structured deeply into the relations of production and reproduction of almost all known societies. Although understanding of the dynamics of gender oppression across class, culture, and time is at an embryonic stage, we know that this oppression is the most profound condition of alienation, the deepest division of humanity within itself and from itself, upon which all other fragmentation and domination has been built. The political emergence of women acting consciously against this domination and fragmentation is therefore not just the activation of a new interest group. It is a major historical event that holds the promise of enabling a more complete challenge to domination than has been possible ever before.

This means that feminist autonomy of organization and theory is necessary not just to enable continued pressure to be brought to bear to improve the conditions of women's lives and challenge our inequality in the world as it is. Feminist autonomy is also essential to the development of a specifically female view of the world and a set of interests, priorities, and values that can articulate the new and deeper challenge to domination that women's growing activism *as women* makes possible. The articles gathered here have been selected from among the Canadian and Québec feminist writing that most clearly expresses this unique female vision and its important liberatory potential.

The work is, without exception, committed scholarship. It recognizes no separation between research, analysis, and practice. For these authors, "the goal of the process of discovery is transformation (self and societal) as much as understanding" (McCalla Vickers), and all would agree with Margaret Benston when she says:

> We are feminists because we believe not only that the evidence shows the oppression of women, but, further, that such oppression is wrong. We also believe that society should be changed to end all forms of oppression. Our scholarship is done in that context, but also in the belief that the closer one gets to the truth the better the cause of women will be served. At the core of the feminist critique of the various disciplines is the attempt to fashion intellectual tools that are freer from the distortions of present male scholarship and that allow us to seek the truth while we recognize our commitment.

Jill McCalla Vickers and Margaret Benston, in the first two articles of this collection, explore the general methodological questions raised by explicitly committed scholarship. The themes they raise are echoed and illustrated by the other authors in both parts of the book. But this commitment to social change, however essential to feminist scholarship and practice, is not unique to it. These articles are distinguished not by commitment to change alone, but by their commitment

18

to a particular type of social change built through the affirmation of values long associated with women and with reproduction[2] and relegated to the margins of male-dominated industrial society. Devalued and subordinated values, characteristics, and activities, such as caring, sharing, cooperation, nurturing, intuition, and emotion, shape the core vision articulated in these articles and give new meaning to established progressive values such as equality, justice, and freedom, which are necessary to feminism but which are not sufficient.[3]

It is the unique focus on women-centred questions and values, for instance, that allows Jill McCalla Vickers' critique of methodology in the social sciences to go beyond that of the post-positivists with whom she acknowledges her affinity, enables Margaret Benston to develop a fuller critique of scientific method than its Marxist or humanist critics have managed to do, and underlies the challenge to established psychology that Jeri Dawn Wine outlines in Chapter Three. In fact, it is the articulation of these female and reproduction-associated values that has provided the framework for the feminist project in general to move beyond simple pressure for women's inclusion in the world to become a full politics concerned with transforming the world.[4]

Women have the most immediate interest in, and are in the best structural position to begin to build, a progressive struggle that can affirm female-associated reproductive concerns and values as the basis for a liberatory integration of life around our human needs and capabilities. In its articulation of these values, feminist struggle speaks to the growing potential for an unprecedented liberatory fusing of individual and collective self-development, of material and cultural production, of production and consumption (reproduction), of work and life, and of the personal and the political, in both its current practice and in the new world to be created—that is, as both means and end of a new politics.

Feminism is thus opening the way for a healing of the industrial fragmentation of life. As a new vision emerges of life and society integrated around the requirements of the reproduction of self-actualizing human beings rather than the production of things, the abstract Marxist notion of non-alienated man*,[5] for the first time, gains real substance as a guide to practice. In this, feminism plays a central role in breaking with male-dominated radicalism's restricted definitions of the world and of politics.

19

Changing material conditions today, in which the motor of social development has extended beyond its industrial locus in the narrow production sphere to the whole of social life,[6] have opened the political stage to significant participation by ever-widening groups of people, transforming and broadening the definition of "the people" in the process. Feminism is the cutting edge of that transformation, transcending and incorporating Marxism's earlier truths to reflect the values expressed in a broader popular struggle waged by a redefined and feminized humanity. I have called the tendency of feminism that most clearly articulates this integrative and feminizing project "integrative feminism."[7] The articles collected here reflect the powerful common themes that link integrative feminists through all their apparent diversity.

There are, of course, many feminists who do not see feminism as a politics that must presume to transform and broaden liberatory struggle in general through the affirmation of a new set of female-associated integrative values and a new vision of the world. Some liberal feminists perceive their struggle as simple pressure for the extension of civil and economic rights to women. Some Marxist, socialist, and anarchist feminists fail to question existing radical politics and definitions. They push instead for the incorporation of women and women's issues into an already existing and presumed complete framework of analysis and struggle. Some radical and lesbian feminists refuse this male-defined framework, not to transform and transcend it in the development of a new and fuller—though feminized—radicalism, but to focus only on women and women's issues as the necessarily separate ground of feminist struggle.

There are, however, large numbers of other liberal, Marxist, socialist, anarchist, radical, and lesbian feminists, who, despite the wide diversity of their concerns and analyses, share a feminism that goes beyond pressure to represent an embryonic new politics of general relevance and universal significance. The activities and views of these feminists are far too varied, and at times even contradictory, to constitute a common acceptance of any single political line. But their sense of feminism as a potentially complete politics nevertheless unites them more closely with each other across liberal, socialist, radical, and lesbian feminist lines than with other feminists of like self-definition.[8] The authors of the articles here are, by label, socialist, Marxist, lesbian, radical, and anarchist feminists. They differ in many of the specifics of their arguments

20

and terminology, and some may even disagree that integrative feminism exists as a tendency of the women's movement or refuse their inclusion in it. Nevertheless, despite the wide variety of subject matter, their work shares major integrative and feminizing themes.

All the authors presume that the female characteristics, concerns, and abilities marginalized in industrial society are necessarily central to the building of a new, more fully human society. The holistic, collective, intuitive, co-operative, emotional, nurturing, democratic, integrated, internal, and natural are affirmed against the over-valuation of the competitive, analytical, rational, hierarchical, fragmented, external, and artificial (man*-made).[9] Long subordinated reproduction-related values and activities are affirmed as the organizing principle of an integrated non-alienated society in which the current deep dualities of life in our fragmented society are overcome. In the articles in this volume the public/private and production/reproduction divides receive most attention. But the personal/political, means/end, man*/nature,[10] theory/practice, commitment/objectivity, mental/manual, emotion/logic, and intuition/reason divides are also common themes.

The authors all presume that feminist revolution/evolution will involve a total integrative restructuring of society and human relations. They accord women and the articulation of women's concerns and values a necessarily central role in the progressive struggle toward that change. Their emphasis on reproduction-related and female-associated values as the key to feminist social change takes their critiques of established social science, psychology, economics, history, anthropology, philosophy, social work, politics, and political theory beyond proscription to prescription. In the process of criticizing established disciplines and politics, most of these articles lay out guidelines for the development of feminist scholarship and politics. The authors present imminent critiques that do not simply reject or negate current thought, but point the way to a whole new level of analysis and action that can incorporate and transcend that thought. This feminism neither accepts male-defined politics and scholarship wholesale nor rejects it outright. Integrative feminism seeks neither inclusion in, nor separation from, that politics and scholarship, but its long-term transformation on integrative feminist lines.

From this, it follows that the authors here advocate neither simply abandoning nor simply entering male-defined and male-dominated contexts. They place absolute priority on autonomous feminist political organization and development as the core of feminist practice; but see participation in male-dominated activities as equally necessary to the pursuit of their struggle. Since the integrative feminist project involves redefining the whole of politics and life, rather than just adding women's issues to existing arenas and agendas, autonomy is essential to building the sisterhood and developing the consciousness and theory to challenge these definitions and contexts. It provides the power base from which women can mass pressure and develop new ideas outside organizations in support of those (often the same) women struggling inside them. All the articles, therefore, maintain a difficult dual stress on the need both to maintain a transforming involvement in male-dominated spheres and to foster autonomous political development and practice. In this they stand together as important examples of the growing capability of current feminism to refuse apparently logical and necessary either/or choices that would reduce our politics to mere pressure.

It is clear that all the authors are writing in the context of an active and widespread social movement whose practice both informs the questions they address and tests their answers. Engaged as they are in a common political project with many thousands of women within and beyond the university, they benefit from the fresh insights, irreverence, and support of those outside their particular discipline and milieu. Common questions of praxis breach the barriers between the disciplines, between intellectual work and activism, and between culture and politics. Dialogue becomes possible and necessary among feminists *as feminists* and not simply as historians, psychologists, anthropologists, social workers, economists, scientists, and philosophers. Insights, information, and theoretical advances in one area are followed, eagerly criticized, and used in others. Themes originating in one discipline or arena are taken up and developed in others. Debates cut across disciplines and move from politics and the movement to the university and back again.

While this political sisterhood provides the inspiration and support to challenge received opinion, it also imposes the discipline and responsibility of opposition. The risk of challenging established power is great, and the costs can be high. The move from "apprentice" to men in academe or social movement and servant of men in the home to autonomous feminist is a painful and dangerous transition. The seas are

22

uncharted, the winds strong, and the port unknown. All the authors here are on this journey. A number write about it:

- Helen Levine records her own and every woman's painful and continuing struggle to move beyond "defining the central and primary task of her life as marriage and motherhood."
- Carole Yawney describes her difficult transition from the "friendly paternalism'" of "university professors, police administrators, government ministers... and Dreadlocks brethren" to a new sisterhood in her anthropological field work.
- Geraldine Finn illustrates the difficult struggle of a woman-identified woman in, but not of, a "male chauvinistic and oppressive" philosophy that presents itself "sometimes unthinkingly, but more often now dogmatically, as the neutral and objective voice of 'reason'."

The immediate personal/political costs of feminist scholarship are the same as those of feminist activism and are required and sustained by the sisterhood and commitment of the same movement. The unity of theory and practice and the refusal of neutrality by feminist scholars is the affirmation of the subjectivity of both observer and observed. The refusal of the absolute division between researcher and researched, between scholar and activist, are two specific instances of the general feminist refusal of the fragmentation and dualism of "male-stream" thought and practice—a refusal shared and explicitly commented on by every author in this collection.

The particular integrative feminist terms of these authors' individual and collective refusal moves them from mere reactive negation of the limited and separative requirements of existing society and politics to a transcendent "negation of the negation" in the active positing of alternatives. The diverse refusals of these authors add up to an early expression of an alternative, as yet embryonic, liberatory praxis that speaks to the most advanced possibilities for human and social progress in our time.

23

The Articles

PART ONE
Scholarship

Jill McCalla Vickers, in Chapter One, examines five basic "methodological rebellions" of feminist scholarship whose challenge to the "underlying ontological order of patriarchal symbol systems," she argues, is its "chief political value."

> The more feminist scholars attempt to understand women's experience under patriarchy, the more apparent it becomes that our venture is more profoundly radical than most of us had ever imagined or, secretly, wished. No longer can we see the venture as one of filling in the blanks with missing nuggets of information here and there about women's experience. No longer can we be satisfied with critiques of the biases and blindness of disciplinary theories and paradigms. Finally, the frightening and exhilarating fact can no longer be ignored—we are embarked on a journey which has as its goal the complete reconstruction of human knowledge... [T]he most fundamental theories of being and knowing within patriarchy must be questioned from the point of view of women.

Margaret Benston, in Chapter Two, envisions a new, more human science in which male norms are no longer defining:

> Men are not expected to mix emotions or aesthetics or concern for the objects of study with rational thought. The male/female split of traits, in fact, makes "pure" rationality the ideal for men while leaving subjective factors as the feminine domain. In such a split, one can be either rational or subjective, but not both... From a feminist perspective, with its goal of transcending the limited human halves represented by male and female norms... what is needed is a methodology that does not, in fact, relegate the non-quantifiable aspects of a problem to secondary status, but instead attempts some kind of integration of this into scientific practice.

Jeri Dawn Wine, in Chapter Three, shows that the "underlying philosophy and methods [of male-stream psychology] are rigidly tied to a view of the nature of *man* that excludes women, and is antithetical to woman-centred values."

24

She goes on to argue that emerging research findings about

> women's connected relational selves, our sense of interdependence, our highly developed sense of responsibility... [have] profound implications for the understanding of the nature of human beings and the conduct of society. It is clear that the development of a fully feminist psychology constructed on gynocentric values and women-centred questions will transform not only knowledge of women but the nature of [a] psychology [based on androcentric values of separation, domination, rationality, and egocentrism] in every respect.

She points out that

> in challenging the individualistic "models of man" that underlie psychology, feminist psychology challenges the very underpinnings of male-dominated society.

Kathleen Lahey, in Chapter Four, shows that patriarchal Western law has developed historically to "define and appropriate women's reproductive, productive, and sexual capacities." She documents and celebrates the many successes women and feminists have won in our centuries-old struggle for reform even while she recognizes that male resistance and subversion have kept the law's essential patriarchal principles and purposes intact. Hers is a powerful and deeply radical argument that the success of current

> feminist legal reforms will depend not only on women's entry into law but also upon changes in the nature of law itself, in the nature of the state, and in the role that law plays. And these changes will require, as a minimum, being able to create the subjectmatter of law from the vantage point of women.

Linda Christiansen-Ruffman, in Chapter Five, identifies two major distortions of patriarchal sociology, which she calls the "either/or syndrome" and the "patricentric syndrome." Using detailed examples from her own research experience she illustrates the importance of rooting out these dualistic and male-centred tendencies in our own work as we develop feminist scholarship and practice. And she outlines specific analytic and research strategies to help us in these "massive remedial and reconstructive efforts [to develop] our knowledge structures."

Marjorie Cohen, in Chapter Six, shows that "economics has evolved a methodology which for the most part cannot 'see' women's economic behaviour."

> The productive nature of women's work is not counted. [Their] economic behaviour as consumers within the "household" generates some interest

but basically the household is viewed as a unit of consumption, not production... Excluding such a huge area of economic activity from economic accounting imposes serious limitations on the validity of what is counted.

[The discipline also presumes that] decision-making in the household is not markedly different than it is in the market... [and thus] reinforces the androcentric view of female behaviour, both in the home and in the paid labour market.

Alison Prentice and Ruth Pierson, in Chapter Seven, trace the movement of feminist historians beyond writing the history of "women worthies," which concentrated "solely on those women who have 'achieved' in terms of patriarchal norms," to "embrace the whole of women's experience of the past." In the process, not just women's lives but the whole of history begins to be re-viewed. The authors argue explicitly for an integrative approach that can encompass both women's equality and our specificity, women's sameness and difference, as a basis for feminist analysis and strategy:

It has been pointed out time and time again that feminist theorists do not agree on whether their long-term goal is to maximize female identity or to reject gender as a primary category. We argue that it is possible and desirable to pursue both goals at once, despite their apparent contradiction.

We, like the maternal feminists of the past, value many traits traditionally associated with the domestic sphere: nurturance, compassion, cooperation, and interdependence, among others. Like them also, we believe that a wider dissemination of these values would have a transforming effect on society...

If feminism is to be a liberating movement, it must not only reject simplistic dichotomies and the compartmentalization of women and men in separate spheres, it must go further and insist on the full complexity of human lives and possibilities... In this sense, liberty joins equality as a watchword of the movement.

Carole Yawney, in Chapter Eight, critiques both the Rastafarian movement and its anthropological observers as "co-conspirators in the patriarchy game," and shows that "the incorporation of women's experience into our study of these movements would transform our understanding of what they are all about."

Geraldine Finn, in Chapter Nine, illustrates the exclusively male definition of philosophy, in its institutions, language, and content, and the damaging consequences of its false presumption of universality. She argues not only that the institutions and practice of philosophy must become more accessible to women, but that its discourse must be transformed to recognize and represent the reality and experience of women

26

if it is to make any legitimate claims to universality. This transformation involves no mere addition of women's themes but a major challenge to the dualistic, abstract, rational, professional tradition of Western philosophy. It is a "reconstruction" of the tradition

> in the light of formerly forgotten and repressed questions and modes of being human, e.g., with respect to birth and reproduction and women's experience of time, space, self, language, etc.

Helen Levine, in Chapter Ten, movingly documents the experience of women in modern industrial patriarchy and shows that an emphasis on this shared experience makes possible a fusion of personal and political, public and private, in our struggle and our vision. In extracts from her diary during a stay in a mental institution she breaks the silence commonly imposed on women, to give voice to women's long-hidden reality: "The point in sharing one woman's experience, I think, is to get at the commonalities in every woman's life, and to fundamentally re-order the priorities of social and political change."

PART TWO

Politics

Angela Miles, in Chapter Eleven, argues that

> it is only if we manage to build a new politics on the basis of our specificity as women that feminism's militant expression of women's sectional interest can represent a major new definition of political discourse and a new departure for humanity as a whole.

An unambivalent recognition of women's specificity is necessary to allow feminists to articulate an alternative set of values "based on the affirmation of the devalued characteristics, concerns and abilities associated with women and reproduction and marginalized in male-dominated society." These autonomously defined female values provide the basis for a new, more human, feminized world, integrated around the requirements of people's self-actualizing reproduction,

27

which can be opposed to industrial male society organized around the alienated production of things.

The Inter-Agency Working Group on Women and Development of the Canadian Council for International Cooperation, in Chapter Twelve, draws on its members' own experience and deliberations, as well as documents from feminism all over the world, to explore the meaning and value of feminism for them as development workers and as women:

> Feminism offers us a wholistic perspective on all issues related to human life... one that strives for the broadest and deepest development of individuals and their societies through freedom from the systems of domination that characterize our world; rich over poor, men over women, North over South...
>
> [It] is a positive and creative challenge to global systems of domination, exploitation, and inequality. As such, it can unite women from North and South; across race, religion, and national boundaries.

Anne Cameron, in Chapter Thirteen, uses myth to invoke the dream of a common struggle for a new world by all the earth's children:

> Some of us, of the far-roaming Rainbow Children, have lost our Dream, some of us had the Dream wrenched from us, some of us had the Dream stolen from us, but the Dream is alive. Some of us have fragments of the Dream, some of us have pieces others of us have lost. Together we can re-form and re-learn the Dream.

But she reminds us that patriarchal race and class divisions are real and we cannot build that unity and that struggle by ignoring them.

Mary O'Brien, in Chapter Fourteen, describes the "feminist socialist theoretical" project as one "to transform [Marx's partial theory] in a way which represents the actual experience of women," rather than to attempt to fit women into existing theory. Feminism must "transcend the academic divisions of labour and the one-sidedness of Marxist theory." The contradictions from which this fuller feminist theoretical synthesis will emerge are those "within and between the social processes of production and reproduction." In her second article she examines the relationship between these two processes more closely, arguing that "the ordering of strategic priorities between the related but opposing needs of class and generic struggle... is not an exclusively women's problem, but a human problem, but women are the progressive social force in the struggle."

Four the Moment, a four-woman a cappella group, is represented in Chapter Fifteen by a selection of songs from a new album in which they fuse Atlantic Canadian and African musical traditions to bring the rhythms of gospel, blues, folk, soul, and reggae to affirm the struggles and the visions of the oppressed and to explore what it means to be Black and a woman in Nova Scotia.

Yolande Cohen, in Chapter Sixteen, describes not just women's exclusion from political power, but women's special relationship to that power and the importance of that special relationship for our development of feminist strategy. She challenges unidimensional analyses of women as absolute victims by analyzing women's sources of (restricted) power in the private sphere, and goes on to argue that "Feminine values are the means of our oppression, the only place we are allowed to be; but they are also potentially subversive because they are so contradictory to the established order outside ourselves." Thus "women's capacity for procreation and our attachment to certain values that follow from this underlies a profound political ambivalence that is, at the same time, women's strength and weakness." These values inhibit women's direct attempts to "seize power" but, at the same time, make it impossible for women to narrow their struggle to this ultimately reformist and assimilationist goal. While acknowledging the importance of pressure for women's access to power as one aspect of movement practice, she suggests that

> there are many ways we can and must resist the power of the oppressor. If we refuse to have one area of struggle imposed on us... we oblige the entire social body to define itself in relation to our demands...
>
> Because we do not have a single political programme which promises emancipation if followed to the letter, we leave the way open for infinitely more total subversion. Because we are not limited to politics, we can overturn politics.

Madeleine Gagnon, in Chapter Seventeen, in the extract (translated by **Wendy Johnston**) from her book *Mon corps dans l'écriture*, reflects feminist attempts to discover/create, out of our historical silence and experience, a specifically female voice—not as a separate and parallel language to men's but as a presence that can transform the existing partial, "divided, compartmentalized, atomized," exclusively male language of the world. Women's presence, too, transforms revolutionary struggle and the fragmenting ideologies where, until now, the phallus has been the dominant fragment.

She is pieces. He is order. She is absence. He is abstract. Let us demand our own right to theory and its practice. The right to be wrong, to come back and to explain. We are not used to it. The right to revolution, to overflowing tenderness, to a new love. The right to desire that joins science and history...

We will never be the sex of others. All of us together will be other and ourselves. Different and similar. Fights and loves. Struggles and tendernesses. Women demand this for everyone. They reach to the heart of the double, of the lining of logocentrism. They add many meanings to the phallic meaning. One, two, three other meanings. They do not simplify, they multiply... It is another kind of logic being born.

Nicole Brossard, in Chapter Eighteen (translated by Marlene Wildeman), writes of the necessarily collective political act of bursting patriarchy's limited and controlling single-sense meaning in an explosion of sense and meanings, and the creation of integrale women whose energy and solidarity names women's humanity, shattering the concept of man as universal. In patriarchal meaning, women are *non-sense*, "whoever aspires to humanity could not know how to identify with women." But radical feminists "have set about claiming the opposite... their humanity is found... in the conquest they make word by word, body by body, of the being, *woman.*" Emerging integrale woman is a collective creation of radical feminist woman for and of herself, a shattering of man's fictive definitions of woman for himself.

For feminists who claim that women's new activism marks the beginning of an emerging more fully human subject, and who argue that women are necessarily the central revolutionary force in this process, the question of men's possible relationship to feminist struggle looms large. The universal claims we make for feminist politics mean that we cannot simply withdraw from male-defined and male-dominated contexts. Our project must be to challenge male hegemony in these areas in the process of attempting major transformation on the basis of new woman-centred values. The project is necessarily one of transcendence that incorporates, transforms, and moves beyond existing dialogue and values. It cannot be mere rejection or substitution, and requires a challenge to the defining powers of established and critical dialogue, not mere abandonment of this terrain.

In addition to this, if a feminist revolution is envisioned as a total human revolution, it must, in the long run, be made by progressive men as well as women. All the authors here speak from this integrative position, and many comment on the problematic role of men in these early stages of a revolution that must be defined at first by women against men and yet ultimately include men. Note that for this tendency of feminism the question is men's relationship to feminism as the central revolutionary process, and not feminism's relationship to a male politics presumed to be central.

Patricia Hughes, in Chapter Nineteen, focuses on this question. She asks, "Is it at all possible that men might have a place in the revolutionary activity of feminism?" and answers that "there is a role for men but it is circumscribed by women in the pursuit of goals defined by women."

> We seek our release and self-affirmation through the act of overthrowing or transcending male political, economic and legal institutions, male concepts, male values, male culture, and the mechanisms that perpetuate them— violence against women, pornography, and ridicule; insofar as they embody those institutions, concepts, values, cultures, as a sex, we also oppose men.
>
> But feminism is far from being merely destructive of malism for self-affirmation can truly arise only out of creation, not out of destruction. Feminism entails a vision which contemplates the metamorphosis of society.
>
> ...This means that while feminist practice does not *require* men, it must recognize their existence and determine their place in the theory and practice because they, too, will be a part of feminist society.

It is precisely their rootedness in the specificity of women's experience and values that provides the basis for these diverse articles to go beyond reaction to redefinition, even to "redefine the definition of definition," as Mary O'Brien says. These articles speak not just to women's condition, but to the whole human condition. Says Margaret Benston:

> Feminism begins with the situation of women and analyzes the way that women's situation has been shaped by and in turn shapes the whole social world. The focus is on women but the basic enterprise is an attempt to understand and evaluate human affairs.

Feminist analysis is, then, not just the analysis of women, nor is feminist struggle just the struggle of women. In representing women's developing autonomous voice and practice, feminism holds the potential for a major transforming step in the emergence of an ever broader and deeper struggle for liberation. The articles in this collection speak in this voice. They present feminism not only as pressure for women, but as the articulation of a transformed revolutionary project for humanity.

31

FOOTNOTES

1. Radical accounts of the emergence of feminism in North America often overlook the fact that feminist radicalism developed in the late 1960s, long after women had begun raising women's issues in the mainstream. Betty Friedan's book, *The Feminine Mystique,* for instance, was published in 1963. The feminism of radical women emerged, as a response to New Left emphasis on personal politics and to the insistence of the Black movement that people would do better to fight their own oppression than provide liberal support for the struggles of others, in a context in which feminist ideas were already in the air and were available to help radical women recognize and understand their oppression in these movements.

2. Reproduction is used here in its broadest sense to refer not only to the bearing of children but to all that is involved in the care, reproduction, and maintenance of people.

3. These are the specific values that allow us to distinguish between feminists concerned with equal rights, and women liberals and democrats, and between feminists concerned with systemic change and women Marxists. The political content of socialism and communism, for instance, is easily distinguished from other non-working-class politics supportive of the "working man," such as populism, progressivism, and red toryism. In contrast, historical studies of the women's movement often use the term "feminism" to refer to all women reformers or all "supporters of women" without distinction. This confusion reigns, also, in our understanding of the feminism of our day. Women have been active today and in the past in a wide variety of politics, including progressivism, liberalism, democracy, socialism, and moral reformism, to name just a few. Aspects of some of these varied politics can, in turn, be found in all expressions of feminism. But feminism as the conscious political articulation of women's revolutionary interests and values is not reducible to these other politics. In order to understand feminism and its significance, it is essential to identify its core defining values and vision. Without this we can have no political analysis of feminism. In fact, most analyses of women's movements and the thought of individual women activists simply identify and list the relative weights of the varying non-feminist components of the politics without in any way defining or assessing the specifically feminist aspects.

4. In my article "Ideological Hegemony in Political Discourse: Woman's Specificity and Equality" in Chapter Two of this book, I trace the emergence of these values in feminism and make the case for their centrality to feminist politics in more detail.

5. The asterisk (*) is used in the text where the word "man" or "men" or a male pronoun might be mistaken for a generic usage but, in fact, refers to men only.
6. It is impossible here to substantiate this point more fully. Those who are interested in pursuing it should see my doctoral dissertation entitled "The Politics of Feminist Radicalism: A Study in Integrative Feminism" (University of Toronto, 1979), in which I develop a general socio-economic analysis of the post-industrial changes that underlie the emergence, the specific nature, and the significance of feminist politics in this period.
7. For a much more developed theoretical analysis of integrative feminism and its emergence in the women's movement, see my article "The Integrative Feminine Principle in North American Feminism: Value Basis of a New Feminism" in *Women's Studies International Quarterly*, IV, 4, 1981:481-495.
8. I do not wish to imply here that integrative feminists always recognize their affinity across the boundaries of movement categories. They are not self-defined as integrative feminists or as a tendency of the movement. My identification of this tendency is based on an analysis of a significant shared perspective that, while evident, remains largely unconscious. Nevertheless, in my experience at feminist meetings and conferences, in women's studies activities, and in such broadly based and diverse organizations as the National Action Committee on the status of women, the Feminist Party of Canada, and Women Against Violence Against Women, integrative feminists of all movement categories tend to welcome and support the initiatives of each other. They also tend, in general, to welcome the tremendous variety of participants, activities, and thinking in the current movement, and to take relatively non-sectarian positions in their practice and writing. Integrative feminists' sense of feminism's historical significance and its embryonic stage of development means they tend to welcome diversity and debate as important contributions to growth and development.
9. As will be seen in the articles collected here, integrative feminists do not reject these separative, male-associated characteristics wholesale in a simple negation. Rather, they seek to develop a more wholistic and balanced vision of humanity and human society through a transcendent affirmation of the feminine side so long devalued and presumed to be less than human. This involves a feminization of the world and of politics but is not simply a substitution of feminine-associated for masculine-associated values, characteristics, and activities.
10. "Man*" is used here advisedly. Women straddle the man*/nature divide. We have a foot in both camps, so to speak, and our struggle must come from both sides of this deep fragmentation. This is one example of the ways in which our struggle is necessarily integrative if we speak *as women* rather than as would-be men.

33

PART ONE

Scholarship:
Theory and Practice

CHAPTER 1

Memoirs of an Ontological Exile: The Methodological Rebellions of Feminist Research

Jill McCalla Vickers

Jill McCalla Vickers is Professor of Political Science and Director of the Institute for Canadian Studies at Carleton University, Ottawa. She is past-president of the Canadian Association of University Teachers, and arbitrator and negotiator with special emphasis on such issues as equal pay, sexual harassment, and maternity leave. She has been active in the New Democratic Party as a federal candidate, member of the Provincial Council, member of the Federal Policy and Foreign Affairs Committees, and co-ordinator of the Federal Task Force on Social Policy in 1980/81. She is a past-president of the Canadian Research Institute for the Advancement of Women and was secretary-treasurer of the Canadian Women's Studies Association. She has also served as Parliamentarian of the National Action Committee on the status of women (NAC).

———————

"It's frightening to set off on new journeys without any maps. Perhaps the hardest bit is deciding what to hang onto and what to shed." (Sheila Rowbotham, *et al.*, 1979, p. 33)

Most of the basic issues which motivate my work as a feminist political theorist fall into the category which Mary Daly has described as the category of "non-question" (Daly 1973:12). Non-questions are those which so fundamentally challenge or question the philosophical structure of a society or civilization (in this case of patriarchy) that they cannot be understood as questions at all by those who work entirely from within an established tradition of thought. Further, they cannot even be asked very clearly as questions by the questioner, whose mind has been trained within and is therefore occupied by the thought of the dominant tradition.

What happens when we begin to ask non-questions? How do we communicate—with one another and with "the others". How do we ask non-questions and how can we ever begin to answer them? Most of us have been trained to use the maps created by what Mary O'Brien has called "male-stream" thought (O'Brien 1976). And yet, as we try to understand more deeply women's experience under patriarchy, it becomes apparent that our venture is more profoundly radical than most of us had imagined (or even secretly wished). Eventually, it becomes clear that the venture is more than filling in the blanks with missing nuggets of information about women. No longer can we be satisfied just with critiques of the biases and blindness of our disciplinary theories, our religions and our ideologies. Finally, the frightening and exhilarating fact can no longer be denied—we are together embarked on a journey which has as its goal the complete reconstruction of human knowledge and human existence. And yet, as Rowbotham says, we seem to have no maps of our own and we seem unable to decide what to take with us and what to leave behind.

In this article, I will argue that feminists may have rather more in the way of maps than we realize. While as a self-declared ontological exile I will argue that even the most fundamental theories of being and knowing developed within patriarchy must be questioned by our Be-ing, I will try to show that the practice of feminist thought and research has already revealed a great deal which can usefully guide us on this monumental journey.

My basic non-question, of course, is why Western man's conception of himself, of us, and of nature so destructive. Why do his ontologies drive me into exile, either from him or from myself? In this very preliminary pursuit of this non-question,

I will briefly present some of the ontological gleanings I have drawn from other feminist searchers who have persuaded me that I am not alone in my exile. I will then more fully outline the methodological rebellions of feminist researchers — rebellions which reveal the determination of feminists to achieve this fundamental restructuring of human knowledge and existence.

1. Dualism and Alienation

Like so many feminists, I cut my intellectual teeth on the study of the "grand tradition" of Western philosophy and culture. And while I felt uneasy with the ideas of an Aristotle, a Hegel or a Nietzsche, the tradition — its tools, its methods and its discipline — afforded me a measure of liberation in the sense that through it I could transcend my being "merely" a woman and "merely" a clerk.* And, perhaps like many of you, I clung to that discipline and to its methods and precepts. The tradition offered me safe haven if — and it is a big if — I left unexplored the basic implications of ontological and episte-mological foundations. Like Queen Elizabeth in Arab lands, I became an honorary male, and certainly my mind worked from within the male-stream thought I had learned. And so, like other feminists, radical in their outlook who still draw back from the notion that their religion or their ideology must also be subject to the scrutiny of our newly ascendent Be-ing, I could not initially believe that these powerful symbol systems of Western thought could not provide a homeland for me. A decade-long excursion into Marxism, which did seem to provide that longed-for homeland, simply delayed the realiza-tion that I was indeed an exile, either from myself or from "the others." It took even longer to realize that my alienation was the potential source of my creativity rather than the cause of the intellectual paralysis I had previously endured.

Many feminists are now exploring in detail the dualisms which have characterized Western (and much of non-Western) thought.[1] Those who have argued that the man/woman, culture/nature set of dualisms are at the heart of Western thought have also seen the seeds of human destruction in the determination of male-stream civilization to dominate nature.[2] To them, the alienation of men from nature and the natural processes of life have created a monster (Reuther's

---

* Why am I still a little insulted when a student mistakes me for a secretary?

"megamachine") which has dominated and can destroy all in its path.[3] To them, only the creation of female-stream thought and the development of female principles of authority and co-existence with nature can save the human species from extinction. This apocalyptic vision identifies man's long-standing alienation from the realms of nurturance and ordinary life processes as the key both to our oppression and to the madness of "the others."

The basic dualism with which I will deal in this paper concerns the categories of reason and non-reason. I use the term "non-reason" with deliberation since the "opponent" of reason in this dichotomy has been described variously: as matter vs. spirit, as passion and its pursuit vs. reason and its direction, and sometimes even as faith, "which passes all understanding," as opposed to reason. The rationalist tradition, within which our scholarly disciplines can be placed, derives its rationale from a presumption that the liberated man can transcend his passions, his prejudices, and even his death, through an elevation of his reason and a suppression of his non-reason. As we will see, the elevation of this premise into canons of method has helped men hide key aspects of human life. It is against such canons and such hiding that the key methodological rebellions of feminist research are directed.

The transcendence asserted for the mind or spirit liberated from the body parallels the transcendence asserted for history over nature. It is as if man's desire to dominate nature requires him to constantly hide the power of nature — her power to woo him to love and her power to erupt in storms and volcanoes destroying his monuments to his longed-for immortality. Women have been identified with nature, with the earth, and with the despised body, with carnality, with the finitude of decaying matter, and with non-reason. There is an enormous temptation for us also to reject those despised things with which we have been associated and to claim our rights to transcendence, spirituality and reason — to reject nature, the body and our human-animal functions. It so often seems that our alienation can be ended thus, and indeed many feminists claim this solution to end their male-imposed exile from the human race. If being human is defined by killing to achieve a project which reason dictates, then let us kill. If giving life defines us out of the human race, then let us turn back on our natural ability to give and nurture life. If reason alone, as defined by male-stream methods, ensures the admission of our thought to the parade of human culture, then let us turn our backs on the non-reasons of intuition, empathy and sentiment.

The project of reconciling spirit and body, which could end the alienation of man from nature and of woman from male-stream culture and thought, is a project of such enormity and daring that it strikes terror in our hearts. And while creeping fingers of thought have emerged (largely from the women's spirituality movement) which say it can and must be done, many of us find a commitment at the level of explicit ontological decision quixotic and painful. And yet, even those of us who have faced the choice and turned away display clear evidence of an underlying commitment in the methodological rebellions which have emerged from our practical attempts to know what female Be-ing is and can be. These methodological rebellions, understood in the context of the insights provided by those who have explicitly accepted the challenge of transcending male-stream thought and reconstructing human knowledge in a way which reconciled spirit and body, provide, for the moment, the best maps and sign-posts for the journey ahead.

2. The Methodological Rebellions of Feminist Research

Feminist researchers have not been particularly preoccupied with abstract methodological issues; at least not in any form recognizable as such to many of our disciplinary colleagues. And yet feminists are highly sensitive to the sorts of issues raised by groups such as those who describe themselves as post-positivists. If pushed to self-definitiion, some would describe themselves as positivists, some as non-positivists, and many as Marxists. The critiques of method (scientific, philosophical, scholarly or theological) engaged in by feminists, moreover, differ from those of other methodological critics because they are largely the product of *hindsight*; that is, they have emerged as *reflections* on research *necessarily* done in a manner which violates many of the methodological canons of the researcher's discipline. These methodological violations are, of course, the basis of charges by disciplinary traditionalists that feminist research is not "real" research, especially in the sense of certifying the researcher for such things as tenure and promotion or in the sense of taking her ideas seriously. For some feminists, therefore, a guerilla war environment prevails, as indeed it does for many prominent natural scientists who voice their "deviant" premises derived through "incorrect" methods in the form of science fiction.[4]

41

Conducting "proper" research for disciplinary consumption, feminists have created an underground in which the norms of feminist research have emerged. Since most have endured a rigorous disciplinary "education" in orthodox method, the sort of open discussions of the newly emerging principles of feminist method which make for logical and normative reconstruction are rare. Rather we can observe a *convergence* which is usually made explicit only in passing or in meetings of the underground.

You will have noticed that observations pertaining to the sociology of science are thus far central to my discussion. This is necessarily so from a feminist perspective. Clearly, the power structures within disciplines and within society are an important starting place for understanding why traditional methods are inadequate for women who wish to understand and change their circumstances, and why male-stream symbol systems offer few guides to revision. Women, after all, have been studied as objects for centuries, just as slaves, barbarians and workers have been studied. What happens, however, when women, slaves, barbarians or workers wish to become *actors* in the discovery process while they remain an oppressed (or at least powerless) group, caste or class? Since there is a high convergence between those who hold power over them and those who make the tools of thinking which "explain" and "justify" reality, they will learn little of themselves useful for achieving change by employing the intellectual tools of their oppressors.[5] Their questions will remain "non-questions," unclear to themselves and illegitimate to those who have the power to create culture and to name things.

Many feminists have followed Mary Daly in her use of the image of a journey to illustrate the process of discovery which has led increasingly to methodological "violations" or transcendences. The first phase of the journey involves studies *of* women within the framework of male-stream thought and disciplinary method. In this phase, the researcher either detaches herself from the objects she is studying (becomes a methodological male), in which case her journey ends, or she identifies with those whom she is studying. This leads to the second phase, in which her "objectified knowledge" (and that of her disciplinary colleagues) concerning women *conflicts* with her personal experience, intuition or aspirations. For example, positivist psychology concerning women will, in the present context of sex stratification, describe us as passive, preoccupied with the approval of others, nurturant, etc.. The theories of the discipline will "explain" these findings as "natural," "mature," "adaptive" and "good" for the human race.[6]

The searcher's dilemma is clear. The weight of her own evidence produced by the methods "proper" to her discipline as "explained" by the dominant theories which express her discipline's rational consensus "prove" either that she is a freak (not being passive, preoccupied with the approval of others, or nurturant); or her "intuitive" knowledge that women are not all alike, that they ought not to be passive, etc., calls into question both her own evidence and the great weight of the disciplinary consensus. If she is an isolate in the social system of science, as many potential feminist searchers are, she may again abort the journey and even take pride in her difference from other women. This "queen bee" syndrome is described in other contexts as producing *compradors* — black white men, scholars from working class backgrounds who despise the working class, etc.. If, on the other hand, the searcher can look to an emerging consensus of other feminists, she enters the phase of critiques in which the main pre-occupation is to discover and illustrate the sexist bias in the theories and paradigms of her discipline.

It is only in the third phase of the journey, aimed at the *creation* of feminist theory oriented to the problems of her Be-ing and that of other women, that the link between patriarchal theories, etc., and the strait-jacket of male-stream "proper" method is fully revealed. In this context, she learns through the experience of searching and discovery that "proper" method hides, deliberately or unconsciously, many of the things she must reveal. In order to reveal that which has been systematically hidden, therefore, she must recognize that method is not neutral even if it is productive and "gets results".

The next step in the journey is both the most crucial and the most difficult. Having been trained to believe that science and scholarship require these methodological canons to produce products with the "good housekeeping" seals of reliability, intersubjective transmissability, capacity to predict, etc., she realizes how truly radical and daring she must be to transcend them without losing sight of the goals of the journey, which involve both understanding and changing what has been called reality. She quickly learns that this is also a dangerous quest. While you don't go to jail or get sick from it, you may well lose status and be punished in hurtful ways.[7]

With these preliminaries, what are the methodological rebellions and transcendences which have achieved the richest tradition of post-positivist or non-positivist research and scholarship? There are five identifiable rebellions, some of which will be more familiar than others. They are taken from a variety of disciplines because the *collective journey* entered into in phase three involves a rejection of disciplinary boundaries which hinder our ability to discover. In many cases they are interrelated.

a) The rebellion against decontextualization

In one of the very few books which looks explicitly at some of the methodological rebellions which feminism involves, Arlene Kaplan Daniels argues that in order to do feminist research "...we are forced to rethink the structure and organization of sociological inquiry..."[8] She demonstrates the impossibility of reconstructing sociological theory (by removing its sexist assumptions) because of the methodological inadequacies of the process of inquiry itself—whether functionalist, structuralist or Marxist theories are involved. Her main complaint is that the "issues," problems and questions which feminists agree are important (even if they wouldn't agree on their ordering or solution) relate to experiences which disappear or are invisible using the decontextualized, analytic method of social science. In the same work, Thelma McCormack (in "Toward a Nonsexist Perspective on Social and Political Change") shows how to recontextualize the study of women's political behaviour in contemporary liberal democracies. She argues that the assumption of a "single society," in which generalizations can be made about all participants, hides the fact that men and women may inhabit different social worlds and that their behaviour can only be understood (and changed) by refusing to adopt techniques of analytic method. She notes, for example, that the sex of an actor is frequently not taken into account as a "factor" in understanding political behaviour although it may often be the most important part of the context of that person's action. Finally, she notes that certain methodologies (frequently quantitative) and research situations (such as having male researchers studying worlds involving women) may systematically prevent the elicitation of certain kinds of information—information which may be the most important for explaining the phenomenon being studied.

McCormack's own research views most women as living in a distinct political culture with quite distinct norms of political behaviour. By recontextualizing women behaving politically, she demonstrates how the big "P" political contexts studied to the exclusion of almost everything else by most male political scientists alienate many women (who are then described as apathetic by the traditional discipline) because "the really important political issues" are not discussed or decided there.

The rebellion against decontextualizing research is dealt with over and over again in many different forms. Clearly the rebellion is most necessary and more intense in the "most scientific" social sciences (or those with the worse cases of "physics envy", as one feminist psychologist has quipped). The "New Scholarship" reviews of feminist work which appear in each issue of *SIGNS: The Journal of Women in Culture and Society*, reveal these differences. In history and classics, for example, method is not generally as decontextualizing. In these disciplines, and to a lesser degree in anthropology, the main task is using methods which do recognize the importance of meaning-in-context to "fill in" the missing half and to research problems and issues which emanate from women's experience. Psychology, on the other hand, offers the hardest case of the rebellion against decontextualizing. Economics, which might be expected to offer the hardest case, does not, simply because of the near total absence of women, let alone feminists, in the academic discipline and the extreme rigidity with which methodological canons are enforced against any "deviants." [9]

The most recent "Review Essay" dealing with psychology by Mary Brown Parlee illustrates the problem well. As Parlee notes, many women psychologists, while ignoring (or critiquing) many of the discipline's conclusions, concepts and questions of the past, keep a basic commitment to a positivist view of scientific method. From a feminist perspective, however, most of the problems of discovery and change so crucial to women cannot even "begin to be completely comprehended by any of the conceptual or methodological paradigms of traditional psychology."[10] Indeed, feminists are concerned with phenomena "which cannot readily be abstracted, even conceptually, from the complex, rich and varied world of human experience—phenomena which clearly cannot be simulated in laboratory experiments."[11] Parlee gives examples of rape, wife-beating and child-battering. I might add Mary Daly's list of witch-burning, genital mutilation, suttee, foot-binding, and genocide which have crucial psychological dimensions but which are not amenable to the methods sanctified by a positivist view of science. Parlee notes that many feminist psychologists have simply accepted as a priority the importance of questions of this sort and have improvised methods which help them find the "best possible version of the truth about the subject matter rather than adhering strictly to a particular method."[12] She notes that this rebellion is perceived as a severe challenge by the discipline, which is "punished" in a variety of ways (exclusion of the searcher, ignoring the findings as non-scientific, trivial, biased, etc.). This assignment of priority based on intuition and the authenticity of individual experience and empathy is increasingly a mark of feminist research.

Parlee also notes that this rebellion is a disciplined rebellion; that is, rules have emerged in which the usual scholarly principles of reliability, consistency, logical inference and honesty are maintained with the additional principle of the investigator continually testing the plausibility of the work against her own experience as well as the experience of other women. This test of subjective relevance and truth is the most condemned aspect of feminist social science, despite the fact that introspection and intuition have always been key parts of the discovery process, although little understood or recognized.

This by-product of the real-life dilemmas of feminist psychologists also displays correspondences with the male-stream post-positivist critiques of the discipline. Parlee, for example, quotes E.G. Mishler's "Meaning in Context: Is There Any Other Kind?"[13] noting that despite the sustained male-stream criticisms of positivism "no new approach or paradigm has emerged." In stating that she can agree with Mishler's general analysis of the problem (context-stripping, in which "Concepts, environments, social interactions are all simplified by methods which lift them out of their contexts, stripping them of the very complexity which characterizes them in the real world."),[14] she concludes that the sterility of male-stream post-positivism "...is because those who are critical and have no analysis of what is wrong with their field have *no subject matter they are eager to explore.*"[15] This insight is, I think, particularly germane. Feminists have a subject matter that they are eager to explore and reject a methodological determinism which insists they not explore a problem they consider crucial because their discipline's "proper" methods cannot aid in discovery. In psychology, context-stripping which portrays the individual as an isolated private entity clashes with the feminist premise that the personal *is* political, therefore giving feminists a basis from which to challenge context-stripping methods, but critiques of what is wrong with the field could come from other sources.

While there are some important correspondences between the feminist rebellions and the critiques of male-stream post-positivists, the context out of which the feminist rebellions arise does not identify as problems, in quite the same way as post-positivist critiques do, such things as "prediction." It is only in the sense that the desire to predict produces context-stripping methods and seems to demand ever "harder" data and ever "firmer" control through laboratory experiments that the ultimate goal of prediction is a problem. Of course, the ability to predict within the context of existing social systems is a limited goal. Rather more common in feminist research is historical prediction such as we see in anthropology when a model of the sex stratification system is constructed from a set of societies and predictions made to be tested in the context of other societies. Attempts at accurate future prediction, on the other hand, probably assume the endurance of patriarchy, and feminists are committed to the idea of social transformations which involve both human choice and agency.

b) The rebellion to restore agency

The next two rebellions are, in fact, aspects of the feminists' efforts to restore context in discovery. They also look to the issues of the language we use and the "power of naming" (Daly 1978).

Mary Daly, following the methodologically important cadre of feminist linguists, has argued that the power structures of societies and civilizations are reflected in the language which is available to discuss reality. To male-stream arbiters of rational methodologies, mathematics is the most consensible language for science, but mathematics as a language for the expression of feminist reality is often the most context-stripped of all. If the goal of the process of discovery is transformation (self and societal) as much as understanding, context must first of all be restored to language. This problem has many aspects, one of which, to quote Daly, is "... the fundamental fact that women have had the power of naming stolen from us. We have not been free to use our own power to name ourselves, the world, or God" (Daly 1973:8). Again we can draw many parallels, such as the progression from "nigger" or "coon" to "negro" and now to "black," to show that the power of naming relates to power and powerlessness. In fact, Daly suggests that so-called women's intuition may involve mental processes for which we haven't invented the words because we haven't had the power of naming.

This attention to language, especially as a device for hiding context, runs throughout the methodological rebellions. Although its roots have only been briefly outlined, it is important to note that these challenges to context-stripping methods are based on feminist research in linguistics which began with the identification of "specious generics" or universals such as "man" and "mankind." To most patriarchal thinkers, "man" does not frequently include woman any more than liberal thinkers meant workers when they talked of men having the right to consent to governments. Nor did the framers of constitutions mean slaves, women or workers when they referred to men with rights. This attention to the actual context-meaning of words is a key part of feminist discovery. In this section, I will deal only with one relevant aspect.

The language, concepts, theories and methods of most academic disciplines abolish agency in their reconstructed images of the world. Mary Daly, who begins by quoting Bergson, "The way back to reality is to destroy our perceptions of it," notes that deceptive perceptions were and are implanted by language—"the all-pervasive language of myth, conveyed overtly and subliminally through religion, great art, literature, the dogmas of professionalism... grammar" (Daly 1978:3). A key element in the deception of language and method for Daly is the elimination of human agency for which are substituted forces, factors, roles, structures, stereotypes, constraints, attitudes and influences. "The point is that no agent is named—only abstractions" (Daly 1978:29). And who can blame an abstraction for starving you, mutilating you, murdering you through suttee (a "custom") or crippling you through foot-binding (an "erotic custom")? Witch-burning is deceptively described as "a process of religious legitimization," genocidal intent as an "attitude" or "prejudice." Examining in detail much academic literature, we would conclude that no human agent is ever to blame, ever profits, or ever plans.

48

Human action is sterilized and pasteurized into a parade of forces, factors, roles, structures, institutions, stereotypes, rites, constraints, customs, attitudes and influences — to name but a few.

Daly illustrates that only a few catastrophic events ever escape this kind of treatment. She suggests that we would be shocked into reality if social scientists talked about the German "custom" of genocide because of the horror conjured up by the event and the word genocide. A description of the Hindu "rite" of suttee which "spared" widows from the temptations of impurity by forcing them to "immolate themselves," Daly observes (Daly 1978:115), seems not to shock male researchers despite the fact that no rite or custom is ever an agent in human life. At some point, human agents (in this case Hindu men) created the "rite" for their own purposes and others continued the rite with some benefit to themselves.

It is clear that categorizing something as a custom, rite or whatever explains little of its origins, purposes or whose interests it serves. In fact, it appears to *explain away* just those things we need to understand. This is context-stripping on a grand scale.

c) The rebellion against reversal

Reversal is the worst sort of context-stripping in which academics engage. In this case, agency in the custom or rite is attributed to the victim through a trick of language or grammar. To continue with the suttee illustration, Benjamin Walker "explains": "At first, *suttee* was restricted to the wives of princes and warriors... but in the course of time the widows of weavers, masons, barbers and others of the lower caste *adopted the practice*."[16] Given the fact that widows were dragged from hiding places and heavily drugged before being flung into the pyre, often by their sons, this is like saying that although the practice of being burned in gas ovens was at first restricted to political dissidents, eventually millions of Jews *adopted* the practice.

Reversal is used to suggest that Chinese women *adopted* the custom of having their feet bound into three-inch festering hooks which required that they be carried or moved on their knees, effectively crippling them, as they might adopt the custom of wearing their hair cut short. This grammatical, theoretical and methodological trick also makes it appear that baby African girls *adopt* the custom of having their genitals mutilated with stones or glass and their vaginal opening sewn up to a tiny hole after having been rubbed with salt. The point is that words like "custom," "rite" or "practice" are neutral, even casual terms which decontextualize hideous events with reversal, making it appear that the victims *embraced* (the term "adopted" is equally casual) their own pain, mutilation or death.

Feminist research works on the presumption that just as the Jews did not willingly adopt the custom of being murdered in gas ovens, women did not willingly adopt genital mutilation, foot-binding, suttee, nutritional deprivation (the "custom" of women eating after the men have finished — if there is anything left) or being burned at the stake. It further assumes that the presence of token females in these events no more proves willing adoption than the presence of some Jews as gas oven attendants proves the willingness of Jews to be massacred. Contextualized research in which agency is established and reversals avoided has the same powerful effect as tours of the death camps had on allied soldiers — it frequently makes students physically sick. Similarly the recontextualized evidence of Hiroshima would abolish forever such hideous social science delusions as mega-deaths and deterrence. Any humane social science must *name* these things for what they truly are.

d) The rebellion against "objectivity"

As should already be evident to anyone who has read this far, feminist discovery rejects many aspects of what the positivists and other male-stream thinkers have called objectivity. This can either mean treating those you study as objects and objectifying their pains in words which hide the identity of their oppressors, or it can mean being detached from that which is studied. The implications of either meaning are unacceptable to feminist researchers who insist on the authenticity of the experience and Be-ing of those studied.

Of course, the concept of objectivity has a deeper purpose in science as the rules it involves are designed to facilitate intersubjective transmissibility, testing, replication, etc.. At the hinge point between phases two and three of the journey I outline above, these issues are not clearly enough exposed to understand very well. Few feminists in the third phase are willing to waste time and effort over the receptivity of traditional disciplines to their discoveries and insights. Far more important is the transmissibility to the community of feminist scholars and researchers, which is taking on the character of a meta-discipline, and to the movement. Hence the process does not "fit" Kuhn's theory of scientific revolutions, since for the moment the traditional disciplines seem largely like stifling tombs, and revolution through persuasion or demonstration seems unlikely. Perhaps a fairly long period of parallel development, rather like that we have seen with Marxist social science, is the likely future. One of the important points, however, is the perceived necessity by feminists that their discoveries be transmissible beyond disciplinary boundaries and beyond the intellectual environment. This introduces rather different goals to which feminist methodological norms are geared.

e) The rebellion against linearity, inevitability and laws

Male-stream theories of method insist on the *unity* of human knowledge with a goal of linear progress towards a set of ever more secure laws capable of permitting us to control ever more phenomena. In trying to understand the separate aspects of this *project* against which many feminists have rebelled, the character of the male-stream project has to be broken down somewhat. The first problem has to do with what has been called the "regularity principle," which holds that there are discoverable uniformities in human behaviour which can be discovered and expressed in the form of laws which have been described as "statement(s) of universal conditional form... capable of being confirmed or disconfirmed by suitable empirical findings."[17] In amplifying the meaning of the universal form, Hempel argues that a sentence can be regarded as a law only if its predicate is purely universal or "purely qualitative in character;" that is, only "if a statement of its meaning does not require reference to any one particular object of spatio-temporal location."[18] Thus, concepts like "soft," "as long as" or "electrically charged" are permissible predicates of general laws, whereas expressions like "Western," "modern," "Greek slavery" or "more oppressed than male workers" are not, because they clearly require some reference to particular objects or spatio-temporal location.

51

The basic point is not that *some aspects* of human behaviour cannot be generalized into laws (clearly they can) but whether the things we want to understand and to change can be dealt with within the framework of the positivist project. To use an example from my own discipline, a law-like statement explaining the phenomenon of revolution can be constructed: "Multiple dysfunctions plus élite intransigence cause revolution"[19]. The point is that not all universal statements are meaningful quite simply because they strip context beyond the point which is useful. Yet some universal statements are both useful and important to the feminist project. The statement "only women bear children" is one such, provided we also recognize (1) that it doesn't mean that women *cause* babies, (2) that it doesn't mean that *all* women bear children, (3) that it doesn't mean women *must* bear children, and (4) that it could well be technologically transcended.

The reason this issue is of real concern to feminists is that many of our core questions hinge on such things as the distinction between sex and gender; since for thousands of years male-stream scholarship and science (from Darwin and Freud through the ethnologists to modern analysts of "hemisphere lateralization" and hormone differentials) have assigned female characteristics to the sphere described as "natural" *about which most would conclude that meaningful universal statements can be made.* Hence the issue in much feminist research is to distinguish between things governed by "laws" (that is, which cannot be changed) and things which have only seemed to have been universal. What is more, since the feminist project is also aimed at transcending some things which empirically *have been universally true* (such as the exclusive responsibility of women for rearing as distinct from bearing children), the regularity principle of male-stream methodologists has a danger beyond its context-stripping character. In general, most feminists seem to view the human species as a self-making species which exists within limiting material parameters. Hence our rebellion against the *exclusive* search for "laws" and our recognition that the *species*, if not individual members, is subject to laws. As an example, while feminists have argued that there is no universal law which dictates that women as a sex or particular women must rear children, they have also recognized thta the species *is subject* to a universal law that its young be cared for, for a distinctively long period of time, and that some significant portion of a species generation must be capable of nurturant behaviour.

The issue raised by the rebellion against linearity is also raised by Marxist feminists against the linearity perceived in dialectical materialism. Inevitably it relates to the assessment of the impact of change. What patriarchal thinkers perceive as progress is frequently viewed quite differently when the searcher proceeds from a woman-centred point of departure. A great deal of feminist research has, for example, documented the loss of power and status and the deterioration of condition which women endured in passages of "progress" from one stage of economic life to another. This, of course, raises the point that descriptions of the process of change in social science are frequently teleological in character despite the ostensible norms of value-neutrality. In general, feminists have argued that androcentric theories of change are assumed to have a universality which they do not, just as androcentric scholars have assumed a unity of "human" knowledge, which can be maintained only by the exclusion of insights and self-knowledge of powerless people. The question of some future synthesis of many partial systems of knowledge into a true unity remains open, of course, although it is not for the moment a stated goal of the feminist project, except in the work of thinkers such as Shulamith Firestone.

Conclusion

The release from the strictures of methodological canons which has been the result of these rebellions has been enormously productive. In the course of less than 15 years, thousands of new works in over a dozen disciplines have appeared in at least five languages. In rejecting the masculine usurpation of universality and masculine appropriations of reality, feminists have also been forced to reject many of the methods and norms which seem so sacred to others. In general, most feminists conclude that the criterion for our methods is productivity in the sense of answering the kinds of questions the project posits as important. There is no particular uniform reconstruction of method which has emerged as yet although that may come—and the dangers of a new orthodoxy with it. That the process is painful is evident and well described by a male feminist, J. Martin Graham:

> Coming out of the "real" closet of mainstream psychology into the bright feminologist's world of "pseudo-science," "fad ideas" and "personal politics" can be a frightening experience... It means giving up

allegiances with a powerful, respected group who have all the "real science," "legitimate ideas" and "value-free logic" on their side. It is perhaps somewhat akin to denouncing the church with all the related stigma associated with the role of heathen and outcast.

(Graham 1980:5)

There is, of course, always the danger that some of the product of these methodological rebellions is and will be "pseudo-science," and faddish. And here the discipline of a collective endeavour in which ideas are openly criticized and discussed is the key, as it is in more traditionally defined science. This is, however, the lesser danger. Far worse is the use of our collective skills and talents to the ends of hiding reality and "legitimizing" the *status quo*.

Despite the important efforts of a number of individual feminists, we remain limited in our attempts to free ourselves from the strictures of male-stream thought. The strength and endurance of patriarchal symbol systems are much greater, and are related in a more complex way to patriarchal systems of dominance and oppression, than most of us have recognized. While it seems both simple and simplistic to state that the hegemony of male-stream thinking makes most of our statements about the nature of our Be-ing, oppositional and reactive, it is important to realize that most of our thought is still conditioned, constrained and limited by the fact that we first learned to think using tools and categories devised by men to understand their reality, not ours. As some women become culture-makers and as we communicate with our own students in a new idiom, we must create new tools of thinking and establish new norms for feminist research and action. Probably the most important *political* value of feminist research at this stage is its capacity to challenge, however implicitly, the ontological underpinnings of male-stream thought and of patriarchal symbol systems.

Much of the work that is currently being undertaken by feminist researchers focuses on the manner in which power and authority are exercised within patriarchy and within patriarchal institutions. Most frequently, as Peggy Reeves Sanday has noted, "a positivist framework is employed in which the causes of relative sex status are assigned to either psychological... or materialist considerations." (Sanday 1981:4) Far too often, however, feminists appear too confident that we have successfully freed ourselves from the constraining categories and norms of the male-stream thought within which all

54

of us in this generation were trained. The fact that we then so often go on to locate our position within a borrowed category of male-stream thought highlights Sheila Rowbotham's point with which we began. It is hard to know what to save and what to discard from male-stream thought as we proceed forward on our journey. Some of us have clearly saved too much and are over-burdened with antique baggage which slows our progress. Others have, perhaps, discarded rather too much too early. It has been the point of this paper to suggest that observation of the practical decisions which feminist researchers make in their efforts to understand and explain the nature *of female* experience reveals a praxis which can be used as an interim guide.

FOOTNOTES

1. Feminist anthropologists like Sherry Ortner 1974; political theorists like Mary O'Brien (especially in her book, *The Politics of Reproduction*, 1981) and Christine Allen 1971; and feminist theologians like Mary Daly, Carol Christ and Rosemary Ruether, have increasingly emphasized this dualism and alienation theme.
2. Dorothy Dinnerstein's 1976, *The Mermaid and the Minotaur* is a powerful, if flawed, attempt to pose this basic "non-question."
3. See Rosemary Ruether's "Motherearth and the Megamachine" in Carol Christ & Judith Plaskow 1979. See also Ruether 1975.
4. The existence of a science fiction underground on the periphery of the natural science disciplines is an important fact in the sociology of science. Exploration of this evidence of the constraints of natural science methodological orthodoxy may also help illustrate the elusive process of "creativity" in science.
5. In this context, Dorothy Smith has argued for the development of a sociology *for* women (i.e., for their purposes), rather than a sociology *of* women.
6. See Jeri Dawn Wine's contribution to this volume, Chapter 3.
7. The case of Marylee Stephenson, fired (i.e., denied tenure) from McMaster University in Hamilton because "feminist research isn't really research" because "it rejects the methodological canons of sociology," is only one of many cases which illustrate the risks involved.
8. In Millman & Kanter 1975:340.
9. See Marjorie Cohen's contribution to this volume, Chapter 4.

10. Mary Brown Parlee 1979:127.
11. *Ibid.*, p. 129.
12. *Ibid.*, p. 130.
13. *Harvard Educational Review* 4a, 1979, pp. 1-19.
14. Parlee, *op. cit.*, p. 131.
15. *Ibid.* (my emphasis).
16. Walker, *The Hindu World*, quoted in Mary Daly 1978:117 (Daly's emphasis).
17. Hempel, "The Function of General Laws in History," first published in *Journal of Philosophy* (1942), reprinted in Patrick Gardiner (ed.), *Theories of History* (Glencoe, Ill.: Free, Press, 1960), pp. 344-356.
18. Hempel and Oppenheim, "The Logic of Explanation" in *Philosophy of Science* 15, 1948, reprinted in Boruch Brody, *Readings in the Philosophy of Science*, Part III, Logical Analysis of Law and Explanation, 1970, pp. 337-350.
19. Chalmers A. Johnson, "Revolution and the Social System," quoted in K.N. Kim, "The Limits of Behavioral Explanation in Politics," in Charles Allan McCoy and John Playford, *Apolitical Politics: A Critique of Behavioralism* (New York: Crowell, 1968), p. 45.

CHAPTER 2

Feminism and the Critique of Scientific Method

Margaret Benston

Margaret Benston has a Ph.D. in Theoretical Chemistry specializing in Quantum Mechanics. She holds a Joint Appointment in the departments of Computer Science and Women's Studies at Simon Fraser University in Vancouver and has been active in the women's movement for almost twenty years. Her publications include "The Political Economy of Women's Liberation," groundbreaking feminist theory that has since been widely translated. She is an active member of the Euphoniously Feminist Non-Performing Quintet, a group that teaches feminist labour and anti-war songs to anyone willing to listen, and is working with a variety of ideas around popular control of work and technology.

Works that explore issues raised in this article and have appeared since it was written include a special science issue of *Resources for Feminist Research* (15:3 1986), *Reflections on Gender and Science* by Evelyn Fox Keller (1985), and *Women's Nature*, edited by Marian Lowe and Ruth Hubbard (1981). For a provocative look at the work done generally on women and science see *The Science Question in Feminism* by Sandra Harding (1986).

Introduction

Feminist analysis is committed to finding answers to important questions about the world and to a development of the best tools possible to arrive at those answers. The growth of feminist theory and scholarship has meant an examination of the basic assumptions of disciplines such as history, economics, literary criticism and the social sciences. Whatever the critique whatever the discipline, however, there is an underlying assumption of the value of "rationality" as the basis for the analysis. It was inevitable, then, that science and the methodology of science could come under feminist scrutiny since the methodology of present science* is widely regarded as the model for rational thought.

A widespread approach to defining science is to examine the methods which work, apparently so successfully, in the physical sciences, with a view to understanding their essential features and generalizing them. The methods of inquiry of these physical sciences are taken as the core of scientific methodology. It is these which exemplify the essence of rational inquiry; it is this methodology which dominates Western intellectual life. Such an approach is widely perceived not simply as one important way of understanding and interpreting the world, but as the only legitimate way. Science is no longer just one form of knowledge; it has become identified with knowledge itself. I will argue that the present view of scientific rationality, of science itself, when taken from its present practice, is an extremely limited one, with irrationalities and inconsistencies that feminists need to understand.

This is particularly true given the dominance of the rationality of present science in both the academic and the radical social sciences. Both apparently accept the equation of science and "truth" since they have explicitly taken the methodology of "present science" as their model in studying the world. This has direct consequences for feminist analysis. While feminist scholars are, in fact, attempting to fashion new intellectual tools, we do not completely reshape them. The various strands of feminist theory draw heavily on the academic social sciences or on Marxism (the major critical social science), or on both. Socialist feminists, for example, may revise or extend classic, male, Marxist assumptions in analyzing the situation of women, but the core of the theory

---

* In what follows I will use the term "present science" to refer to the methodology and practice of science now, since I believe that ultimately feminist and other critiques will lead to a quite different conception of what science can be.

ordinarily goes unchallenged. Insofar as classic Marxism is actually modelled on the present practice of science in its assumptions and methodology, an understanding of the implications of that is crucial for feminists.

While present science *is* the dominant model for rationality, it does have its critics. These describe present science as "scientism,"[1] "technism"[2] or "technist science,"[3] and they raise some fundamental questions about it. They challenge its claims to objectivity and ethical neutrality, and offer evidence for the importance of subjective and ideological factors in scientific practice. Gould, for example, argues that a tendency to bias is intrinsic to any scientific practice.[4] He holds that this occurs because science is necessarily done in the context of commitment to a theory or model or paradigm. His argument is that the problems for present science lie not in the existence of this commitment (and consequent tendency to prejudge results), but in an assertion that the tendency to bias is, in fact, not there. Ignoring this tendency makes it impossible to deal with it. Other aspects of the critique of present science explore the extent to which scientific practice reflects capitalist social relations and the extent to which it is shaped by the social uses of science.[5]

If we take as our view that "whatever is established by sound reasoning and evidence may belong to science,"[6] whatever its source, be that literature or physics, then the critical work cited above is extremely valuable. It offers not just a critique of the science that now exists, but gives the beginnings of insight into what exactly we might mean generally by "sound reasoning" and "evidence." Almost none of it, however, has any feminist content. It has been left to feminists themselves to begin that task. Recently, a number of feminist scholars have begun to add this dimension to the critique, examining the implications of the fact that present science is not only the dominant paradigm for knowledge, but it is also almost entirely a male enterprise.

If feminist scholarship generally is about the answers to important questions, then this implies an attempt to find not just the answers but the questions themselves. Feminism begins with the situation of women and analyzes the way that women's situation has been shaped by and in turn shapes the whole social world. The focus is on women, but the basic enterprise is an attempt to understand and evaluate human affairs. As scholars, feminists are explicitly committed. We are feminists because we believe not only that the evidence shows the oppression of women, but, further, that such oppression is wrong. We also believe that society should be changed to end all forms of oppression. Our scholarship is done in that context, but also in the belief that the closer one gets to the truth the better the cause of women will be served. At the core of the feminist critique of the various disciplines is the attempt to fashion intellectual tools that are freer from the distortions of present male scholarship and that allow us to seek the truth while we recognize our commitment. We are, in fact, developing new ideas about rationality in these specific areas. This alone is a sufficient reason for a careful examination of the basis for rationality generally.

A final reason for trying to come to some understanding of the nature of science lies in its importance in practical terms. Present science and the technology it supports are central to our society and will continue, in some form, to be central to any practical future. A feminist analysis of science is necessary in trying to understand whether or not science and technology, as they are now shaped, are compatible with feminist goals for the future. One obvious question, for example, is whether there would have to be major changes in scientific practice, and even scientific methodology, before women could fully participate.

The argument in what follows begins from the premise, basic to all the critical work on science cited above, that science is not independent of social context; both the practice and kind of science which exist now reflect the fact that the society which has given birth to modern science is both capitalist and male-dominated.

Sex Roles and Science

Many of the forces that keep women out of present science are not unique to it. Discrimination in science is in many ways similar to discrimination in other professions; a growing body of feminist scholarship describes and documents such discrimination.[7] In addition, problems can arise because of women's minority status in science or because of responsibilities in marriage or child-rearing. With its claims to universal relevance, however, science is not simply another profession. The practice of rational thought is upheld as a quintessentially human activity, and yet from its beginnings a continuing tradition in science has maintained that only men are capable of becoming scientists. Men are identified with culture, with rational thought, and with science; women are identified with nature (Merchant 1980; Griffin 1978; Ortner 1974).

None of the above is to say that individual women cannot and do not do science as competently as men. But we live in a society with strong and clearly articulated norms for appropriate behaviour and characteristics for men and women that are very different. Of course not all individual behaviour matches these norms, but the crucial fact is that they exist as the standards by which individuals judge themselves and are judged as either normal or deviant in some way. An important factor in the different relations that men and women have with science lies in the fact that the characteristics required to practice science are, in an almost one-to-one correspondence, parallel to normal male characteristics. The norms for typical feminine behaviour are, on the other hand, almost entirely opposite.

It is assumed that men are or should be aggressive, strong, independent, logical, dominant, in control of their physical environment, handy with tools and mechanical systems, in control of their emotions, and capable of abstract, objective thought. (This list may vary slightly in different Western cultures but the core of it remains remarkably constant.) Women, in contrast, are assumed to be intuitive, nurturant, emotional, dependent on and with strong connections to those around them, loving and caring, passive, and with limited capability for rationality and objectivity.

The stereotype of scientists themselves is as loners, coldly logical, committed only to their investigations, uninfluenced by personal desires, social factors or qualms about the uses of the work. Such scientists are objective in the sense of an assumed complete separation from the objects of their study. They are skilled in mathematics—the epitome of abstract thought—and in experimentation; thus, they both understand and control the physical world upon which they experiment. While not expected to be physically aggressive, they are expected to aggressively promote and defend their scientific results. Whether or not this view is correct in all its details, it is not only the popular stereotype but also provides the ideal that most scientists use to model their own scientific behaviour.[8]

The extent to which a man or woman has been socialized into a proper sex role will clearly affect ability to do science in this mode. However, independent of actual socialization, the simple existence of these norms is important. Men can do present science with little or no role conflict, no need to

61

examine or change basic assumptions about their world. The opposite is true for women.

According to Miles, one of the most important common tendencies in a wide variety of feminist theory and practice is to be found in the attempted synthesis of the dichotomized view of humanity (Miles 1979). She found as a recurrent theme the idea that in all areas of human endeavour one must strive for an integration of the attributes and points of view now split into the "male" and the "female." Feminism, like many other types of liberal or radical social thought, including Marxism, is the inheritor of the humanist tradition in its insistence on the centrality of human interests and the primacy of human worth and development. A powerful argument can be made that not only does feminism continue the humanist tradition, but that the attempted synthesis of the "male" and the "female" means that feminism is at present the most creative and progressive part of radical political thought since it is attempting to create a wider view of what it might mean to be human and so to create a "whole" humanism (Frieze 1978). In terms of the analysis of science, this means that the basic feminist enterprise is the investigation of the effect that the male/female split has had on scientific methodology and practice. Ultimately, if successful, such an enterprise will mean the development of modes of rationality and scientific investigation that take into account both subjectivity and the interactions between the knower and the known in a context of care and responsibility for both natural processes and other creatures.

The spread of present science as the dominant world view has been part of an anti-humanist tendency; it has been accompanied by tendencies to mechanization of the material world and dehumanization of the social one — people increasingly become means to ends outside themselves. While the roots of this lie in capitalist social relations, the expression of such tendencies is found in terms of the imperatives of technology and a "scientific approach." Humanism in its many forms has been the major counter-force to such tendencies, asserting the value of non-technical rationality as well as other modes of thought and experience. Humanism has provided a constant critical look at the uses of and claims for science and technology. Feminist analysis continues this tradition and brings a major new dimension to the critique.

In what follows, then, we will (1) examine features of present science which are incompatible with such a feminist/humanist approach to the world (this is not identical with

62

examining the different relations that men and women have to present science but this latter offers insight into the nature of science and will be a feature of the analysis), and (2) examine the extent to which present science fails in fulfilling its own methodological claims, and show how this failure is related to a masculine bias in present science itself.

Science—Postulates and Practice

Science can mean several things: the social institution made up of scientists plus the relations between them; the total body of propositions and information about the world; or a methodology describing how to carry out investigation of the world. These are all aspects of a whole; we study them separately but need to take the interrelations into account also. Further, science is not monolithic; it is a complex social institution and not even all scientists agree on the body of propositions or even the methodology. Science is also connected in complex ways with the rest of society—for example, the questions prominent on the scientific agenda from the very beginning have been those raised by industry, war or ruling class needs for controlling other parts of society. A critical understanding of the nature of present science requires setting any analysis of specific aspects of science into this larger picture, if it is to be complete. In this paper, my focus is on the methodology of present science; as necessary, some attention is paid to the social practice of that science and to the questions important to it—but the analysis must be understood in this wider context which is that of the radical and feminist critique cited earlier.

Present science works. It is a powerful method of obtaining specific kinds of knowledge about the world; scientific knowledge of material processes has allowed human intervention in an incredible range of activities. Practitioners of this science do not necessarily understand exactly how they get their results, and the practice of science may not be the same in all areas, but there is a core of assumptions that seems to characterize what is now meant by science and to be common to much present scientific practice. These assumptions are:

    1. There exists an "objective" material reality separate from and independent of an observer. This reality is orderly.

2. The material world is knowable through rational inquiry and this knowledge is independent of the individual characteristics of the observer.
3. Knowledge of the material world is gained through measurement of natural phenomena; measurement in a scientific sense consists of quantification, i.e., reduction to some from of mathematical description.
4. The goal of scientific understanding is the ability to predict and control natural phenomena. (This postulate often takes the form of the equation between science and power.)

This is a set of propositions that probably all working scientists would agree with; it is the core that is explicitly taken over into the social sciences in an attempt to model themselves on the physical sciences. There is an additional subset of premises that consitutes a working philosophy for most scientists:

a) The specific sciences are arranged in hierarchical order, varying from high level ones like sociology and psychology through biology and chemistry to particle physics at the base.
b) The sciences at the base are more fundamental. Phenomena in higher level sciences can be reduced on the basis of a one-for-one correspondence to phenomena, and hence laws appropriate to the lower level sciences; ultimately, physical laws, beginning with ones for the particle level, can be derived which will subsume and explain sociology, for example.
c) The phenomena to be studied can be isolated out from their surroundings; the essential features of these phenomena can be described by a mathematical theory that offers some insight into the workings of physical reality.

This set of postulates, which can be generally characterized as the "reductionist" paradigm, is not as fundamental as the first four postulates given, but, in fact, constitutes the working methodology of Western science.[9]

As the model for rational thought, present science is more than just a methodology. In important respects it is also an ideology in that it is both prescriptive and offers, in its fundamental postulates, false notions of how it functions. It is prescriptive not just because of the technocrat who claims that a "scientific" approach is better, but because this claim is implicit in scientific methodology itself. This is particularly true of the third of the assumptions given above. Measurement requires, among other things, that the object or phenomenon under study be "prepared" for such measurement by being stripped of all non-quantitative content, whether experiential, metaphysical, ethical, or whatever. Implicit in that postulate is an "axiom of impoverished reality"[10] which asserts not only that objects can be so stripped of non-quantitative aspects, but that they *ought* to be—that such a view is somehow better or truer than any alternative.

This ideological aspect of the postulate is not simply a perversion of proper scientific practice. The seeds of the notion are inherent in the idea of objectivity which is so central to present science. Scientific pratice is to be devoted strictly to abstract, quantifiable knowledge of the world where one strips down the phenomenon of interest to "basic" measurable quantities which can be observed undistorted by subjective factors. No part of present scientific methodology deals with integration of any social or individual values into scientific practice. In fact, consideration of such factors is, in principle, forbidden as unscientific. Though the assertion is made that such factors are not therefore to be considered as inferior but are simply separated out for others to deal with and to integrate with the scientific results, the actual inference is clear: the quantifiable, "scientific" aspects of the phenomenon under consideration are in fact, the important ones. More than that: it is implied that the introduction of subjective or ethical or non-quantitative factors of any kind is incompatible with objectivity and rationality. Working scientists would agree, by and large, with the basic proposition that such a scientific description is somehow "truer" than the other possible descriptions. This ideological aspect is an intrinsic part of present science.

This "impoverishment of reality" has been consistently rejected by humanists, who point out the range of important aspects of human culture which cannot be reduced to quantification and measurement, while the critics of science cited above point out the extent to which subjectivity actually enters into scientific practice even at present. What neither of these criticisms points out, however, is the extent to which the acceptance of an "impoverished reality" as the best truth about the world is compatible with male norms rather than with female ones.

Men are not expected to mix emotions or aesthetics or concern for the objects of study with rational thought; the male/female split of traits, in fact, makes "pure" rationality the ideal for men, while leaving subjective factors as the feminine domain. In such a split, one can either be rational or subjective, but not both. Given this perspective, the fact that the male norms are the dominant ones then becomes of critical importance. A number of studies have shown that male traits are those generally associated with desirable human traits. This makes it easy for a science to develop which includes impoverishment of reality as a good. It further means that no challenge to that view is likely to be viewed as legitimate. Such a challenge from a feminist perspective does not say that one should never attempt to isolate and measure phenomena, but that one should try to understand when such isolation is appropriate and when it is not.

The problem raised here, though, is not one of simply trying to understand the areas of appropriateness of a scientific approach, although this is clearly necessary.

From a feminist perspective, with its goal of integrating the halves represented by male and female norms, this is not sufficient. What is needed is a methodology that does not, in fact, relegate the non-quantifiable aspects of a problem to secondary status but instead attempts some kind of integration of this into scientific practice. We get additional support for this stance when we try to come to grips with the question not just of the appropriateness of the quantified approach to reality but with the assumption of objectivity that goes along with that.

Science and Objectivity

The axiom of impoverished reality holds that a quantitative description of reality is the truest one; the first two of the postulates given above assert that such a description is, in fact, possible to achieve. These two postulates embody the assumption of scientific objectivity — particularly the idea of the objective observer. Traditional views of science begin with the objective nature of experiment — that given the same conditions the same results will be obtained by any observer — and go on to assume further that in all other aspects of scientific investigation as well, the observer can remain completely independent of context. No individual factors or influence of specific historical times and places are considered to be important in the choice or formulation of problems, the interpretation of results, or, most fundamentally, in the development of the theories which are the core of science. As for example:

66

> But, basically, modern science is surely identical under every meridian. There is only one logic of controlled experimentation, only one application of mathematical hypotheses, and their testing by statistical methods. There are canons here which cannot be transgressed; the basic method of discovery itself, which was discovered in Galileo's time.[11]

(This very mainstream view of scientific methodology is, in fact, written by a critic of science in its social aspect.)

The idea of the objective observer needs further investigation. Just who is it who is competent to be such an observer? From the traditional scientific view, it cannot be just anyone. The observer must be disciplined to his part.[12] A general and standard attitude of impersonality or distance must become the dominant way of responding to objects. Natural objects are viewed as fixed and possessed of invariant quantities which are the objects of study—the way that the observer feels about these objects is not just irrelevant to a scientific approach but must be rigorously excluded. The ideal scientific investigator stands aside in his own person and becomes the impartial judge of the data and their relation to the particular theory under consideration. A second feature of the observer is that he is a measurer; much of present scientific training consists of learning standard methods and procedures in the use of measuring instruments. The ideal observer, then, is one who is able to be detached, unemotional, completely rational in approaching phenomena, and who is, in addition, skilled in the use of scientific instruments. In this traditional view of science, such an observer is one who clearly delineates and detaches his self from outside objects and, further, is someone who assumes the right of mastery over objects.

As mentioned earlier, the qualities required for the practice of such a science are those assumed to be possessed by "normal" men in this society, with the addition of special training. This does not, in itself, constitute a valid criticism of present science. If we assume that such behaviour is, in fact, the way that such science is practised, it might be that women should simply learn to behave in this fashion and that the feminist vision of an integration of characteristics is inappropriate here. Such a position is untenable, from a feminist point of view, on two grounds: first, even as an ideal, such an objectivity is incompatible with a feminist vision of the world; and second, this objectivity is another of the ideological features of present science in that it is a myth rather than a description of actual practice.

Regarding this second point: a relatively large body of recent work has challenged the possibility of scientific objectivity in the traditional sense.[13] In perhaps the best known of these, Kuhn examines the way in which scientific theories are formed and the problematic relationship that such theories have with experiment.[14] The widespread view of objectivity given above seems to rest on the assumption of a relatively straightforward formulation of theory or hypothesis on the basis of experiment. If experiment is dependent on some theory, however, then this simple view (which is that outlined in almost all introductory science texts) is not a description of scientific practice. If experiment is no longer simple and independent of theory, then the one apparently firm claim for objectivity in present science becomes problematic also.

This is not to say that the same controlled experiment, done under the same conditions, will not provide the same raw results to any two observes — but one observer may pick one part of these results as important while the second chooses other parts, or the two observers may interpret the results in very different ways, applying different theories or different statistical assumptions. A paper by Gould, re-analyzing the data on which Morton based his asssumption of the superiority of caucasians, provides as excellent example of this.[15] In most of physics and chemistry, such variations between observers are small, mostly because the problems ordinarily tackled in these sciences are relatively simple compared to those in such other disciplines as biology, even, or psychology. In many of these disciplines, experiments cannot even be controlled; the necessity for attempting to extract conclusions from such a welter of factors clearly exacerbates the whole range of problems with theory/experiment. In all cases, however, the conclusions are clear: to a greater or lesser degree, the observed is not completely independent of the observer — the theory itself guides what is seen and how results are interpreted. Subjective factors are intrinsic to the very act of observation.

The claims for objectivity in present science become even less tenable when we look at the ways in which problems are formulated and the subjective factors that enter into the choice of the relatively few aspects of nature that we can hope to study intensively.

...of necessity we can tackle only the few, limited aspects of nature of which we take sufficient notice that they arouse our interest or curiosity to the point where we begin to examine them more closely. The scientific modes of thought and action therefore elevate some things and events to the rank of "facts," indeed of "*scientific* facts," while being oblivious to the existence of others, and actively relegating yet a third category to the foggy realms of supposition or, worse yet, superstition.[16]

The questions of interest to science have, in large measure, been those of interest to industry and to the military. This alone would lead to a distortion of the objectivity claimed by present science, and it is clear that all of the factors destroy the idea of detachment and independence of context in the practice of science now. What *is* practised in present science is a kind of "pseudo-objectivity" where, because they are not taken explicitly into account, subjective factors are uncontrolled and unaccounted for.

There are a number of factors which lead to the continuation of this ideal of pseudo-objectivity. On the institutional level, the objectivity myth is encouraged by the ruling class which uses science to legitimate the subordination of human beings to anti-human ends which serve the purposes of those with power disguised in a kind of technological determinism. The idea of objectivity supports the actual use of science to gain control of and domination over a world viewed by those in power as being made up of manipulable objects — both human and non-human. Indeed, the assumption that the observer can be completely separated from the phenomena being observed, and that such phenomena can be treated entirely as objects with no relation to the observer, becomes more and more problematic as the scientific method is applied to human matters or even to questions involving any living creatures.

First of all is the problem of getting valid conclusions at all — the inability to do controlled experiments, particularly in medical science, psychology and the social sciences, was mentioned above, but there is also the problem of separating out the observers' biases from the design of experiments and interpretation of results. Male/female differences in brain function, sociobiology, or even animal behaviour, raise such problems. The most frightening of the problems, however, comes with the abrogation of responsibility that the pseudo-objective stance allows. In the name of science, anything is allowed, from the medical treatment of women's reproductive organs as disposable (after their reproductive years, of course) through the game theory approach to nuclear warfare where millions of deaths become counters in a global game of terror, to the psychosurgery used to "cure" homosexuality in men and promiscuity in women.

69

The functioning of such pseudo-objectivity, with its denial of the subjective factors with do enter into scientific practice and the human factors which ought to, is possible only in a context where the view of humanity, and in particular the human observer, has been already equated with the (male) logical and rational functions. This particular myth of objectivity depends on a co-existing ideology that legitimizes the idea of pure intellect. Men, who are brought up to deny their own emotions and to be separated from their own selves, find it easy to believe that a pure, isolated rationality is possible. As a consequence, it is easy to believe that their science is, in fact, as objective as it claims to be.

As noted above, even if such objectivity were real, however, it would still be unacceptable to feminists, since it is this assumption of isolated rationality that leads to the systematic treatment of other human beings as objects and, indeed, that allows scientists to take no responsibility for the uses of science in any area. One current in feminism these days does not, in fact, advocate a rejoining of "male" and "female" halves, but, in effect, advocates a rejection of male characteristics and attributes as intrinsically anti-human. A number of expressions of this tendency exist which reject scientific knowledge, methodology, and any attempt at scientific objectivity, as irreclaimable, anti-human and male.[17] For the integrative tendencies in feminism, the problem is not quite so simple.

As Keller points out, such a rejection of science is a capitulation. It accepts a division imposed by a male tradition and makes a virtue out of the exclusion of women from science. Such a position abandons any attempt to reclaim science for women and elevate the female half of human characteristics as that which ought to be characteristic of humanity instead of the male half which is at present taken to represent a complete human. However, such a retreat in the subjectivity assumed to be the realm of women leaves too much behind. Objectivity, however distorted into pseudo-objectivity, is too important to abandon; it is a "quintessentially human goal,"[18] and a true objectivity can only be achieved by an observer who is not cut off from half of human experience.

> Objectivity consists in so fully realizing the countless intrusions of the self in everyday thought and the countless illusions which result — illusions of sense, language, point of view, value, etc. — that the preliminary step to every judgment is the effort to exclude the intrusive self. Pseudo-objectivity, on the contrary, consists in ignoring the existence of self and thence regarding one's own perspective as

immediately objective and absolute. Pseudo-objectivity is thus anthro-pocentric illusion, finality — in short, all those illusions which teem in the history of science.[19]

Science and Power

The goal of scientific understanding at present is to predict and hence be able to control natural phenomena. The direct search for results, whether they be in ballistics, birth control technology, textile dyes, drugs, recombinant DNA experiments, or cognitive psychology, is a major part of present scientific effort. Even realms of "pure" research eventually are tied to this quest for power over the world — through such factors as allocation of research money, training of scientists in "interesting" questions, and direct control of research by industry. Science rests on an assumption of the legitimacy of control and domination of the natural world; in examining this relationship of science to power, we can see another consequence of the male origins of present science.

As Gorz and Weizenbaum both point out, scientists are allowed one expression of self — the exercise of power.[20] Scientists are, in fact, *expected* to exercise power, both in the practice of scientific research itself and in the social institutions in which that research is done. Questions of power within the social organization of science, with its hierarchies, discrimi-nation against women and minorities, the scramble for grant monies, and the connections with the military and big business, are clearly important for feminists to understand. Of direct concern for this discussion, however, is the question of the exercise of power as a factor in scientific research itself. This is particularly true since one of the consequences of the assumed objectivity of present science and its assertion of the legitimacy of control over the natural world outside the observer is the reduction of other human beings to objects to be controlled and manipulated. Given the widespread cultural identification of "women" with "nature," this is particularly liable to happen when women become the objects of scientific study.

Little boys grow up encouraged to make things happen. Their parents encourage them to practise mastery over material objects, particularly machines, and to develop inde-pendent problem-solving skills. Girls are not encouraged to develop their confidence in manipulating the world; they learn to be more dependent on others, particularly in solving problems. This is another aspect of the general situation noted above, where the practice of present science is compatible with male norms and not with female ones. In this case, the practice at issue—the exercise of power over the world—combined with the ideal of a "pure" and hence irresponsible rationality, gives that power the characteristics of dominance and exploitation that together pose one of the main problems with present science.

The scientific reduction of women and men to objects of study and manipulation is a consequence of the general technique of reductionism in science (the postulates of which are outlined above). Generally, in fact, power and reductionism in science are linked. The basis of scientific prediction and control is the construction of a "model" of the phenomenon or system under study. (Such a model may be a single scientific theory or one constructed of several such theories which are used to describe the various aspects of the model world.) The model is a stripped-down version of the world, in the sense described earlier, in that it focuses on the quantifiable, measurable aspects of the world. Further, it assumes that the phenomenon can be broken up into simple components and understood in terms of these (relatively) simple parts. Properly constructed, the model is completely understood and unambiguous. It allows prediction of processes within the model world, since, if initial conditions are assumed to be set in a certain way, one can predict what will follow in terms of results. To the extent that such a model does, in fact, mirror the actual phenomenon of interest, the model tells one how to arrange the initial conditions to get the desired results.

The essence of the present scientific method lies in this limitation of the problem to a manageable size—in reducing the complexity of the real world by the construction of a model that represents an isolated, small part of that reality. In many cases this is an extremely powerful tool for achieving the desired results—the selection of certain aspects of reality as the only ones important for study and the neglect of all others means a reduction of problems to a manageable size. Central to understanding the practice of present science is the fact that science is not simply about knowedge, but is intended to lead to power over the world. The almost exclusive reliance on the reductionist approach in present science can be traced to the desire to achieve certain specific effects or products. The lack of interest in any "side" effects or related effects is intrinsic to this approach.* There is no established part of scientific methodology that deals with interactions, processes, complex effects or levels of significance of results.

A good example for the reductionist approach can be found in medical science. Medicine is based on a mechanical reductionist view: (a) the human body is viewed or analyzed as a set of quasi-mechanical parts, operating according to the laws of physics and chemistry rather than as an organically related whole; these parts are assumed to function independently of the mind of the organism; and (b) each disease is assumed to be caused by a specific agent (generally either mechanical damage or some sort of germ). This model has provided the basis for some very real accomplishments of medicine—vaccination, antisepsis, anaesthesia, antibiotics, and birth control technology. However, the limits, even when dealing with infectious diseases, have become more and more evident. Critics such as Dubos have presented a multiple cause model of disease where body, mind, and an environment which includes more than "germs," interact to produce or cure disease.[21] The tendency of reliance on present scientific methodology is evident in the tendencies of medical researchers and practitioners to dehumanize others—patients are treated as objects, not as participants in their own health. The treatment of women's reproductive organs as simply disposable parts and the lack of research on side effects of birth control technology are consequences of this reductionist medical model. Further than that, however, such a model results in the very narrowest of definitions of the boundaries of medical science. Present medical research concentrates almost exclusively, for example, on a search for the cure and treatment of cancer by understanding the basic biology and biochemistry of tumour growth or by testing heroic drug treatments. It is clear though, that many, if not most cancers result from interaction between body and environment.[22] Research into cancer prevention (as opposed to cancer detection) is not a part of the medical model. Treatment of such conditions as depression (particularly for women) by prescription of drugs like Valium is another result of the reductionist model of health or illness.

---

* In fact, there are no "side" effects: there are only effects. The definition of some of the results of the process under study as unimportant is done in terms of the intent of the investigator rather than the reality of the process. The "pill" is a good example—suppression of ovulation is one of its effects, while another is a change in body chemistry that may make blood clotting more likely. A less distorted methodology would not dismiss this second effect as easily as present medical science does.

The importance of a critique of reductionism for feminists is twofold. First, insofar as reductionism and the associated search for power are central to science and as long as the norms for male and female roles are different, women will be exceptional in science. Second, if feminists do not want to reject either the male half or the female half of humanity, then they must reject a kind of science which rests exclusively on the practice of male traits.

Toward a Different Science

We cannot afford to give up the struggle to understand and to come to terms with our world. As women and as feminists, we must begin to deal with the science and technology that shapes our lives and even our bodies. We have been the objects of a bad science; now we must become the makers of a new one. What is needed in such a new science is, first of all, a sense of the limits of appropriateness of reductionism and the development of a methodology which can deal with "systems that flow so smoothly and gradually or are so profoundly interwoven in their complexities that they cannot be broken up into measurable units without losing or changing their fundamental nature."[23] Difficult as this may be in practice, its very adoption as a goal must mean a major change in scientific methodology. With this must come a consideration of the connections between the knower and the known and an understanding of the ways in which subjective factors are important in science. With this also must come a sense of limits—of what is not known or cannot be known or is not appropriate as a subject for scientific approach. We will need an understanding of appropriate levels of discourse—of when it might be appropriate to offer explanations in terms of basic physics or chemistry, for example, as opposed to when an explanation in terms of the relationship of an organism with its environment would offer more insight. This is not to say that these approaches are never encountered in present science, but the central core of present scientific methodology simply does not take them adequately into account.

The distortions and limitations of present science arise out of its social context. Science clearly shows its origins in a hierarchical, class-based society, and, more than that, just as clearly shows the marks of its origin and practice as a male enterprise. The claim that science is value-free, objective and purely rational is ideology and not reality.

The task that seems of primary importance — for women and men — is to convert science from what it is today, a social institution with a conservative function and a defensive stand, into a liberating and healthy activity. Science needs a soul which would show respect and love for its subjects of study and would stress harmony and communication with the rest of the universe. When science fulfills its potential and becomes a tool for human liberation, we will not have to worry about women "fitting" into it because we will probably be at the forefront of that "new" science.

(Arditti 1980:367)

FOOTNOTES

1. David Dickson, *Alternative Technology and the Politics of Technical Change* (London: Fontana, 1974).
2. J. Davis, *Man and Technology* (Baton Rouge: University of Louisiana Press, 1976).
3. Barrington Moore, "Tolerance and the Scientific Outlook" in R.P. Wolff, B. Moore & H. Marcuse, *Critique of Pure Tolerance* (Boston: Beacon Press, 1969).
4. Stephen Gould, "Morton's Ranking of the Races by Cranial Capacity" in *Science*, Vol. 200, 1978, pp. 503-509.
5. H. Rose & S. Rose (eds.), *Ideology of/in the Natural Sciences* (Cambridge, Mass.: Shenkman, 1980); B. Easlea, *Liberation and the Aims of Science* (London: Chatto & Windus, 1973); R. Arditti, P. Brennan & S. Cavrak 1980; R. Hubbard & M. Lowe (eds.), *Genes and Gender II* (New York: Gordian, 1979).
6. Barrington Moore, *op. cit.*, p. 55.
7. *International Journal of Women's Studies*, Vol. 4, 1981; *Women's Studies International Quarterly*, Vol. 3, 1981; Kanter 1977; Choices for Science: Symposium Proceedings (1980).
8. H. Lowe, "Cooperation and Competition in Science" in *International Journal of Women's Studies*, Vol. 4, 1981; Roe 1956; D.C. McClelland, "On the Dynamics of Creative Physical Scientists" in *The Ecology of Human Intelligence* (London: Penguin, 1962).
9. S. Rose & H. Rose, "The Politics of Neurobiology" in Rose & Rose 1980, *op. cit.*.
10. I. Jenkins, "Postulate of an Impoverished Reality" in *Journal of Philosophy*, Vol. 39, 1942, pp. 533-547.
11. J. Needham, "History and Human Values" in Rose & Rose 1980, *op. cit.*, p. 245.
12. J. Davis 1976, *op. cit.*, p. 157.
13. Thomas Kuhn, *The Structure of Scientific Revolutions* (Chicago: University of Chicago Press, 1970); B. Easlea 1973, *op. cit.*, and references therein.
14. Kuhn 1970, *op. cit.*.

15. Gould 1978, *op. cit.*.
16. R. Hubbard, "Introductory Essay" in Rose & Rose 1980, *op. cit.*, p. xvii.
17. Griffin 1978; Gearhart 1979; Charnas 1974, 1976.
18. Keller 1980.
19. Jean Piaget, *The Child's Conception of the World* (Totowa, N.J.: Littlefield & Adams, 1972), quoted in Keller 1980:269-270.
20. J. Weisenbaum, *Computer Power and Human Reason* (San Francisco: Freeman, 1976), Chapter 4.
21. J. Ehrenreich, "Introduction" in J. Ehrenreich (ed.), *The Cultural Crisis of Medicine* (New York: Monthly Review Press, 1978), p. 13.
22. *Ibid.*
23. Hubbard, *op. cit.*, p. xvii.

CHAPTER 3

Gynocentric Values
and Feminist Psychology

Jeri Dawn Wine

Jeri Dawn Wine teaches psychology and feminist studies at the Ontario Institute for Studies in Education, Toronto. Her major interest lies in feminist analysis of social interaction and human relationship and in working toward an inclusive feminism that recognizes and affirms differences among women yet transcends the barriers of sexuality, race, and class. She was a member of the Feminist Party of Canada. She is active in the Centre for Women's Studies at OISE, is on the editorial board of *Resources for Feminist Research*, is active in the Canadian Women's Studies Association, and sits on the board of the Canadian Research Institute for the Advancement of Women.

Since publication of this chapter, a number of works have represented the efforts of feminist psychologists to explore women's experience from a gynocentric perspective. Perhaps the most prominent of these publications are Belenky, *et al.* (1986), *Women's Ways of Knowing*, and the Boston Lesbian Psychologies Collective's (1987) *Lesbian Psychologies: Explorations and Challenges*. Strongly recommended also is the special issue on Women's Development and Education of the *Journal of Education* (1985). Work from a gynocentric perspective that uses the qualitative and interpretive methodologies favoured by scholars working within such a perspective is still coming under considerable attack both by mainstream academics and feminist scholars (e.g., see *Signs* 11:2, pp. 304-33, discussion of Carol Gilligan's research), primarily for its deviation from positivist criteria for good research.

Feminist perspectives in psychology are slowly emerging, a process that is a painful and controversial one, but one that is beginning to provide important ovarian theory and data for the broader feminist struggle. The process of emergence of fully feminist scholarship is a particularly difficult one in psychology for a variety of reasons that have to do with the nature of psychology's underlying philosophy, "scientific" methods, accepted subject matter, and its extensive investment in documentation of the inferiority of women. Equally important, though less obvious, are the inextricable linkages among these and the androcentric values inherent in prevailing psychological views of the nature of human beings—or in the disciplinary vernacular—its "models of man." As Jill McCalla Vickers has noted in Chapter One, it is markedly difficult for a fully feminist psychology to emerge that has the defining features of feminist scholarship in other disciplines, including its interdisciplinary character, contextualism, and concern with the female experience guided by woman-centred questions and values.

In the first part of this article, I examine some of the dimensions of "male-stream" (to adopt Mary O'Brien's and Jill McCalla Vickers' apt term) psychology that render it a particularly inhospitable environment for the growth of feminist work. An ontogeny of feminist scholarship suggested by Showalter[1] is then used to examine the development of feminist psychology, an ontogeny that proceeds from *imitation*, through *protest*, to a *focus on female experience*. In the second part of the paper I discuss work in psychology that explores a woman-centred or gynocentric perspective. "Relationality" is the organizing principle I've used in this discussion, a principle I consider centrally representative of women's experience and values. In essence, relationality refers to consciousness of the necessary interdependence of human beings, to a sense of connectedness to others, to awareness of one's embeddedness in human, social and historical contexts, to the maximization of well-being for all persons, and to commitment to non-violence. Relationality contrasts markedly with the individuality principle that underlies male-stream psychology's models of man. Examination of work on social interaction, human relationships, development of individuals in the human context and resolution of interpersonal moral dilemmas from a gynocentric relationality perspective makes it clear that gynocentric values challenge not only the androcentric models of psychology but the very essence of patriarchal society.

Male-stream Psychology

There are certain central features of male-stream psychology that render it a particularly barren and hostile environment for the growth of feminist work. Psychology has a peculiarly rigid adherence to a naïve brand of logical positivism that, in Sherif's[2] estimation, is symptomatic of an advanced case of "physics envy."[3] The "scientific methods" that are predominantly used in psychology require removal of the individuals under study from the contexts of their natural human environments, reduction of the units of observation to readily classifiable simple behaviours of individuals, a detached rational worship of control and "objectivity," an extremely narrow ahistorical, non-contextual space and time framework, and reverence for quantification and for so-called "basic" (meaning physical) levels of analysis. Though psychology is purported to be concerned with understanding the individual, it is an abstracted, idealized individual based on group averages. Any real individual differences that do appear are considered as "noise" or error in the data. The relationship between researcher and researched is a distant, detached one. More often that not, research "subjects" are deceived as to the purposes of the research on the grounds that accurate knowledge might "contaminate" their responses. The tightly controlled experiment with its clearly defined "independent" and "dependent" variables is the *sine qua non* of psychological method. Though other research methods are condoned, the measure of their worth is the extent to which they approximate the control, objectivity, and quantification of the experiment. The nature of the human being that is evident in psychology's models of man is directly tied to its methodologies, i.e., the abstracted, separated, self-interested, context-free individual.

The extent to which positivist philosophy and methods affect the growth of feminist psychology can readily be detected in an examination of the contents of the two major psychology of women journals, *Sex Roles* and *The Psychology of Women Quarterly*. The majority of the studies reported in these journals are of the highly controlled, context-stripping, experimental variety. This observation attests not only to the criteria used by reviewers in selecting articles, but to the research methods in which psychologists are intensively and almost exclusively trained. The only major alternative research approaches used to any extent by psychologists are phenomenological in nature. In my view, researchers who use the latter methods are likely to err in another non-feminist direction, that is, in the reification of the unique individual experience, independent of context and without explicit linkages to the experiences of others. In the context of the feminist dictum that "the personal is political," phenomenologists' reports are likely to suggest that "the personal is highly personal."

The debate regarding the proper research paradigm for the conduct of feminist psychological research is an extensive and heated one. It is not likely to yield a single "correct" paradigm; there are undoubtedly a variety of approaches appropriate at different stages of the feminist research process. Our research methodologies must, however, become more flexible, contextual, and interdisciplinary. From a feminist perspective, it is essential that the relationship between researcher and researched be a collaborative, non-deceptive, non-exploitative one. We are learning a good deal from sociologists and anthropologists regarding interpretive contextual research approaches. It is my fond hope that the controlled experiment will come to be seen as the very limited method it is, useful at best for confirming, in a quantifiable fashion, with a sizeable group of women, a specific aspect of research findings previously explored in more contextual depth with a small number of women.

Another important feature of male-stream psychology that has rendered it especially inhospitable for feminist work, especially work directed towards exploration of woman's specificity, or the unique female experience, is psychology's history of the documentation of the inferiority of women. No other discipline has invested more time, energy and money in demonstrating that women are different than men, and therefore inferior to men. It has been amply documented that psychology is a male-centred and male-defined discipline.[4] Well over two-thirds of its human research has been done on males and generalized to all humans, while females have been studied exclusively only in devalued, purportedly feminine areas. In sex differences research, women have served as a convenient "other" to aid in defining the essence of humanity, the male. In Judith Long Laws' estimation, psychological theories of human functioning are predicated on "the assumption of male as normal and female as exception, of man as essence and woman as accident."[5] The large literature on psychological sex differences is highly problematic from a feminist perspective because of its apparent demonstration of the inferiority of the female. In this work, the guiding assumptions are that any characteristic that males have more of than do females is an essential characteristic, a mark of superiority, while any characteristic that females have more of is a sign of weakness, of inferiority. Thus we find this literature replete with such ludicrous interpretations as visual-spatial abilities being considered more important than verbal abilities, of single-minded achievement behaviours and aggressiveness being highly prized while nurturance is viewed as weakness, of environmental responsiveness being labelled "field dependence" and devalued, and so on; the list is endless. Given psychology's profoundly misogynous history in sex differences, it is apparent that any propositions focused on woman's specificity are likely to be greeted with suspicion by feminist psychologists.

Androcentric Interactional Models

The embeddedness of androcentric values in theories of human functioning is obvious when we look at recent human interactional theories in psychology. The individualistic models of man are translated into views of the individual acting on or against other people in order to achieve personalistic goals — a "man against his social environment" image. The image can most readily be detected in the popularized assertiveness model. It is probably inaccurate to label this very large literature as representing a model, as it is quite diverse and loosely connected, consisting of speculations, experimental studies, attempts at definition, treatment studies with non-assertive persons, etc.. There is very little semblance of unifying theory or analysis. The literature is based on the unquestioned assumption that assertiveness, considered to be a male trait (itself a dubious proposition), is by definition good and desirable. There are a variety of definitions of assertiveness in the literature, those that do and those that do not include aggression as a component of assertiveness, those that include positive expressiveness as well as negative expressiveness, and so on. They are all characterized by an almost exclusive focus on the individual's self-centred pursuit of goals, expression of self-defined needs and emotions, constrained only by avoidance of infringement on the rights of others. This androcentric individual rights orientation to evaluating effective social behaviour is reflective of the principles on which males base moral decisions, an observation that will become apparent in a subsequent section of this paper.

An excellent example of the unquestioned androcentric bias in the assertiveness literature is provided by a study that is frequently cited by assertiveness researchers for its supposedly elegant analysis of cognitive and behavioural components of assertiveness.[6] The university students who participated in the research were sorted into groups labelled as low, moderate and high assertive on the basis of their scores on a questionnaire measure of refusal of "unreasonable" requests. In the experiment proper, the students reponded to unreasonable requests that were presented with three sets of instructions. In one set they were instructed to give "model refusal responses," that is, they were instructed to refuse, while in the second they were instructed to imagine that they were giving advice about what to say to a friend who had asked for help in refusing the requests. With these two sets of instructions, of course, all of the students gave refusal responses. The third set of instructions was intended to simulate reality; the students were told to imagine that the situation was really happening and to respond as they naturally would in that situation. They also completed a questionnaire about their thoughts, consisting of "cognitive self-statements" that had been previously classified as "positive"—ones that would facilitate request refusal, and "negative"—ones that would make it harder to refuse a request. With these reality-simulating instructions, the students classified as low assertive were less likely to refuse requests than were the high assertive students; they also reported more negative cognitions while the high assertive students reported more positive cognitions.

These data were interpreted as indicating that low assertive persons know "correct" assertive responses but their performance is blocked by negative thoughts. The results were compared to other research in which a "variety of *patients* had thought patterns characterized by negative and *maladaptive* self-statements,"[7] with suggestions for treatment of low assertive persons to restructure their maladaptive thought patterns. In order to explicate the androcentrism of this research, it is essential to examine the content of the positive and negative self-statements. Examples of the positive self-statements are: "I was thinking that it doesn't matter what the person thinks of me. I was thinking that I am perfectly free to say no." Examples of the negative self-statements are: "I was thinking that it is better to help others than to be self-centred. I was thinking that the other person might be hurt or insulted if I refused."[8] These positive and negative thoughts are reflective of very different value orientations to social interaction, the former indicating egocentric autonomous pursuit of self-defined goals and the latter reflecting concern for others and acceptance of responsibility for the effects of one's behaviour on others. There is clearly nothing inherently inferior or maladaptive about the low assertive students' orientation to social interaction. Indeed, from a pro-social perspective which emphasizes the welfare of all, it is much to be preferred to that of the high assertive students. The unquestioned androcentric bias of the assertiveness construct dictated that this pro-social orientation be devalued; that those who hold it be compared to patients, described as maladapted and in need of therapy.

The individualistic man against his social environment model is also evident in much of the social competence literature, especially the literature that is based on a social problem-solving approach to explaining effective social behaviour. In this approach, often used in remedial social skills training, social interactions are defined as problems to be solved; individuals are trained to identify their own goals in interactions, to generate specific kinds of behaviour as means of reaching those goals, and to observe the actions of others in order to assess the impact of their behaviour on them. This is a somewhat more genteel and sophisticated version of the assertiveness approach. Another prominent example of an androcentric model is the social exchange theory which foreshadowed the assertiveness and problem-solving approaches. Thibaut and Kelly first introduced social exchange theory in 1959, and it has been so influential that many of its propositions and language conventions have been absorbed into the lore and language of psychology. The basic propositions were apparently so intuitively self-evident (to men) that they became "common knowledge" in androcentric psychology. In essence, social exchange theory postulates that individuals engage in social interaction to exchange the commodities of reward and punishment, each individual striving to maximize the former and minimize the latter. Each social interaction is considered a zero-sum game, a win-lose proposition with participating individuals vying with each other for the limited reinforcements available. It is assumed that individuals maintain a running tally of personal gains and losses in interpersonal interaction. The possibilities of mutuality, harmonious relationships, and recognition of the interdependence of human beings are precluded by the very nature of the theory.

Development of Feminist Psychology

Showalter's description of developmental foci in feminist scholarship is an ontogency that is helpful to understanding the development of feminist psychology.[9] The first stage of development that she identifies has an *imitation* focus. It accompanies women's early awareness of the male-centredness of a particular discipline, and does not include a questioning of androcentric values. The problem for those concerned about women is defined at this stage as one of the under-representation of females as objects of research. Research problems are not reformulated from women's perspective, rather male-centred research is replicated on women. Females are plugged into male theories, or the theories are altered slightly to accomodate women, without questioning the implicit androcentric assumptions of the theories. The second phase of Showalter's ontogeny is the *protest* focus which is concomitant with feminists' growing consciousness of the historical pervasiveness of misogynous bias in extant bodies of knowledge, and takes the form of concerted attacks on these bodies of knowledge. The androcentric values underlying choice of research problems and interpretation of research results are still not seriously challenged, however. In the third focus, feminist scholars are concerned with *exploration of the female experience guided by gynocentric concerns and values.* As Judith Long Laws has noted, this ontogeny is often recapitulated in the careers of individual feminist scholars.

Much of the work on the psychology of women, as the area is known in the discipline, can most accurately be described as focused on imitation or protest. This is not a surprising observation considering that feminist scholarship in psychology is only a little over a decade old. (There were some superb feminist psychologists just after the turn of the century, but it is some time since their influence has been felt.) We have made considerable progress for women as a function of work in these foci: the establishment of publication policies that support equal opportunities for female authors and equal representation of female and male subject populations in research reports; regulations regarding non-sexist language usage; the establishment of statistical criteria for reporting sex differences; the founding of organizations committed to women's needs in psychology; the questioning of longstanding empirical generalizations regarding differences between the sexes, and so on. I consider it essential at this stage of the

84

feminist journey in psychology to re-examine the process of that journey, being especially attentive to androcentric assumptions and values.

The early position of most feminists working in the psychology of women can be described as a simple victimology that accepted the male as standard and saw the female as inferior but malleable. It was believed that if she was given the same learning experiences, societal opportunities and rewards, she could be as good as a male; that is, she could acquire valued male characteristics. The analyses implied that the explanations for women's oppression lay in women's deficiencies — psychological characteristics of individual women that were the result of faulty sex role socialization or deficient learning opportunities. The analyses were focused on changing socialization experiences, on providing learning opportunities so that women might individually be less defective. The "blaming-the-victim"[10] fallacy is very difficult to avoid when researchers accept conventional male-stream psychology's methodologies and the associated subject matter of the decontextualized individual. Three bodies of work in the psychology of women that represent Showalter's imitation focus are the work on the motive to avoid success, research and theory on androgyny, and the early surge of assertiveness training for women.

The "motive to avoid success"[11] was an effort to patch up a male theory of achievement to accommodate women without questioning the masculinized definition of achievement and without recognizing that it is a victim-blaming construct.[12] I know no feminist psychologists who were unmoved by this apparent breakthrough for women in an important theoretical area. Perhaps we should have recognized something was wrong when Horner's 1969 doctoral dissertation was, within a very short period of time, presented widely in the popular media and appeared in every introductory psychology textbook. Briefly, Horner's major hypotheses were that the motive to avoid success was more likely to characterize women than men, that it was a stable motive established in childhood, and that bright women were especially likely to experience it. Though the extensive research literature on this motive has failed to replicate Horner's early results or verify any aspect of her theory, the motive to avoid success has become part of the folklore in psychology. It obviously serves the male-centred purposes of explaining away women's under-representation in advanced educational and occupational pursuits as our own fault.

The extensive work in androgyny, which presents the view that *both* rigidly held feminine *and* masculine sex roles are maladaptive and that an androgynous combination is most adaptive, appeared initially to offer considerable promise for the development of feminist psychology. Recent feminist critiques of this work have made it clear that androgyny involves prizing of stereotypically masculine characteristics, even in the structure and origin of the term, [13] and that the measurement operations treat as real entities stereotypes of what masculinity and feminity mean, reifying the stereotypes rather than attacking them (Eichler 1980). The inadequacy of the term as an index of mental health, suggesting something akin to "John Travolta and Farrah Fawcett Majors scotch-taped together," is becoming glaringly apparent. [14]

The third example of the imitation focus is the wave of assertiveness training for women that began in the early 1970's. Again, the immediate popularization of this approach should have alerted us to its problems. Assertiveness training was so quickly embraced and widely disseminated through established organizations (in most major cities in North America, Y's offer programmes geared especially to women) that it must be serving some highly useful social control function for patriarchal society. Again, I submit that this approach is representative of the blaming-the-victim fallacy to which male-stream psychological theory and research so readily lends itself. In this instance, the fallacy is that the power imbalance between men and women is a result of individual women's lack of assertiveness. Assertiveness training work with women assumes that (1) assertiveness is a unitary masculine characteristic and is thus to be valued, and (2) that women are deficient in it. In other work, my colleagues and I have questioned both of these assumptions. In the present context, my immediate concern is with the over-emphasis on assertiveness to the exclusion of other aspects of human functioning. Women *do* need encouragement to develop an autonomous sense of self and to have a healthy respect for ourselves and our own rights. I think it is important, however, that feminist work directed toward these goals be embedded in a broader gynocentric model of human functioning that emphasizes women's positive qualities and capacities, such as the models proposed by Jean Baker Miller (1976) and Nancy Chodorow (1978).

The protest focus in psychology is represented by a number of broadly based critical reviews of existing theoretical and research literature that have attacked longstanding empirical generalizations about women's inferiority vis-à-vis men. Perhaps the best known of these efforts is Maccoby and Jacklin's (1974) careful examination of *all* the sex differences research literature over an eight-year period. In this volume, they poked holes in many of the widely accepted myths regarding sex differences. It has long been "known" and reported in social psychology texts that females are more persuasible and readily influenced by social pressure than are males. Alice Eagley (1978) reported a mammoth review of all of the available research on short-term persuasion and suggestibility, revealing that there is simply no evidence for the blanket generalizations regarding women's suggestibility. Her review indicates that when some aspect of a person's integrity or self-concept is threatened, neither women nor men are readily influenced in brief encounters. When responsiveness to the situation seems more important at the time than maintaining one's concept of self, persons of either sex may be readily influenced. Other reviewers have been concerned with demonstrating that under certain specified conditions women equal men in some culturally valued masculine characteristic such as aggressiveness, or, like Eagley's review, that women are similar to men on some devalued "feminine" characteristic. This work has been valuable in demonstrating the extent to which existing psychological theory and research are simply naïve reflections of our misogynous androcentric societal structures, and in dispelling many patriarchal myths regarding the inferiority of women on male-defined dimensions. My concerns are that it does not seriously question the dimensions themselves, and that it seems implicitly to be guided by the goal of demonstrating that females and males are, after all, essentially the same.

Psychological feminist work that is not readily classifiable according to Showalter's foci is that which is concerned with women's oppression in areas unearthed in the broader feminist struggle. These areas include feminist psychological work on rape, pornography, woman-battering, the exercise of social power, and so on. Social power research is an area that I consider to be very useful to the feminist struggle and yet highly problematic from a gynocentric perspective. A large body of work has revealed a variety of strategies that males use to maintain power in interactions with women that range from controlling conversations through interruptions, topic changes and poor listening, to the use of non-reciprocal touching, sexual harassment, etc.. Knowledge of these strategies is important to us in male-defined power struggles.

However, to limit our analyses of social interaction to the androcentric definitions of power and win-lose strategies is to preclude the emergence of a gynocentric perspective that is concerned with mutuality and interdependence. In the next section I discuss work that I consider representative of a fully feminist perspective, the gynocentric construct of relationality.

Gynocentric Values and Relationality

Feminist psychology is beginning to make contributions to research and theory in Showalter's third focus, that of the exploration of the female experience from a woman-centred perspective. Much of this feminist work bears quite directly on views of the nature of the individual and the relationship between the individual and society. Work that is particularly rich in its implications is that which deals with humans as social beings — on the values, behaviour and development of individuals in interpersonal contexts. The interpersonal realm has traditionally been woman's domain. Women have, historically and cross-culturally, been responsible for interpersonal caretaking, while men have busied themselves with the impersonal "real" work of the world. In male-stream psychology, women's interpersonal orientation has typically been devalued, our nurturance and interpersonal sensitivity defined as weakness. In other disciplines, women's interpersonal caretaking has been redefined through feminist scholarship as the most essential and basic activity in any society. Feminist psychologists are slowly beginning to recognize women's interpersonal orientation as a reservoir of positive social skills and sensitivities with profound implications for the conduct of society.

In this second half of the present chapter I discuss feminist work that presents gynocentric perspectives on interpersonal interaction, the development of a sense of self in the interpersonal context of the family, a woman-centred view of moral development emphasizing women's connectedness to others, women's orientation to interpersonal interaction and the relational nature of female concepts of self. "Relationality" is the term I've chosen to describe the major feature of woman's existence that is revealed by these findings and suggestive theoretical work. Relationality refers to a sense of one's connectedness to and responsibility for others, to the necessary interdependence among human beings.

Many feminist scholars, and not only feminist psychologists, react strongly and negatively to references to woman's specificity. To suggest that women and men are somehow different implicates those differences in women's oppression, suggesting that women collude in their own oppression. It has been considered far safer to view women and men as malleable in the face of social, historical, and economic forces, and any differences that may appear as temporary artifacts of these forces. Further, the most obvious explanations of differences between the sexes are biological ones, and we are fully aware of the social control uses to which biological explanations have been and are being put. Sociobiology is a current, dangerously Fascist version of such an explanatory theory. However, human beings are not static, instinct-ridden creatures continually at the mercy of biological forces, but are rather social creations, themselves actively creating and constructing their own realities within the limits of the social, political and economic conditions imposed on them. Commonalities in women's experiences across time, classes and cultures render superfluous the biological explanations of woman's specificity. These experiences are partly a function of women's reproductive capacities; Mary O'Brien (1981) considers woman's connected experience and investment of labour in the birth process — in contrast to man's distant, alienated, intellectualized contribution to reproduction — to be the most important source of differences in our orientations to experience. It is unnecessary, however, to resort to biochemistry, genetic make-up, brain functioning and the like as explanatory devices. Another commonality in women's experience, as noted above, is our responsibility for the domain of interpersonal caretaking. A shared set of experiences lies also in the mother-daughter dyad. All women are daughters, and most of us are mother-raised. According to the object relations theorists, the experience of being reared by a woman has markedly differing effects on the developing selves of girls and boys.

Object Relations Theory and Relationality

Nancy Chodorow (1978) and Dorothy Dinnerstein (1976) have proposed theories regarding gender differences in self development that have been broadly influential in feminist scholarship. These theorists present psychosocial analyses of deep differences between females and males in their sense of self and their orientation to others and to the world — differences that the object relations theorists consider to result from virtually all children being mother-raised. Being a feminist of anti-Freudian persuasion, I must admit to a profound uneasiness regarding the dangerous possibilities of these theories adding ammunition to the timeworn great mother-blame myths. Indeed, Dinnerstein's ahistorical analysis, though brilliant, is quite flawed in this regard. She does seem to hold women, as mothers, largely responsible for the patriarchal mess the world is in.

Chodorow's analysis is more sophisticated and more socially and historically contextual. The processes affecting gender differences in self development that she discusses are *contingent on features of male-dominant industrialized societies*, those in which there is clear demarcation between the public and the private spheres. In such societies, differences between the genders are marked, and gender identity is established early. Reproduction, child-care and interpersonal nurturing are carried on in the private sphere in such societies. Most often, the biological mother is the primary caretaker of the children, while fathers assume little or no responsibility for child-care. Mothering is devalued and societal structures provide virtually no child-care support or recognition for mothers' societal contributions. When paid caretakers are involved in child-care, they are typically other women.

The basic premise of object relations theory is that people create mental representations of important persons in our early development that shape our sense of ourselves and reactions to others throughout our lives. The experience of the first relationship with the primary caretaker, likely a mother, creates an image for ourselves and a model for our future relationships with others. In Western societies, in which virtually all children are parented by a female adult, the development of self-identity and of core gender identity is markedly different for girls than for boys. The child's earliest identification, whether girl or boy, is with its mother. However, a girl's gender and her gender role identification processes are continuous with her earliest identification, while the boy is required to shift his identification from the mother to the father in later development.

Dinnerstein focuses primarily on the development of male ego differentiation and its relationship to the deperson-alized power structures and destructive dominance practices of patriarchal society. The young infant experiences many overwhelming emotions, from engulfing awe and love, to terror, pain and rage, all of which are associated with the woman who cares for him. During early infancy, the important stage of developing a sense of self individuated from his surroundings, the little boy typically has only the mother with whom to identify. There are deep ambivalences in this identification process, however, associated with mother's omnipotence and the terror and pain he connects to her. As the boy grows older and becomes aware of his sex — the same as father's, different from mother's — he begins the difficult identification process with the often absent father. The most important bond between the son and his father in this identification process, in a male-dominant society, is that "we are both better than she who takes care of us." Masculine identity is developed primarily in opposition to mother. The boy identifies with a distant, abstract male standard; his masculine identity is tenuous, as the presence of mother is a constant reminder of his former identification which he must repress. He must continuously fight for masculine identity, and it is experienced primarily through separation from and rejection of mother. These early common experiences among mother-raised male children in male-dominant societies lay the bases for the male separated self as well as for the exercise of male power in human relationships, especially in opposition to women.

More pertinent to the purposes of the present paper is Chodorow's expansion of object relations theory that focuses on the uniqueness of early female experience. In contrast to the sharp break between the boy's early identification processes and establishment of a core gender identity, these processes are much more continuous for girls. The girl's primary attachment is with the same person, her mother, with whom she later identifies in establishing a core gender identity. The process of developing a clearly separated sense of self is more difficult for the girl, but is carried out in the realistic context of an ongoing relationship with the mother. The relationship between the girl and her mother is a complex one in its mutuality; a woman is more likely to identify closely with her female child in her sameness than she is with a boy. The process of empathy is a frequent maternal experience with daughters. This, too, is a mutual process, one in which daughters learn early to experience empathy with another human being. The daughter's sense of self is thus developed in continuous context within relationship with mother: she, like the son, must struggle with the infantile experiences of terror and utter dependence associated with her early interactions with mother, but does so in the more realistic context of an ongoing, interdependent relationship with her. As the primary caretaker, one of the mother's characteristics is interpersonal nurturance, a prominent feature in the daughter-mother identification process.

"Girls and boys develop different relational capacities and senses of self as a result of growing up in a family in which women mother. These personalities are reinforced by differences in the identification processes of boys and girls that also result from women's mothering" (Chodorow 1978:173). Girls define their sense of self in the context of continuous interdependent relationship with mother, while boys' self-identity is developed in opposition to the mother. As the evidence in the remainder of this paper indicates, females' self-identity continues to be defined in terms of the quality of their relationships with others, while males become increasingly individuated, one might say distanced and alienated, with age.

Gynocentric Study of the Development of Values

The acknowledgment of a valued female specificity has also led to important developments in the feminist study of moral development. Kohlberg's[15] model of moral development, a derivative of Piagetian cognitive-developmental theory, has dominated the area since the early 1960's. The six-stage model was developed on a sample of male adolescents. It proceeds from a first hedonistic egocentric stage through the definition of "the good" as defined by interpersonal relationships, to stage 6, in which moral judgments are made on the basis of abstract, universal principles disembedded from interpersonal and social contexts. Researchers have found that women's responses to Kohlberg's standard moral dilemmas tend to cluster around stage 3 — not surprising in view of the fact that all references to emotions such as compassion, sympathy and love are automatically coded in this system as representative of stage 3. Kohlberg's system can be described as an extreme individual rights orientation built on a legal-rational model, with the most moral individual being the most thoroughly separated from his social milieu.

Carol Gilligan (1977, 1979) has very recently begun to document a specific female path of moral development. She worked with Kohlberg for some time but became dissatisfied with the failure of his theory to deal adequately with the female experience. Gilligan is doing or has done research that involves interviews with females ranging in age from six to 60+, cross-sectionally as well as longitudinally, in which she is learning about self-generated moral dilemmas as well as females' responses to standardized moral dilemmas. She has completed an intensive interview study with women contemplating abortion, a moral decision uniquely representative of women's experience. She has learned that the principles of *responsibility* and *care* underlie women's moral judgments, responsibility for the effects of one's actions on others and care and concern for other people. Non-violence, avoidance of harm to people, is an important concern in shaping women's moral decisions. The developmental sequence for women's moral judgments seems to proceed from a focus solely on personal survival, to a concern for the welfare of others excluding oneself, and finally to acceptance of responsibility for one's own welfare as well as that of others.

A fascinating aspect of her findings is the contextualism which women demand in making moral judgments. Women find it ludicrous to suggest that such decisions could be made without full information about the people involved and the situation they are in. When presented with Kohlberg's standard dilemmas, women typically ask for considerably more specific information (in Kohlberg's system, a sign of deficient development!). For example, in response to the well-known Heinz dilemma in which Heinz's wife will die without a rare, expensive drug hoarded by a certain druggist, females often refuse to consider what Heinz should do until they know more about the situation. Why doesn't the druggist want to give him the drug? Are there other, perhaps younger people more in need of the drug? Why doesn't Heinz work out a time payment plan? Why doesn't he try other sources for the drug? Why is the drug so unavailable? Is it because it's dangerous and unproven, like laetrile, etc.? In contrast, males at Kohlberg's stage 6 typically pit the abstract universal principles of the value of human life and the value of law and order against each other in order to make a decision about what Heinz should do.

Research reported by others supports essential features of Gilligan's theory. For example, girls' responses to Kohlberg's dilemmas are typically characterized by concern for consequences for others as well as references to love, welfare, affection and intimacy. Girls' self-created moral dilemmas are likely to involve relationships between friends, while boys write about acquaintances and distant others. Women's self-esteem is tied to their perceptions of their own morally good *and* bad behaviour, reflecting concern for the consequences of their behaviours on others, while men's self-esteem is tied only to self-perceived good behaviours.

In sum, this work supports the position that the bases of moral judgments are very different for females and males. Females' judgments reflect our gynocentric values, our sense of a connected self, of the interdependence of human beings in relationship, of the responsibility of each human to care for others and to be aware of the consequences of one's actions on others. In contrast, male moral judgments reflect a separated sense of self, are focused on individual rights, and assume that people are essentially interchangeable in an abstract system of justice.

Gynocentric Values and Interpersonal Interaction

Growing appreciation of male/female behaviour differences has led, also, to a re-evaluation of social competence and social interaction literature. In 1980, my colleagues and I undertook a literature search to see if there existed any evidence regarding the superior social competencies and interpersonal sensitivities of females. The research we reviewed was not conducted by feminists, and is primarily of the controlled experimental variety in the suspicious sex differences area, most of it based on the usual androcentric assumptions of male-stream psychology. So it is not surprising that we did not find supportive evidence under the obvious rubrics of social competence or interpersonal skills. As discussed earlier in this paper, these areas are so accommodated to male-centred values that any differences between the sexes are typically washed out. Women's investment in the interpersonal realm has, in fact, been consistently devalued in psychology, our connectedness with others seen as pathological dependency needs, nurturance and interpersonal sensitivity defined as weakness. However, we did find evidence, some of it interpreted in the original reports as reflecting negatively on women, under rubrics such as non-verbal communication, proxemics or personal space, influence and power tactics, eye contact, and differences in specific social behaviours.

Our search was guided by gynocentric questions and values; we were interested in interpersonal sensitivity, including attentiveness and responsiveness to social cues and the ability to understand them, ability to transmit social-emotional messages and the interpersonally relevant content of such messages. We used a gynocentric definition of pro-social skills as ones that would be likely to result in positive consequences for all individuals in an interaction.

Briefly, the literature we reviewed indicated that females surpass males in attentiveness to visual, auditory and tactile social stimuli, in being better listeners, and in showing greater responsiveness to variations in the characteristics of other people and of social situations. Females more accurately interpret the content of emotional messages and are more effective communicators of emotional-social messages. Females show pro-social patterns of social behaviour, such as reward-ingness and empathy, that foster the well-being of all persons in interactions as opposed to anti-social patterns of social behaviour.

Stark-Adamec and Pihl[16] have published a study that provides an excellent example of the differences that appear between females and males in their interpersonal interactions. The study was designed to test the effects of smoking cannabis on social interaction. Same-sex pairs of strangers smoked either cannabis or a placebo while interacting with each other, and a good deal of behavioural and self-report data was collected. The most striking set of results from the study was the difference between the female and male pairs. Regardless of substance smoked, the quality of the female interactions was simply more pleasant and positive than that of the male pairs. The women had fewer silences, were more positively reinforcing of each other, smiled more frequently, discussed more personally relevant content, and made greater expressive use of body movements to emphasize conversation. After the interaction, the women reported themselves as happier than the men and as having more positive impressions of each other.

Women's self-descriptions correspond with our inter-personally sensitive, pro-social actions. As early as adolescence, girls have more positive self-images with regard to such characteristics as congeniality and sociability. Cross-cultural data suggest that women are more likely than men to use adjectives to describe themselves that reflect an interpersonal orientation such as being loving, affectionate, compassionate and sympathetic, while men are more likely to describe themselves as assertive, dominating, and competitive. Lilian Rubin's (1980) qualitative interview study of American women in mid-life included a question regarding self-identity. The women invariably described themselves in the context of their human relationships with their families and others, frequently using such adjectives as generous, helpful, considerate and thoughtful in their self-descriptions. A comparison group of men responded to the same question with descriptions solely in terms of their work ("I am a... I do..."), never in the context of their human relationships.

Conclusions

In the first part of this paper I explored some of the features of male-stream psychology that render it particularly hostile to the development of a fully feminist psychology. The nature of its underlying philosophy and methods is rigidly tied to a view of the nature of *man* that excludes women, and is antithetical to woman-centred values. The androcentric values of separation, domination, rationality and egocentrism are embedded in the philosophy, methods and models of psychology.

I have explored the implications of some emerging research findings and feminist theory for the nature of gynocentric values, women's connected relational selves, our sense of interdependence and our highly developed sense of social responsibility. This work has profound implications for an understanding of the nature of human beings, as well as for the conduct of human society. It is clear that the development of a fully feminist psychology constructed on gynocentric values and woman-centred questions will transform not only our knowledge of women, but the nature of psychology in every respect. Gynocentric connectedness, interdependence and integration have implications for views in all areas of this highly fragmented discipline. Indeed, in challenging the individualistic models of man that underlie psychology, feminist psychology challenges the very underpinnings of male-dominated society.

FOOTNOTES

1. Elaine Showalter, "Is There a Female Aesthetic?" in *Women, Advocate and Scholar:* Proceedings of the Conference at Montclair State College, 1974.
2. Carolyn Wood Sherif, "Bias in Psychology" in Sherman & Beck 1979.
3. See Margaret Benston's Chapter 2 of this volume for a more detailed feminist critique of scientific method.
4. For example, *Canadian Psychological Review*, January 1977 (entire issue) and Carolyn Wood Sherif, *op. cit.*.
5. Judith Long Laws, *Feminism and Patriarchy: Competing Ways of Doing Social Science*. Paper presented at the Annual Meeting of the American Sociological Association, San Francisco, 1978, p. 4.
6. Robert Schwartz & John Gottman, "Toward a Task Analysis of Assertive Behavior" in *Journal of Consulting and Clinical Psychology*, 44, 1976, pp. 910-920.
7. *Ibid.*, p. 919 (emphasis added).
8. *Ibid.*, p. 913.
9. Showalter 1974, *op. cit.*.
10. William Ryan, *Blaming the Victim* (New York: Pantheon, 1971).
11. Matina Horner, "Toward an Understanding of Achievement-Related Conflicts in Women" in *The Journal of Social Issues*, 28, 1972, pp. 157-175.
12. David Tresemer, *Fear of Success* (New York: Plenum Press, 1977).
13. Kathryn Morgan, *Androgyny: Vision or Mirage? A Philosophical Analysis*. Paper presented at the University of Toronto and York University Research Colloquium, December 1977, p. 10.
14. See Mary Brown Parlee, "Feminist Psychology in the 80's" in Caplan 1982; Sandra Pyke, "Androgyny: A Dead End or a Promise" in Stark-Adamec 1980; and C. Stark-Adamec, *et al.*, "Androgyny and Mental Health: The Need for a Critical Evaluation of the Theoretical Equation" in *International Journal of Women's Studies*, 3, 1980, pp. 490-507.
15. Lawrence Kohlberg, *The Development of Modes of Moral Thinking and Choice in the Years Ten to Sixteen*. Unpublished doctoral dissertation, University of Chicago, 1958; Lawrence Kohlberg, "Stage and Sequence: The Cognitive-Developmental Approach to Socialization" in D. Goslin (ed.), *Handbook of Socialization, Theory and Research* (Chicago: Rand-McNally, 1969), pp. 347-480.
16. Connie Stark-Adamec & R.O. Pihl, "Sex Differences in Response to Marijuana in a Social Setting" in *Psychology of Women Quarterly* 2, 1978, pp. 334-353.

CHAPTER 4

Celebration and Struggle: Feminism and Law

Kathleen A. Lahey

Kathleen A. Lahey is a feminist lawyer, teacher, writer, scholar, and activist, currently a professor in the Faculty of Law at Queen's University. She has participated in the development of an integrative feminist approach to legal scholarship, working on topics that range from child abuse, the Charter of Rights, lesbian jurisprudence, and criminal law to taxation and liberal economic theory. She is one of the initiators and organizers, now co-editor, of the *Canadian Journal of Women and the Law*, has consulted in lesbian and feminist litigation, and dreams of working in a law school that exists for women instead of against them.

Introduction

In contrast to the nihilism, individualism, and determinism of contemporary (masculist) legal thought, feminist activists in law have a great deal to celebrate. After centuries of struggle, many laws that oppress women have been repealed or amended, some laws that actually promote women's equality have been conceived and enacted, and increasing numbers of women are gaining access to the kinds of knowledge, structures, and processes that continue to make these changes possible.

These three strands of women's activism in law have combined, in recent years, to form the area of legal scholarship sometimes referred to as "feminist legal theory" or "feminist jurisprudence." Feminist legal activists and scholars are far from agreeing on the precise meaning of these terms but it is possible to sketch out the main conclusions that have been drawn by women who do this kind of work.[1]

The concerns of feminist legal theory can be expressed at the levels of knowledge, method, doctrine, and structure. At the level of knowledge, feminists know the Western legal system as just one of the many faces of patriarchal domination.[2] At the level of method, feminists have concluded that the terms in which legal discourse is conducted are projections of masculist subjectivity, which men are able to transform into (false) universals by virtue of the power they can exert to enforce their views.[3]

Doctrinally, feminist legal scholars have concluded that legal theory or (masculist) jurisprudence is basically nothing but an ideology of male supremacy[4]—when the subjectmatter of legal doctrine is women, that doctrine is about the uses that men make (or would like to make) of women. And structurally, feminist lawyers are struggling in their own lives with the realization that in education and access, only women who meet male-defined criteria and who speak in voices acceptable to men are really welcome to participate in legal discourse; while in legal practice, sex-role stereotyping still blatantly defines women's roles and marginalizes women who challenge or disrupt these roles.[5]

Feminists have thus come to understand that the Western legal system is fundamentally patriarchal in every aspect—method, content, theory, personnel, process, and outcome. Having pushed their critiques to these conclusions, women have ultimately had to confront the sexual politics of patriarchal law: in a patriarchal context, what roles can feminist activists play? Is feminist law reform even possible? Exactly how do feminist analysis and political action around law affect the material conditions of women, determined as they are by centuries of male privilege?

In this essay I will attempt to produce, if not answers to these questions, then at least some working hypotheses women can use to better understand the relationships between women and law and between feminism and law. I will propose a feminist theory that focuses on the patriarchal use of Western law to define and appropriate women's reproductive, productive, and sexual capacities. I will then outline women's struggles to free themselves of patriarchal law with feminist law reform since the 1790s. In the sections on male resistance and feminist lawmaking, I will attempt to articulate a radical feminist theory of law reform ("feminist lawmaking") that takes into account the persistence and transformation of patriarchal law in the face of two centuries of feminist activism.

My central focus is the precise relationship between structures of patriarchal and Western domination—of which law itself is paradigmatic—and women's liberation. Although law has never been the sole cause of women's disadvantaged status, it has operated powerfully to define the terms of women's oppression and therefore to form part of the material base of that oppression. Women have learned all too well that reform of existing law is not, by itself, enough to improve the material condition of women, even though reform is a necessary precondition to such improvement. If women are to avoid the worst excesses of cooptation and backlash in law-reform processes, however, the success of feminist legal reforms will depend not only on women's entry into law but also on changes in the nature of law itself, in the nature of the state, and in the role of law. And these changes will require, as a minimum, the ability to create the subjectmatter of law from the vantage point of women.

A Feminist Theory of Women and Law

Historically, men appear in law as subjects and women as subjectmatter. In Kantian terms, women are the means, while men are the end. Specifically, women appear in patriarchal Western law as the embodiment of productive, reproductive, and sexual capacity. Thus, despite women's historic

101

resistance and reform attempts, law is about the definition, appropriation, and exploitation of women for the benefit of men. A feminist theory of women and law, then, is about the ways in which law reflects and reinforces the social, economic, and political structures that surround subject women in liberal patriarchy.

Until the 1980s, feminist analysis of patriarchal law tended to be fairly ahistorical, concentrating on the effects of present laws on present women. This has had the advantage of producing detailed information on the way in which law contributes to women's subjugation in the present tense. It has had the disadvantage, however, of obscuring from women those larger structures of domination particularly associated with the emergence of the liberal state, as distinct from the emergence of patriarchal culture more generally.

As women find and create knowledge about the relationship between women and law in the history of patriarchal culture, certain features of law have emerged as crucial to maintaining women's dispossessed status:

(1) Women are not persons: this ensures their treatment as subjectmatter.
(2) As things, women cannot enter into the legal relations that count in patriarchal culture.
(3) As things, women cannot participate in social, economic, and political processes.
(4) As the means of human reproduction, women are denied the reproductive self-determination that would detract from male control of reproduction.
(5) As sexualized things, women's "sexuality" is determined by men for the benefit of men.

Feminist historians have uncovered increasing evidence that these features of women's status in patriarchal culture are present to some degree (usually more rather than less) in ancient as well as in contemporary civilizations.[6] Perhaps more important for understanding the economic basis for women's status, however, structures of sexual domination resonate markedly with historic structures of racial and ethnic enslavement during the very period associated with the emergence of liberal patriarchy.[7]

The role of law in defining women's social, economic, and political status in the liberal state illustrates this theory of women and law. During the period that began in the 1600s (and which, according to some critics, continues even today), the focus of law on relations and institutions of private property, combined with the legal regulation of women's reproduction and sexuality and the nonenforcement of either criminal or civil law on behalf of women, ensured not only women's subjugation, but also that the particular ways in which they were subjugated would suit the needs of men in the liberal state.

Production

The political economy of women is characterized by two durable features: (1) the feudal organization of women's productive activities; and (2) the virtual exclusion of women from the cash nexus. Both features are rooted in the history of Western economic relations. Both have been largely unaffected by the monetization of the economy and the emergence of institutions of private property. And both have been remarkably resistant to law reform.

The virtual exclusion of women from the cash nexus dates back to the use of money in bourgeois economic relations. Under feudalism, women as well as men devoted large amounts of time to productive subsistence activities. They also frequently shared control over work processes, over tools used in the work, and over the products of that work. Around the thirteenth and fourteenth centuries, however, this sharing gave way to a new principle of social, economic, and legal organization as an emerging bourgeois class moved from a barter system of trade to a system that involved money. This new principle, of course, was male ownership of the means of production.[8]

By the 1600s and 1700s, in England, the bourgeois revolution was underway in both theory and practice, but this did not substantially change the status of women. Relations between women and men were still nonreciprocal and appropriative. In liberal theory, these relations were described as "dependency" relations in order to draw attention away from the very nonreciprocity and appropriation used to justify the abandonment of feudal relations among men. Political and economic ideologies of liberal patriarchy were constructed to justify sex-based appropriation within the family unit even while men decisively challenged the patriarchal organization of the state.[9]

By the 1900s, the industrial revolution was nearly complete for men, most of whom had moved out of feudal subsistence relations into the monetized economy. Women, however, were still largely excluded from the cash nexus. Only twelve percent of Canadian women had access to wages.[10] In the nineteenth and early twentieth centuries, women of the ruling classes fought hard for—and sometimes obtained— some of the prerogatives enjoyed by men of their class: ownership of property, participation in public affairs, admission to the professions, control over their own incomes. But for most women, cash was something they neither owned, nor— as with one woman whose husband even today will not let her see or touch money—were allowed to use. For most women, their entire economic identity, as well as their political identity, was constructed through their dependency in the family unit, as wives, mothers, daughters, spinster aunts.

Looking back over time, we can now see that the combination of physical domination of women in so-called private relations and their exclusion from ownership of wages, property, and means of production in early patriarchal law perfected male appropriation of women's productive capacity centuries ago. That appropriation is now nearly invisible in the content of law itself. All we see today, when we look at the continuing fact of women's impoverishment, is the (gender neutral) use of law—primarily family property law, but also criminal, income tax, and employment law—to defend the present distribution of wealth and income, and the use of modern legislation such as pay-equity laws to partially redress the small part of the economic gap thought of as wage discrimination.

About the complete poverty—and therefore the very real dependency—of millions of nonwaged women, there is only a thundering silence in law: the enslavement of women has been the point of patriarchal law—including liberal law— and therefore has never been considered a serious legal problem. And, not surprisingly, contemporary law reform has been notoriously ineffective, for a whole range of reasons, in interfering with the violent and abusive behaviour that men use to dominate women, to stop women from escaping from the family, and to punish defiant women.

Reproduction

Women's relationships to their own reproductive capacity and activities have been particularly difficult. Most women procreate and nurture under conditions of such unrelenting male control that it is fair to say that all of women's reproductive arrangements are subject to some form of patriarchal domination.

104

In each reproductive event, male control is mediated by either individual males (or male proxies) in the household or an array of state workers who administer, establish, or interpret the terms of particular arrangements. Known more popularly as the institutions of marriage, childbirth, motherhood, law, and medicine, these forms of mediation obscure the fact that individual women are not acting in a self-determined(ing) way, but are playing out the appearances of choice in a social, legal, and economic context that is simultaneously founded upon and dedicated to the instrumentalization and appropriation of women's reproductive capacities.[11]

Historically, men have used law—especially criminal law—to resist women's reproductive self-determination. A good example of this resistance is found in an unlikely place: obscenity legislation. When the first federal consolidation of Canadian criminal law was enacted in 1892, for example, the criminal-abortion prohibition was backed up by the first "obscenity" prohibition:

> [Everyone who] offers to sell, advertises, publishes an advertisement of or has for sale or disposal any medicine, drug or article intended or represented as a means of preventing conception or causing an abortion...

was guilty of "obscenity" and was liable to imprisonment for two years.[12] This definition of obscenity equated it with women's reproductive self-determination; to male legislators in the 1890s, women's independence was obscene.[13]

As this passage from early anti-abortion legislation makes clear, resistance to anti-abortion law must be a crucial component of feminist strategies for self-determination. Legal historians have demonstrated that women's abortion practices predated the colonial period in North America, and that information on abortifacients was once part of the knowledge that women acquired as they matured. But women gradually lost access to that information and the right to use it on their own behalf, as medical, political, and legal specialists increasingly assumed control over women's reproductive activity in industrialized cultures. Thus women were reduced to their present state of dependency on male professionals for the very skills and knowledge that women themselves had developed.[14]

The early-1970s "decriminalization" of abortion in Canada was heralded by feminists as a breakthrough. However, that legislative exception restored to women, on quite restricted terms, only a tiny fraction of their historic knowledge and access.[15] In the 1980s, Ontario women finally challenged this monopoly by establishing a free-standing abortion clinic—operated by and for women. The history of legal attacks on that clinic illustrates all too clearly that, despite decades of activism, patriarchal control over women's reproduction persists.[16]

The story of male control of alternative (artificial) insemination (AI) is similar to the abortion story. Of all reproduction "technologies," alternative insemination is the most women-empowering—yet the very knowledge of AI has been effectively lost to contemporary women. Although traces can still be found in mythology and religion, most women think of AI as new "technology." AI is woman-empowering just as abortion is woman-empowering: it makes it possible for individual women to make direct personal decisions about whether or when to engage in reproduction. In the 1970s, however, AI became a "reproductive technology" in the vernacular sense as women became the subjects of male technology—technology developed in the veterinary practice of animal husbandry.

The real motivation behind the technological development of mass AI has been medical treatment for male infertility. The cure for such infertility is the medical and legal means for these men to appear to have impregnated their wives. And while law "reform" is being used to ensure that such men are treated as legal fathers, it is also being used to criminalize the use of AI by nonmarried women.[17]

Attempts to legalize and regulate contemporary reproductive arrangements ("surrogacy contracts") reveal the dimensions of male desire to control women's reproduction. The very term "surrogate motherhood" nullifies women's biological role in reproduction,[18] while it places the knowledge of motherhood on the same shaky foundation on which rests the knowledge of paternity: legal presumption.[19] The trend in legal practice and law "reform" proposals is the development of legal devices that would guarantee purchasing fathers (and their wives) legal title to contract children and that would force the mother to surrender custody.[20]

Sexuality

The use of law to exploit women's sexuality for the benefit of men is relatively visible in contemporary law. Feminists have long understood that rape laws exist not to protect

106

women but to protect male interest in women's reproduction capacity (Clark 1977). For feminists, the nonenforcement of rape laws has served to ensure that as male property interests in women has been eroded, they have received in return less restricted access to women's sexuality for "entertainment" (nonreproductive) purposes.

Similarly, the principle of nonenforcement of criminal law on behalf of women now extends well beyond mere rape law—now known as sexual assault—to apply also to assault, battery, murder, obscenity, domestic violence, domestic terrorization, and pimping laws. Even when anti-prostitution laws have been expanded to apply to male customers as well as women prostitutes, male police and judges have found ways of exempting them from actual application.[21]

Feminist Law Reform

Women's struggles in law have had two distinct objectives: to obtain the repeal of laws that themselves form part of the material conditions of women's oppression; and to obtain enactment of laws intended to improve the status of women. Activists have employed several strategies in pursuit of these objectives: critiques of political and legal theory; social and political activism; law reform; litigation; and, whenever possible, feminist lawmaking.

I would distinguish law reform for women from feminist lawmaking by referring to the political perspective and content of the measure in question. Law reform for women—even when it is radically conceived to eliminate laws that actively oppress women—generally tends to accept patriarchal constructs of law by reallocating interests within existing frameworks. As part of the processes of liberal legalism, law reform—even when it is used to promote women's interests—tends to fall short of addressing the material conditions of women's actual inequality. It can therefore even become part of the problem.

Feminist lawmaking, in contrast, begins with women's experiences of oppression—whether by law or by the social, economic, or political arrangements enforced by law—and seeks to articulate remedies for those harms while radically challenging the structures that produce them. These two processes are certainly not separable but seem, in practice, to have reinforced and informed each other.

Beginning with Mary Wollstonecraft's brilliant deconstruction of the legal status of women in 1790, it has taken Western feminists nearly two centuries to uncover and understand—at the level of theoretical critique—the role that law has played in constructing the material condition of women. In the first half of the 1800s, women in the abolition movement in the United States developed a practical critique of the status of Afro-American women.[22] By the middle of the 1800s, North American white women had crystallized their understanding of the role of law in the *Seneca Falls Declaration of Sentiments*.[23]

Feminist challenges to patriarchal law have also had an activist aspect in North America since the 1800s. Women in the second half of the 1800s organized around male abuse of alcohol, women's right to vote and hold office, abuse of women in the name of "prostitution" laws, and exploitation of women in industry. As women who were involved in these movements slowly began to redefine women's role, women also began to understand that men's absolute monopoly over formal political processes—and especially over legal processes—formed one of the biggest barriers to structural reform.

Relative to women in other Anglo-infuenced countries, propertied women in English-speaking Canada were rewarded somewhat earlier for their efforts at law reform. In the 1870s and 1880s, the provinces began enacting legislation that allowed married women to hold property and to enter into contracts. Canadian women were admitted to the practice of law in the 1890s. Some women obtained the right to vote in municipal elections as early as the 1890s.[24]

Despite these early breakthroughs, however, Canadian women generally continued to be nonpersons well into the 1920s. Sporadic legislative successes in obtaining the vote, employment protection, child-custody rights, and other incidents of legal personality were simply not enough to remove all the legal barriers that had been constructed over the centuries by men for women.

In 1930, the era of "blanket" reforms began when the Privy Council in England (overruling the Supreme Court of Canada) ruled that women were persons in law[25] and the Québec civil code was amended to remove the worst of women's legal handicaps.[26] Women continued to work for particular reforms in property, custody, employment, wages, pensions, taxation, and other areas of law throughout the 1940s and 1950s, but they also focused increasing political energy on those blanket reforms, beginning with enactment of the Canadian Bill of Rights sex-discrimination provisions in 1960 and culminating with the inclusion of sex-equality guarantees in the Canadian Charter of Rights in the 1980s.[27] While women were constructing the terms of their legal (civil) existence, they were also participating more in the monetized economy. In 1980, women received 31.5 percent of all salaries in Canada—a dramatic increase over the 12 percent figure for 1900.[28]

Because women were so successful early in the century in eliminating legal incidents of their nonpersonhood, feminists in the contemporary movement have been able to concentrate less on women's civil status and more on their social, political, and economic status. The focus of women's activism has shifted to trying to understand how it is that women can be so systematically disadvantaged relative to men after a full century of legal activism and feminist-inspired law reform. In Canada, the Charter of Rights has given this focus a solid base from which to argue for reforms contributing to the elimination of the effects of centuries of legal, social, political, and economic dispossession.

By any standards, Canadian feminists have enjoyed significant political and legal success, the reasons for which are not difficult to find. Despite the wave of economic and political conservatism engulfing the Western hemisphere, Canada remains committed to public ownership and regulation of natural and productive resources; and guarantees, as well, a minimum standard of living and health care for all. As an economically-deprived group, women have benefitted from such commitments.

Of equal importance is the fact that women have been increasingly active in the legal profession for more than fifteen years. Beginning with the formation of women-and-law caucuses in the early 1970s and the first national women-and-law conference in mid-decade, Canadian women lawyers have combined a strong commitment to feminist activism with both their legal education and their legal careers. This has produced a climate in which feminist insight into the ways in which contemporary laws oppress women can be translated rapidly into law reform. The stock of active feminist lawyers in Canada is continually growing, with enrolment of women students now reaching fifty percent at some schools. The launching of the *Canadian Journal of Women and the Law* in 1985 and the growing interest in women and the law, feminist legal theory, feminist jurisprudence, and, more recently, feminist advocacy, are all indications of the seriousness with which feminists are taking law in Canada.

Male Resistance

When the positive accomplishments of feminist struggle in law are analyzed in their historical context, the story is indeed worth celebrating. But women's struggle for liberation is ongoing: from an historical perspective, all that has really changed is the level of struggle. Although women are now legal persons in Canada, and even enjoy minimal social security and human rights protection, the material conditions of women's existence are still marked by inequality, while male resistance to feminist law reforms—combined with male domination of the legal process and profession itself—undercuts and subverts these reforms.

By way of exploring the material conditions of women's inequality, think back to 17 April 1982—the day on which the Charter of Rights became effective and on which the three-year moratorium on implementation of the sex-equality guarantees became effective.[29] While women activists, politicians, and lawyers thought about how best to use these provisions to improve women's position, most women carried on as usual. They continued to drudge through their hundred-hour work weeks—working more than twice as many hours in the average week as men—meeting the dual and competing demands of home and workplace.

Street workers walked their beats, looking without seeing, giving head or whatever the customer wanted, getting out of the car at the next corner. A woman whose husband never lets her see or touch money and brings home weekly starvation rations rather than let her go shopping begged from the neighbours and checked through the garbage in the alley as usual. Native women, dispossessed first by white occupation of Turtle Island, endured further dispossession by the status rules of the Indian Act.[30] A woman whose boss liked to have sex with her once again kept her in his office after work. Women were raped, hassled on the street, and displayed in pornography; daughters were violated in incestuous acts; women were threatened with loss of support if they did not obey their husbands. Canadian women received thirty percent of all income that year, while men got seventy percent—for working one third the number of hours. Women

110

enjoyed only thirty percent of all speech time, received thirty percent of special-education spending, and owned but a tiny fraction of productive wealth. Rosa Becker discovered that she could not get her historic Supreme Court of Canada judgement enforced.[31] A lesbian mother living underground because she had taken her children from their abusive father moved to yet another city, staying one step ahead of his search.[32] A woman whose husband beats her was once again slammed up against a wall. A man whose wife had finally left him because of his abuse ransacked her house, smashing all the windows as he went.[33]

While women continued to suffer the violence, poverty, and overwork that are their lot, judges charged with implementing feminist law reforms confused attempted murder with expressions of love and breasts with beards,[34] while male lawyers began looked nervously over their shoulders, complaining about "radical feminists" in the law.

When the three-year moratorium on invoking the sex-equality guarantees of the Charter came to an end in 1985, women indeed gave men something to be nervous about. On the advice of her feminist lawyer, the woman who is never allowed to touch money charged a graduation dress for her daughter at a neighbourhood store. The lesbian mother living underground decided to turn herself in and contest the criminal charges as sex discrimination. Street workers protested the new prostitution legislation and asked feminists to see it as sex discrimination. Native women who had struggled for repeal of the status rules continued to expect equal treatment on the basis of culture and race as well as on the basis of sex. Women began to say that sexual intrusions like sexual harassment, pornography, prostitution, and rape are forms of sex discrimination. Rosa Becker began to think of her problem as an issue of sexism. Women in every province began to understand that "freedom of speech" may well construct their inequality in pornography, while "freedom of contract" constructs their inequality in sexual harassment, reproductive contracts, and prostitution.

But the reality remains that patriarchal institutions can incorporate and coopt a certain amount of feminist law reform simply because men dominate the legal system. Even when women began to think they finally had a legal as well as ethical basis for equality claims, for example, judges and legislators continued to attack and undermine the fragile gains that women had made for themselves over the last century and began to give sex-equality guarantees the narrowest possible application.

In property law, reproduction law, sex law, and liberation law, women have learned that real redress can be achieved only by reconceptualizing the basis for legal remedies themselves, not by applying to women existing male-defined principles. Women have learned this at great cost, but the cumulative effect of male resistance in each area of law produces a powerful statement of the need for feminist lawmaking.

In property law, women are ending up with smaller shares of family property, even though the first round of family-property reforms in the 1970s gave women a presumptive fifty-percent share in everything (except a man's "business" assets); women are receiving smaller support payments, because they are presumed to be capable of earning equal wages; women are finding it more difficult to collect support arrears because evidence that they can somehow survive when their husbands are in arrears is being used to show that they do not really need their support; husbands are being given tax incentives to keep property out of women's hands; when tax provisions are "gender neutralized," they turn out to be of great value to men and of no value to women; tax benefits that are theoretically of value to women actually shift the burden to other women, and are in fact of little use to the average woman; men are receiving million-dollar damage awards for the loss of wage-earning women's services, while women who are injured in compensable ways get low awards because women are not, in economic terms, worth very much to themselves.

In reproduction law, women are losing custody of children under a variety of ruses (if they work outside the home, they are not at home with the children; if they are at home with the children, they do not earn enough to support them adequately); women are having joint custody imposed on them involuntarily; birth mothers are losing their presumptive right to legal custody of children born under reproductive contracts; women are losing even more "privacy" and reproductive rights with judge-ordered surgical births "for the good of the child."

In sex law, feminist-inspired reforms of rape laws are being used to protect the "rights" of accused rapists; sexual assault provisions are not being enforced in clear cases; now that soliciting is an offence for both women and men, customers charged under the new rules are getting absolute discharges because "they did not know that the law had changed," while women charged with prostitution are finding it more difficult to get out on bail; women who win sexual harassment cases find that litigation costs them more than they win; women who lose such cases are being slapped with punitive defamation suits.

In liberation law, classification by sex is being struck down almost automatically whenever it burdens men relative to women,[35] yet upheld as "not discriminatory," "reasonable," or "justified" whenever it imposes some sort of burden on women.[36]

Because the meaning of sex equality is being so distorted—turning it into "equality with a vengeance"—some women think that Charter litigation actually puts women at risk. Some equality theorists are dealing with this risk by holding back on equality arguments until "ideal" precedents can be established, which means that greater substantive gains are being made for women under the due-process and security-of-the-person guarantees of the Charter than under the sex-equality guarantees. As a result, women's equality claims are being silenced at the precise moment that we should be asserting them loudly.

While women are experiencing this very real backlash in litigation, masculist legal theorists are all too eager to explain to them the inevitability of these results. Critical theorists are telling women who act in law that their efforts are futile, that women lawyers are immobilized by their own dread, that they are substituting action for responsibility for their own conspiracy with the forces against which they say they are contending. Liberal theorists are telling women that as autonomous, undifferentiated, gender-neutral, self-maximizing individuals they are the equals of men, it is improper for them to ask that women's particularities be recognized in law ("special treatment"). Conservative theorists are telling women that as "persons" whose (subordinated) biology and (subordinating) social construction just so happen to complement the (dominant) position of men, women's equality lies in accepting—and here *is* affirmation—women's differences, so long as difference is not occasion for oppression (and oppression will, of course, continue to be defined by men).

To the very real fact of this male resistance—at the levels of both practice and theory—are added the doubts of women who see how powerfully patriarchal imperatives affect even feminist law reforms. Conservative women are saying,

113

"We told you so." Some liberal feminists are saying, "Maybe men *are* more oppressed than women." And some socialist women are saying, "See—feminist law reform really *does* hurt women."

The same experiences with law reform that have revealed the resilience of patriarchal structures, however, have helped some feminists understand and more effectively resist patriarchal laws. The most significant factor in the continued use of law to enforce patriarchal privilege is that men still control not only the legal process and the interpretation of laws, but also the subjectmatter and vantage point of law. This is such an obvious point that it is nearly transparent, but I will make it anyway: if the subjectmatter of law is male concerns (such as the appropriation of women's productive, reproductive, and sexual capacity), and if the perspectives employed within the legal process are those of men, then women should actually have no reason to expect that mere reform of existing law will materially improve the condition of women.

This is particularly true when attempts to improve the status of women are made through incremental reforms that are not grounded in an understanding of how women's oppressions are constructed. Reform of rape laws will not materially improve the status of women when the point of rape laws is their nonenforcement. Rationalization of murder and assault laws will not materially improve the status of women when those provisions are applied and interpreted in a way that treats masculist subjectivity as the objective norm. Revision of obscenity laws will not materially improve the status of women when nonenforcement and masculist subjectivity combine to ensure that these laws are applied first to silence women by turning them into pornography and then to privilege that silencing by calling pornography "free speech." Amendment of criminal prostitution laws will not materially improve the status of women when its only accomplishment is to give the state a share of the pimp's control. Introduction of criminal sanctions for reproductive arrangements ("surrogacy contracts") will not materially improve the status of women when the point of those sanctions is to add the duress of criminal penalties to the economic duress that led women to enter into such contracts in the first place.

114

Feminist Lawmaking

Women activists have not yet succeeded in ensuring that women receive equal treatment in law or in life. The husband of the woman who is never allowed to see or touch money found the dress that she charged at the neighbourhood store and tore it up. The underground lesbian mother was found guilty of kidnapping, and although the judge listened to arguments based on sex discrimination, she refused to consider the effect that judicial homophobia had on the woman's ability to protect her children in the first place. Native women have discovered that the new status rules dispossess many of their children just as powerfully as the old status rules dispossessed them. The feminist community has scarcely started a revolution over the new prostitution laws, even though they potentially threaten the liberty of all women. Rosa Becker committed suicide. Free trade has now joined the ranks of free speech and freedom of contract in intensifying the conditions of women's inequality.[37]

Having said all this, what directions can feminist struggles in law take? In the long run, law reform will really begin to make a concrete difference to women only when the content of the law, as well as its perspectives, reflect women's realities. This implies a heavy agenda.

(1) Women must look at the whole theory of law from a completely unfettered women's perspective.

(2) Women must obtain the repeal of all provisions that perpetuate male appropriation of women's productive, reproductive, and sexual capacities: this includes, *inter alia*, abortion, childcare, AI, reproductive contracts, and prostitution provisions.

(3) Women must subject every remaining aspect of the law to close scrutiny, not only for disparate impact and differential application to women, but also for nonneutralities in the language of legal thought: the public-private dichotomy; *mens rea*, and "objectivity"; the nature of abstraction and codification.

(4) Women must develop methods of preventing existing legal provisions from being applied in a discriminatory manner: this might include remedies for discriminatory nonenforcement of existing laws.

One important strategy for feminist lawmaking that flows from and incorporates all these tasks is the conceptualization of harms to women—as women—as wrongs, when recognition of those harms will actually promote equality. This means nothing less than saying that when the categories of law (*assault, battery, obscenity*) do not apply to or deal with women's experiences, new categories must be created and given legal expression as well as social meaning. Some of these harms might include *domestic terrorization, enslavement of women, abuse of prostitutes*, and *use of women as reproductive chattels*.[38] Along the same lines, Christine Boyle[39] has suggested that judges be liable for *contempt of women* if judicial use of contempt powers to abuse women cannot be curbed.

As a corollary to this strategy, legal enforcement mechanisms must be revisioned around the realities of women's experiences with law. The artificial boundaries between criminal and civil law, for example, dissolve when the necessity of enforcing one or another of those types of remedies is confronted: the real problem, in most cases, is in the gender identity of the enforcers. Liability for costs, for another example, ensures that women do not have access to the legal process at all, thus guaranteeing not only that proaction in the legal process is reserved almost exclusively for male use, but also that men can use it against women.

Finally, there is the matter of personnel. It is becoming increasingly obvious that many law professors, lawyers, and judges are behaving very destructively toward women in the legal profession as well as toward women generally. Women should not have to undergo five years of sexual abuse in order to be admitted to the legal profession. Nor should women have to tolerate sexist or discriminatory remarks from other lawyers or from judges. This area of struggle will also have to continue.

Conclusion

For possibly the first time in history, there are in the West enough women in the legal profession, with support from women outside, for women to speak in the law. No doubt this will affect the nature of law itself, the nature of the state, and, ultimately, the role that law plays. And no doubt women will disagree on the specific direction that feminist lawmaking should take in particular situations. But imagine, if you can, a world in which women who are being abused can simply walk away from the abuser, and feel safe while walking; in which women can exercise full reproductive self-determination; in which women who remove their children from the presence of an abuser are not arrested for kidnapping; in which women receive enough income to support themselves, and their children, in dignity and comfort. So long as law is used to enforce values and social choices, it is much better that it should enforce women's dignity and self-determination than racial, sexual, heterosexual, and class oppression.

FOOTNOTES

I delivered an earlier version of this paper at the University of Windsor Faculty of Law 1987 Kathleen A. Lahey Feminist Legal Lecture Series. This series was founded by the Windsor Women and Law Caucus and was funded by Nancy Jackman of the Jackman Foundation. This paper summarizes and formalizes some of the main conclusions I have reached about the effects of women's activism on law over the last century. It is also a statement of an approach to law and to feminism that I have found useful in integrating feminist theory with legal practice.

Many women have given me insight into this work. I would particularly like to thank my feminist students at Windsor and Queen's for working with me. I would also like to especially thank Angela Miles, Geraldine Finn, and Sarah W. Salter, whose work has made it possible for other women to think and talk about integrative feminism; Diana Majury, whose personal politics have deepened my understanding of feminism and of law; Mary Lou Fassel, whose legal-aid practice has reached women who had never had access to legal representation; Pat Marshall, whose sense of what women can say in law as well as about law continually astounds me; Lorenne Clark, who taught Canadian feminists how to think about patriarchy, politics, and law; and Marguerite Russell, who practises integrative and critical feminism in law and in politics.

1. See Kathleen A. Lahey (1985) for an overview of some of the tensions in feminist thinking about women and law. For general references to this literature and bibliographies of feminist legal scholarship and theory, see Kathleen A. Lahey (1984), also Susan B. Boyd & Elizabeth Sheehy (1987).
2. Janet Rifkin (1980) first made this observation. This article has been the starting point for most radical feminist legal scholars.

Other faces of patriarchy include religion, government, and education. I am not suggesting that feminists are not disrupting these institutions; indeed, they are, and it is one of my contentions that the legal system is being similarly disrupted.

3. For discussions of feminist knowledge and method, see Jill Vickers, "Memoirs of an Ontological Exile: The Methodological Rebessions of Feminist Research," *infra*; see also Lahey (1985:525-30); Sandra Harding & Merrill B. Hintikka (1983).

4. Lorenne Clark (1976) was among the first to formulate this insight.

5. For a discussion of forms that sex discrimination can take in the legal profession, see Faith A. Seidenberg (1985).

6. See Gerda Lerner (1986); Janet Rifkin (1980); Ruby Rohrlich, "Law and Disorder: Impact on Women of the Early Laws in Mesopotamia and Mesoamerica," paper presented at the Third International Interdisciplinary Congress on Women, Dublin 1987.

7. See generally Stanley M. Elkins, *Slavery: A Problem in American Institutional and Intellectual Life* (Chicago: University of Chicago Press, 1976); cf. Nancy E. McGlen & Karen O'Connor (1983). So powerful was the device of legal nonexistence in maintaining the underclass status of women that when English and American legislators needed a legal model for the social and economic status of African slaves, who also were to be civilly dead and therefore exchangeable as forms of productive property, they looked to the legal status of married women. Being property themselves, African slaves could not own property, nor even tools; they could not enter into contracts, being the subjectmatter of contracts themselves; they could not move freely, reproduce by choice, speak without permission, work for money, own their own labour power, have custody of children, nor marry. Compare this status with what Mary Eberts has called the status of womanhood: women could not own property, enter into contracts, initiate or be a party to law suits, engage in monetized crafts or businesses, have custody of children, establish a residence or domicile, nor participate in the political processes of the so-called public sphere, including, of course, the practice of law. See Mary Eberts (1979).

8. See Janet Rifkin (1980) for a review of the research on this use of law.

9. See John Locke, *Two Treatises of Government*, ed. by Thomas Cook (New York: Hafner Publishing, 1947), for the clearest statement of these obviously inconsistent positions.

10. These figures include all women over the age of ten. See Carole Swan (1982). It should also be noted that within that twelve percent were many women whose husbands felt they "owned" those wages.

11. This is not to suggest, of course, that women are mere "victims" or "objects" in this process. On the contrary, women have resisted

118

these processes of appropriation and exploitation, have survived them, and have exercised considerable agency in making choices that are open to them.

12. Criminal Code, 1892, 55-56 Vict., c.29, section 179(c).

13. This amendment was enacted in the same year that Clara Brett Martin persuaded the Ontario legislature to let women practise law as solicitors. See Constance B. Backhouse (1985).

14. See Constance B. Backhouse (1985) for a detailed account of how this process was carried out in Canada.

15. Until the Supreme Court ruling in the 1988 Morgentaler case, a Canadian woman seeking an abortion had to secure the written agreement of three licensed physicians (overwhelmingly males) affiliated with an authorized hospital; she had to have the abortion in an approved hospital, and the procedure had to be performed in an approved manner by a licensed physician. If she could obtain geographic access to such facilities (many women could not), and if she had medical insurance or enough money, then she was usually given a general anaesthetic, was called "Mrs." even if she protested, and was exposed to anti-abortion pros-elytizing as she lay in the hospital bed. In free-standing clinics, women can decide whether and how to have an abortion. In some, they are also able to decide whether to have an anaesthetic, who will perform the procedure, and how they will deal with the emotional effects of the event.

16. Immediately after the Toronto clinic opened, the doctors who worked there were indicted for violating the criminal abortion prohibitions. In R. v. Morgentaler (1984), 47 O.R. (2d) 353 (Ont. H.C.J.), Parker J. ruled that the criminal prohibition did not violate the Charter of Rights. The jury acquitted the defendants, but in R. v. Morgentaler (1985), 11 O.A.C. 81, 52 O.R. (2d) 353 (Ont.C.A.), a full panel of the Ontario Court of Appeal ruled that the Crown was entitled to a new trial because the jury had heard inappropriate evidence and arguments (essentially, the defence of necessity). The Supreme Court of Canada vacated the order for a new trial and declared the criminal abortion prohibition unconstitutional, thus ending this part of the abortion struggle. But the ruling clearly contemplates that the provinces are empowered to regulate most of women's reproductive ac-tivities, and new restrictions on abortion will doubtless be enacted.

17. See Kathleen A. Lahey (1987a, 1987b), for discussions of these law "reform" measures. Generally, these measures make it a criminal offence for anyone but a licensed medical practitioner (or an employee—usually a nurse) to perform AI, and impose a marriage or stability test on women who want AI. Similar proposals have been made by the Ontario and British Columbia law reform commissions, but have not yet been legislated.

18. In experiments on mother-child attachment, which test the extent to which baby monkeys attach emotionally to terrycloth-covered lightbulbs, the lightbulbs are referred to as *surrogate* mothers because they were not the genetic/uterine mothers. The usage *surrogate mothers* in relation to human reproductive arrangements reverses the knowledge of maternity and thus cancels the role of genetic/biological mothers by putting them into the same category as terrycloth-covered lightbulbs. This reversal has the convenient effect of conferring the status of *mother* on the woman who is in reality the human equivalent of the lightbulb: the woman who is really the human surrogate mother (because she adopts the child of another woman) becomes the mother, and the genetic/uterine mother becomes the surrogate mother. This is a flip or reversal of shattering proportions.

19. For example, the Ontario Law Reform Commission's 1985 report on reproductive technology recommends that the mother of an AI child "should be conclusively deemed to be the child's legal mother." Without the double-think that lies behind the reversed meaning of surrogate mother, such a legal presumption would be completely unnecessary, even ludicrous. But once the central (and to men, threatening) legal principle of *mater semper certa est* (the mother is always certain) is abandoned, then women can know their maternity only through male legal and cultural constructs.

20. In contrast even with abortion law, which generally tends to treat at least the first few months of pregnancy as the woman's to control, criminalization of reproductive contracts denies women who enter into these contracts all claims to privacy, security of the person, and self-determination. Jurisdictions that do regulate these arrangements either have enacted criminal penalties for participating in such contracts (United Kingdom; Victoria, Australia) or allow women to engage in these contracts only under judicial supervision (the Canadian recommendations fall into this category). No legislature that has considered the issue has proceeded on the basis that women should be allowed to decide whether to engage in such transactions nor to decide whether they should perform such undertakings.

21. For example, when the criminal anti-prostitution provisions were amended to apply to customers as well as to prostitutes and pimps, women lawyers began to report, anecdotally, that the number of (male) customers arrested was much smaller than the number of (female) prostitutes, that prosecutors were routinely dropping charges (with the approval of judges), and that the few customers who were actually convicted were frequently given absolute discharges.

22. The fullest statement of this critique was written by Sarah & Angelina Grimke and published as Theodore D. Weld, *American*

Slavery As It Is (New York: Arno Press, 1968; first published in 1848).

23. Published in Elizabeth C. Stanton, Susan B. Anthony, & Matilda J. Gage, *History of Woman Suffrage* (Rochester, N.Y.: Charles Mann, 1881), reprinted in Rossi (1972).

24. This process was not complete until 1941, however (Altschul & Carron 1975).

25. Henrietta Muir Edwards v. A.G. for Canada, [1930] A.C. 124, reversing in the matter of a reference as to the meaning of the word "Persons" in section 24 of the British North America Act, 1867, [1928] S.C.R. 276. This principle of law is now codified in federal and provincial interpretation acts, which stipulate that words of the male gender in legislation are to be read as including women, "unless the context indicates to the contrary."

26. An Act to amend the Civil Code and the Code of Civil Procedure respecting the civil rights of women, 21 Geo. V., c. 101. In parallel developments in the United States, the National Women's Party began to lobby for the enactment of a blanket equal rights amendment (at the state and federal level) that would have roughly the same effect as the civil code amendments.

27. Even during this period, women continued to press for particularized reforms. In the 1970s, feminists continued to focus on substantive reform of rape, family property, and evidence law, for example.

28. Kathleen A. Lahey, *Women in the Canadian Economy* (Ottawa: CACSW, 1986).

29. See Penny Kome (1986) for a history of the drafting and adoption of the sex-equality guarantees of the Canadian Charter of Rights and Freedoms.

30. See Janet Silman, ed. (1987) for a detailed account of the effects that section 12(1)(b) of the Indian Act has had on Native women who married non-Native men. Defining Indian status by reference to marriage to Native men, Native women and their descendants who lost status under this regime have been disadvantaged in non-Native culture because of racial discrimination and have been denied the benefits of the Indian Act because of sexual discrimination. The reform of that provision has not entirely solved the problem, but has made it more difficult to see the problem.

31. Rosa Becker was the first woman plaintiff in Canada to obtain legal recognition for a woman's right to a share of assets that are built up during the course of a cohabitation. The ruling in Pettkus v. Becker partially nullified the Supreme Court of Canada's disastrous ruling in Murdock v. Murdock, which deprived a farm wife of any share in the farm assets regardless of her huge contributions. Despite her historic victory in the Supreme Court of Canada, however, Rosa Becker never collected a penny under the Supreme Court judgement because her husband was

able to hide and encumber her assets and otherwise avoid execution. The nonenforceability of her order was, in the end, paradigmatic of women's rights in these kinds of property divisions. And although Rosa Becker clearly saw this ruling as a victory for all women, she never received as much support from women lawyers as she did from men lawyers.

32. Gail Bezaire was the first openly-lesbian mother to win a custody case in Canada. However, the Ontario Court of Appeal upheld the reversal of the custody order when she began to live with another woman, despite substantial evidence that the children were being abused by their father. After she lost custody of the children and had exhausted all administrative and legal remedies, she took the children "underground" in the United States for five years, and lived the life of a fugitive in order to avoid detection.

33. These are all cases and situations that in some way touched my life or the lives of my friends at that time, and are by no means a completely representative sample of women's condition in 1982. Other women could, I suspect, make similar lists, but would give different examples.

34. Christine Boyle, "Sexual Assault and the Feminist Judge" in *Canadian Journal of Women and the Law*, Vol. 1, No. 1, 1985, p. 93.

35. For example, statutory rape rules; paternity tests (unless the man wants paternity and the woman contests it); drinking age; retirement age; insurance rates; breathalyzer rules; damages for consortium; legal presumptions relating to possession of premises; rape consent rules.

36. For example, paternity rules (when women want the man to pay support); abortion rules; affirmative action orders and provisions.

37. Marjorie Cohen, *Free Trade and the Future of Women's Work: Manufacturing and Service Industries* (Toronto: Garamond, 1987).

38. A draft civil statute called the Sex Equality Act under discussion among feminists in Canada addresses many of these points, and attempts to articulate these harms not only in terms of women's experiences of such abuse, but also in terms of judicial abuse of women's claims under existing civil, administrative, and criminal laws. This draft statute incorporates the anti-pornography ordinance developed in the United States.

39. Christine Boyle, *Feminist Reform of the Canadian Criminal Code* (Ottawa: NAWL, 1987).

CHAPTER 5

Inherited Biases
Within Feminism:
The "Patricentric Syndrome"
and the
"Either/Or Syndrome"
in Sociology

Linda Christiansen-Ruffman

Linda Christiansen-Ruffman is Professor of Sociology at Saint Mary's University in Halifax, Nova Scotia, and has a Ph.D. from Columbia University. She is past-president of the Canadian Research Institute for the Advancement of Women, both at the national level and in Nova Scotia, and president of the Canadian Sociology and Anthropology Association (1989-90). She organized and chaired the Social Science Federation of Canada's Task Force on the Elimination of Sexist Bias in Research, has written on women's organizations and women's political activism and community participation, as well as on feminist theory and methodology, and has been actively involved in women's action caucuses and groups in the community, the university, and professional organizations.

Similar versions of some sections of this article will be included in a forthcoming book on appropriate methodology for feminist analysis.

Introduction

Feminists live and work in a world that is permeated by patriarchal knowledge and institutions. It is not surprising, therefore, that we have inherited theories, ways of thinking, methodologies, research procedures, political ideas, and action strategies that are seriously flawed, especially for feminist purposes. This essay discusses some of the major distortions that characterize theory, research, public policy, and common-sense knowledge, and explores possible alternatives using examples from the sociological literature and from my own research and activism.

More specifically, the essay focuses on two interrelated syndromes or clusters of patriarchal distortions, which I call the "either/or syndrome" and the "patricentric syndrome." After a brief discussion of each of these syndromes, the essay will illustrate theoretical, political, and methodological distortions that result from their combined effect. The essay will suggest several analytic strategies to eliminate features of patricentric bias, to avoid the worst features of the either/or syndrome, and to improve conceptualization from a feminist perspective. Use of these strategies will help to overcome theoretical and methodological problems, not only within feminism, but within sociology and the social sciences in general.

Identification of these syndromes, their manifestations, and ways of overcoming them will allow feminist scholarship, research, and practice to avoid some of the patriarchal traps that will confront us as long as structural inequality continues and until feminist transformation is successful.

The Either/Or Syndrome in Practice

Intellectual thought stems partly from personal experience and partly from working with the language, logics of argument, and systems of relevance that are part of our society and our scholarly discipline. Personal experiences are often rendered invisible, however, as human understanding is transformed into "objective science." As Vickers points out in this volume, intellectual and theoretical development in the social sciences has suffered from glorification of abstractions, from false claims to objectivity, and from depersonalization.

I will begin by reflecting upon some of my own experiences of one-dimensional, simplistic, dichotomous thinking, or what I call the "either/or syndrome." Symptoms of the either/or syndrome within sociology are dichotomous variables, bivariate tables, and pairs of concepts such as urban versus rural, public versus private, production versus reproduction, traditional versus modern, and primary versus secondary relationships. The either/or syndrome is characteristic of the basic structure of theorizing and research methodology in sociology and dominates public debate and the ways in which policy is formulated. Because either/or thinking is so dominant in North America, feminists, including myself, have also become victims of its misplaced logic. As a practising feminist, I have encountered the either/or syndrome and other biases within feminism as a researcher in the field, as a theorist working with theories produced by others, and as an activist.

Feminism has often been uncritical of stereotypical ways of thinking about "traditional versus modern" women. My research on citizen participation in Nova Scotia during the 1970s had made me uneasy about some of the biases inherent in the "traditional versus modern" dichotomy, but I was inescapably confronted by them while doing consulting work in Labrador Straits, an isolated and rural part of Atlantic Canada. The Labrador women participants in a public meeting, and the employment-oriented projects they had produced, fit my stereotyped expectations in some ways but departed radically from them in others. For example, consistent with my expectations of traditional women, at the meeting the women sat on one side of the room while their husbands sat on the other. Labrador Straits women, however, were not marginal and conservative housewives; they played a vital role in the community. This was confirmed later when I returned and interviewed a number of women organizational leaders, using the same questionnaire I had administered in the more urban Halifax area to leaders of women's organizations. The women's organizations in Labrador Straits were more likely to be focused on issues such as employment and child care, which were identified as important community issues by their leaders, than were organizations in Halifax in 1975.

This research and my experience with these women and their communities led me to identify and to question three interrelated assumptions prevalent in feminist literature at the time:

(1) that women in rural areas, often called "traditional women" and characterized by relatively rigid sex-role segregation, are deprived of personhood compared to their more sophisticated urban counterparts;

(2) that there is gradual progress toward personhood as communities become more urban and industrialized; and

(3) that women in rural communities and in Atlantic Canada generally are conservative and are not innovative or politically active in community life.

All three of these assumptions were contradicted by comparisons between Labrador Straits and other parts of Canada (see Christiansen-Ruffman 1980).

Once the inaccuracy of assumptions like these is revealed, underlying conceptualizations are undermined. In this case the distinction between so-called traditional and modern women was seen to be laden with parochial urban bias; the idea of continual linear "development," or "progress" for women, along a unidimensional continuum from traditional to modern, was recognized as ethnocentric; the debate about whether women are "by nature" conservative or innovative was revealed as a meaningless exercise based on the abstracting of women's actions from their context.

In retrospect I realized that all these false assumptions were part of what I now call the "either/or syndrome." They were all based on dichotomies in space, in time, and/or in social or personal organization which helped obscure rather than analyze the position of rural women in particular and women in general.

My problems with the either/or syndrome emerged again in an examination of the theoretical literature related to women and politics. Dichotomies developed to understand women's positions in society—public versus private, domestic labour versus wage labour, production versus reproduction—also serve to hide the ways in which women have participated in the political process. For example, the association of men with the public sphere and women with the private sphere masks the fact that women's important role in reform movements is political activity. Moreover, one can be misled into the stereotypical thinking that all women's activity is domestic or private. Analyses focusing on women's emergence from the private to the public sphere also often imply incorrect unilineal assumptions of continual progress. In short, uncritical feminist acceptance of dichotomies, in conjunction with traditional male-defined academic fields, were leading me to a formal, narrow, institutional definition of the political which decreased rather than increased understanding.

The detrimental effect of the use of the public/private dichotomy in analyses and the discrimination that it implies has been well documented by Rogers (1980). She shows that this ideology has become institutionalized in the ideas and practices of development agencies and in public policy, and that it has contributed to development failures, to underdevelopment, and to what she calls the "domestication of women" as opposed to their development. It leads to systemic crises and to the feminization of poverty (DAWN 1985, Scott 1984). As an activist struggling to achieve a just society envisioned by feminists, I have become painfully aware of how the public/private distinction and the association of women's experiences with the private has been used to keep women's issues off the public agenda and to delegitimize them.

The Patricentric Syndrome Within Feminism

Contemporary feminist scholarship is being conducted within a scholarly tradition that is fundamentally sexist. As the authors in Spender (1981) and in this book indicate, androcentrism and sexist bias permeate contemporary scholarship in every discipline. The Canadian Psychological Association (1977), Armstrong & Armstrong (1983), Christiansen-Ruffman (1985), and Eichler (1988) have pointed to ways in which sexist biases enter the research process, resulting in bad, incompetent, inferentially unsound, biased, and/or unethical research. The Task Force on the Elimination of Sexist Bias in Research, which I chaired (1983-1986),[1] discovered that sexist biases tended to be recognized and resisted by women's caucuses or committees in some disciplines but not to be recognized by leaders of many of the professional social science organizations, disciplines, and publishing outlets in Canada. Thus, patriarchal knowledge and practices continue to permeate our intellectual heritage.

127

The patricentric syndrome refers to the scholarly and institutional practices that reproduce sexism and androcentricism in scholarship and in our daily lives—practices that underlie the invisibility and undervaluing of women and women's experiences and the exclusion of women's needs, work, lives, values, and interests from consideration in scholarship, public policy, and popular consciousness. For example, "universal suffrage" is described by historians as having taken place when men's vote was no longer based on property, well before women achieved suffrage. Other symptoms include the glorification of men and what are defined as "manly" features and the devaluation and/or servitude of women; this treatment of women occurs both theoretically and in practice. Because of the patricentric syndrome, our current knowledge system and our current sociological theories are an ineffective starting point for theoretical work, for research, for defining women's reality, and for political practice.

Sociology's theoretical basis was developed by the "fathers of sociology"—Comte, Spencer, Marx, Durkheim, and Weber—who sought to develop a theory of social order, social change, and "man in society." The patriarchal conceptualizations that were produced continue to be perpetuated in the discipline's teaching and research traditions. Concepts such as the sociology of work and social stratification, which were developed without any reference to women's activities, perceptions, and experiences, have been central to the discipline and enforced by patriarchal gatekeepers.[2] The work of contemporary feminist scholars trained in rigid, sex-biased disciplines cannot easily escape the many layers of patriarchal heritage embedded in scholarship. The number of women scholars working in the social sciences is still relatively small, the preferred subject matter and research subjects are still male-defined, and there is scholarly resistance to feminist scholarship that challenges existing paradigms. It is not surprising, therefore, that many major theories and concepts used by contemporary feminists are based on intellectual concepts and assumptions that are fundamentally sexist. These sexist assumptions enter both unconsciously and out of the need to do "legitimate" work. They are based on concepts and issues of importance to men, defined by men, using males, often implicitly, as theoretic actors. It is problematic for sociology that this male bias is often implicit rather than explicit.

Feminist theories that are generated as adjuncts to other theories and that do not treat women as central are usually based on assumptions that exclude women and women's experiences, but the patricentric assumptions are sometimes hidden from view. Because the currently acceptable way of working as a theorist is to base one's work on that of others, and because the work of both male and female theorists contains patricentric bias, some feminist theorists have chosen to base their work on male theorists who display brilliance in theorizing. For example, O'Brien (1984:87) suggests that "neomarxism, which marginalizes women but does not obliterate them, may hold heuristic and analytical possibilities which its current androcentrism conceals." She reviews the work of Gramsci even though she recognizes that he has "no notion of patriarchal hegemony and the reality of gender conflict" (O'Brien 1984:92) and that Marxism "has nothing to say about the value of individuals [and]... nothing to say about gender struggle" (O'Brien 1984:94). In recognizing the need to replace inadequate assumptions, she points out that "we have not yet started to assert the need to pose our materialist problem specifically from our own experience, to ask the forbidden questions and to proclaim that, if the theory does not fit, then the theory is inadequate" (O'Brien 1984:94).

One of the major purposes of theory is its ability to direct the researcher to interesting questions and answers in the empirical world. The dramatic disjunction between empirically interesting phenomena to me as a feminist scholar and theoretical questions raised by the current neo-Marxist framework was illustrated at a conference sponsored by the Social Sciences and Humanities Research Council of Canada (SSHRCC) aimed at identifying interesting research questions in Newfoundland and Labrador.[3] The implicit association of the public sphere with the world of wage labour rendered theoretically uninteresting the political decision-making of women, the vibrant women's political culture in Newfoundland and Labrador, and the economically-relevant components of women's organizational activities that my research and that of others had identified (Davis 1979; Porter 1983, 1985). The framework also excluded from attention case studies replete with descriptive details of the activities and perceptions of women in their outport communities as they deal with their lives and families in communities (Murray 1979).

At this stage, we need case studies like these, which describe the diverse reality of women's lives from women's perspective. Such studies are necessary if we are to understand the different and changing relationships of women within and between communities as community structures change over time and under different historical circumstances. While there are no doubt important hypotheses from Marxist theories that should be tested empirically in Newfoundland, it is inappropriate to limit research attention to such theoretically-derived questions, especially given the poverty of feminist conceptualization, the presence of patricentric assumptions, the lack of comparative empirical studies, and the sexist nature of some of the anthropological work that has been done. To limit research to that based on biased theory has the consequence of perpetuating sexist assumptions and sex-biased research in sociology.

·The patricentric syndrome also includes interactional and structural mechanisms that reproduce sexism and androcentrism in our daily lives. For example, Berit Aas (1985) points to "master suppression techniques": mechanisms at the interactional level used by men to make women invisible, to ridicule women, to withhold information from women, to attribute shame and guilt to women, and to define women's behaviour in such a way that she is damned if she does and damned if she doesn't.[4] At the structural level, all institutions, such as church, state, the media, and the military, perpetuate patriarchal control and devalue women's experiences and systems of relevance through what Dorothy Smith (1987) calls "relations of ruling." Vickers (1984) and Boyle, *et al.* (1986) point to the negative policy implications of these current patriarchal practices.

Joint Effect of These Two Syndromes on Feminist Scholarship

The either/or syndrome and the patricentric syndrome are often found together, mutually reinforcing each other. Thus while these two syndromes may be separated analytically, their joint effect has a particularly negative effect on scholarship, including some feminist scholarship.

Theoretical problems

The either/or syndrome and the patriarchal syndrome combined underlie many sets of concepts. In most cases, the separate category or concept into which women are placed implicitly or explicitly has the specific character of being not autonomous and virtually invisible and/or secondary. Action

130

originates in the male arena. Women are implicitly or explicitly compared to what is defined as the male "norm" and found lacking, or they are located theoretically to service men. For example, the public myth of women's private role is accompanied by an assumption that private activity is off-bounds for real analysis and interesting only insofar as it serves the public sphere. Hence scholars have tended to treat women stereotypically and functionally and to place greater value on the male sphere of activity. As Okin (1979) points out, political philosophers have asked what are men *like*? What are women *for*? Women's activities are not considered important in their own right. Women are not considered to be autonomous subjects, but merely objects of analysis, serving the interests of others.

Perhaps some of the most interesting feminist work in sociology to date has been done using a neo-Marxist framework (e.g., Benston 1969; Hamilton 1978; Connelly 1978; Luxton 1980; Armstrong & Armstrong 1984). The historical and/or dialectical approach of some of these authors allows them to escape some of the worst features of simplistic either/or thinking, but in most of these cases, women and women's experiences are forced into Marxist analytic categories as domestic labourers, as reserve armies, or as part of the reproductive sphere. As in the functionalist example above, the analytic function of these categories is either residual or to service the male-based activities and priorities. Even Dorothy Smith, a pioneer in treating women's standpoint as theoretically significant (1978, 1987), occasionally in her analysis seems to retreat into Marxism for her description of the structures of oppression, which results in a situation wherein women's decisions are no longer theoretically central. The secondary and residual nature of concepts related to women within these theoretical frameworks connote secondary status for women's activities and perceptions. Women are there, but their activities and perceptions count only insofar as they contribute to male-defined systems of relevance.

The broad, crude dichotomies into which women in society are sometimes slotted—private versus public, domestic labour versus wage labour, reproduction versus production— also tend in their use to obscure and hinder women-centred theorizing and to render invisible large portions of women's activities. They are not useful in theorizing, in conceptualizing, or in creating operational definitions, and, in fact, they may create misleading findings. Miller (1982), for example, criticizes the public/private theorists for underestimating women's participation in achieving "social good" within the public domain. She continues to use the dichotomy, however, rather than develop new ways of orienting her work conceptually.

A related problem with contemporary broad and crude concepts such as the public/private dichotomy is that the nature of what is considered private and public changes, but use of the same concepts may lead the researcher to assume as constant the socially-meaningful nature of this dichotomy over time. It is likely that Stacey and Price's book *Women, Power and Politics* (1981) ignores women's "grassroots politics" at different historic periods, largely because the public versus private dichotomy—and the gradual trend towards women's involvement in the public arena—is the conceptual basis for their work.

I have already pointed to the way in which the public/private dichotomy has tended to obscure women's social and political activity by identifying men with the public and women with the private. Such a conceptualization violates the three misplaced assumptions identified above and ignores women's community-based political activities and longstanding public volunteer work as well as women's community-building work in a variety of contexts. In one recent attempt to overcome the restrictive dualistic nature of the above dichotomies and to highlight important features of women's experiences, Leslie Brown and I initially posited women's community work as a "Third Part of the Puzzle" in terms of women's work experiences. Upon reflection and analysis, however, we recognized that adding a third sector to the existing categories of public and private is not an adequate corrective. We must question the theoretical assumptions on which these conceptions are based. Our analysis of the third part of the puzzle "led us to a recognition of the need to develop a new puzzle, solidly grounded in women's work experiences" (Brown & Christiansen-Ruffman 1986).

Politically inappropriate concepts

The other difficulty with these broad and crude dichotomous concepts is their use in ways that are divorced from context, that are implicitly conservative and simplistic in approach, and that enforce stereotypical thinking. Eichler (1980) made this point in her critique of masculinity-femininity scales and the ways in which they idealize sex-stereotyped behaviour.

As she points out, such concepts are not in the political interest of feminists:

> Paradoxically, the literature dealing with androgyny and with sex identity, while explicitly attempting to overcome current limitations of sex roles and sex identity, nevertheless contributes to and even cements their continued existence. (p. 62)

The dichotomy of traditional versus modern with its even more fuzzy, ethnocentric, and self-righteous basis is also detrimental to the women's movement at this stage of its development.[5] Implicit use of this dichotomy has led urban feminists to treat other women with paternalism, and I have seen this happen in Labrador, in Nova Scotia, and in rural Ontario. Incidentally, I am using the word "paternalistic" intentionally here since the "we" versus "they" attitude engendered by this dichotomy is probably more characteristic of a hierarchical and patriarchally-organized approach to the world than one based on women's culture.

This "paternalism" and the damage it does is sometimes evident when urban feminists speak to rural women. Often the feminist speaker "from away," having bought the patriarchal myth of unilinear "progress" and improvement of women's status through modernization, presumes rural women to be less "liberated" than herself. She accepts uncritically the patriarchal categories that devalue these women and their work and fails to see their strength, their self-respect, and the central role they play in the community. In doing so, she fails to challenge patricentric and dualistic definitions that construct rural women as "other" and "backward" and that hide her own continuing dependence and oppression in the modern, urban setting. The resulting blindness may lead to an arrogance that is insulting to rural women. It will certainly leave her without anything useful to say to them and with a feminism that appears to them to be irrelevant at best and threatening at worst and that cements rather than undercuts patriarchally-constructed and imposed divisions among women.

Methodological problems

Contemporary social-science research methodology, based on survey research and the psychological experiment, is riddled with sexist and dichotomous thinking and is largely responsible for many of these theoretical and conceptual problems within feminism as well as the analytic poverty of contemporary social science. In an attempt to eliminate many potential biases, these two types of methodological approach have been oriented almost exclusively to measurement, and in turn the measurement model of research has dominated social sciences in general and sociology in particular.

In spite of the current orientation towards measurement, sociologists at present are not very good at it. Contemporary research approaches are used to measure concepts in valid and reliable ways that assume that measurements are objective and gender-neutral. If gender does make a difference, it is assumed that gender will be treated as a variable and that its effect as an independent variable will be apparent on a questionnaire. What such a model ignores, however, is the taken-for-granted sexism and ways of looking at the world that are deeply embedded in social structures and that are invisible if one follows generally-accepted quantitative-survey techniques.

This problem of taken-for-granted contextual variables is illustrated by my study of newcomers in Halifax (1968-1976).[6] As a minor part of the study, I sought to discover why individuals in my sample moved. This information would provide background descriptive information on the characteristics of newcomers, to be included in an appendix, and would be a way in which to relate my study to other work done on migration.

When I asked people why they made both their recent and past moves, and calculated the stated reasons given for all moves in the lifetime of these residents, I found that almost eighty percent moved for reasons primarily related to the "job" as opposed to the "family."[7] Since the data appeared to be consistent with findings from all other studies I had examined, which "found" the dominance of economic reasons over family ones, this finding would not normally be considered a candidate for further exploration. It was only upon qualitative examination of the data from one respondent that I recognized an inconsistency and biased interpretation that these data were leading me and others to make. One male who said he moved for family reasons explained that he moved because his wife had a job. The women who moved because of their husbands' jobs stated that the reason for the move was the job. Although the linguistic construction of the situation was different, the situations were equivalent. The women had taken the conjugal family commitment for granted. The objective fact that most of these women and children would not have moved except for family reasons was taken for granted to such a degree that is was systematically not stated.

The implications of this qualitative analysis of one "strategic case" are tremendous, and, in fact, totally reverse the findings. The nuclear family, not the job or occupation, was why a majority of the individuals in my study moved although almost no one stated this fact. It was an accepted feature of the social structure among women in my Halifax sample at the time. The job-related reasons, which I and others were reporting, were, in fact, the most frequently articulated reasons for moving.[8]

Methodologically, this example points to the ease with which women's experiences remain hidden and unrecognized in this sexist society, and the facility with which currently-practised measurement-oriented research methods adopt sexist assumptions as part of their findings. This case is not a simple example of not talking to women, but of women not having named part of their reality and thus its remaining unrecognized in formal speech and in research. Although women have since begun to resist being moved at the whim of a spouse's employer, and the actual findings might be different today, this case should alert us to the presence of other taken-for-granted features of social reality that our analyses should not ignore. The newcomer study also indicates that the apparent replication of findings may, in fact, turn out to be artifacts of the methodologies used. Consistency, it should be noted, is not a measure of validity.

This case also raises an issue about the data to be expected from the relationship between researcher and respondents. According to standard survey research, we ask some relevant questions and then take the answers uttered by our respondents (usually limited to one choice) to be the "stuff" of our analysis. This case study illustrates the limits of the strategy of asking only fixed-ended questions and indicates that we must take the multi-dimensional experiences and perceptions of our respondents more seriously, on the one hand, and, on the other hand, that we cannot rely only on the language of the survey, on what is "questionable" in a particular society at a particular time, as an empirical basis for our analysis.[9]

The study of why people move also points to problems with our current conceptual apparatus. Because of the either/or syndrome, we often divide even nominal data into apparent dichotomies, conceived along a continuum of one level of reality through our instructions to form mutually-exclusive and exhaustive categories. We assume that data from an individual may be coded into either "job" or "family" reasons, but not both. Perhaps a more legitimate—and corrective—assumption would be to see how both "ends" of such dualisms might apply to an individual in different ways and over time and space. This might counter the tendency common in contemporary social science of reducing the world to one dimension, taking people and concepts out of context and then forcing one choice of a dichotomy. Even such a conceptual strategy has its drawbacks, however, because it assumes a binary world of opposites as a starting point.

Another implication of this example from the newcomers study is the ease with which apparently precise quantitative findings may be totally reversed when a different assumption is introduced. This is not a unique situation. Part of the problem is that currently accepted research approaches tend to take contextual variables for granted analytically and methodologically, and in their emphasis on measurement they ignore inferences. This problem, in turn, stems partly from the analytic strategy of hypothesis-testing, which usually requires focusing on independent and dependent variables that are divorced from context and often dependent on dichotomous, either/or conceptualizations.

Let me provide an example from a study that used a variety of methods to collect descriptive historical data on the tenant movement of New York City from early in this century to 1978. In an article in *Signs*, Lawson and Barton describe the differing contributions of men and women to the tenant movement and raise the problem of sexism within this social movement.[10] In the qualitative descriptive portions of the article, they discuss a relatively complex and multi-layered pattern of organization in the tenant movement and a variety of strategies and initiatives followed over time. They focus on leadership by men and women, sometimes as individuals and sometimes as groups, in terms of (a) organizers or "activists," or the "active core," (b) leaders of formal tenant organizations, and (c) members, or the rank-and-file. However, problems with the patricentric and either/or syndromes emerge when they produce "findings" by constructing, asserting, and explaining two hypotheses. They claim to have found that the leaders of the tenant movement were generally male, and they identify a pattern of leadership succession wherein men lead and women follow.

136

As I pointed out in a comment on their work, also published in *Signs* (Christiansen-Ruffman 1982), it is possible using Lawson and Barton's own descriptive data on women organizers and their own conception of leader to come to diametrically-opposed findings. These opposite findings are produced by my including activists as leaders, as is implied by the researchers' definition of leaders but not by their empirical practice, and by my not assuming the greater importance of federation leaders in contrast to leaders of building associations and/or activists.[11] It appears that when Lawson and Barton organize their "findings" and analysis into "legitimate" dichotomous categories in order to count leaders for their first hypothesis, their patricentric bias leads them to see leaders as men in positions on top of organizational hierarchies, in spite of their definition of leaders as decision-makers, in spite of their data, and in spite of their statements about the importance of activists and women organizers. In "testing" the second hypothesis, they give a few illustrations of occasions when male leaders occupied "leadership positions while new directions are evolving" (p. 237) but fail to treat seriously their own findings that women were leaders in the initial stages of organizing. As they point out, "At the outset—in 1904, 1907 and again in 1917-20—[women] were organizers whose prominence was usurped by the men who formed the first [neighbourhood organizations]" (p. 246). When women clearly take the initiative, their leadership qualities are not seen and not counted.

Thus, even if one had to generate "findings" according to their dichotomizing hypotheses, the data in their article, in fact, indicate that women, not men, were the leaders of the tenant movement in New York City and that women initiated the movement and the men followed. But rather than succumbing to the either/or syndrome and being limited to analysis by hypothesis, more interesting insights would be generated by describing the types and processes of leadership by women and men.

Feminist Analytic and Research Strategies

The frequency, prevalence, persistence, intellectual power and authority of the patricentric and either/or syndromes implies that enormous remedial and reconstructive efforts are needed in our knowledge structures. This paper will close by suggesting several analytic and research strategies to counter these syndromes and to develop feminist scholarship and practice.

One might think that in light of problems with the either/or syndrome, it could profitably be banned from use. Total elimination, however, would not be appropriate because dichotomies and the comparisons they imply are important theoretical tools. Dichotomies are useful for clarifying ideas, constructing taxonomies, developing complex concepts, and uncovering hidden assumptions as well as faulty logic. [12] The systematic examination of similarities and differences at different levels of abstraction—and of the dichotomies that are implicit or explicit in such an endeavour—is an integral part of the process of theorizing in that it helps develop new ideas and questions.

Dichotomous thinking should not, however, continue to use stagnated and paralyzing sexist categories or to dominate scholarly work to such an extent that our thinking is determined by dichotomies and the assumptions they imply. Two strategies are suggested as a corrective to the overemphasis on establishing and reifying dichotomies in contemporary social sciences and society. (1) When scholars want to use dichotomies, they should theorize how both sides of the dichotomies they produce in fact might be appropriate. [13] For example, Lawson and Barton might examine the apparently opposite findings that may be derived from their data and develop the argument that both female and male leadership could be seen as dominant and could be seen as coming first. Such an analytic approach would lead to a far more interesting analysis because it would involve examining the data in context rather than abstracting it from context, as was necessary in their hypothesis-testing approach. Such an approach might also lead to the development of more complex variables. (2) Because of the current excessive use of dichotomies, we should try to avoid them. We should challenge ourselves to think in terms of three, four, or five categories and to conceptualize curves or circles rather than straight lines. For example, Lawson and Barton would have been better advised to develop their official "findings" in terms of organizers, leaders of formal organizations, and members rather than attempt the leader/follower dichotomy. Their analysis might even have been enriched had they begun to think of different types of members as well. Clearly, in this case they should have "listened" to their data and developed appropriate categories rather than forced their data inappropriately according to the either/or syndrome.

Feminists have already suggested strategies that are relevant to combatting the patricentric syndrome. For more than a decade in Canada, feminist scholars and women's caucuses have identified various problems of sexism and androcentrism in research and suggested solutions. Blatant examples of sexism at every stage of the research process have been identified and correctives suggested (Eichler 1983, 1988; Stark-Adamec & Kimball 1984; Vickers & Eichler 1987). The earliest and most obvious examples identified were those of language bias, and feminist scholars have sought to eliminate the so-called generic use of the masculine and to adopt non-sexist positional titles. A major step would be taken if social scientists learned to avoid making sloppy sexist inferences and generalizations in terms of gender. Guidelines for non-sexist research have been developed and publicized by Margrit Eichler and Jeanne LaPointe in the booklet *On the Treatment of the Sexes in Research* (1985), distributed by the Social Sciences and Humanities Research Council, the major funding source for social science research in Canada.

These efforts at non-sexist research, which avoid biased inferences and overgeneralizations, are necessary,[14] but they are not sufficient. Eliminating sexism in each study and making the gender of the sample and the theoretic actor explicit is important but inadequate at present. Years of men theorizing about "man" on the basis of male data has created a body of theory riddled with sexism and a discipline wherein the patriarchal biases are perpetuated by current gatekeepers and by methodological practice. So much of our language, ways of thinking, values, theories, and assumptions are permeated with patriarchal influences that an enormous effort of feminist scholarship and feminist consciousness is required even to begin to "see" and to articulate women's reality. We need concerted radical measures to offset the scholarly inheritance of the patricentric syndrome.

One of the greatest needs at present in feminist sociology is for new conceptual frameworks and assumptions that allow women and women's activity to become central and to remain so. The following strategies are likely to generate such theories. (1) The first strategy is one of developing new concepts and new names for features of women's reality and experiences, which have to date been unarticulated. Patriarchy's silencing methods over the centuries must be reversed, as Mary Daly's work (1978, 1984) has demonstrated. These efforts at reacquainting ourselves with our own realities must be made on a global scale and then compared in order to identify features of women's specificity and diversity. (2) A second strategic approach might be called "radical reconceptualization." Such an approach would begin at the theoretical level, rather than the empirical one, and radically challenge the bases and assumptions of major theoretical frameworks, suggesting a new problematic and set of assumptions on which to base enquiry (see Mary O'Brien 1984 and in this volume). (3) A third alternative—theorizing anew—is to ask ourselves afresh some of the theoretical questions that have challenged intellectuals for centuries, such as the nature of society and its relationship with individual members, the nature of change, the important features of social activity, and the foundations of social structure. Feminists and non-sexist researchers could then develop ways of thinking that base answers to these questions solidly on women's experiences.

Feminism's need to break from the inheritance of the either/or syndrome and the patricentric syndrome also requires the use of appropriate methodologies. Feminist scholars have begun to recognize both the ways in which methodological biases in research are being created (Christiansen-Ruffman 1985) and the ways in which the standard research rules are inappropriate. For example, feminists have recognized that the researcher cannot adopt a neutral role and so have begun to explore alternative descriptions of the ways in which researchers approach and participate in the interview or field situation (see, for example, Roberts 1981; Stanley & Wise 1983; Bowles & Klein 1983; Reissman 1987; Harding 1987).

The either/or and patricentric syndromes lie at the basis of contemporary methodologies focused on measurement of variables and testing of hypotheses using independent and dependent variables.[15] In order to break this scholarly inheritance and to ground feminist theory in women's experiences, we must develop analytic and methodological approaches that do not orient all of their rules of procedure to verification and measurement. What I am proposing is an "appropriate methodology" that is consistent with our current need to develop useful conceptual frameworks and assumptions based on women and women's experiences. Feminist research strategy should recognize the importance of inference and develop a means of gathering data that maximizes the possibility of theoretically-useful inferences. The concepts developed in feminist research should not only be useful analytic tools to grasp the reality of women's experience, treating women as subject and not as object, but they should also be useful in feminist praxis.

Appropriate methodological rules are in need of development. New feminist paradigms require new assumptions, research questions, forms of analysis, and logics of argument. This will involve experimentation with a variety of models and research approaches. For example, the Canadian Research Institute for the Advancement of Women is experimenting with comparative, collaborative participatory research aimed at developing a research approach that is empowering, action-oriented, and potentially useful to the women's movement. *Women's Involvement in Political Life: A Pilot Study* (CRIAW, 1986) reports on the process and findings of one such collaborative research project.

A number of feminist scholars have found the "grounded-theory" approach to research particularly appropriate in these early stages of our work when generating new theory must be given priority. Grounded theory orients the research enterprise toward developing theory rather than testing it. It stresses the development of ideas and theoretical sampling, the selection of cases for specific theoretical purposes, and emphasizes the importance of inference.[16]

The grounded-theory approach can be used in strategic comparative case studies. Although the theoretical use of empirical detail has a long history among sociological theorists, including Marx, Durkheim, and Weber, it is interesting that discussion of strategically-selected ethnographies or case studies for the purpose of generating theory tends to be absent from textbooks on research methodology with the exception of a brief mention of grounded theory. Given the current needs of feminist theory, case studies and inductive analysis are potentially fruitful ways of examining, describing, and explaining women's experiences within their social structural, contextual, and historical setting. Until we have conceptual frameworks and theories devoid of patriarchal imprints, measurement-oriented approaches are not likely to provide the most appropriate methodologies.

Some feminists have already made theoretical strides, avoiding the limitations of the either/or syndrome and following other feminist principles, such as treating women as subject and treating analysis as relevant to praxis. The recognition by writers in this volume that women's specificity and equality are not dichotomous, mutually-exclusive qualities is a good

141

example, as is the book's focus on scholarship and action. What we need are more analytic frameworks, concepts, and theories that are not based on an overtly masculine agenda, on patriarchal either/or assumptions, or on patriarchal theories, concepts, assumptions, logics of argument, or methodological rules of procedure. As feminism and feminist analysis begin to whittle away patriarchy's defences, a more humane society becomes possible for both men and women. Women must be active participants, and women's activities must be recognized as important, in order for feminist theory and analysis to flourish.

FOOTNOTES

This is a revised version of a paper on the "either/or syndrome" presented at the annual conference of the Canadian Research Institute for the Advancement of Women (CRIAW) in Ottawa, November 1982. I wish to thank Angela Miles and students in my Feminist Analysis Sociology course (1987-88) for their helpful comments.

1. The Task Force was established by the Science Policy Committee of the Social Science Federation of Canada (SSFC), of which I was a member, representing the Canadian Sociology and Anthropology Association. Data were gathered from presidents of all the professional associations in the SSFC, from a woman contact in each professional association, and from editors of all social-science journals and publishers. See Christiansen-Ruffman (1986).

2. While at graduate school at Columbia University in the mid-1960s, a number of us tried to name eminent women sociologists whose careers were not dependent on eminent male sociologists— as spouse or mistress. The fact that we were unable to name any woman who did not have such sponsorship is indicative of the strong presence of patriarchal gatekeepers.

3. Pat Marchak, who was invited to the conference "from away" in British Columbia, used neo-Marxist theory as a basis for generating research questions she felt should be pursued in studying women and the Canadian economy in Newfoundland (Patricia Marchak, 1982, "Women in the Economy: Debates and Directions for Research," keynote address to the Newfoundland SSHRCC Conference on Women and the Economy, July 28).

4. A much more detailed description of these techniques has been published in Norwegian, and an English unpublished manuscript

is available. Berit has also discussed these techniques at lectures throughout Canada.

5. One should not be surprised that some dichotomies that are particularly useful at one stage of development become counterproductive. From the viewpoint of the sociology of knowledge, the traditional/modern dichotomy may illustrate a pattern in the development and use of dichotomies. At first, the dichotomy is identified, is used in theorizing, and commands its own scholarly importance or dies in obscurity. The traditional/modern dichotomy was useful in recognizing important analytic differences in the social organization of two types of society. At a second stage, some dichotomies that have gained scholarly importance become recognized and used in public discourse. Early in that process such dichotomies provide new insights, but as they gain political use and are applied in ways that are divorced from context, they become what might be called inappropriate public stereotypes. It should be recognized, of course, that this process of knowledge dissemination happens within a political context and those that are most consistent with prevailing ideologies and in the interest of those in power are most likely to progress through the early stages, are least likely to be transformed in the process, and are most likely to be reinforced and maintained as inappropriate stereotypes in later stages of the process. The traditional/modern dichotomy is now at this later stage.

6. See Linda Christiansen-Ruffman, 1976, "Newcomer Careers: An Exploratory Study of Migrants in Halifax," Ph.D. dissertation, Columbia University.

7. When I first examined the data qualitatively, the job reason appeared to be given added weight. I examined the fourteen couples in this subsample who did not give job reasons directly, and my thesis reports that "the importance of the job becomes even greater." One male respondent who replied that he did not know why they came to Halifax in fact arrived in the area just as graduate school started; one could infer that in this case school and ultimately the future job of the male was of some importance in the decision to move. Members of the other thirteen couples mentioned family reasons for their move to the Halifax area, five citing reasons connected with the nuclear family and eight with the extended family. I explored their reasons, multiple reasons, and the relationship of their responses to class position. Occupational reasons were clearly important in many of these cases and I found that all five of the couples who had given the nuclear family as a reason for the move also had a very clear job-related reason for the move.

8. In my thesis, this discussion occupied only two paragraphs of the six- to eight-page section on the Reasons for the Move (see Linda Christiansen-Ruffman, 1976, "Newcomer Careers: An Exploratory Study of Migrants in Halifax," Ph.D. dissertation,

Columbia University). The full theoretical implications of this finding for the migration literature and for our understanding of the taken-for-granted nature of nuclear-family ties in the late 1960s were not developed. Even though the thesis was methodologically oriented, it is only in retrospect that the full methodological implications are beginning to emerge.

9. This criticism is not limited to survey research. In fact, in discussions of qualitative versus quantitative research, reliance on the sample's responses is often described as intrinsic to qualitative research (see, for example, Alan Bryman, 1984, "The Debate About Quantitative and Qualitative Research: A Question of Method or Epistemology?" in *British Journal of Sociology*, Vol. 35, No. 1, pp. 75-92). To some extent, this reliance on members' responses is more taken-for-granted in survey research and therefore more open to inappropriate assumptions.

10. Ronald Lawson and Stephen E. Barton, 1980, "Sex Roles in Social Movements: A Case Study of the Tenant Movement in New York City" in *Signs: Journal of Women in Culture and Society*, Vol. 6, Winter, pp. 230-247. The fact that this article was published in *Signs*, was written with a focus on sexism, and had been approved by the review process indicates the layers of patriarchal thinking that are invisible even to many feminists.

11. Despite their hypothesis-testing either/or formulation, complete data are not presented and data in the article are not consistent with the hypothesis. For example, two tables of contemporary information are presented where percentages indicate that "among core activists, women outnumber men at *all* levels. However, the situation is different when leaders are separated from other activists: the higher the structural level, the more likely are the leaders to be male" (p. 234). This statement is accurate, but what is left unsaid is interesting. The article did not give raw figures, and when these are calculated from percentages and "n"s given, it turns out that when leaders at building, neighbourhood, and federal levels are taken together, a majority of those counted by the authors as leaders are, in fact, women. When leaders and activists are included together, women are present in larger numbers than men in all three structural categories.

12. Dichotomies have also been useful illustrations to women of how objectively similar behaviour is perceived as different in men and women in a patriarchal society.

13. The analytic approach of focusing on the overlap between two apparently opposite concepts is not entirely new to feminist analysis. Consider, for example, how the personal and political have been asserted by feminists not to be opposites but to be intertwined in theory, in intention, and in action. "The personal is the political" is a basic orientation of the feminist movement

and has been used to inform, to plan, and to shape actions at the individual, group, community, and global level.

14. As long as women and women's experiences are not central, feminists as women scholars will be making their contribution to other bodies of knowledge rather than to feminist scholarship. One should not belittle this effort, since existing theories will also be of great benefit as some of their layers of sexist biases are whittled away.

15. For example, our incredible over-emphasis on reliability tries to erase the fact that an interview is an interaction between two people and tries to keep all interview discussion on a superficial, simplistic level that ignores the complexity of social interaction. Another of our problems, stemming from linear, either/or thinking, is our glorification of quantitative measurement. It leads researchers to try to give quantitative meaning to nominal data and to assume that more is more relevant. Problems stem as well from over-zealous attention to measurement strategies that idolize quantitative ratio data and that worry more about sampling error than the representativeness, or features of the social structural context from which the sample was drawn and to which the inferences are being made. The choice of place from which to draw the sample is too important a decision to be treated as incidental to research design.

16. See Barney Glaser and Anselm Strauss, 1967, *The Discovery of Grounded Theory* (Chicago: Aldine). This methodological account was based in part on Barney Glaser and Anselm Strauss, 1965, *Awareness of Dying* (Chicago: Aldine) and also has its roots in Aaron Cicourel, 1964, *Method and Measurement in Sociology* (New York: Free Press) and Harold Garfinkel, 1967, *Studies in Ethnomethodology* (Englewood Cliffs, N.J.: Prentice Hall).

CHAPTER 6

The Problem of Studying "Economic Man"

Marjorie Cohen

Marjorie Cohen, an economist, teaches at the Ontario Institute for Studies in Education. Her most recent publications include *Free Trade and the Future of Women's Work* (1987) and *Women's Work, Markets and Economic Development in Nineteenth Century Ontario* (1988). She has been actively involved in economic and labour issues in the feminist movement through the National Action Committee on the status of women and other feminist organizations. She is also co-chair of the Coalition Against Free Trade.

Feminists are familiar with the androcentric biases of the disciplines which have something to say about women's condition. The power which these disciplines have, in simply defining what they see as the problem and then explaining the issues with a male concept of society and social relationships, is well known. Feminist criticism has put us on our guard against accepting the well established viewpoints of literature, history, medicine, psychology, and even politics. But no one has written about the biases of one of the most thoroughly male of all disciplines—economics. Of course, women, like most men, tend to distrust economists and economic analysis; nevertheless the discipline itself has had extraordinary power, both to shape social institutions according to its own objectives, and to instill in the subconscious of individuals an analytical approach which inevitably leads to conclusions based on apocryphal notions about human behaviour.

The point to be developed is that economics has evolved a methodology which for the most part cannot "see" women's economic behaviour. However, when women's economic behaviour does conform to that which theory can say something about, the assumptions on which the theory is based are false. In short, economic theory has little that is useful to say either about what is happening to women in the economy or why it is happening. My criticism will focus on the theories of neoclassical economics because of their dominant position in economic literature, economic departments in universities, and in social policy. Neoclassical methodology is studied by all students who enter the discipline, and even if they do question its assumptions in later life, a certain amount of mental baggage is retained so that its notions pervade even new fields of economic consideration such as the problem of discrimination, an issue which will be discussed later.

Economists have defined their area of study very widely. One of the most famous definitions is that of Alfred Marshall, the father-figure of neoclassical thought: "Political Economy or Economics is a study of mankind in the ordinary business of life; it examines that part of individual and social action which is most closely connected with the attainment and with the use of the material requisites of well being."[1] The ordinary business of life takes in quite a bit of territory, and with such an inclusive definition one would be tempted to think that "mankind" is used in the generic sense—it is not. The real range of the subject is clarified by Marshall when he says it is concerned "chiefly with those motives which affect, most powerfully and most steadily, man's conduct in the business part of his life."[2] Economists can deal with "facts which can be measured and recorded" and problems which "relate specially to man's conduct under the influence of motives that are measured by a money price."[3] However, there is a great deal of the ordinary business of life which does not lend itself to being measured by a money price. The way economists have coped with this fact has been to assume that although a facet of life does not have a money value established directly on the market, it can nevertheless be determined indirectly by the market value of what one must forego in order to pursue or realize a non-monetary objective.

Some economists have felt that a definition of economics which sees the discipline as dealing with the material requisites of well-being is too restrictive. In an attempt to make the subject include choices between the economic and the non-economic, Lionel Robbins introduced the notion of scarcity as the distinctive feature of the discipline. He defined economics as being "concerned with that aspect of behaviour which arises from the scarcity of means to achieve given ends."[4] With this definition, presumably, the discipline was interested in the economic problems both of the individual and of social economic behaviour on markets.

Paul Samuelson, in his textbook for first year students, restricts Robbins' definition by adding the materialist definition. But he claims it is a definition of the subject on which economists basically agree: "Economics is the study of how people and society end up choosing, with or without the use of money, to employ scarce productive resources that could have alternative uses, to produce various commodities and distribute them for consumption, now or in the future, among various persons and groups in society."[5] It is necessary to pursue the way economists define their field since they claim to study society in a way which would include the economic activities of everyone in the society, including women.[6] There is a tendency for economists to see their analysis as having the widest application to human behaviour and to include activities which do not at first glance appear to be economic.[7] While most of the nitty-gritty of economic analysis deals with the market mechanism, the economists, by defining the scope of the profession widely, use the tools they have developed to explain the market to deal with non-market areas. There are two significant issues here to be discussed: first, that economists are relatively uninterested in non-market behaviour, although they believe that their methodology is sufficient to analyze it should they wish to do so; and second, that the tools which have been developed to explain market behaviour are exceedingly blunt instruments for an analysis of non-market behaviour.

By now, people interested in the study of women are attuned to the fact that the productive nature of most women's work is not counted by economists. Women's economic behaviour as consumers within the "household" generates some interest, but basically the household is viewed as a unit of consumption, not production. Having noticed that excluding women's housework from economic accounting (GNP) creates some problems, economists usually express their regret with a little exclamation point after having repeated A.C. Pigou's puzzled observation that if a man married his housekeeper the GNP goes down! "Or if a wife arranges with her neighbour for each to clean the other's house in return for $5,000 a year, then the GNP would go up by $10,000."[8] But the problems of trying to count non-market work, while not insurmountable, are clearly not considered worth the effort; as Samuelson explains, "So long as the number of women working at home does not change much in relative importance, the ups and downs of GNP will be about the same whether or not we count in this or similar items such as home-grown vegetables and other do-it-yourself activities."[9] Unfortunately, he doesn't discuss how one knows whether the relative importance of what is going on in the household changes if no one measures its productive activity. The implication here, too, is that women's housework is roughly of the same proportions as work involved in hoeing the carrot patch or messing around on the tool bench. In fact, housework is the single largest "industry" in terms of the number of people working at it, and estimates of its *value* range from one-quarter to one-half of the gross national product.[10]

But what are the consequences of excluding housework from the GNP? Would including the value of this work be anything more than a symbolic gesture in recognizing women's work as productive activity? Its juridicial significance *is* often recognized, particularly for evaluating matrimonial property settlements, pension benefits, entitlement to family wealth, and even as a measure of value should the issue of wages for housework become a reality.[11] But women's work has economic significance as well: excluding such a huge part of economic activity from economic accounting imposes serious limitations on the validity of what is counted. It also raises questions as to what we know about how effectively the system allocates resources. If a productive activity is not counted, then neither is the cost of that production. Efficiency is an important issue for economists, and it can be determined only if total production and total costs are known. For example, if total production increases even though there has been no change in the number of the factors of production used, then the economy has become more efficient, and presumably welfare increases. Both the total amount of production and the efficiency of production are critical indications of an improvement or worsening of the economy. If economics is really concerned with notions of efficiency and employing scarce productive resources to alternative ends, it cannot confine its analysis only to those alternative ends which can be given a value through the market.

By not counting the nature of production in the household, society does not know the cost or benefits of that production, and is thus not able to make rational decisions about alternative uses of resources. For example, because all economic activity within the household is treated as consumption, items like washing machines and stoves are not considered factors of production, hence are not costs of production. There are huge capital costs involved in having kitchens, laundries and playrooms in each individual household, just as there are huge expenditures of labour involved in raising children one at a time by one adult. However, by simply labelling this activity as consumption, the economist is able to say that activity within the household is rational because the household is maximizing its own total utility. But clearly, if this activity were considered as part of the production process, its rationality would be examined in a different way. The fact is that economists have no way of dealing with efficiency outside the market mechanism unless they look at an economic unit in isolation.[12] The whole significance of a market equilibrium (i.e., the optimum use of resources in the economy) becomes quite meaningless if a huge portion of economic activity is not part of the calculation. The policy implications of not seeing activity in the household as production are significant for women because alternatives to production in the home (for example, day-care centres) will be considered only in terms of the cost and benefits of their impact on the market; not in consideration of the total use of resources.

While women's economic behaviour in the household has not been integrated into mainstream economic analysis, this does not mean that neoclassical theory is felt to be inadequate to deal with the issue. When the household is examined, the same methodology which is used to explain market behaviour is applied. My contention is that there are serious difficulties in using an analysis which was designed to explain market behaviour to explain non-market activity as well. Economic theory is based on a notion of human behaviour which in the early days of neoclassical theory building was given the label "economic man." Economic man is a fantastic creature whose wants are insatiable and whose capacity for calculation is perfect. His motivition for action is gain, so he will be consistent in his choices and will "maximize" everything. Over the years, economic man acquired a rather nasty reputation as a money-grubbing individual whose whole system of values is directed by the profit motive. So economists for some time, mostly for publicity reasons, have avoided the term "economic man": they try to emphasize that they do not believe that a money profit is the sole motive for anyone's behaviour. Nevertheless, the idea of maximizing utility remains fundamental to neoclassical economic theory: on the market the central assumption is that producers will be profit maximizers and consumers will be pleasure maximizers.

This discipline of maximizing gain, which is so critical to a market analysis, is assumed to apply to all behaviour whether or not the ultimate objective is measured in terms of psychic happiness or monetary rewards. In order to maximize behaviour, individuals must be able to determine the relative utility of all possible courses of action and make choices so that total utility is maximized. If this can be done (and economists have no doubt that it can), then the economist feels that emotional needs can be compared with material needs and decision-marking in the market can be compared with decision-marking in the household. So the most basic assumption on which a neoclassical analysis of the household rests is that decision-making is not markedly different within the household than it is on the market. This is a heroic assumption about the nature of human motivation which is treated as constant through time, but which became true even of market behaviour only after a considerable period of discipline. It is likely that the motivation necessary for the successful functioning of the market system was learned behaviour: that is, the economic calculations of individuals are not governed by an immutable natural law but are culturally determined. Karl Polanyi maintains that the great transformation in society brought about by the domination of the market was the change in the motive of action from one of subsistence to one of gain.[13] Other economic historians have shown that this change was not a natural process and that participants on the market, particularly workers, resisted being motivated by gain.[14] If the motive of gain is an economic law peculiar to market behaviour, then any theory which bases its analysis on this assumption but applies it to a non-market situation is beginning with a very questionable premise. Yet any analysis of economic behaviour in the household has this premise as its underpinning. Understanding the assumptions used to explain household behaviour becomes particularly important now as economists are more interested in determining how time is allocated between market and non-market activities. When it is assumed, for example, that the allocation of time within the household or between the household and the market is based on maximizing total utility, then it is fairly easy for the economist to show that the division of labour by sex within the household is the result of a purely rational economic calculation.[15] The social implications are significant: if behaviour is based on some economic law, then what exists is rational and becomes a powerful argument for justifying the *status quo*.

The analysis of household behaviour, particularly with regard to problems of production, is not an issue with which an economist would normally deal. However, in those few cases when the household is examined, it is approached with premises assumed valid for market behaviour. I maintain that these do not necessarily apply to behaviour within the household — behaviour which has not been made to conform to the requirements of the market. But the examination of economic behaviour within the household does not rely simply on the assumption of gain as the motive to explain the relationship between the household and the market. It is also dependent on other tools which neoclassical economics has developed to explain the market mechanism. The most important of these is the explanation of the distribution of income.

When women work for money, their activity comes under the scrutiny of mainstream economic analysis. One issue we might expect an economist to clarify is why women are paid less than men. Neoclassical analysis tells us that except in unusual circumstances we are paid exactly what we are worth. The notion that the wage paid is really indicative of the worth of labour is a belief of our society which has been "proven" by economic science. The theory of wages rests on the economic proof that in normal circumstances, when the market is in equilibrium, workers will be paid a wage equal to their marginal productivity.[16] So if a woman is paid less than a man, it is basically because she is less productive. This conclusion also involves an important assumption about the nature of the market itself—that it is perfectly competitive. Now, no economist today would actually claim that perfect competition exists, rather it is seen as an abstraction where all kinds of inconvenient, distracting complications like unemployment are removed so that the basic mechanism of the market can be explained. A perfectly competitive economy is one where all economic units are small enough so that no one individual or group of individuals can have an effect on the price. It is a market where, among other things, there is total freedom of contract, labour is perfectly mobile, and full employment is the rule. Everyone gets a wage exactly equal to the value of his labour because any wage less than that would force the individual to seek out another employer—one who was behaving more rationally. In a perfectly competitive market, an employer who tried to pay some workers a wage less than the marginal productivity of their labour would have to accept a lower profit because he would be forced to operate with a smaller labour force at a scale of production which was less than optimal. To the neoclassical economist, discrimination is an irrational economic action for which the discriminator pays by receiving a lower profit.

Much of the prejudice regarding the worth of female labour stems from the notion of neoclassical economists, based on the assumption of perfect competition, that labour will be paid a wage equal to its marginal productivity. This idea has so permeated the thinking of society over such a long period of time that it has become a difficult mental hurdle to dissociate women's wage from the true value of women's work. Economists who are interested in the problem of discrimination (it is still considered a fringe field) are still firmly in the grip of the neoclassical model and cannot quite comprehend why competition does not eliminate discrimination in the long run.[17] In the short run, prejudice (which the economist tactfully labels "taste") might permit discrimination, but in the long run, prejudice would constitute extremely irrational economic behaviour.

Neoclassical economic analysis, then, explains wage differences between men and women as arising either from differences in the productivity of labour or from economic man not behaving true to form. Of course this analysis flies in the face of reason and (to echo Galbraith) is the sort of thing one can believe only after very careful training. We would suspect that someone must be profiting from paying lower wages to women, but neoclassical analysis will not let us come to that conclusion. The neoclassical explanation of wage differences has had ramifications both for an analysis of women's condition and for political action. If wage differences are a result of differences in productivity, then a great deal of effort must be expended to discover what causes these differences in productivity. This gives rise to the whole supply-side analysis of female labour which explains female labour force participation rates and wages according to characteristics of their labour supply. The explanation for women's lower wages is that women's labour is not invested with as much human capital as is men's labour. So improving the quality of female labour and making women more attractive as workers will eliminate the problem. Practically, this leads to all sorts of policy initiatives of questionable efficacy,[18] but particularly important is the notion that it is the individual woman all by herself who can determine her employment fate.

Feminists tend to be skeptical of an analysis which explains total wage differences between men and women on differences in productivity. With the neoclassical model this leaves only one other conclusion: that discrimination is simply an irrational, anachronistic practice; a matter of prejudice, and not a structural feature of the system. This is comforting to some because it implies that, in fact, equality between men and women is perfectly compatible with the economic system: it is just that some people are not behaving rationally, so it is necessary to point out to them that discrimination is bad business; when everyone understands this, there will be no problem.

The conclusions of neoclassical analysis are perfectly correct *if* the assumptions on which the analysis originates are true. I maintain that the theory takes as "given" precisely those conditions which most affect female labour. For example, theory states that the total number of labourers is given. J.R. Hicks explains this by saying that any question of changes in the total numbers of workers available "is one which modern economists are content to treat as lying outside the theory of wages. It may be regarded as belonging to the theory of population."[19] The best neoclassical theory can do is to tell us that with a given labour force the number employed will vary directly in response to changes in the real wage (which is equal to the marginal product). If people are unemployed, then it

155

means they are unwilling to accept the wage they are worth. Of course the validity of the theory of the direct relationship between the level of employment and the real wage in all instances was disproven by Keynes some time ago, but it still remains a basic assumption of all neoclassical explanation of wage differences. For women, one of the most important issues is why the size of the labour force changes; this is an issue which economics feels is beyond its purview. If the size of the labour force varies and unemployment does exist, which we know it does, then the whole framework of assuming that employers are competing against each other for scarce workers simply is not true: the result is that the whole neoclassical analysis falls. While the most serious problem with neoclassical analysis is the assumption that the size of the labour force is given and that full employment will be the normal condition of the economy, there are other assumptions of the model which are specifically unrelated to the conditions of female employment. These are the assumptions of freedom of contract and mobility of labour. Women, for most of the history of industrialized countries, have been restricted from access to all but a handful of jobs, so freedom of contract cannot be seen as ever having applied to the condition of female labour. Female labour, particularly for married women, is also severely restricted in its mobility, so the notion that labour is free to move from place to place in search of the wage equal to its marginal productivity is ludicrous when applied to women in general.

That pure competition has been an approximation of any real condition is doubtful; but as an approximation of the female condition of the market, it is surely false. Women simply have not had access to the market under the same conditions as men, yet this fact is not recognized by economic analysis. For example, Alfred Marshall, that pioneer of neoclassical thought, was one of the most ardent defenders of a free unfettered market, yet he clearly did not understand that his view of women was a contradiction of this notion. Beatrice Webb describes a conversation with him in which he expressed his views.

> It opened with chaff about men and women: he holding that woman was a subordinate being, and that, if she ceased to be subordinate, there would be not object for a man to marry. That marriage was a sacrifice of masculine freedom, and would only be tolerated by male creatures so long as it meant the devotion, body and soul, of the female to the male. Hence the woman must not develop her faculties in a way unpleasant to the man; that strength, courage and independence were not attractive in women; that rivalry in men's pursuits was positively unpleasant.

> Hence masculine strength and masculine ability in women must be firmly trampled on and boycotted by men. *Contrast* was the essence of the matrimonial relation; feminine weakness contrasted with masculine strength; masculine egoism with feminine self-devotion. If you compete with us we shan't marry you, he summed up with a laugh.
>
> (Webb 1971:350)

There is a real danger when neoclassical ideas are used by economists who appear to be sympathetic to women and who seem to want to truly understand the economic condition of women. Ultimately, they merely reinforce the androcentric view of female behaviour. All of the economic theories of discrimination use the neoclassical methodology without questioning its assumptions.[20] In addition, the neoclassical theories about how individuals in the household allocate time between the market and the home, and between the sexes, is predicated on the market as being perfectly competitive.

The neoclassical model was developed with a blind eye toward women. Women's economic activity was not a part of the original conception of the model, and fitting them in the existing analysis now does not work. The methods are simply misleading when they try to explain why women earn less than men, why more woman are working for pay, why women do some jobs and men others, and why women do housework.

FOOTNOTES

1. Alfred Marshall, *Principles of Economics* (London: Macmillan, 1927), 8th edition, p. 1.
2. *Ibid*, p. 14.
3. *Ibid*, p. 27.
4. Lionel Robbins, *An Essay on the Nature & Significance of Economic Science* (London: Macmillan, 1935), 2nd edition, p. 24.
5. Paul Samuelson, *Economics* (Montréal: McGraw-Hill, 1976), 10th edition, p. 3.
6. Jacob Viner is a notable exception to this. For him, "economics is what economists do," quoted in Kenneth Boulding, *Economic Analysis* (New York: Harper & Brothers, 1948), p. 3.
7. Gary Becker, for example, states most explicitly that economic theory is well on its way "to providing a unified framework for *all* behaviour involving scarce resources, nonmarket as well as market, nonmonetary as well as monetary, small group as well as competitive." "A Theory of Marriage: Part I" in *Journal of Political Economy*, July/August 1973, p. 814.

8. Samuelson, *op. cit.*, p. 199; also Richard G. Lipsey and Peter O. Steiner, *Economics* (New York: Harper & Row, 1966), note 4, p. 151.
9. Samuelson, *op. cit.*, p. 199. This is a point of view which is echoed even by women who are sympathetic to the inclusion of housework in the GNP. Gail Cook and Mary Eberts say "since activity within the household does not change markedly over the period of business cycles, its inclusion has not been essential to appropriate policy decisions." Cook and Eberts, "Policies Affecting Work" in Cook 1976:146.
10. A.B. Atkinson, *The Economics of Inequality* (Oxford: Claredon, 1975), p. 164.; John Kenneth Galbraith, *Economics and the Public Purpose* (Boston: Houghton Mifflin, 1973), p. 33. In Canada, the estimates of the value of housework range from 34-40% of GNP, depending on the method of calculation used. See Hawrylyshyn 1971:33.
11. Judith Alexander, "Women and Unpaid Work: The Economic Consequences" in *Atlantis*, Spring 1979, pp. 204-5; Cook & Eberts *op. cit.*, p. 147; Hawrylyshyn 1971:10.
12. This is not a problem which is peculiar to capitalism. Market analysis is so central a part of economic thought that even socialist economic theory does not escape it. In socialist economic theory there is no *theoretical* basis for rational economic decision-making without a market mechanism, and so far the only solution to this is to treat non-market economies as if their activity were governed by a "shadow" market. See Oskar Lange and Fred Taylor, *On the Economic Theory of Socialism* (New York: McGraw-Hill, 1964); also J.G. Zielinki, *On the Theory of Socialist Planning* (Ibadan: Oxford University Press, 1968).
13. Karl Polanyi, *The Great Transformation* (Boston: Beacon Press, 1957), p. 158.
14. Sidney Pollard, *The Genesis of Modern Management* (London: Edward Arnold, 1965), Chapter 5; E.P. Thompson, *The Making of the English Working Class* (Harmondsworth: Penguin Books, 1963), especially Chapter 6; Harold Perkin, *The Origins of Modern English Society 1780-1880* (London: Routledge & Kegan Paul, 1969), especially Chapter VIII.
15. See Gary Becker, "A Theory of Marriage: Part I" and "A Theory of the Allocation of Time" in *The Economic Journal*, September 1965, pp. 512-516.
16. For those who have managed to avoid all economic courses, or who have suppressed the experience, the term means that workers will be paid a wage equal to the value of the increase in total production as a result of their labour.
17. Francine D. Blau and Carol L. Jusenius, "Economists' Approaches to Sex Segregation in the Labor Market: An Appraisal" in Blaxall & Reagan 1976:185. For an explanation of the economists' difficulty, see Kenneth Arrow, "Economic Dimensions of Occupational Segregation: Comment I" in Blaxall & Reagan 1976.

18. Isabel V. Sawhill, for example, feels that special programmes should be designed for inexperienced workers. What she has in mind are "special apprenticeships at below-market wage rates" so that employers would have an incentive to hire workers they normally discriminate against. "On the Way to Full Equality" in Cohn 1979:46.
19. J.R. Hicks, *The Theory of Wages* (London: Macmillan, 1963), 2nd edition, p. 2.
20. Specifically I am referring to the following approaches to discrimination: the crowding hypothesis explained by Barbara R. Bergman, "The Effect on White Incomes of Discrimination in Employment" in *Journal of Political Economy*, March/April 1971; the human capital approach found in the work of Gary Becker and Jacob Mincer; the statistical theory of sexism of Edmund Phelps; and the internal labour market approach of Blau and Jusenius.

159

CHAPTER 7

Feminism and the Writing and Teaching of History

Alison Prentice and Ruth Pierson

Alison Prentice is a member of the Department of History and Philosophy of Education of the Ontario Institute for Studies in Education (OISE) and has published widely in the history of women teachers and the history of women in education. She is a member of the Canadian Women's History Committee of the Canadian Historical Association and of the Canadian Research Institute for the Advancement of Women. She is general editor of the Documentary Series in Canadian Women's History of New Hogtown Press and co-author and compiler of the volume for the years 1713 to 1867. She has co-edited books on Canadian women's history and, with five others, is an author of the women's history text *Canadian Women: A History*, published by Harcourt, Brace, Jovanovich in 1988.

Ruth Roach Pierson teaches women's history and the history of feminism in the Departments of History and Philosophy of Education and the Department of Sociology in Education at OISE. She has worked with the St. John's Rape Crisis Centre in Newfoundland and has served as Newfoundland representative on the Board of the Canadian Research Institute for the Advancement of Women. She is the author of *They're Still Women After All: The Second World War and Canadian Womanhood*, editor of a collection of articles on women and peace, co-writer and compiler of a collection of documents in Canadian women's history from the 1920s to the 1960s, and is currently co-editing a collection of essays on the history and sociology of mothering.

This article has appeared in *Atlantis: A Women's Studies Journal*, VII, 2 (Spring 1982).

Any discussion of feminism and history must begin with definition. What does feminism mean in the context of the contemporary women's movement and for feminist historians? We will begin with a definition of feminism and a discussion of the problems that arise with the use of this term. Needless to say, we recognize that there are many feminisms and that our definition cannot encompass all of them. We hope, rather, to establish what it has meant and means to us as historians. From definition, we will move to an examination of how feminist perspectives affect the writing and teaching of history.

I

Feminism is at once a movement and an ideology, and insofar as some of its followers have engaged in extended philosophical analysis, it also gives rise to theory.[1] Intrinsic to feminism is women's sense of grievance, an awareness of oppression, an awareness that women suffer from systematic social injustice because of their sex. This awareness of injustice depends, in turn, on a belief in and commitment to the ideal of equality. In a world where there existed no concept of equality, we would argue, there could be no feminism.[2] As an ideology, feminism is premised on the belief that women suffer from oppressive inequalities in a number of specific and interrelated areas and puts forward the ideal of a world in which the sexes would be equal. As a movement, it strives to make the achievement of justice, perceived as the attainment of women's equality with men, a political and economic reality.

While we recognize that inequality is not necessarily synonymous with oppression, we believe that systematic inequalities lead to abuses of power and therefore to oppression. Feminists, by definition, are particularly concerned with systematic inequalities based on sex.

The critical task of feminism, therefore, is to examine the structures of women's oppression. When and where has systematic subordination of women existed? What have been the mechanisms of women's oppression? Feminists want to understand how social and political institutions and economic systems, and their accompanying ideologies, have worked to subordinate and oppress women. But because an exclusive preoccupation with these mechanisms could lead to a distorting and purely negative picture of women as victims, it is equally a

162

task of feminism to reclaim, elucidate and re-evaluate the positive aspects of women's experience in the present and in the past. In fact, one of the basic oppressions that women suffer is the silencing, marginalization and devaluing of their whole experience, both negative and positive. An injustice that feminists wish to redress, therefore, is inequality in terms of visibility. What feminists demand is the right to know and understand the experience of women and to have it analyzed, taken into account, recorded and valued, equally with the experience of men.

Women's invisibility is rooted in the language itself. Often embedded in conventional language are usages that marginalize the experience of women or leave them out of the picture altogether. The most frequently cited case in the English language is the use of male pronouns or prefixes whem both sexes are intended, as when "he," "his" and "him" are used as supposedly genderless terms which could refer to either sex, or when "mankind" is used to refer to the entire human race. Although some have argued that the issue is a trivial one, or that past usages enshrined in our literary inheritance should not be challenged, most feminists insist that the question is far from trivial and that, without in any way detracting from the heritage or beauty of our literature, the living language must both evidence and promote a new sensitivity to the equality of women.[3]

Another, more subtle form of devaluing women and their experience, which current language usage reflects, involves assigning from a pair of related terms the exalted one to an activity usually performed by men and the lowly one to a similar activity usually performed by women. A case in point is the use of the words "chef" and "cook." A more complicated case has resulted from the historical emergence of a distinction between "art," seen as the creative act of "men of genius," and "craft," which has been reserved for smaller, less significant and often collective and anonymous productions. Although nothing in the language logically assigns art to men or craft to women, the fact is that few women have made it into the domain of high art, as this has been defined historically, while many have devoted themselves to the creation of works to humanize the domestic environment. Contemporary feminists have sought to open our eyes to the excellence of design and execution in such objects as hooked rugs and patchwork quilts and thus to abolish the distinction between craft and art altogether.[4] This aim is part of the larger feminist insistence that all domestic matters, including childbirth, sexuality, child-rearing, family relations and domestic labour, should be accorded attention and importance.

Invisibility because of the traditional usages of language, or marginality because of a lower value implied in words attached to women's activities, feminists perceive as structurally based in the patriarchal organization of society. A major focus of feminist research, therefore, is the examination of the origins and perpetuation of patriarchy. In such analysis, the modern division between the public and the private spheres is seen as serving to reinforce patriarchy by circumscribing women within the domestic realm, or, insofar as they are drawn into the public domain, relegating them to menial and low status positions. For insistent as feminists are that the domestic sphere is important, we also recognize that we ignore at our peril the larger world outside the home — the realms, for instance, of the State and its military, of institutionalized religion and education, or of space science, computer technology, and the multinational corporation.

Crucial decisions affecting the lives of all human beings are made in the public realm. And insofar as decisions made there impinge on private and domestic life, it cannot be said that the two spheres are equal in power. It is this recognition of the interconnectedness of the public and private spheres, and the subordination of the latter, that drives feminists to demand that women move into the public world. And here the concern of feminism with personhood comes into play. For so long as women do not participate or represent themselves directly in the public realm, we are not persons in our own right. Systematic inequality of representation or participation in any field of endeavour is, in the present order of things, diminishing to women. In order to be at least as autonomous and self-determining as men, whether it be in respect to marriage laws, the price of bread, or the possibility of nuclear war, women need to be able to participate in public power equally with men.

Feminist goals are not without their attendant problems. It has been suggested, for example, that by seeking an autonomous selfhood for women, equal to men's, feminism promotes a further atomizing of society. The self-sufficient woman, living alone, unencumbered by intimate ties to or responsibilities for other human beings, however, is not necessarily a feminist goal. Feminists insist, rather, that women have a human need equal to men's for affection and emotional support but that for satisfaction of this need women should not have to make a greater sacrifice of autonomy than men. That it is difficult in a patriarchal society for any man and woman to achieve and maintain an intimate relationship based on equality no feminist would deny.[5]

Another major tension arises out of the co-existence of the demand for equality with the acceptance or celebration of difference. How does one reconcile the ideal of equality with the fact of difference? For the feminist, a more important question perhaps concerns how socially significant and ramifying are we going to allow the irreducible biological differences between men and women to be, and who is going to define them and say how limiting they should be. As George Eliot sardonically observed in her Prelude to *Middlemarch*:

> ... if there were one level of feminine incompetence as strict as the ability to count three and no more, the social lot of women might be treated with scientific certitude.

Woman's personhood is curtailed insofar as definitions of difference are established by a male-dominated "science" and are used to set limits to women's expression and development.[6]

A crucial example of the different but equal dilemma concerns birthing. If women demand control of the birth process, is this because they have a superior claim on the grounds of biological role or inherited or socialized traits not shared by men? Or should women demand, rather, an equal share in the government of childbirth—with fathers, doctors, hospital authorities and the like—on the grounds of an equal right to govern a process that affects all of us intimately? As feminists, we should like at the moment to live with this as an open question. Our fear is that the answer will be pre-empted by a male-oriented sociobiology with theories of genetic determination or mother-infant bonding, for example, or by male judges issuing injunctions against abortions in the name of fathers or foetuses.

We recognize that all too often women's choices have been circumscribed by rigid categories and dichotomies, positing irreconcilable conflict between two solutions, two interpretations, or even two supposedly opposite types of feminism that force women into one camp or another. It has been pointed out time and time again that "feminist theorists do not agree on whether their long-term goal is to maximize female identity or to reject gender as a primary category."[7] We argue that it is possible and desirable to pursue both goals at once, despite their apparent contradiction.[8] We think that having to make choices of that nature is analogous to the traditional choice forced on middle class women between career and marriage. We want to argue that women can be both different and equal, separatist and assimilationist; that women have a right in certain situations and moments in their lives to their own organizations and the creation of sisterly solidarity at the same time that we have a right to integration with men in the public domain of power. If this is seen as a demand to have our cake and eat it too, we agree that it is.

And we recognize that the achievement of these goals depends on a radical re-organization of the social order and the division of labour and responsibility between women and men. We, like the maternal feminists of the past, value many traits traditionally associated with the domestic sphere: nurturance, compassion, co-operation and interdependence, among others. Like them, also, we believe that a wider dissemination of these values would have a transforming effect on society.[9] We go beyond these past feminists, however, in recognizing the negative impact of the isolation of women within the domestic world, and, in particular, of women's monopoly of certain roles such as cleaning and child-rearing.[10] We insist that women should have a wider, indeed a genuinely equal share in public power; but we also insist that the domestic sphere should be opened up to genuinely equal participation by men.

Are we therefore advocating androgyny in all spheres of human activity? Not necessarily. For androgyny, too, can be seen as yet another strait-jacket.[11] If feminism is to be a liberating movement, it must not only reject simplistic dichotomies and the compartmentalization of women and men in separate spheres; it must go further and insist on the full complexity of human lives and possibilities. Freedom of choice for men and women, the recognition of complexity, as well as of a multitude of possible contexts and arrangements for the realization of human potential, should be among the goals of feminism. In this sense, liberty joins equality as a watchword of the movement. Women should have an equal right with men to be free.

II

How does feminism apply to the writing and teaching of history? Is there a legitimate connection between our feminism and historical study? We contend that there is. We are convinced that no student of the past entirely escapes from her or his rootedness in the present, and thus that a complete separation of one's scholarly enterprise from one's personal and social reality is impossible. We further argue that present-day concerns frequently suggest new lines of inquiry or new perspectives which serve to enliven historical discourse.[12] Hence a feminist consciousness is compatible with the historian's task, and, indeed, the present-day women's movement, by exposing bias against women and raising questions of concern to women, has had a stimulating impact on the discipline. For feminism challenges all existing knowledge in every discipline on the grounds of possible sexist bias.

Thus it is the feminist perspective that has exposed the preoccupation with men in, and the general absence of women from, most official, published and academically respectable history. Insofar as conventional history has been about politics, military affairs or macro-economics, and therefore about realms dominated by men, it is understandable that men have figured as the chief or sometimes the only actors on the historical stage. Conventional history has been criticized because it left out all kinds of groups of people excluded from power, not just women. But when the new social history, to which that critique gave rise, does not take the experience of women into account, the failure to do so seems unwarranted. The eminent socialist historian Eric Hobsbawm failed to include women in his 1971 theoretical plea for a social history so all-encompassing that it would become a history of all society.[13] In 1978, he admitted the justness of the criticism "that male historians in the past, including Marxists, have grossly neglected the female half of the human race," and included himself among the culprits. But then, as the feminist historians among the editors of *History Workshop* have pointed out, Hobsbawm proceeded to make sweeping generalizations about women's aims and perceptions, betraying a cavalier disregard for the "bewildering range of experience in working, political and domestic life for nineteenth century British women" revealed in recent feminist scholarship.[14] Another example of bias is Philippe Ariès' path-breaking study of the history of childhood, which deals almost exclusively with male children. A much more recent book, *Youth in History* by John Gillis, does not pretend to deal with other than male adolescents, leaving the history of adolescent girls to some other historian.[15] If this state of affairs were allowed to persist, women would continue to have at best an incomplete history.

The feminist perspective is also responsible for our growing understanding of the fact that women, like men, need their history. The sense of self depends on having a sense of one's past, and to the extent that modern women have been denied, in the historical canon, all but the faintest glimpses of their own history, they are like victims of amnesia. The fact is that the experience of women and men in the past has not been exactly the same. Woman cannot be subsumed under the general category of "Everyman." The nature and implications of the differences between the histories of the sexes have got to be discovered and examined if women are to repossess their past.

The first task of the feminist historian, then, is the simple retrieval of women from obscurity. This task is necessarily compensatory, at this stage of the undertaking, because there is so much lost ground to be made up. A certain kind of feminist consciousness has focused on the female heroines of the past, "great women" in the public sphere, comparable to the "great men" of history. In the same vein, feminist historians are re-examining historical movements, revolutions, wars, intellectual and artistic endeavour — indeed nearly every facet of public life in the past — to ferret out the ways in which women have participated but which traditional histories have overlooked. Both of these enterprises have an important morale-building value in that they reveal to women precedents for their participation in the public realm. To the extent that women's roles have been hidden in traditional historical writing, women are deprived of inspirational models, and indeed of any examples of the public exercise of female energy and competence in the past.

Writing women into history is not a problem-free enterprise, and certainly not all women's history has been as comprehensive or as sophisticated as we would want it to be. Many studies of "women worthies," for example, have verged on the hagiographic.[16] Equally, we must recognize the flawed nature of analyses which assign importance to women only insofar as they have contributed to or supplemented the work or achievements of men. Concentration solely on those women who have "achieved" in terms of patriarchal norms, it has been pointed out, will produce at best a truncated history.[17] The best women's history will try to understand the whole of women's experience in the past and will be wary of the temptation to plug women into historical chronologies or outlines that were established with other priorities in mind. The "Renaissance," for example, is not a category which sheds much light on the lives of many women in early modern Europe. Nor does relegating the turn-of-the-century women's movement to a small part of a supposedly wider and more significant phenomenon of "social reform" capture the full implications of pre-World War I feminist aspirations.

Feminist historical analysis necessarily helps to establish new schemes of periodization considered within the purview of scholarly research. Among these are women's domestic work and the domestic arts, childbirth and child-rearing female networks, and female sexuality, as well as women's health and reproductive lives, including menstruation and menopause. Many of these subjects are also being explored by historical demographers, but all too often the female experience is muted or lost altogether in the tendency to focus on macro-levels of historical change, such as the impact of fluctuations in fertility on the overall growth of population. Similarly, historians interested in family structures who ignore power relations between male and female members omit a dimension of crucial importance.[18]

But getting at the actual experience of women in the past is not an easy task. Much valuable work has been done in examining prescriptive literature directed to women. Equally valuable examinations exist of medical, legal, educational, religious and other texts which reflect norms and prevailing attitudes towards women and their roles in various periods.[19] Insofar as women followed or participated in public debate over the nature and role of their sex, it was an important part of their emotional and intellectual lives. But it must always be recognized that women's actual behaviour did not necessarily coincide with such projected images and pronouncements.[20] These, therefore, must be studied with caution, for they raise many questions, not the least of which is the extent to which ethnicity, literacy, or economic or social class might have affected the exposure to and internalization of what was prescribed.

Historians of women thus recognize the necessity to go beyond the prescription of and debate over roles wherever possible, in order to examine women's actual behaviour and their lives through whatever sources are available. New approaches to the problem of sources have been discovered: official statistics and their categories have been challenged, different questions have been put to old sources, and new sources have been found. Without unusual detective work resulting in interviews with the descendents of Lancashire suffragists, for example, much about the contribution of these working class women to the British suffrage movement could not have been known.[21] Similarly, the provision of *salles d'asile* for children of working mothers in 19th century Montréal went unnoticed until historians began to examine lives of working class women and the archives of female religious orders.[22] A commitment to getting at the actual experience of women underlies the collection and publication of such primary sources as the letters and diaries of ordinary women, their recipe books, scrapbooks and photograph albums, and reminiscences recorded in writing or on tape.[23]

But women's private lives and women's activities in the private domain, as we have suggested, do not proceed in radical isolation from the society at large. Changes in ways in which the public impinges on the private world and in the functional relationship of the one to the other also require historical investigation. For instance, women's lives in the 20th century will remain partially obscured if studied outside the framework of the emerging welfare state. One new study has examined the meaning of mothers' allowances for Canadian women and a number of others have demonstrated how the State's provision and withdrawal of child-care facilities have manipulated female participation in the paid labour force.[24] The socialist feminists' concern with analyzing the nature of unpaid labour performed by women in the home and its relationship to the capitalist mode of production has stimulated historical research and analysis on the interaction between changes in a society's overall economic system and changes in women's familial and domestic responsibilities.[25]

Indeed a radical split between the public and private spheres has not been a universal phenomenon, but rather one specific to certain classes in certain places and periods. It is also an obvious but important point that men's and women's lives are intertwined and affect each other in all areas. "Men and women interact as part of the same world."[26] Feminist historians have shown that in many milieus the sexes have worked side-by-side or, even when there has been a strict sexual division of labour, men's and women's economic activities have been interdependent. Under industrialized capitalism, the labour performed by women in the home preparing meals and cleaning clothes has been shown to perpetuate and replenish the publicly employed labour force. The development of the professions in which men have been dominant are increasingly seen to have depended on the decline of women's participation in those professions, or on their entry as low status workers or paraprofessionals in related fields. Finally, it has become clear that the education provided for boys in any given society or class must be compared with that provided for girls, and vice versa, if either are to be fully understood.[27] Indeed a full understanding of what has happened historically to males, in any field, at any time, simply cannot be gained without equal consideration of the impact of those developments on the females in that society—the reverse, of course, being also true.

III

We have concentrated above on the problems of defining feminism and on the relationship between feminism—or more correctly, perhaps, a variety of feminisms—and the writing of history. Feminists, historians, and indeed feminist historians, are recognized in this account as being inevitably the products of their time and place, and, most importantly for the purposes of this paper, of their own personal and social lives as women and men. Feminist perspectives, we have argued, have much to offer to historians, both male and female. We have outlined a number of serious methodological problems that arise in the doing of feminist history and we recognize that, for male historians, the imaginative leap required by a feminist perspective is a large one. Nevertheless, we would submit that the leap can be made and that, in fact, it has been. No less than the male novelist whose insight enables him to create believable female characters, the open-minded and imaginative male historian should be able to overcome the biases of his discipline and his socialization. But the very structures within which knowledge is created and disseminated still militate against a feminist approach to history. No analysis of the relationships between feminism and the historical discipline can avoid, therefore, at least some brief comments on the structures within which historical research, teaching and learning take place.

The most obvious problem is the sex structure of the historical profession, which, as is well known, is male-dominated at all levels of the educational system. Men are in the majority in high school, college and university history departments, and in archival and other research-related positions. Male historians tend to monopolize the full professorships and department headships, while the women are clustered in the bottom ranks. With the exception of women's history courses — and these are still rare and taught mainly by women on the fringes of academia — the history curriculum at all levels is still heavily biased towards the traditional. Potential feminist historians are therefore deprived of opportunity in numerous ways; as a result, women are denied their history.

Feminists question many aspects of traditional education, although they are not the only critics to do so, and opinions among them obviously vary according to their particular perspectives. Are hierarchical teaching structures with men dominant at the top conducive to learning, for either sex, but particularly for women? Should the teaching of history be as print-oriented as it currently is, or is it time that the techniques of oral history, material history, or even genealogy, be more widely adopted by learners as well as researchers in history? How effective is the lecture, in which an expert (usually male) defines what is to be learned and how? Does the competitive seminar or the competitive grading system lead to the best development of scholarship in history? Why are students kept from collaborating, or penalized if they do, when more and more established academics are finding collaboration productive? Finally, how are feminist students to find mentors in scholarly environments that are only marginally welcoming to women's history or feminist scholarship?

From the schools, colleges and universities, we turn to the archives, funding agencies and publishers. In these areas, as in the most progressive history departments, the light is beginning to dawn. But there remain the projects not funded, the repositories without an archivist responsible for women's history and the studies that have not been published — not to mention the poverty and isolation of feminist presses and of some of the journals that do publish women's history. But even in the relatively enlightened environment of the academic society, feminist scholars struggle to make an impact. Their numbers are small and their professional lives are often stretched to the limit as they strive, without sufficient institutional support, to meet the needs of their students, their own scholarship, and the demands that arise out of the growing interest in the field of women's history.

All of this is not to deny the remarkable progress that has been made. We do have feminist publications and journals that are receptive to feminist scholarship; articles and books in women's history increasingly see the light of day; archivists are becoming interested, as are learned societies and funding agencies. Feminist historians feel pressed on every side, nevertheless, not least by the fact so many students of history continue to question the very validity of their enterprise. Under these circumstances, is a feminist history viable and can it flourish? If not, we believe that both sexes are the losers. If yes, we would submit that it has an important contribution to make to the liberation of both men and women.

FOOTNOTES

1. We do not use the term "ideology" perjoratively nor in the narrow sense of a system of values and beliefs imposed by a ruling class. Karl Mannheim in *Ideology and Utopia* (New York: A Harvest/ HBJ Book, 1936) has made the distinction between ideology as a complex of ideas serving to maintain an existing order and Utopia as a complex of ideas calling for transformation of an existing order. If we followed this distinction, we would find ourselves among those of Utopian bent. But partly because the term "Utopia" implies a value judgment of unrealizable from the point of view of the upholder of the *status quo*, we choose to employ the term "ideology" more generally to include sets of ideas and values which call into question and seek to change a prevailing social system as well as those which work to preserve an existing order. In accepting this view of ideology, we take issue with many aspects of Lewis Feuer's definition, especially the notion that all ideologies are closed systems that are inimical to scholarly inquiry. Lewis S. Feuer, *Ideology and the Ideologists* (Oxford: Basil Blackwell, 1975).
2. Awareness of this point derives from conversations with the anthropologist Jean Briggs in which she has argued persuasively that in Inuit society one thinks in terms not of equality between the sexes, but rather of complementarity and interdependence.
3. On the question of bias in language, see Kramer (1978), and Robin Lakoff, who has written of "The personal identity of women" as "linguistically submerged" in *Language in Society*, 2, April 1973.
4. The idea for this discussion of craft and art came from conversations with Giovanna Peel and her unpublished essay "Woman's Art." Contemporary women artists' efforts to bridge the gap between art and craft may be seen in the work of Joyce Wieland in the quilt form and in Judy Chicago's *The Dinner Party*, which combines, among other skills, the techniques of pottery and embroidery.

5. A woman's high intelligence, ambition, and dedication to larger social goals do not necessarily make her immune to affective need any more than they increase her chances of overcoming the obstacles to filling that need in an egalitarian relationship. See, for example, *Comrade and Lover: Rosa Luxemburg's Letters to Leo Jogiches* (Ettinger 1979).

6. The defects and bias of much so-called scientific research related to gender are blatantly obvious in examples drawn from the past. See, for example, Elaine and English Showalter, "Victorian Women and Menstruation" in Vicinus (1972, pp. 38-44). For discussion of more recent studies which parade as "scientific" while serving to buttress a challenged *status quo*, see Wini Breines, Margaret Cerullo and Judith Stacey, "Social Biology, Family Studies and Antifeminist Backlash" in *Feminist Studies*, 4, 1, February 1978, pp. 43-67; and Marian Lowe, "Sociobiology and Sex Differences" in *Signs: Journal of Women in Culture and Society*, 4, 1. Autumn 1978, pp. 118-125. See also Margaret Benston's Chapter 2 in this volume.

7. Ann Barr Snitow, "The Front Line: Notes on Sex in Novels by Women, 1969-1979" in *Signs: Journal of Women in Culture and Society*, 5, 4, Summer 1980, p. 718.

8. This is an instance of our disagreement with Lewis Feuer who, in *Ideology and the Ideologists, op. cit.*, p. 134, argues that ideology by definition forces choice. "To the ideologist, it is always an either-or, with only two alternatives, two extreme choices." On the possibility, and, indeed, necessity of a pluralist feminism, see Gerda Lerner's contribution to "Politics and Culture in Women's History: A Symposium" in *Feminist Studies*, 6, 1, Spring 1980, pp. 48-54. The whole symposium illustrates the variety of points of view among contemporary feminist historians. On the value of different points of view among feminist literary critics, see Annette Kolodny, "Dancing Through the Minefield: Some Observations on the Theory, Practice, and Politics of a Feminist Literary Criticism" in the same issue of *Feminist Studies*, pp. 1-25. "The fact of differences among us proves only that, despite our shared commitments, we have nonetheless refused to shy away from complexity, preferring rather to openly disagree than to give up either intellectual honesty or hard-won insights", p. 20.

9. This was certainly the view of Nellie McClung, one of Canada's leading suffragists. See Strong-Boag 1972.

10. See Dinnerstein 1976 and Chodorow 1978.

11. "A Critique of the Concept of Androgyny" in Eichler 1980, Chapter 3, "The Double Standard Internalised: The Inadequacy of the Sex Identity Approach."

12. This point has been made admirably by M.I. Finley in "Slavery and the Historians" in *Social History/Histoire sociale*, 12, 24, November 1979, pp. 247-261.

13. E.J. Hobsbawm, "From Social History to the History of Society" in Felix Gilbert & Stephen R. Graubard (eds.), *Historical Studies*

Today (New York: Norton, 1971), pp. 1-26.

14. Eric Hobsbawm, "Man and Woman in Socialist Iconography" in *History Workshop: A Journal of Socialist Historians*, 6, Autumn 1978, p. 121; Sally Alexander, Anna Davin & Eve Hostettler, "Labouring Women: A Reply to Eric Hobsbawm" in *History Workshop*, 8, Autumn 1979, pp. 174-182.

15. Philippe Ariès, *Centuries of Childhood: A Social History of Family Life*, translated by Robert Baldick (New York: Vintage Books, 1962); John Gillis, *Youth in History: Tradition and Change in European Age Relations* (New York: Academic Press, 1974).

16. The expression "women worthies" was coined by Natalie Zemon Davis, who was one of the first critics of this approach to the history of women. See her " 'Women's History' in Transition: The European Case" in *Feminist Studies*, 3, ¾, Spring/Summer 1976, p. 83.

17. See Gerda Lerner 1979.

18. Miranda Chaytor, "Household and Kinship: Ryton in the Late 16th and Early 17th Centuries" in *History Workshop*, 10, Autumn 1980, especially pp. 26-30.

19. Barbara Welter, "The Cult of True Womanhood: 1820-1860" in *American Quarterly*, 18, 2, Part 1, Summer 1966, pp. 151-174, was one of the earliest examinations of 19th century American prescriptive literature. In a critique of Welter's approach, Ronald Hogeland pointed out that the early and mid-19th century literature presented not just one, but at least four possible models of behaviour to women although some were more obviously accepted and acceptable than others. Hogeland, " 'The Female Appendage': Feminine Lifestyles in America, 1820-1860 " in *Civil War History*, 17, 1971, pp. 101-114. Valuable studies of the literature on women in Canada and Britain respectively are Wendy Mitchinson, "Historical Attitudes Toward Women and Childbirth" in *Atlantis*, 4, 2, Part 2, Spring 1979, pp. 13-34, and Donna Andrew, "Female Vice and the National Welfare: Some Eighteenth Century Opinions About the Role of Women." Paper presented at the Annual Meeting of the CHA, Fredericton, N.B., June 1977.

20. See, for example, Carl Degler, "What Ought To Be and What Was: Women's Sexuality in the Nineteenth Century" in *American Historical Review*, 79, December 1974, pp. 1467-1490.

21. Jill Liddington, "Working Class Women in the North West II" in *Oral History*, 5, 2, and "Rediscovering Suffrage History" in *History Workshop*, 4, Autumn 1977, pp. 192-202. Liddington & Norris 1978 call attention to the way in which the barriers between the compartments of history — and life — break down in women's history. "Our decision to concentrate on local rather than national history, and to use the research methods that we did has meant questioning the historians' habit of compart-

mentalizing everything neatly into 'suffrage history,' 'labour history,' 'political history' and 'social history.' The lives of the radical suffragists overlapped into all these categories. Their attitudes to winning the vote for women, like their commitment to the labour movement, was dovetailed into their experience of growing up in working class families. They emerge not only as a group but also as women who were not deterred by the perennial problems of combining political activity with their family commitments" (Liddington & Norris 1978:18-19).

22. D. Suzanne Cross, "The Neglected Majority: The Changing Role of Women in 19th Century Montréal" in Trofimenkoff & Prentice 1977:74-77; Micheline Dumont-Johnson, "Des garderies au XIXe siècle: les salles d'asile des Sœurs Grises à Montréal" in *Revue d'histoire de l'amérique française*, 34, 1, June 1980, pp. 27-55.

23. For Canadian examples, see Rasmussen 1976; Knight 1974; Light & Prentice 1980.

24. Veronica Strong-Boag, "Wages for Housework: Mothers' Allowances and the Beginnings of Social Security in Canada" in *Journal of Canadian Studies*, 14, 1, Spring 1979, pp. 24-34; Ruth Pierson, "Women's Emancipation and the Recruitment of Women into the Canadian Labour Force in World War II" in Trofimenkoff & Prentice 1977:125-145, and "'Home Aide': A Solution to Women's Unemployment After World War II" in *Atlantis*, 2, 2, Part 2, Spring 1977, pp. 85-97; and Patricia Vandebelt Schulz, "Day Care in Canada: 1850-1962" in Ross 1978:137-158.

25. Tilly and Scott 1978 is perhaps the most comprehensive attempt to date to relate the domestic lives and work of women to the larger social and economic trends. See also Julie A. Matthaei 1982.

26. Alexander, Davin & Hostettler, "Labouring Women," *op. cit.*, p. 174.

27. Alison Prentice, "Patriarch or Public Servant? Teachers and Professionalism in Mid-Nineteenth Century Ontario," paper presented to the Workshop on Professionalization in Modern Societies, University of Western Ontario, March 1981, and "Towards a Feminist History of Women and Education" in David Jones and Neil McDonald (eds.), *Proceedings of the First Conference of the Canadian History of Education Society* (University of Manitoba Press, forthcoming); Joan Kelly, "Did Women Have a Renaissance?" in *Women History and Theory: The Essays of Joan Kelly* (1984).

CHAPTER 8

To Grow a Daughter: Cultural Liberation and the Dynamics of Oppression in Jamaica

Carole Yawney

Carole Yawney teaches anthropology in the Dept. of Sociology and Anthropology at Atkinson College, York University (Toronto), a special facility for mature and part-time students. She did her graduate research and wrote her doctorate on the Rastafarian movement in Jamaica. She has acted as an expert witness on numerous occasions for Rastafarian defendants in Canadian courts and has published on the movement in both academic and journalistic contexts. For the past few years she has been actively involved in field-work and teaching in the area of health care and alternative approaches to healing. She combines this interest with a healthy life on a small farm in rural Ontario where she watches stars, grows herbs and designs banners for posterity.

This paper deals with the ways in which the patriarchal imperative has distorted a contemporary movement of liberation. It is about how I myself came to realize the extent to which such a fundamental contradiction existed in the particular movement that I researched, the Rastafarians of Jamaica.[1] It is motivated by a concern for the future of this movement, which offers so much of a creative and cultural nature to inspire black people living in the West. Sometimes these patriarchal assumptions are so well hidden in the otherwise egalitarian ideology of such movements that it requires a special kind of diligence to recognize their ramifications. In my own case, this was not so. The general exclusion of women from the central ritual activity of the Rastafarian movement — reasoning over a glowing herbs pipe — was clear. For a long time, I simply chose to ignore its import. After all, the academic problem that I had defined for myself — the relationship between visionary experience and movement ideology and behaviour — was far more significant to me than wondering why women were usually so obviously absent on these occasions. In the context of Rastafarian culture as I came to understand it, this seemed "natural."

The patriarchal bias of such movements generally runs counter to their stated goals. If male dominance is institutionalized in these social movements, they cannot possibly represent real alternative social forms, because they share, in common with the social systems to which they are opposed, a fundamental oppression of women. While there is an extensive anthropological literature on social movements, there is no serious examination of the extent to which patriarchy is integral to them. The example with which I am familiar is just one case in which all of its major researchers assume a definition of its participants as essentially male. And built into the definition of the nature of the Rastafarian struggle is the subordination of women. What is generally accepted as Rastafarian culture is actually the beliefs and behaviours of Rastafarian brethren, to which many sisters subscribe. The major historical figures of the movement and its contemporary leaders — called "Elders" — are all brethren. We need to ask ourselves how the collective experience of years of field-work by these anthropologists results only in the reflection of a partial reality. If we are to incorporate women's experience into what these movements are all about, then we will have to change our understanding of them.

The Rastafarian movement is not being singled out for special criticism. The problematic female-male dynamics in

Rastafarian culture are evident in all societies. In Rasta, however, we find a highly polarized version of them. While many liberation movements have an ideology of egalitarianism but in fact practise sexual hierarchy, the Rastafarian movement, in addition to its espousal of universal human values, actually has developed an explicit ideology about the subordination of women. This is based primarily upon the Bible. Its basic self-definition, then, as a movement of liberation, is distorted. Rastafarianism is also of special interest because of the international reputation it has gained as a movement of the oppressed through the vehicle of reggae music. But, like different versions of "youth culture" in our own society, and although many women identify with it, Rastafarianism is dominated by men. Its limitations in regard to women could be particularly instructive for our understanding of other kinds of progressive social movements. Barbara Burris, for example, has discussed the subordination of women in groups as various as the American Left and the Algerian Liberation Movement (Burris 1973). Michele Wallace has written at length about the problems which women experience in the American black movement (Wallace 1979).

In the following section I will describe the kinds of situations that I encountered as a woman trying to do anthropology in West Kingston, Jamaica. Then I will go on to discuss female-male relationships as they have developed in Jamaican society. Finally, I will deal with the role of women in the Rastafarian movement. Having first-hand experience of such a movement, and realizing the extent to which accounts of it are biased or neglectful on the subject of women, one can only wonder about the competence of countless other texts on social movements in this regard. But more importantly, one questions why the patriarchal basis of such movements has rarely been examined.

Field-work in Jamaica

Jamaica is entirely an artifact of imperialism. Its indigenous inhabitants were killed off in the early days of colonization to be replaced by white colonizers and black slaves. These slaves were intended to provide the labour force for a highly specialized mode of production, the plantation. A key feature of the plantation economy is its need for abundant labour. Following Emancipation in 1834, the colonizers turned to India and other Asiatic countries for non-white indentured labour. As a result, in Jamaica and in other West Indian nations today, the population consists of predominantly non-white groups, visibly stratified along class-colour lines. This, in turn, has bred hostility among the various segments.

The legacy of all this has been continuing under-development, increasing poverty and unemployment, and greater dependency upon foreign sources of capital and goods. Following the granting of independence from Britain in 1962, Jamaica exhibited a typically neo-colonial pattern of development. It is against this background that we have to understand the genesis and growth of the Rastafarian movement.

The Rastafarian movement started in the 1930's during a decade of widespread political and economic unrest. It was clearly based on the philosophy of Marcus Garvey and pan-Africanists who spoke to the unity of all people of African descent, the autonomy of Africa, and the return of diasporic Africans to the Continent. The Italian adventure in Ethiopia in the mid-1930's gave further impetus to the movement and focused attention on Emperor Haile Selassie who was to become its dominant spiritual symbol. We shall see below that monarchial symbolism informs ideal notions about female-male roles within the movement.

Generally, we can say that Rastafarian ideology is characterized by four major themes: Ethiopianism, a philo-sophical tradition with roots in Africa in the last century, which for some Rastafarians means demands for repatriation; a Biblical fundamentalism, including both the Old and the New Testament; a determined anti-colonialism; and an appeal to such universal values as love, truth, justice, etc... It is impossible to know how many Rastafarians live in Jamaica today, but various estimates put their numbers in the tens, and even hundreds of thousands. There is also a substantial following in large North American and European cities such as London, New York, and Toronto, not to mention reported accounts of the movement's success in Africa. We are obviously dealing, then, with a movement of some social significance. Moreover, these estimates are generally based upon the movement's most visible members, the brethren.

In the context of Jamaican society, the Rastafarian movement is an innovative development, radically different from other kinds of progressive social movements there. In a society visibly stratified by the co-factors of class and race, the Rastafarian insistence on the solidarity of people of African descent undermines the hegemony of the ruling class. Rastafarians have developed distinct cultural forms which fly in the face of middle class conventions. Their refusal to participate in the two-party system and to vote places them in a vulnerable situation politically. Their support of African liberation movements is clear and unequivocal. Elsewhere I have described extensively the creative adaptations which Rastafarians have made in their poverty-level lifestyle.[2] For all these reasons, then, we are dealing with a movement which is struggling to define its reality in terms which are more compatible with human freedom and dignity. Thus it becomes especially problematic if Rastafarian women are not able to share equally in defining these developments.

Sociologically, the movement is organized in a very decentralized and heterogeneous kind of way. Some groups within the movement follow hierarchical principles in their social relationships, while other groups may be only loosely associated as social networks. The movement in general, though, has no one leader or dominant faction. This is partly related to the value that the movement places upon the individual's responsibility for defining his own role within it, and for developing his own ideological orientation based upon general precepts. This individualism is at once the strength and the weakness of a social movement which purports to be collectively oriented in its goals, but which in practice has a great deal of difficulty overcoming factionalism.

Because of its anti-establishment and possibly subversive image, the Rastafarian movement traditionally has been portrayed as a kind of threat to law and order. Rastafarians have been cast variously as madmen, terrorists, anarchists, drop-outs, and criminals. Their central ritual activity — the smoking of cannabis, or "herbs", in the local argot — is illegal in Jamaica. And most of their adopted lifestyles are oriented towards undermining the dominant cultural values of Jamaican society. None of this has helped to foster a sympathetic understanding of the movement. However, since the success that many Rastafarian reggae performers have had there has developed a more accepting attitude on the part of the Jamaican public. This has naturally introduced the possibility of co-optation as a means of taming the movement.

When I began my own research in 1970, the Rastafarian movement was not extensively known outside Jamaica. There were very few scholarly studies available about it, and the particular problem that I wanted to study — herbs smoking and reasoning, and the visionary experience in relation to movement ideology — was generally treated as another

181

sensational aspect of the Rastaman's eccentric lifestyle, not warranting much serious investigation. My own interests had been shaped by the period of the late 1960's—the anti-war movement, the New Left, and alternative sub-cultures. I visited Cuba in the summer of 1968, and I spent the summer of 1969 in Berkeley. For a self-confessed seeker, the Rastafarian movement seemed to offer the ideal combination of radical politics and radical culture.

Doing participant-observation field-work in West Kingston in the early 1970's posed several problems for the anthropologist. But when that person is a single young white woman trying to do independent research, she is exposed to rather more occupational hazards than her male counterpart. Elsewhere I have outlined in detail the kinds of research strategies that I adopted.[3] Here I want to confine my comments to the problems of being a woman in that situation. Since I was not willing to compromise my original interests when faced with the reality of life in the West Kingston ghetto, I had to make certain choices which naturally affected the course that my research would take. If I wanted to study the relationship between the visionary experience and movement ideology, I simply had to be present when herbs were smoked and to partake of this communion with the brethren. Frequently this meant staying up all night, reasoning until dawn, and then carrying on with the day. It meant accompanying the brethren on their travels, attending their meetings, and joining their celebrations. It meant negotiating safely through the West Kingston maze. At that point in time, Rastafarians had not been much exposed to scholarly investigation, nor had the Jamaican establishment adjusted to the interest of the international academic community in a home-grown phenomenon. Frequently, therefore, I found myself walking the narrow line of suspicion between insiders and outsiders.

I was the recipient of abundant fatherly advice from university professors, police administrators, and government ministers about how best to proceed under the circumstances. There was a whole coterie of sugar-daddies standing by if I should ever need them. But in order to get on with my work I decided to substitute one form of friendly paternalism for another. My university training to that point had socialized me to appreciate male authority figures. The alternative sub-culture had legitimized patriarchal gurus. I had avidly read about the adventures of Carlos Casteneda with his teacher, Don Juan. It seemed "natural" once again to learn in the way I

182

knew best. I gradually became associated with a network of dreadlocks brethren (the radical orthodox members of the movement who wear their hair in long, unruly locks) who had been on the scene a long time and whose activities were central to the on-going definition of the movement as it was evolving during that period.

In my opinion, there was far more to be gained by settling down and adopting one yard as a base than in wandering about and engaging people in chance encounters. This latter method was employed quite successfully by a young Jesuit priest who was studying the movement at the same time; but that kind of approach was simply too risky for a woman, and besides, the kind of data I wanted was predicated on the establishment of long-term relationships. Given the constant tension of life in an urban ghetto and its very real perils, I was only too relieved to seek refuge in the Rastafarian community where people were trying to apply the principles of peace and non-violence in everyday life. Carrying guns, for example, a common practice among some Jamaican youth, was never tolerated in the yards with which I was associated. The brethren had something very genuine to teach me about surviving with dignity and joy in an environment of widespread poverty and dehumanization. It was not so difficult to understand the appeal of the Rastafarian way of life for women under such circumstances. The establishment of righteous nuclear households based upon patriarchal principles and a clearly defined sexual division of labour offered a certain degree of security and stability in an otherwise tumultuous setting. When one recognizes the kind of oppressive responsibilities inherent in matrifocal family arrangements, it becomes clear that there are no other acceptable options for women in Jamaican society as it is presently constructed.

I can only surmise what motivated this group of brethren to adopt me more or less as an apprentice in their midst. Clearly, their openness, flexibility, and tolerance made it possible for me to begin my field-work. Certainly I had an explicit understanding with them that I was a student and somewhat of a fellow-traveller. Again, it seemed "natural" for me to be spending most of my time with brethren. They went out of their way to instruct me and make me feel comfortable. Once I had established that I was serious, and that I would probably be with them well over a year, we had a more solid relationship. They were committed to making connections with outsiders in order to tell the world the truth about Rasta.

But they were also genuinely interested in my spritual welfare as a person, since they realized that I, too, had made some sacrifices in order to be there among them. Sometimes they were exposed to threat and abuse from less tolerant brethren who charged them with collaborating with a white person. Because this particular network of brethren was of a more orthodox orientation within the movement, they believed that the freedom of black people lay partly in the ability of black men and black women to re-establish sexual and familial relationships exclusively with each other. As a result, they never made sexual demands upon me. On the other hand, being defined as unavailable sexually was surely an enabling factor in the kind of apprentice role that I adopted. They would even intervene on my behalf if a stranger was being abusive. Thus they offered me both protection and guidance, as there were many circumstances which they helped me to navigate successfully. It was through this network that I came to know the rest of the movement. Although my relationship with other brethren was mediated by my association with this particular group, I was nevertheless able to get about quite extensively. Thus the data upon which this paper is based are drawn from a broad range of experiences within the movement, and cover a span of well over 10 years. It does not reflect the orientation of any one group within the movement.

The main focus of my research, however, was the one area in which I experienced my greatest conflicts. Conforming to the extent that I could to the modest Rastafarian dress code for women—wearing my hair braided and my head tied in a kerchief—I was there with the brethren as much as possible, smoking and reasoning, always present in situations where sisters were mostly absent. Obviously the brethren with whom I made my primary contact were the most progressive in this regard, for they did accept myself and a few other sisters into their ritual circle. There was definitely a handful of sisters, personally strong and independently-minded, who also sought to draw the chalice with the brethren. They were tolerated if they accepted the male definition of the situation, but they rarely engaged in reasoning with them in the fullest sense. Reasoning is a stylized form of dialogue in which movement ideology is formulated and tested. A good session may demand several hours of concentration before an issue is resolved. Some sisters were simply too busy with domestic duties to spare that kind of time, while others even expressed a total lack of interest in this activity, something I could not understand

184

at that time. Now, of course, we know that women respond very differently to the use of cannabis (and to alcohol, for that matter) and thus exhibit different patterns of smoking than men. This kind of research would have profound implications for a social movement like Rastafarianism where the culturally acceptable form of behaviour is based on conforming to male norms. If women are ever to be included in the Rastafarian culture as full participants, it would require a restructuring of its central activities to incorporate their special experience.

In retrospect, it is apparent that the kind of research subject in which I was interested — ritual behaviour and the formulation of ideology in a social movement — was the result of a lengthy educational process and learning to recognize what was a significant problem for study. Of course I had to focus on male behaviour, because it is men who largely define ritual propriety and who coin appropriate ideology. It is only by re-assigning research priorities that women's experiences and how they look at the world will become academically relevant in the proper sense. It may mean, for example, that we will have to reformulate our theoretical understanding of colonialism if we take seriously women's experience of it. Turning to the subject of social movements, we will have to restructure the analytical frameworks that we use in order to expose certain fundamental assumptions in their ideology that many of us take for granted. Now we shall move on to a discussion of female-male roles in Jamaican society and within the Rastafarian movement in order to explore how firmly this patriarchal orientation is embedded there.

Patterns of Sexuality and Reproduction in Jamaica

The title of the classic work on Jamaican sex roles and family patterns describes a common social experience: *My Mother Who Fathered Me* (Clarke 1966). In a passage inspired by George Lamming's book, *In the Castle of My Skin*, Clarke comments that:

> It has, however, to be said that examples of paternal devotion, and kindness were far outweighed by the cases where he was either no more than the man "who had only fathered the idea of me" or someone remembered for neglect or harsh treatment.
>
> (Clarke 1966:161)

Lower class family life in the British West Indies in general is characterized by various styles of matrifocality. This is taken simply to mean situations wherein women ultimately assume responsibility for the raising of children. Far from being a matriarchal system, which implies that women have power, matrifocality, in fact, contributes to the further exploitation of women. According to the 1970 census, at least a third of Jamaica's adult women headed households (Mathurin 1977), and at the same time in Trenchtown, a slum area of Kingston where my own research was conducted, more than 45% of the household heads were women. Yet Jamaican lower class women hold the lowest paying and most unskilled jobs in the society, many of which bar them from union activity. These same women also have the highest rate of unemployment. What, then, is the basis of the contradictory image of the Black Matriarch? Jamaican women share this situation with colonized women everywhere, as described by Eleanor Leacock in *Myths of Male Dominance:*

> [Over-worked and under-paid, women] bear the brunt, psychologically and sometimes physically, of the frustration and anger of their menfolk, who, in miserable complicity with an exploitative system, take advantage of the petty power they have been given over the women close to them. Perhaps the most bitter reality lies with the family, which is idealized as a retreat and sanctuary in a difficult world. Women fight hard to make it this, yet what could be a center of preparation for resistance by both sexes is so often a confused personal battleground, in which women have little recourse but to help recreate the conditions of their own oppression.
>
> (Leacock 1981:311)

In Jamaica it is only within the context of slavery and the poverty that followed Emancipation that we can understand female-male relationships. While a good argument can be made historically for the cultural inheritance of certain African social patterns, there is no doubt that economic factors continue to foster certain social adaptations in family and kinship arrangements. Leonard Barrett has outlined the major contributions to Jamaican folk culture made by the Ashanti-Fanti peoples of Ghana, the source of most of the Jamaican slaves.[4] Mathurin has argued that rebel Jamaican slave women built upon an African cultural tradition of relative independence (Mathurin 1975). In a comparative study, McCaffrey has shown the many similarities of women's culture in Ghana, Senegal, Haiti and Jamaica due to shared historical experiences (McCaffrey, no date). In particular, she points out that the culture area from which the majority of Jamaican slaves derived was noted for its matrilineal form of social organization, where married spouses lived with their respective kin and not with each other (McCaffrey: 200-201). Motherhood, once a highly respected ideal of African cultural life, then denigrated as "breeding" in the slave regime, nevertheless continued to be rewarded in Jamaican peasant culture. In contemporary Jamaica, barren women are called "mules" and their childlessness is regarded as some form of divine punishment for their transgressions. Jamaican women are simply expected to have children.

A matrilineal form of social organization does not necessarily imply the isolation of women in single-parent households and the absence of male responsibility, as in the case of matrifocality. In the African context, extended families were more the norm, and the role of the mother's brother was socially significant. In the Jamaican situation, while extended families are common, they frequently consist of a responsible core of related women, since men cannot be relied upon to make a long-term commitment to the welfare of their children. While there is a culturally institutionalized type of female-male relationship called the "visiting union," where men visit their children and their "baby's mother" periodically, and may even contribute to their support, nevertheless they are not responsible on a day-to-day basis. The organization of the family and child-rearing practices actually militate against this. In Jamaica, boy children are valued far more highly than girl children, and sisters are obliged to cater to their brothers as they grow up. Mothers bind their sons to them to the point where mutual dependencies exist far into the children's adult lives. Clarke describes several examples of this (Clarke 1966: 162-164). Merle Hodge has argued that under the right kinds of circumstances the extended family affords its members a security and a quality of experience which is far superior to the attenuated nuclear arrangement. She goes on to say:

> All of which would seem to suggest that the Caribbean is right there in the avant-garde of the social revolution where it affects family, for what the avant-garde sociologists seem to be pointing to is good old West Indian fluidity of possible relationships. But have you noticed that in the Caribbean all the fluidity of patterns, as the wide range of options, are for the men, in the final analysis, and not for the women? At both levels of the society—the respectable upper class which marries, and the deemed-not-so-respectable lower class which does not consider marriage compulsory—the image of womanhood is strangely rigid. Girls are still borne along, as on a conveyor belt, into what is presented to them as the only possible fulfilment for a woman— marriage and or child-bearing. (sic)

(Hodge 1977:41)

187

There undoubtedly exists a double standard of sexuality for men and women in the Jamaican situation. This double standard is common throughout the West Indies. In their survey of the status of women in Caribbean societies, Henry and Wilson cite evidence for this (Henry and Wilson 1975:178-181). Men and women are pressured into complementary social roles which have quite different consequences for each sex. Women, for example, frequently bear children without being married. In fact, a woman might have several children with different fathers. Men, too, might commonly father children by engaging in a series of relationships. In Jamaica, the terms "my baby's mother" and "my baby's father" are used by such parents to refer to each other. However, the responsibility for rearing these children ultimately falls upon the woman and her family. Therefore, while men are expected to demonstrate their virility by fathering children, women may be motivated to have yet another child for economic reasons. Perhaps this father will make a commitment to the relationship.

> Just as a woman is only considered "really" a woman after she has borne a child, so the proof of a man's maleness is the impregnation of a woman. There is, therefore, no incentive for either men or women to avoid parenthood even in promiscuous relationships: on the contrary, it is the hall-mark of adulthood, and normal, healthy living... The man is satisfied by the proof of his virility and does not necessarily accept any of the obligations and duties of parenthood.... At the same time women are acutely aware of the economic burden which children represent if they have no male support for them.
>
> (Clarke 1966:96)

Clarke then goes on to discuss the ambivalence of women towards contraception and abortion, and men's outright opposition to these practices. McCaffrey has also noted the paucity of literature dealing with the same theme (McCaffrey:179). Another study by Roberts and Sinclair on fertility in Jamaica points to the widespread ignorance among women about the biology of reproduction (Roberts and Sinclair 1978). On the other hand, in assessing the impact of Edna Brodber's research on child abandonment, Mathurin writes:

> The single most disturbing social phenomenon of contemporary Jamaica is the physical and/or moral abandonment of children by single young mothers... More than any other human indicator, abandonment of a child signals near social collapse: it points to a growing sense of desperation and despair in a group historically perceived as a main effective source of human power.
>
> (Mathurin 1977:6)

Clearly, this is a corollary of the widespread cultural opposition in Jamaica to the use of birth control, and, in effect, evidence of the society's abandonment not just of children, but of women.

As in many other societies, the nature of Jamaican women's sexuality is not well understood, nor is it considered of sufficient interest to be a problem. Women are frequently described as having the status of an object rather than a person in a sexual relationship. In Jamaican parlance, one will hear the phrase "to sex a woman" or "to breed a woman" to describe sexual intercourse. A controversial aspect of female-male relationships, then, concerns the apparent need for sex and expectations about fidelity. While polygamy was practised in West Africa, it had quite different implications for women there than any approximation of this social pattern would have for women in Jamaica. Yet while women are expected to be faithful to their partners, a well documented aspect of West Indian life is the institutionalization of the "other woman," whether in the form of the mistress or the mother. Henry and Wilson discuss at length some of the strategies women have devised for coping with this problem in an attempt to hold on to the man as an economic resource (Henry and Wilson 1975:185-186). However, given the unstable economic situation of many men, it appears that other factors such as social status and cultural values are working here. It is common to hold women responsible if their partners have sexual relations with other women, on the grounds that they have not done enough for their man at home (Henry and Wilson 1975:179-180).

This kind of attitude towards women — blaming them for their own oppression, objectifying them as "breeders" or "mules" — reaches its extreme form of expression in patterns of culturally sanctioned violence towards women. In *The Shadow of the Whip*, Merle Hodge asks the question of how a society whose history is so saturated with violence can appear so politically stable? She then argues that:

> ... the violence of our history has not evaporated. It is still there. It is there in the relations between adult and child, between black and white, between man and woman. It has been internalized, it has seeped down into our personal lives. Drastic brutality — physical and verbal — upon children is an accepted part of child rearing in the Caribbean... And the fact that a physical fight between a man and a woman — or more accurately, a woman-beating — may erupt into the open air and rage on for hours without any serious alarm on the part of the onlookers for the safety of the woman, without attracting the intervention of the law, is a strong comment on our attitudes.

(Hodge 1974:111-112)

Many of the attitudes towards women that we have discussed above, but in particular the association between sex and violence, are expressed in some of the popular reggae recordings. Honor Ford-Smith has pointed out that male

189

reggae singers even threaten rape, "advertising masculinity as something which by definition is intimidating and violent towards women."[5]

Women in the Rastafarian Movement

The relationship between Rastafarian men and Rastafarian women can be understood only within the ideological context of Rastafarian attitudes towards women, sexuality, and the family. In general, we can say that the brethren's behaviour in this regard is directed toward the end of controlling women's sexuality and their reproductive capacity, for purposes and in ways that men have defined. A recent major study on the Rastafarian movement by Barry Chevannes demonstrates the degree of cultural continuity between Rastafarian ritual and belief, and the peasant origins of the movement—something the brethren would probably rather ignore, given their emphasis on cultural innovation and African values.[6] In this section, I intend to argue that Rastafarians, in their attitudes and behaviour toward women, share a common cultural heritage with other Jamaicans. And I intend to show that when the brethren do take a divergent stand—that is, around their advocacy of a male-dominated family structure—they mirror the culture of the European colonizers to whom they are ideologically opposed.

The Rastafarian ambiguity towards women is common to patriarchal cultures everywhere. While there exists in Rastafarian ideology a Utopian conception of the ideal woman, in reality the behaviour of women is frequently cast in a less complimentary light. There are several cultural models upon which the brethren draw to make their points. One derives from Ethiopian culture, the notion that the roles of Emperor-Empress can be mapped onto male-female roles. In fact, Rastafarians speak of their "king-man" or "queen" to refer to husbands and wives. This concept is appropriate if they are speaking in the context of the patriarchal nuclear family. On the other hand, Old Testament family forms and notions of African polygamy are used to support the double standard with which most cultures are familiar. Clearly, the models available allow the brethren to swing either way depending upon the circumstances.

Women are eulogized as symbolically equivalent to Mother Africa. When I had just started my field-work, several brethren with whom I was associated had committed to memory a poem published in the *Ethiopian Observer* entitled "Black Mother." They were in the habit of reciting it to women and to sisters whenever they wanted to make a point about the proper conduct of women. The poem projected an especially dignified image of African women struggling for their survival. It provided a vision of possibilities, along with the brethren's implied message that Rastafarianism would be the path to achieve these ends. One would have to experience the degrading conditions of life in an urban ghetto to comprehend the power of this image for women. Yet to take it up is to intensify the contradictions of women's lot — from matrifocality to patriarchy.

The other kind of model for women emphasizes her fallen nature. The source of many of these attitudes is the Bible. Various versions of the Biblical creation myth as elaborated by the brethren introduce us to Eve and Lilith, or to Eve's daughter, fathered by the serpent. They play with puns on women — woe to men — and on Adam — a damned. Somehow they work the seductive nature of women into the genealogy of the entire human race. We meet this sister again and again, in the form of the Whore, from the Fall of Babel to the Revelations of St. John. This theme, expressed in a variety of ways, is consistent with traditional Jamaican ambiguity towards women, and has parallels in our own culture.

Elsewhere I have discussed how the concepts of Babylon and Zion are major organizing principles in Rastafarian ideology.[7] These are related to notions of contamination and purity, respectively. While holding up the ideal of the African woman who steadfastly supports her man, brethren argue that women's way to God is through man — "the dread is the head" — and that unless their behaviour is "controlled" by a man they will fall into the pits of corruption. Rastafarians actually use the expression "to control a daughter" to refer to a woman who is under their influence. In fact, a culturally approved way for a Rastafarian to obtain a female partner is to "grow a daughter." This refers to the process of courting a young woman, often a girl considerably younger than the brother, while she still lives in her parents' home, and influencing her in the ways of Rastafari. Later, the young woman will leave her home for that of the brother. In the case of one Rastafarian couple, as the brother assumed the status of an elder dread in the neighbourhood he became progressively alienated from his wife.[8] The sister, who was a fairly

191

independent, outspoken sort of a person, had difficulty coping with his changing role. The couple had three young children. For several months the wife continuously complained about her husband's relationships with several young girls who spent a lot of time in the yard, while one of the young teenagers moved into the yard as the dread's wife. This relationship continues to be stable years later. The brother had, in effect, "grown a daughter" right under the nose of his wife, one who was far less likely to cause friction in his household.

Such adventures are not without problems, however, especially when the daughter becomes a woman and wants to assert her own independence. During the period of my field-work, I unwittingly provided accommodation for a young married country sister who wanted to spend some time in town shopping and visiting. Sister Miriam was a daughter who had left her parents' home at a very young age to live with a brother several years her senior. In this particular case, the brother was especially solicitous of the younger sister and always treated her with a great deal of tenderness and respect. However, the sister felt to find her own bearings in the world. After the sister had stayed with me for a few days, I was called to a conference in one of the yards where I had been working. Present were the elder dread in this yard, his wife, and a few other brethren, all of whom were long-term associates of Sister Miriam's husband.

Sister Miriam was not present, but she had apparently announced her intention to all to leave her country home for the time being and to move into town. Now the question was, to what extent was I complicit in this decision? The main issue seemed to be that this sister did not realize that I was a *white* woman. Here she was, a lockswoman, carrying on this way in a white woman's yard. It just didn't look good. The brethren reasoned that something *had* happened between her and her king-man, but it looked like I was encouraging her to stay. I was criticized for letting people get too close to me and was told that in order to protect her *and* me, they would have to find her somewhere else to stay until the problem could be resolved. The sister who was present pointed out again that Miriam was dreadlocks and this behaviour reflected poorly upon her. In fact, this sister, who was a much older woman, said that she herself had not grown dreadlocks yet. The elder dread present emphasized that no sister should grow locks just for her king-man, that she should do it only out of a commitment to Rastafari. And here we had the case of a daughter who had

192

perhaps locksed too early in her development, and was now suffering the responsibilities of the role. The brethren found Miriam another place to stay, and told me that from the moment I dropped her off there I was no longer responsible for her. But for several weeks afterwards they continued to muse about how this sister just couldn't seem to understand that I was a *white* woman. Obviously, our identification as women had overridden our differences as black and white, something that the brethren found difficult to comprehend. Shortly afterwards, the sister returned to her husband in the country and this relationship, too, continues to be stable.

Most written works which deal with the Rastafarian movement project men's culture as characteristic of the entire movement. This tendency has been carried furthest in a series of popular accounts of reggae music, which conveys the impression that male culture is the only reality.[9] Where sisters are mentioned, their treatment is often superficial and misleading. For example, in a section entitled "Sisters and Daughters," Nicholas writes:

> It is a goal of Rasta brethren that their sisters and daughters be relaxed, contented, at ease with themselves and their way of life... None of the sisters or daughters of Rastafari seemed to foster the jealousy, competition, or negative infighting which prevail among women in Western cultures, who have predominantly been socialized to believe that their worth lies in competing for and catching a man.... While the Rasta moral code allows for sex between man and wife... many sisters and daughters nonetheless become pregnant without a man to depend upon. In most cases the Rasta community comes to their assistance, to prevent their dependence upon Babylon in a time of need.[10]

The Rastafarian culture has been the subject of considerable romanticization and projection, based on the data of a few informants rather than prolonged field-work. There are those who, disillusioned with Western culture, look to the Rasta as the "natural man." Without providing contradictory data at this point, we can observe that when the Rastafarian brother is present, we find a patriarchal system, and when he is absent, a matrifocal one. In either case, women are disadvantaged. Nicholas also notes that women rarely engage in reasoning, much less "serious ganja smoking," or for that matter "any serious business."[11] In other words, women are excluded from the central activities of the movement, yet they are expected to be "at ease with themselves and their way of life"!

Finally, while Nicholas applauds the fact that Rastafarians use two terms of respect for women of all ages, "daughter" and "sister," as opposed to using popular slang words, she neglects to mention that only one term, "brother," is used for men of all ages. For young Rastafarian males, the term "youth" is used, but it would never be applied to an adult brother. In Jamaican parlance generally, the terms "brother" and "sister" are quite commonly used. However, it is only the Rastafarians who use the term "daughter" to refer to adult women. When pressed, some brethren argue that "daughter" is equivalent to prophet. But while it may not be the conscious intention of the user, who may mean it as a term of endearment, structurally the language reflects the subordinate status of women within the movement and serves an ideological end by disguising their objective condition. Could this term be an oblique reference to the Daughter of Babylon?

When we turn to more serious and scholarly studies of the Rastafarian movement, we do not find women's experiences treated in any depth. There are very few references to women in the social science literature on the movement. Owens follows Barrett in limiting his comments to noting that the membership is largely male, with women playing a minor role.[12] Chevannes documents in a little more detail the subordinate status of women in the groups that he studies.[13] There is one reference to women in Nettleford's book, another major source on the movement, although he does acknowledge that the role of women and the family have been neglected as areas of study.[14] He even suggests that women may be the major social link between Rastafarians and the non-Rastafarian society, as well as the "prime breadwinners." With regard to female-male relations, Nettleford writes:

> Mating habits in an ethos where common sharing is an ideal may even reveal that the Rastafarian is no less fastidious than his Jamaican compatriots in his belief that "sexual exclusiveness is the ideal mode of behaviour." The strong emphasis on the male suggests a patrifocal organization and a possible solution to what some people view as a major problem of Jamaican family organization, viz. the household without a man at the head.[15]

Here Nettleford has overlooked patriarchy as the basis for restricting women's sexual behaviour.

The only person to spend some time discussing women, sex, and the family within the movement is a woman anthropologist, Sheila Kitzinger. While she recognizes that women are peripheral to the movement, she argues that "this institutionalized masculine dominance runs counter to the general pattern of relations between the sexes among the Jamaican poor."[16] Without disputing Kitzinger's data, we have seen above that it is a question of interpretation whether or not Jamaican women are powerful.

194

We have argued that in this regard the Rastafarian movement tends to fit the general cultural pattern of ambivalence toward women. Certainly my own data suggest that brethren's most significant social ties are with like-minded brethren, especially those with whom one "came up in the faith" i.e., became Rastafarians together. I was frequently told that the kind of love experienced collectively among the brethren was far superior to the "fleshy" kind of involvement experienced with a woman. Women and their sexuality seem to represent a threat to the established bonds between males; hence the need for their control. On the other hand, there is a fear of homosexuality on the part of the brethren, which is reflected in their use of the term "bati man" (Patois for "gay") as the ultimate form of insult. Women then become a necessary evil because they help men to establish their virility.

We have already noted the fact that the Rastafarian movement is a heterogeneous social phenomenon which allows the individual a great deal of flexibility in interpreting and operationalizing ideology. There is a wide variety of groups with which to associate. Needless to say, this is a flexibility afforded the brethren, but not the sisters. While brethren tend to be recruited through male peer groups, sisters tend to affiliate with Rasta through the influence of a brother with whom they have established a relationship. Sisters generally do not participate in the daily rounds of smoking and reasoning, and their attendence at ceremonial occasions is limited to a minority. They are, in fact, discouraged from seeking the associations of other sisters on any scale. One way to intimidate women in this regard is to define their business as inconsequential. For example, while discourse among the brethren has the status of "reasoning," women's communications are often described by the cultural term "petty-petty." Cast another way, we can see that ideology is the signal, gossip is the noise. While brethren circulate on their daily rounds from yard to yard, sisters are expected to be involved in domestic responsibilities. I have seen sisters held accountable for their time when they dallied too long at the corner shop or were tardy in returning from the market. On the other hand, even brethren who have a nuclear family situation might stay up all night reasoning and not reach home to their yard at all. The behaviour of one particular brother was frequently held to be exemplary by other brethren because, regardless of what was happening in his smoking yard, he returned home every night, however late the hour, to be with his family.

195

It is my observation that brethren rarely spend time with sisters in a companionable kind of way. This can lead to serious breakdowns of communication. One particular episode is instructive in this regard. A brother had committed himself to the responsibility of trying to provide for a woman who had several children by other fathers. He operated a small shop in downtown Kingston, and was fairly active in movement projects. He seldom spent much time at home at all, yet the sister was isolated at home daily. One day he went home to discover that somehow the sister had managed to arrange passports for all the children and with the help of relatives had emigrated abroad. The brother was devastated. There was only a note left behind. In trying to come to terms with this problem, the brethren never thought to consider why the relationship had deteriorated to this extent. The sister was blamed for her cowardice and her opportunism, while the brother received much sympathy. On another occasion, a great deal of social pressure was brought to bear on a brother who had abandoned his wife and family for a younger woman. The brethren were genuinely concerned with their welfare and the manner in which this would reflect negatively on the movement. His second liaison would be tolerated, but only if he carried out his responsibilities to the first sister.

Among the brethren with whom I worked closely there was clearly a high value attached to a man's ability to be responsible for his family or dependents, and if the brother in question could also spend time engaged in reasoning and other kinds of movement activities, that was ideal. However, little thought was given to how all these demands would affect the quality of the couple's relationship and day-to-day family life. This was rarely defined as a problem. So we end up with a situation wherein men and women pursue their interests in parallel, and not together. The brethren, though, do so collectively, while sisters function more in isolation from each other. And surprise is expressed when things do not work out.

Onto the conceptual distinction between Babylon and Zion can be mapped Rastafarian attitudes towards women. There exist a great many rules, which, if followed, will protect brethren from the contaminating influence of women. When carried to an extreme, there is a Rastafarian cultural pattern which legitimizes a celibate, monastic-like lifestyle for Rastafarian men. Here the physical separation is complete. On a broad scale, this is expressed in terms of the "yard" and the "camp", the former being the collective, mixed-sex dwelling unit, the latter a men-only retreat centre. While some brethren live exclusively in camps, all brethren have privileged access to them; but admittance is generally denied to women, except as visitors. Brethren have the opportunity to move back and forth between these two kinds of living arrangements, while sisters do not.

Less dramatically, there are provisions for brethren who cannot separate themselves from a life with women. In order to control contaminating energies under these circumstances, there are a number of prohibitions concerning pregnancy and menstruation. Brethren tend to regard blood as impure in itself, but special kinds of blood are particularly dangerous. In Jamaican parlance, certain curse words refer to this subject, such as "bloodclot" and "rassclot" which I was told mean menstrual "rags." The continued use of such terms as part of a lifestyle which is so dignified in other ways partially reflects the peasant roots of the culture. There is an avoidance tabu surrounding menstrual blood and menstruating women. It is said that women may not cook for men when they are "unclean." Not all members observe this prohibition, but while many brethren appear to ignore it, it is nevertheless part of the ideology. Some brethren never allow women to cook for them under any circumstances. Once, when visiting the yard of some youthful brethren who were living a monastic-style life, I chanced to lean upon a table which held a small kerosene stove. I was immediately chastized and told that in some camps I would be held responsible for contaminating it. Chevannes describes the case of the Ethiopian International Congress, a Rastafarian community which lives in the country, which has established menstrual huts in their compound, where women retire for two weeks of the month.[17] While some feminists argue that this may constitute a holiday for women, in this context it is denigrating.

Although fertility and child-bearing are highly valued, there seems to be some ambivalence about the state of pregnancy. Not only is giving birth considered "women's business," but it is said that pregnant women might attract malicious spirits. I was once present during a smoking and reasoning session where the elder dread called out at a pregnant woman who passed nearby in order to protect himself. Here again we might have an example of the kind of cultural continuity with peasant roots which Chevannes discusses.

On the other hand, in the very rich symbolism surrounding the act of smoking, there exist several references to the procreative act. Lighting the pipe itself symbolizes the act of creation, because all the essential elements are present: earth, water, fire and air. A more veiled allusion is to sexual intercourse. Oblique jokes were occasionally made in this regard, although my presence may have been inhibiting. Terms such as "rape the chalice" and "go up on it" are used. I.M. Lewis had noted that

> ecstatic communion is thus essentially a mystical union: and, as the Song of Solomon and other mystical poetry so abundantly illustrate, experiences of this kind are frequently described in terms borrowed from erotic love.[18]

Lewis goes on to discuss the use of sexual imagery in spirit possession behaviour, where people "mount" spirits or spirits "mount" people, and where the language of the stable is applied. Lewis also describes the concept of mystical marriage in this context.[19] Rastafarian brethren frequently speak of their marriage to Rastafari, the herbs, and their pipe. It is not uncommon in many cultures for men to usurp procreative symbolism to refer exclusively to their own activities (see Mary O'Brien 1976, 1981). Possession by spirits, which is fairly common throughout Caribbean culture, is defined by the brethren as a female form of expression. It is regarded as excessively emotional and thus a lower level experience than reasoning and meditation. I witnessed many attempts to censor behaviour that tended in this direction. To the brethren, it smacked of Pocomania, which is what such cults are called in Jamaica. The identification of Pocomania and spiritual emotionalism with women is clear in the minds of the brethren.

It is in the area of sexuality and reproduction that brethren make their greatest efforts to control women's behaviour. There are several behavioural prohibitions which are designed to de-emphasize women's sexual nature. The Rastafarian dress code, for example, requires sisters to cover their heads at all times, while brethren may or may not display their locks. Brethren, in fact, are required to remove their tams while smoking. Sometimes they even doff their caps and shake their locks in an intimidating manner—something sisters would never do. This is related to the Old Testament motif of Sampson and Delilah, wherein men might lose their power through the cutting of the locks. Loose hair is also suggestive of unrestrained sexuality. Sisters are expected to dress modestly, to cover their bare arms and legs, and to wear clothing which does not emphasize or expose bodily parts. No such restrictions exist for brethren, who may even adopt the local custom of wearing tight-bottomed pants. Rape and other forms of abuse are frequently attributed to women's flaunting of immodest attire.

Brethren also oppose the use of birth-control and the practice of abortion. However, they make no distinction between programmes of birth-control directed to the under-developed countries as a form of genocide, which they under-stand politically and condemn, and an individual woman's right to choose whether or not to have children, something they also deny. Their position supports reproduction, but denies sexuality for its own sake. Some will even ask why have sex if children are not desired. This poses a very complex dilemma for women in the movement—in terms of the kinds of choices they can make within a relationship.[20]

Relatively speaking, Jamaican women generally have enjoyed greater freedom of movement than have women who are part of traditional patriarchal cultures. As heads of households, they can manage their own affairs, travel, trade, take part in public life, and relate to other women. Rastafarian brethren, however, prefer a nuclear family arrangement as the ideal type, as described in Biblical and patriarchal terms. Institutionalization of patriarchal culture generally means restricting women's movements and to some extent cloistering them in the home, accompanied by economic support by men. In the Jamaican context, economic pressures have made this development impossible on any large scale, especially in relation to a man's ability to support more than one household. In cases where it does work, the households often take on extra responsibilities such as caring for younger dependents who may be relatives or children of other brethren. This inevitably means extra domestic labour for the woman.

More research has to be done on the nature of women's experience when they become involved with the Rastafarian movement. We need to ask ourselves to what extent sisters continue to do the same things they have always done in a context that has been redefined for them, and to what extent they actually change their behaviour in significant ways. Is it possible that the "righteous nuclear family" works because women continue to do what they have always done? Brethren can take advantage of the strengths of traditional Jamaican women's culture and redefine the context in a way that supports patriarchal privilege. In one case, two sisters who had children with the same father came to know each other and provided mutual support in traditional ways, such as

199

caring for each other's children over extended periods of time. They cooperated not because they were committed to a patriarchal ideology, but because they recognized their shared predicament and the need to establish a stable situation for their children. This kind of mutual support and solidarity is essential for survival, and it is part of traditional women's culture in Jamaica.

It should be apparent that it has been possible to analyze the patriarchal assumptions underlying Rastafarian ideology and practice without examining in detail the experiences of women in the movement. One obvious question is to what extent do Rastafarian sisters comply with this definition of the scheme of things. On the one hand, we have the attitude expressed by Sister Farcia in a commentary in a Rastafarian newspaper:

> ... Remember Daughters, you have an important role to play in the downfall of Babylon. The dread is the head but men are beneath a righteous daughter and by virtue of their corruption and loss of masculinity, cannot stand our wrath. It is written in the book of Isaiah, "In the last days, a woman shall encompass a man." These are the last days. Bring down Babylon, do not uplift it. Strengthen your Kingman in his struggle against the evil forces dominating the world. Play your part in the liberation of Africa. Forward up Daughters. Forward ever. Backward never.
>
> (Farcia 1976:16)

The image is that of the supportive wife identifying with the man's definition of the situation. On the other hand, there is some discussion by Rastafarian sisters who are beginning to confront these contradictions. They appreciate the radical cultural message of the movement, with its emphasis on an integrated way of living in dignity and peace. However, their own experience tells them that there is a long struggle ahead in regard to women's autonomy within the movement. In an interview with the magazine *Yard Roots*, Sister Ilaloo describes the changing situation: "You never use to have a Rastawoman; you use to have a Rastaman Woman" (Ilaloo 1981:6).

Many women are starting to affiliate with the movement independently of a relationship with a Rastafarian brother. Some of the sisters who have been raised abroad or who have lived some time abroad are asking very pointed questions about their role within the movement. As Rastafarianism gains more momentum outside Jamaica we will need to study the kinds of influences such developments will have on the movement. In July 1982, the First International Rastafarian Conference was held in Toronto. While the delegates from the West Indies were men, there were several sisters in attendance from Canada and the United States who played an active part in the proceedings. The one workshop which ran well past its allotted time was on "Rastafari and the Family." It was well attended by both brothers and sisters, and constituted, in effect, a family-style dialogue on the relationship between brothers and sisters in the movement. Many sisters were very eloquent and vocal in pressing forward their assumptions about themselves. They challenged the brethren's notions of the "nature" of women and made demands of their own. The independent behaviour of some of the sisters raised the question for a few as to whether or not they were "real" Rastafarians. It remains to be seen the extent to which other kinds of cultural alternatives will develop for women in Jamaica. Clearly, no liberation struggle will be successful unless the patriarchal imperative is effectively eliminated. This issue is bound to arise again and again until the contradiction of patriarchy within a movement of liberation is resolved.

Finally, it should also be clear that in order to conduct research from a feminist perspective, the field-worker must be involved in social relationships with women. A shift to a feminist viewpoint involves new personal associations. To what extent the establishment of such ties with other women will be perceived as threatening by men remains to be seen. But if we are to effectively deal with the problem of freedom and humanity for all people, such commitments are essential.

FOOTNOTES

1. The original field-work was sponsored by grants from the Canada Council and the Centre for Developing Area Studies, Montréal. I would like to thank A. Miles and D.W. Smith for a critical reading of the manuscript and useful suggestions. I would like to express my appreciation to F. Forman of the Women's Resource Centre, Ontario Institute for Studies in Education, Toronto, for calling my attention to several sources.
2. C. Yawney, "Dread Wasteland: Rastafarian Ritual in West Kingston, Jamaica" in R. Crumrine (ed.), *Ritual Symbolism and Ceremonialism in the Americas*, University of Northern Colorado Occasional Publications in Anthropology, No. 33, 1979, pp. 154-178.

3. C. Yawney, *Lions in Babylon: The Rastafarians of Jamaica as a Visionary Movement.* Unpublished Ph. D. dissertation, Dept. of Anthropology, McGill University, 1979, pp. 137-158.
4. L. Barrett, *The Sun and the Drum: African Roots in Jamaican Folk Tradition* (Kingston: Sangster, 1976).
5. Honor Ford-Smith, *From Downpression Get a Blow Up to Now: Becoming Sistren.* Mimeographed talk, c. September 1979, p. 6.
6. B. Chevannes, *Social Origins of the Rastafari Movement.* (Mona, Inst. of Social and Economic Research, 1978).
7. C.D. Yawney, "Remnants of All Nations: Rastafarian Attitudes to Race and Nationality" in F. Henry (ed.), *Ethnicity in the Americas* (The Hague: Mouton, 1976).
8. I have changed names and taken care to protect the anonymity of my sources.
9. See T. Nicholas & B. Sparrow, *Rastafari: A Way of Life* (New York: Anchor Books, 1979), and A. Boot & M. Thomas, *Jamaica: Babylon on a Thin Wire* (London: Thames & Hudson, 1976).
10. Nicholas & Sparrow, *op. cit.*, pp. 64-66.
11. *Ibid.*, p. 65.
12. L. Barrett, *The Rastafarians: Squads of Cultural Dissonance* (Boston: Beacon Press, 1977), p. 106; J. Owens, *Dread* (Kingston: Sangster, 1976), p. 23.
13. Chevannes, *op. cit.*, p. 201ff.
14. R. Nettleford, *Mirror, Mirror* (Kingston: Collins & Sangster, 1974), p. 106.
15. Ibid.
16. G. Kitzenger, "Protest and Mysticism" in *Journal of Sci. Stud. Rel.*, 8, 1969, 252.
17. Chevannes, *op. cit.*, p. 197.
18. I.M. Lewis, *Ecstatic Religion* (Harmondsworth: Penguin, 1971), p. 58.
19. *Ibid.*, pp. 59-60.
20. The Rastafarian position on dress codes and birth control is discussed in more detail in Yawney 1976, *op. cit.*, pp. 255-262.

CHAPTER 9

On the Oppression of Women in Philosophy—or, Whatever Happened to Objectivity?

Geraldine Finn

Geraldine Finn has a B.A. in Philosophy and English from Keele University in England and an M.A. and a Ph.D. in Philosophy from McMaster University and the University of Ottawa, respectively. Her Master's and Doctoral studies focused on Marxism, phenomenology, and structuralism. She has taught philösophy at the CEGEP de l'Outaouais Heritage Campus in Hull, Québec, since 1975, and has been active in the Canadian Society for Women in Philosophy and the Committee on Socialist Studies and the Radical Philosophy Group of the Canadian Philosophical Association. She has written feminist critiques of science and technology, socialism and Marxism, the media, and sex and representation, and is currently developing feminist theory in the areas of fiction, music, and moral and political philosophy. She teaches courses in the Women's Studies Programme at the University of Ottawa and is affiliated on a part-time basis with the Graduate School of Social Work at Carleton University. She is editing the collection *Women's Studies: A Canadian Introduction*, soon to be published by Garamond Press.

Interesting works on feminism and philosophy that have appeared since this article was written include *Philosophy and Feminist Thinking* by Jean Grimshaw (1986) and *Discovering Reality: Feminist Perspectives on Epistemology, Metaphysics, Methodology, and the Philosophy of Science* by Sandra Harding and Merrill Hintikka (1983).

*This paper was originally written for and presented to
the philosophy department of the University of Ottawa where I
was at the time completing my doctoral studies. The department
consisted of about 30 full-time male professors and no full-time
female professors, though it had recently refused to grant tenure
to a very good female philosopher who had taught there for two
years. The following should be read with this in mind for it
presumes an audience which is largely male.*

The first thing I should say is that this, "strictly
speaking," will not be a "philosophy paper" in the conventional
sense: it is about philosophy, philosophers, philosophies and
philosophy departments, and it is written by a philosopher, for
philosophers, to be presented to philosophers in a philosophy
department—but, strictly speaking, it is not philosophical
because it does not present *an argument* to defend a position.
Rather, what I shall be doing is trying to convey to you
something of the experience of being a woman in philosophy—
it is that experience, i.e. my own, which has led me to the
conclusion that philosophy is oppressive of women. It is my
experience of the philosophical world as masculist and sexist
that I would like to give you a taste of in the time allotted to me.

I do not resort to arguments because I do not believe that
you convince anyone of the truth of a proposition by argument.
You may *predispose* someone to "embrace" that truth (my
metaphors are not lightly chosen and the topic will be
returned to later) by a good argument, but the final acceptance
of any truth claim, I believe, is the consequence of personal
experience and a function of practice and vision, if you would.
Inductive empirical truths are like deductive "rational" truths
and psychoanalytic truths in that, ultimately, their self-
evidence is seen, acknowledged, acquiesced to—and not forced
upon you by the strength of a good argument. So I shall try to
convince you of my claim—that philosophy oppresses women—
not by force of argument (for someone can always redefine the
terms, object to the concepts, etc.), but by a series of
observations, anecdotes and asides. (What, you may indeed
ask, has happened to objectivity—or philosophy, for that
- matter?)

Because I an speaking personally and specifically—of
my experience *as a woman* in the supposedly public forum of
philosophy—what I say may (and frequently does) cause
offense to (male) philosophers. This is because men rule out-of-
order any discourse which transgresses the(ir) separation of
the public and the private spheres. And the intrusion of

personal considerations into professional or academic and "learned" debate (and vice-versa)[1] is particularly offensive to them and sufficient to invalidate whoever is speaking. In philosophy, the *ad hominem* fallacy sees to that. But this very possibility itself only illustrates the truth of one of my principal claims: that the philosophical world is and is assumed to be male (yet at the same time undifferentiated sexually); and that the philosopher presumes (and must presume to be heard *as* a philosopher) that she (in this somewhat special case) is addressing men when speaking to philosophers. Because, if there is offense, it is men who will be offended, and they are offended precisely because they are men. It is only because (a) I am presenting this paper, and (b) because the topic is (unusually) relevant to women who nurse philosophical aspirations (or indeed philosophers themselves — as wives, lovers, secretaries, mothers, students, etc. — again, not a lightly chosen metaphor) that I can assume with some confidence that there are some women in my audience. If (a) and (b) were not the case I would have to presume otherwise, i.e., that I was addressing an exclusively male audience. This is not an irrelevant detail, since if it were not true I would not have written the paper in the first place, and since it *is* true the paper runs the risk of being offensive. The offense will be to the listener's philosophical sensibilities or to his masculine sensibilities — which, I believe, are the same at this point in history, as subsequent observations may make clear. What I say may also cause offense to those women who have been admitted into philosophy, or to those who perceive themselves as likely candidates, but that is far from my intention and the nature of the offense should in no way be assimilated to that caused to men.

Explication of the Claim that Philosophy Oppresses Women

What am I referring to, then, when I talk about the "oppression" of women in the context of philosophy? Well, I am not being metaphorical or exotic in my choice of words, I am using "oppression" in its everyday, common-or-garden, O.E.D.

sense; it refers to the condition of being oppressed, where, to oppress, means:

> to *put down*
> *crush*
> *overwhelm*
> *check*
> *suppress*
> *conceal*

1. *to press injuriously upon or against; to subject to pressure with hurtful or overpowering effect; to press down by force; to crush, trample, smother, crowd; to bear down or crush in a battle; to overwhelm with numbers;*
2. *to affect with a feeling of pressure, constraint or distress; to crush (the feelings, mind, spirits, etc.);*
3. *to put down, suppress, crush, quell, subdue, overwhelm, check, extinguish or put an end to (a thing, a state of things, feeling, disposition); to suppress, keep out of sight, conceal ;*
4. *to trample down or keep under wrongful exercise of authority, or superior power or strength; to load or burden with cruel or unjust impositions or restraints, to tyrannize over;*

....
....

9. [*and finally, of course*] TO CLOSE, TO SHUT UP. This is what I have concluded philosophy has done and continues to do to women. It puts them down, crushes them, suppresses them, smothers and conceals them, etc. —and usually succeeds (though clearly not in this particular case) in finally shutting us up.

I am using the expression "in philosophy" (as in "the oppression of women in philosophy") in its widest possible scope to include personalities and theories, as well as the formal structures of both the activity itself and the institutions in which it takes place (universities, conferences, associations).

The sexist and misogynist content traditional to philosophy has been fairly comprehensively documented in the last few years, showing how women have either been concealed in the history of philosophy, i.e. rendered invisible; or quite literally abused; or, at best, appeared as the less than "rational" sex (and we are always "sex") and therefore as less "human" than men, and relegated to the realm of "nature" rather than "culture," and so on, and so forth. Plato, Aristotle,

Aquinas, Hobbes, Locke, Rousseau, Mill, Nietzsche, Sartre and (even) Marx refused to take the "woman question" seriously, and excluded women from philosophy (in its broadest sense); or they denigrated us *en passant* and thus maintained our effective exclusion by this means. A few examples will suffice to remind us of some of our appearances in philosophical theory:

Kant

Women will avoid the wicked not because it is upright, but only because it is ugly... Nothing of duty, nothing of compulsion, nothing of obligation! ...They do something only because it pleases them... I hardly believe that the fair sex [sic] *is capable of principles.*

Her philosophy is not to reason but to sense.

All the other merits of a woman should unite to enhance the character of the beautiful which is the proper reference point... all education and instruction should have [this] *before its eyes... A woman who has a head full of Greek, like Mme. Dacier, or carries on fundamental controversies about mechanics, might as well have a beard.*[2]

Fichte

[she] *is subjected through her own necessary wish—a wish which is the condition of her morality—to be so subjected...*

The woman who thus surrenders her personality, and yet retains her full dignity in so doing, necessarily gives up to her lover [of course!] *all that she has. For, if she retained the least of her own self, she would thereby confess that it had a higher value for her than her own person; and this undoubtedly would be a lowering of that person... The least consequence is that she should renounce to him all her property and all her rights. Henceforth... her life has become a part of the life of her lover. (This is aptly characterized by her assuming his name.)*[3]

Schopenhauer

[woman] *is in every respect backward, lacking in reason and reflection... a kind of middle step between the child and the*

207

man, who is the true human being... In the last resort, women exist solely for the propagation of the race.[4]

Rousseau

The search for abstract and speculative truths, for principles and axioms in the sciences, for all that tends to wide generalization, is beyond woman's grasp; their studies should be thoroughly practical. It is their business to apply the principles discovered by men, it is their place to make the observations which lead men to discover those principles... The men will have a better philosophy of the human heart, but she will read more accurately into the heart of men. Woman should discover, so to speak, an experimental morality, man should reduce it to a system. Woman has more wit, man more genius; woman observes, man reasons.[5]

Hegel

Women are capable of education, but they are not made for activities which demand a universal faculty such as the more advanced sciences, philosophy and certain forms of artistic production. Women may have happy ideas, taste and elegance, but they cannot attain to the ideal. The difference between men and women is like that between animals and plants; men correspond to animals, while women correspond to plants because their development is more placid and the principle that underlies it is the rather vague unity of feeling. When women hold the helm of government the State is at once in jeopardy, because women regulate their actions not by the demands of universality, but by arbitrary inclinations and opinions. Women are educated—who knows how?—as it were by breathing in ideas, by living rather than by acquiring knowledge. The status of manhood, on the other hand, is attained only by the stress of thought and much technical exertion.[6]

Comte

It is in order to better develop her moral superiority that woman must gratefully accept the rightful practical domination of man... First as a mother, and soon as a sister, then above all as a wife, and finally as a daughter, marginally as a maid-servant, in these four natural roles woman is destined to preserve man from the corruption inherent in his practical and theoretical existence.[7]

It is my opinion that revising the views of women in these thinkers, or indeed putting women into those theories from which they are conspicuous by their absence, is not philosophically feasible — as has been recently demonstrated in the cases of Plato, Rousseau, Locke, Hobbes, Hegel and Marx, in Clarke and Lange (1979). You cannot "doctor" these theories with respect to women and at the same time save the theory. The philosophical system does not survive the doctoring. The exclusion or denigration of women is integral to the system, and to give equal recognition to women destroys the system. The demonstration of this point is, of course, philosophical work in the strictest and most traditional sense, and not, therefore, to the purpose of this particular paper.

Anecdote

What motivated this presentation? Well, a whole personal history of oppression as a woman — both within and outside philosophy; but the particular motivation occurred as follows.

I arrived early for a Philosophia meeting in the Fall of 1979. The organizer of the meeting, M., was setting up coffee and doughnuts, and another person was already there for the meeting. Evidently a philosopher; the person was silent (did not offer a greeting); smoking a pipe (therefore thoughtful); and reading a book — and, of course, he was male. Although he did pass an occasional comment to M., he did not offer to help with the fetching and carrying. I was inclined to do so, but I did not because I was damned if I was going to reinforce the sex-stereotyping so abundantly evident and available upstairs. (The meeting took place in the basement of the philosophy department which, as indicated above, consists of about 30 full-time male faculty members and *no* female faculty, plus about six female secretaries serving those professors.) This caused me some conflict and discomfort — not unfamiliar in kind — which I do not believe a male philosopher would have experienced.

M. asked me to present a paper next semester in Philosophia and I was happy to do so. Looking down the list of presenters, I noticed that, predictably, they were all men except for one L.: *I wondered if this L. was the girlfriend of Professor K.?* You may not be able to draw the relevant conclusion from this *pensée* so I will elaborate a little to make myself quite clear

I was not, in posing this question, making the familiar sexist assumption that women in general are philosophically or otherwise incompetent, and therefore that any who are visible in philosophy must be there despite their inadequacy and in return for sexual favours rendered. I was simply acknowledging the reality that women, even brilliant women, usually gain access to male terrain through their association with men, and even if this is not the case are presumed to have gained their access this way.

As part of my claim that women are oppressed in philosophy I have asserted that they are excluded from it — both as a theoretical and as a practical enterprise. In philosophical theory they either do not appear or they are essentially dehumanized in their appearance, while in philosophical practice they are just not there — with a few exceptions, of course: I am one, and I thought that L. was another. In the history of philosophy there are perhaps a handful of women who did gain access to philosophy and of whom we have heard. Diogenes Laertius (I am told)[8] speaks well of *Hipparchia* and Crates; Descartes had his *Elizabeth*; and Sartre his *de Beauvoir*. Others are emerging with the new feminist scholarship — Abelard and Héloise? Rosa Luxemburg and Jogiches?[9]

What these woman have in common should be self-evident: their access to philosophy was/is *mediated by men*, i.e. their relationship to philosophy passed through their love for/commitment to a particular man, a particular philosopher with an independent reputation. This legitimized their involvement in philosophy and paved their way into its history books. It is this point, which taken wrongly, could offend women who perhaps like to think that their presence in philosophy was not mediated by their commitment to or connection with a particular male philosopher. And perhaps in their case it was not. But in my experience this is rare. It tells us something crucial about women's credibility and confidence; it tells us more about the internal operations of the philosophical credit system with respect to women. We have to earn our credits and establish our credibility differently from our brothers. We may be excellent philosophers but this fact

210

will not be acknowledged on its own merits; our excellence is validated only if it is mediated by a particular relationship with a particular man—and this relationship, since it is across the sexes, is invariably "romantic" in one form or another. This does not give us an "unfair" advantage, as our fellow philosophers sometimes argue: it simply means that our relationship to philosophy is rarely direct, and our recognition as philosophers always suspect—not only by others, but also *by ourselves*. For we are taken seriously as philosophers only when we are being taken seriously "as women"; and when the sexual interest diminishes, so does the philosophical.

Such a situation is not peculiar to the world of philosophy, of course. Women have a hard time becoming visible and a harder time getting themselves heard without a male mediator/protector/facilitator/legitimizer/in every aspect of life defined as social. It has serious consequences in philosophy because it means that women have a particularly difficult task attaining any direct access or relationship to philosophy, especially since there are so few professional women in the field to act as mediators. It also means that any relationship we do establish remains essentially *amateur*, non-professional and personal, in that it is frequently rooted in a personal "erotic-transference relationship" with a particular man (just as the philosophers prescribed!) (LeDoeuff 1977:3).

Of course, men gain access to philosophy, and often their reputation in the professional world, in similar ways: they establish an allegiance with a particular teacher, imitate his ways, do his research for him, try to impress him, and proselytize on his behalf (I am referring to the "guru-disciple syndrome" in academia). But this takes place within an *institutionalized* framework, is not necessarily exclusive, is more readily available, and rarely involves the erotic or romantic complications which "muddy" women's relationship to philosophy. Breaking the relationship between male student and male professor is not nearly so personally shattering, and the separation of public/professional from private/personal life ensures that the personal *in his case* is *not* political.[10] Sartre said to Simone de Beauvoir early on in their relationship, "From now on I will take your hand," and Simone quotes this with pleasure in one of her works. Both the gesture and the acceptance of it speak volumes to me—about the nature of woman's relationship to philosophy, and philosophy's relationship to her.

211

Second Anecdote: Same Occasion

I was about to write "History" as the topic of my presentation but found myself writing the title of this paper in the allotted space. I had been in the philosophy department only about five minutes and had encountered only two philosophers — and was already "angry," feeling my difference, and "oppressed."

The scheduled paper began. The presenter was male, the audience (excluding myself) was male, and the philosopher under discussion was male. The topic was social interaction, and we were asked to imagine two people, A and B, interacting socially. We had been told that one of the conditions of a social interaction was that there be a "face-to-face" encounter. I naturally tried to think of this face-to-face encounter as one between myself, A, and a hypothetical other B.

Now this supposedly sexually neutral other, B, is actually male: "he" always is, no matter what stipulation you make — people are either male or female in our society, and unless otherwise specified "he" means male. Along with the nominal "man," the pronominal "he" is accepted in philosophy as a neutral indicator of a token person of no specific sex. But of course this is nonsense. He is always male and so was B to me — and I am sure to all the others in the room.

This meant, however, that my experience of the complete paradigm — a face-to-face encounter with B — was unique, because I am female and my face-to-face encounter with B was a male-female encounter — never a neutral affair. There was no way I could live this encounter differently. The supposed neutrality of this harmless example was lost on me, and therefore its usefulness as a paradigm. For I was involved in an essentially sexual and political relationship with B, and the rest of the people in that room were not.

I then realized that the same could be said of my entire philosophical experience. Women doing philosophy are engaged in a male-female — and therefore a sexual and political — relationship, and men are not. This is not accidental, but constitutive — as is the sexism of philosophical theories; it conditions and directs the whole exercise:

> It may be the great dignity of philosophy that keeps women away from it; conversely, for this great dignity to be maintained women must be kept away... When a respected activity admits women it loses value.
>
> (LeDoeuff 1977:5)

Practically all philosophers are men, certainly all traditional and "great" ones are. Women, if at all present, are on the margins: in existentialism (Mary Warnock — herself married to a distinguished philosopher, de Beauvoir, Iris Murdoch, Marjorie Grene), or moral philosophy (Phillipa Foot — also married to a distinguished philosopher, de Beauvoir, Murdoch, Warnock) — philosophical disciplines considered by many *not* to be philosophy at all. This is especially true of Anglo-American (analytically orientated) philosophy. Apparently philosophical commentary has a similar secondary status in France, and there are proportionately more women visible and acknowledged in this field. "Who better than a woman to show fidelity, respect, remembrance?" (LeDoeuff 1977:10)[11]

Philosophers therefore speak as men, to men, about men, and the very process and institution of philosophy is determined by this. Schultz, the philosopher under discussion on this occasion, lost me — I could not go along with *his* phenomenology of social interaction from the moment he introduced face-to-face encounters, since he involved me in a personal and necessarily political male-female encounter — just as Aristotle lost me in the early pages of *Politics* when he relegated women and slaves to servile functions by virtue of their "intrinsic" nature. Indeed, phenomenology is especially vulnerable to this critique because it has assumed that the phenomenology of male-consciousness is tantamount to the phenomenology of consciousness as such. But one's philosophical consciousness can only reflect one's everyday consciousness, and since that consciousness is male, chauvinistic and oppressive of women, so is the philosophical consciousness entrenched in our culture and institutions. And it is continuing to be perpetrated, sometimes unthinkingly but more often now dogmatically, as the neutral and objective voice of "reason."

This particular example effectively excluded me as a female and thus made it difficult, if not impossible, for me to make any contribution to the philosophical dialogue it generated about social interaction. I was stuck at the paradigm. And this, I maintain, happens to women all the time in philosophy. We either get stuck at first base, as the men would have it, or we must suspend our disbelief — as we frequently do — giving men the benefit of the doubt instead of ourselves — as we should — for the sake of what must inevitably become a purely academic exercise instead of a genuine, authentic, philosophical inquiry into meaning, truth and understanding. Or, of course, we get involved in a transference relationship, i.e. an erotic relationship with the teacher (to mediate our identification, etc.), and still we do not *do* philosophy.

Lest you should think that I am making too much of a particular example let me remind you that this is not an argument but a demonstration. This happens all the time. To emphasize the generality of this experience and to show that it is not a special case, but absolutely central to women's relationship to philosophy, consider the following examples from logic.

Logic

It is tempting to imagine that at least in logic — stripped of social and political content — women would not necessarily get struck out as soon as they come up to bat (more on metaphors in the next section), as they might say. But consider the following first line of a very familiar syllogism. And remember that this is where most of us are initiated into the rational necessity, inevitability and universality of deductive reason and logical analysis:[12]

All men are mortal

Most people would agree that the occurrence of "men" here is intended to be neutral, and that this, therefore, is a statement about the whole of the human race.

But if this is true, then the syllogism associated with it, the paradigm (I remind you) of all valid syllogisms, is clearly invalid on the grounds of equivocation. For the second line, which usually reads:

Socrates is a man

does not use "man" in the same neutral sense, but in the gender-specific sense of male of the species. If it were the neutral "man" of the first premise, then

Sophia is a man

would be acceptable as a substitute, and it is not.

Philosophy is shot through and through with this equivocation on supposedly neutral terms like "man" and "his" and "humanity." A thoughtful, "philosophical" and intellectually honest woman is sensitive to these ambiguities and biases which confuse what to men must be crystal-clear meanings and principles, and they therefore exclude her from the philosophical tradition and from current philosophical discourse which is but a continuation of the tradition.

Consider another similar example—one more serious in terms of its consequences for the status of women, especially for those struggling with philosophy:

Man is a rational animal

Again, most people would agree that "man" in this context is intended to be neutral and not gender-specific. But then consider the resulting syllogism:

Man is a rational animal

Sophia is a man

Sophia is a rational animal

The second premise is simply false; Sophia's rationality, unlike the rationality of Socrates or any other male, cannot be demonstrated syllogistically. Socrates, by virtue of his sex, is a man and therefore rational. Sophia, by virtue of her sex, is not a man and therefore her rationality cannot be "proven" syllogistically and is therefore suspect.

Imagery

Whenever philosophers are called upon for examples, analogies, metaphors, illustrations, etc., they draw them from the male world, presuming a masculine point of view and assuming masculine sympathies and concerns in their audience or whatever—as in the examples already referred to above: Schultz's face-to-face encounters; Socrates' rationality. The point I want to emphasize is that in most of these cases you cannot just replace the male-specific gender term by female-specific terms and retain the sense of the example. For replacing male terms by female terms (and there are few really neutral terms) *changes the meaning of the paradigm* or demonstration. It is in this way that women are "ignored," "squeezed out," "concealed," "crushed," i.e. oppressed, in the very activity of philosophy— to say nothing of its institutions which I have not yet really discussed.

215

About hypothetical cases, paradigms, examples: the agent in philosophical discourse is always male. Women appear, if at all, only as adjuncts of men's lives along with their private property, their essential needs and so forth; but always as objects vis-à-vis male subjectivity — as men's wives, men's mistresses, men's mothers, men's sisters and daughters, or, most importantly, as mothers of men's sons. They appear most often and most consistently as occasions of male weakness or irrationality — as occasions of "sin," temptation, immorality or passion — and most especially as occasions of men's *anger* or violence. (We are told to imagine that John Doe has just had a row with his wife...)

A very good example which illustrates all these points was provided by John King-Farlow in the paper he read at the University of Ottawa, just a few weeks before this presentation, on *Akrasia, Self-Mastery and the Master Self.* He offered three, what he called "common garden" examples: first, a small Greek polis "out of whom 40 adult males comprise the political assembly," which was the focal point of the illustration; next, a "Here and Now" common garden example consisting of "two travelling salesmen who are middle-aging bachelors... negotiating how to spend an evening away from home" whose options were as follows:

Ted

1. *Having a lot to drink slowly with a companion (85)*
2. *Search for a motherly wife in Victoria's better drinking lounges (75)*
3. *Feeling good for work tomorrow on Vancouver Island (70)*
4. *Sober long distance conversation with mother (65)*
5. *Having a lot to drink quickly with a companion (35)*

Bob

1. *Having a lot to drink quickly with a companion (70)*
2. *Sober long distance conversation with mother (65)*
3. *Search for a motherly wife in Victoria's better drinking lounges (60)*
4. *Having a lot to drink slowly with a companion (55)*
5. *Feeling good for work tomorrow on Vancouver Island (50)*

The message is clear: women, like alcohol, are ways to spend the time when a man is at loose ends. Women are distractions, pastimes and caterers to men's needs. Man is the agency, woman the adjunct. To add insult to injury, these options were then *quantified* as indicated in the brackets.

Finally, his last and "central case of Akrasia" was the following:

> In Dallas a distinguished, but overweight, diabetic guest speaker with high blood pressure is offered a huge plate of chocolate mousse at a large, hard-drinking party with a Texasly lavish buffet. Hermes has confined himself to celery sticks and clam juice for hours of mingling with long winded, pseudo-egalitarian hostpersons. [Guess what sex these supposedly neutrally identified persons were.] A *Persona*, Hermes-as-desirer-primarily-of-any-refreshing-and-fortifying-food-immediately-lest-he-drop, is giving a less crude version of the same message ... Hermes experiences a strain within himself from many conflicting messages, arguments and urges. The Master Self, Hermes-as-committed-to-various-virtuous-goals (which-rule-out-the-mousse), continues with admirable effort to strive to uphold his health and his vows to his worried family. He refuses the mousse graciously but suddenly notices that his wife is holding hands a few yards away with a man he has told her to avoid [sic!]. He is shaken by anger... the Master Self loses almost all that sense of well-being and recognized authority which usually makes striving a welcome business. The plate of mousse, it happens, is offered again by an attractive admirer from a local college for young ladies. And so, like a hired giant on a tug-of-war team, whose sudden pique induces him to strive on, yet to strive just a little too fatally less hard, Hermes' Master Self labours on for abstinence but still lets Hermes reach out for the mousse...[13]

Notice that the occasions for weakness of will are precipitated ultimately by women—in their conventional roles as wife or temptress—and this is a very typical example.

The ironic thing about this particular case is that before hearing the paper, or even knowing its title, I had asked the speaker if he knew of any systematic work that had been done on the sexism of philosophical imagery. He gave an immediately defensive response... asking what could I possibly mean, what did I have in mind, how could an image be sexist, etc., etc.? (He must have been embarrassed about his Master Self!) But he then proceeded, patronizingly, to make unintelligent and unintelligible concessions to my suggestion by referring at the beginning of his paper to the "Master *or Mistress* Self". But of course that was laughable—Mistress is not the female equivalent of Master—and especially laughable given the role of women in this particular paper. He soon stopped trying to modify or conceal the implicit sexism of his paper, for even he could hear its ludicrousness. But he was right to see something objectionable in the choice of terminology. A Master Self is

217

peculiarly masculine. For a woman to accept this kind of talk and attribute to herself a Master Self would be for her to internalize and reproduce *within her psyche*, within her own self-consciousness, the male domination and oppression she experiences in the public world. As far as I was concerned as a woman, King-Farlow's *Akrasia, Self-Mastery and the Master Self* was another non-starter of a philosophy paper which no amount of doctoring could save. Its very substance depended upon the notion of Mastery; and women do not master, they are mastered.

This particular example reveals all of what I wanted to show about philosophy's imagery but I can add a few more general cases for emphasis.

Sartre

It is clear on reading Sartre that the For-itself, the essentially human, is really essentially male. It is threatened by and can be compromised, consumed, sucked-in and possessed by the In-itself, the essentially non-human and contingent, which is consistently identified with the feminine in Sartre's work — both philosophical and literary. The women in his novels and plays, for example, *do* nothing: they are passive recipients of the actions of others — they are done to, or things happen to them, but *they* do nothing. And in both forms of work, the In-itself is associated with holes and slime, just as is the female sex. For example

The For-itself is suddenly compromised. I open my hands, I want to let go of the slimy and it sticks to me, it sucks at me... It is a soft, yielding action, a moist and feminine sucking... I cannot slide on this slime, all its suction cups hold me back... It is a trap... Slime is the revenge of the In-itself. A sickly-sweet feminine revenge which may be symbolized on another level by the quality sugary.[14]

The obscenity of the feminine sex is that of everything which gapes open... In herself woman appeals to a strange flesh which is to transform her into a fullness of being by penetration and dissolution. Conversely, woman senses her condition as an appeal precisely because she is "in the form of a hole." This is the true origin of Adler's complex. Beyond any doubt her sex is a mouth and a voracious mouth which devours the penis... The amorous act is the castration of the man; but this is above all else because sex is a hole.[15]

218

I played distractedly with her sex... Ants were running
everywhere, centipedes and ringworm. There were even more
horrible animals: their bodies were made from a slice of toast,
the kind you put under roast pigeons; they walk side-ways with
legs like a crab. The larger leaves were black with beasts. Behind
the cactus and the Barbary fig trees, the Velleda of the public
park pointed a finger at her sex. "This park smells of vomit," I
shouted.[16]

Ryle

A very quick (three-minute) survey of a very few pages
of Gilbert Ryle's *Concept of Mind*, his chapter on "Knowing
How and Knowing That," produced the following list of
images — all of them drawn from a world which is pretty well
exclusively male: doing anagrams, climbing mountains,
training soldiers, scoring bull's eyes, and reading maps; a
drunkard playing chess, a schoolboy learning geometry; the
boxer, the surgeon, the poet, the salesman, the judge's bench,
the lorry-driver's seat, the studio, the football field, the
railway signal-box; tying a clove-hitch, pulling a trigger,
high-diving. References were also made to the following:
Napoleon, Boswell, Aristotle, Plato, Johnson... and, finally,
Jane Austen.[17]

Strawson

An even briefer glance at the first few pages of
Individuals, where there is, in fact, little imagery, proferred
just two examples, but both fitted the masculine stereotype:
we were introduced to a man and a boy standing by a fountain,
and a paternal grandfather. (Note their exclusively male
orientation.)[18]

Various

Unfortunately, I have not been able to do a systematic
study of the sexist imagery in philosophy — there are, needless
to say, more urgent demystifications to be realized — but I
have always balked at the following peculiarly,

and perhaps exclusively, masculine ways of interpreting the world:

- Hume's billiard-ball theory of causality
- the "battle-field" imagery of philosophical discourse, whereby you "advance" an argument or proposition, "defend" it against inevitable "attack" from the "opposition," "marshall" your evidence, "reduce" your opponent, or "destroy" him, or "retreat" to a safer position... etc.
- Plato's "philosopher-king," Hegel's "master-slave," and everybody's "Master Self"
- Austin's preference for "trouser-words"
- the definition of liberty in terms of private property and the selling of labour, and of moral and political rights and obligations in terms of contracts—all of which women have been excluded from until very recently and only in certain special circumstances even now do they have access to these "necessary conditions" of "civil" life
- the appropriation of reproductive labour and value by philosophers who "give birth" to ideas and the mystification of this essentially ideal and illusory "creativity" into the "truly human" creation of a "truly human" nature—non-sexual and non-physical, and therefore, we are told, superior to natural forms of creativity.

Institutional Exclusion

Finally, more biographical anecdotes to show how women are excluded from philosophy as a practice and a social institution: by intimidation; by not being taken seriously (neither as persons nor as philosophers); and by simply not being seen.

Undergraduate experience: At my undergraduate university in England it was common knowledge that the professor of the department, a well-known international philosopher and therefore someone whose approval and respect could stand you in good stead, did not like women. In fact, I did take his course and found him patronizing—not so much to myself, but to the two other women in the class, with whom he was "kind" and condescending in argument, while he was usually quite acerbic and witty. A second member of the department was known to "like" women, favour them in his class, and invite them to his house for tea. In fact, he sought their "pity" and sympathy, having recently been left by his wife, who had a reputation for, as they say, running around with the students. A third professor, again of international repute and a rising young star at the time, was also known to "like" women; but he liked to "bed" them and seduce them into the "guru syndrome." He was especially fond of the first year students, who were courted and bedded with speed and incredible heartlessness. A fourth professor, advisor to graduate students, responded to my requests for information on graduate school with: "We only like to recommend serious candidates for Master's scholarships." I wondered why he considered me unserious — I had an excellent record in the philosophy department, though I was, and am still known to be capable of laughing at some of the more ponderous pomposities of philosophers. It was clearly my sex which counted against my seriousness. And still people wonder why there are no women in philosophy!

Master's level: Recognizing that it would be difficult to establish credibility in England, I came to the New World. Again, the same story — X doesn't like women. I took X's class and found him very patronizing and incapable of seriously criticizing my paper. He had only one comment upon it, which was that I argued eloquently; but, of course, he could not agree with me. Of course not, for that would be like being like a woman, right? And I was arguing against dualism, after all. I came to the university with a man who was at the time my husband. I met him in England when I had already bought my air-ticket and had established my place in Canada. Nevertheless, the assumption in the department was that I had followed him here (he was doing nuclear physics), and had decided to do a Master's degree in philosophy while I was here (instead of playing bridge or doing voluntary work, I suppose). One graduate, who subsequently went off to Oxbridge — where people do "real" philosophy — constantly accused me of not being a "real philosopher" because I was so iconoclastic towards the tradition and because I rejected the dualisms of most philosophic discourse and didn't think it was important to teach first year undergraduates Plato, Aristotle or Descartes. By this time, parties were getting difficult, too, because I had more to say to the men, who were my colleagues, yet despised and deplored their attitudes to their wives or women who were expected to stand around and listen to this in-talk. In many respects I had more in common with their female friends, by virtue of being a woman, but they mistrusted me because I was not playing my part. Isolation. Nevertheless, I managed to complete my three courses and write my thesis within a year—and at the same time entertain both parents and parents-in-law for a total of six weeks while my husband was tied up, often for 18-hour days, in the heady man's world of nuclear physics. Nevertheless, I liked it better in Canada and wanted to stay and continue to do my Ph.D. But the same husband did not like it and refused to stay any longer. So I quit and disappeared to Africa for two years. He did not like it there either and returned to England. But this time I did not follow him. After a three-year absence, I returned to Canada to do a Ph.D.

Doctoral level: By this time, I had accumulated four years' teaching experience and a Master's degree and applied to teach a course to assist me with my doctoral studies. I did not get one; I was told that no courses were available. I had made my application in writing in February, and orally again in July, so I was not late. In the course of the academic year I learned of several students who were teaching courses. (I was working in the library at night and weekends at $2.40 an hour.) These students had two things in common: they were male and they had wives (though only one of them had children). Some of them had not even completed Master's degrees and some had never taught before. This is when I began to realize that I was *invisible;* or if not invisible, *not welcome.* I made a fuss about this distribution of courses among graduate students, and was given one to teach in the summer. When I went into the department to submit my book-order list, the secretary looked surprised and observed that I was not teaching this course. More outrage, more protest. The excuse: professors don't always make up their minds, and they had forgotten that they had promised a course to a particular professor for the summer. I observed that I had no other source of money and perhaps they could be less indulgent towards their professors and more concerned about the welfare of their graduate students. I was told, by the dean of the faculty himself, that it was not the business of the department to worry about their students' welfare. I suggested that it was. I was also told that the particular course I was supposed to teach was a "sensitive" one—it was a compulsory course—and therefore they needed to express how seriously they took it by assigning a "fully fledged" professor. It turned out that the professor in question was less fully fledged than myself in many respects: he had little, if any, teaching experience, and had not yet completed his doctorate degree, yet was hired as a full-time teacher for the following academic year. But he was, of course, a man. I learned that there was one precedent for what had happened to me. Some years previously, a graduate student had been given a course, then had it taken away. That student was also female; and East Indian.

I went to my first Canadian Philosophical Association (C.P.A.) meeting. Just prior to that, I met a professor of political science while I was reading *Capital*. His opener went something like this: "What's a nice young thing like you doing reading *Capital*...?" Despite this, I welcomed his attention (like a fool), since no-one else from my own department had considered having a philosophical conversation with me. This professor warned me against going to the C.P.A. because everyone assumes that women go there only to carouse and be caroused and curry favour with some influential academic and that I would be expected to sleep with professors there, and if not, presumed to be doing so anyway. Now, all of this may be a pile of nonsense, i.e. it may have little basis in fact; but as an ideology it's pretty powerful and in many respects quite paralyzing for a woman. At the C.P.A. I was aware of one woman who gave a paper (things have improved since then) and she was the girlfriend of a better known and well established figure in the philosophical world. I was also caroused, as they say. Q.E.D.

In my remaining five years as a doctoral student, only one professor in the department of philosophy took me seriously as a philosopher — read my material with interest, and exchanged ideas; and he I met socially rather than professionally. I accumulated many more anecdotes, of course, but I think the point in question has been made. Women are excluded from philosophy, one way or another — either by intimidation (X does not like women; X Y does like women; X Y Z cannot speak or even see women unless they are appended to a man, or seeking to be so); or by negation (what's a nice young thing like you doing reading *Capital*?); or by discrimination (we are just invisible as possible philosophers); or by out-and-out rejection (it is not the business of the department to worry about students' welfare; the voice of Man is the voice of Reason, so either speak like a Man or get out of philosophy... etc.).

What is to be done?

Both theoretical and practical work within institutions is called for. With respect to theory, there must be more feminist criticism of the history of ideas and of the institutionalized systems of exclusion in philosophy to reveal the deep structures of patriarchy which constitute them both and maintain the exclusion of women from philosophy and their oppression within it. In addition, feminists must reconsider and reconstruct philosophical thought in the light of *women's specific experience* and those modes of being human which have been systematically excluded from "serious" philosophical discourse in the past.

In particular, women's relation to *reproduction* must be made central to both the critique of the old and the creation of a new philosophical discourse. Although philosophers have been traditionally concerned with "universals" and with the "essentials" of being human, they have, up until now, seen no place in their wisdom for a discussion of the cultural relevance of sexuality, birth, childhood or reproduction—or of the specific consciousness which goes along with these modes of being human. These central and pivotal moments of existence have been traditionally relegated to the "particular," the "accidental" or the "biological" *natural* life of "man," and on that account excluded from any philosophical reflection which aspires to focus on the essentially human or cultural aspects of his (sic) existence.

These omissions occur, I presume, because men themselves play so small a part in the reproductive process. (Only copulation requires their active participation.)[19] They cannot afford to grant to it any *essentially* human significance, for then they would be obliged to concede that theirs is, after all, only a *partial* and incomplete perspective on humanity and thus hardly an appropriate basis for their assertion and articulation of supposedly universal and/or objective truths. (If he cannot do it, then it cannot be human, for he is the self-appointed norm of humanity; if she can do it, then she must be Other than human in this respect, and she and her processes must be controlled, mastered by those in whom essential humanity resides.)

Yet birth is both universal and necessary, and sex a necessary foundation of birth, and reproductive practice necessarily social and socially necessary: it creates value, provides for the continuity of the species, is historical, conscious,

224

intentional... and so forth.[20] However, instead of acknowledging the reality and human significance of these *real* material reproductive processes and relations, philosophers, scientists and politicians alike have continually posited and aspired to *ideal* cultural and non-biological principles of beginning, self-determination and independence; and granted no social, moral, intellectual, physical or historical significance to real biological reproduction in return. It is held (by those who know so little about it) to have nothing in it that could move humanity to thought or action (transcendence); to be not *praxis*, therefore, but mindless biological process. And indeed social and political institutions have done their best to make this true by penalizing women who attempt to assume autonomous and self-determining control over their own sexuality and reproductive possibilities. Marriage, abortion, prostitution and rape laws, for example, strip women of their reproductive *praxis* and subject them to a process which they neither determine nor control.

At the level of ideology, birth, for example, has never been considered a worthy subject for philosophical reflection (in my opinion, this is because men are not its agents), while death has always been so dignified (and men have exercised their physical and mental prowess through the ages devising myriad ways of administering it). The ideological hegemony of death over birth is so fundamental to our ways of thinking the human that even Simone de Beauvoir pays homage to it in what many consider an explicitly feminist work, *The Second Sex*. She assumes that "it is not in giving life but in risking life that man is raised above the animal," and makes this the premise of her supposedly historical (?) and dialectical explanation of women's oppression and female "immanence." Birth has been denied, negated, denigrated and concealed at the level of ideas so that Man can "make himself." From Plato to Sartre the philosophical and political subject has constituted himself as autonomous subject without ever getting born. And even revolutionary Marxist man conceives of "material," "history," "labour" and "liberation" in exclusively *productive* terms, leaving no room for women's reproductive labour in its account and thus excluding women once again from the project of "human" liberation.

This systematic obfuscation of reproduction in philosophical discourse renders that discourse ideological — both mystifying (presenting partial truths as the whole truth) and reifying (presenting those partial truths as non-historical timeless truths). Feminist philosophers must explode that ideology from *below* by asserting the difference between men and women which has been traditionally suppressed (their different relation to reproduction, as praxis and consciousness) and the value of the experience (women's) which has been obfuscated. Our consciousness of self, time, space, nature, the other, language, knowledge, freedom and necessity, etc., is rooted in a quite different experience (both productive and reproductive) from that of men, and its articulation must be one of our foremost goals.

We must at the same time acknowledge the *political* dimension of a feminist philosophical praxis and remind ourselves continually of the threat to philosophy which admitting women into it *as women* (and not as female men) poses — and prepare ourselves to cope with these political realities (LeDoeuff 1977). For example, like any other institutionalized knowledge, philosophy will lose status and men will lose some of their male privilege if women are admitted. More importantly, philosophy (and philosophers) will be exposed: they will lose their mask as the repository of universal, objective, impersonal, abstract, rational, ordered, apolitical knowledge or truth. And objectivity will be revealed as itself value-laden, serving the interests of male (and class) superiority; as do the concepts of rationality, justice, equality, freedom, knowledge, progress... and so forth. Traditional dichotomies will be similarly exposed (and once more men themselves), and discredited as intellectual or phenomenological givens.

The presumed splits between public and private, rational and emotional, cultural and natural, mental and physical, objective and subjective, universal and particular, sacred and profane, knowledge and belief, subject and object — and male and female, of course — are constitutive of philosophical discourse and academic discourse generally (as other articles in this collection indicate). The first element in each pair of opposites (according to the tradition, differences are oppositional) is aligned with "Man" as the essential human nature; and the second element with that which threatens "Man's" uniqueness, order and freedom. It is associated with Man's "eternal" Other, against whom, or which, he pits both brain and brawn — conquering nature, as they are wont to say. Woman appears along with this Other, as that which threatens the uniqueness of Man.[21]

It is not surprising, then, that women are not welcome in philosophy. For in many respects philosophers will lose their *raison d'être* if they admit women into their discourse; they will lose their Other, their object, and therefore their own identity as Subject, Reason, Order, Norm—Humanity itself. And they will be forced to be truly *reflective, i.e. to reflect upon themselves*. In the dialectic between master and slave, the master's (ontological?) need of the slave is far greater than the material dependency of the slave on the master. Without the slave, the master is nothing. Admitting women into philosophy will oblige the former masters to contemplate this—their own nothingness. And, finally, admitting women into philosophy will deprive the larger patriarchal social system of its traditional rationalizations and legitimations of the sexual division of labour which is the condition of possibility of institutionalized male dominance, in philosophy as much as anywhere else. There are very real, immediate and personal, social, and political consequences to admitting women into philosophy. Who, for example, will do the family maintenance work for philosophers once philosophy is demystified? And so the *economics* of the "logocentric-phallocentric illusion of omnipotence" of abstract knowledge will be exposed (Le Doeuff 1977).

Finally, feminists have to constantly wrestle with the problem of language and traditional theory: from what position can one speak as a feminist philosopher? One cannot assume the alienated and alienating, falsifying and oppressive language and voice of the tradition. Yet one must address one's critique and creative work to that tradition, for that is where our historical and immediate social and philosophical reality lies. Somehow we have to straddle that fine line between co-option and separation, both of which render us invisible and ineffective in our efforts to create new forms of thinking, speaking and being our humanity. Quite a task.

With respect to practical institutional changes, the task is more formidable and my suggestions more tentative. Ruling institutions can be changed only from the inside, and women are not yet within philosophy. Nor will they be so, nor will philosophy change significantly, unless the larger context of social and material life is radically transformed. But we must work where we can, and in philosophy we must agitate for the following:

1) At the institutional level there must be compensatory praxis, i.e. purposeful efforts to admit women into philosophy. However, one recommends this with some caution, knowing how entry into and survival within an institution more often than not lead to

co-option and the adoption of the institution's values and practices; and we do not want women to be institutionalized in philosophy along with men. But preferential hiring must be encouraged, not only in fairness to women and to redress past injustices, but for sound pedagogical and philosophical reasons. Women must be *invited to* teach, sought out and encouraged to participate in the field.

2) Job-sharing should be established as a possible option. This would permit more women into philosophy — two instead of one — as well as contribute to the breakdown of the prestige structure of academia, and provide something of a basis for undermining the individualism and competitiveness of philosophy, which, as in other professions, operates to the disadvantage of women who are not socialized for success on these terms. Joint authorship of papers should also be introduced for similar reasons, whereby no one person is considered the single "subject" of the philosophical enterprise — as indeed no one person is.

3) Women themselves must unite and organize and act together in recognition of their shared specific interests in philosophy, to seek out the structures of their oppression and strategies for combatting it. Men will not willingly give up their position of advantage, their "world-historical victory" over the female sex. They will not admit women *on their own terms* without a fight because they really do have a lot to lose by doing so. If we have a presence in philosophy now it is only at men's discretion and for as long as they choose to permit it. But feminists know that men also have a lot to gain from admitting women *as women* into philosophy. It is up to us to make them realize this — not with an argument, but through a collective authentic feminist philosophical praxis.

Post-script

Interestingly enough, the paper did have some positive effects on the philosophy department in question. First, it generated discussion by naming the previously un-named. More importantly, it united the women (not all of them, of course) in the department. For example, the one full-time (one-

year replacement) female professor, whom I had not seen at any previous weekly session, introduced herself, expressed solidarity with the contents of the paper and committed herself to giving a paper—which she did. Likewise, L. expressed solidarity and also committed herself to giving a joint paper, which she also subsequently did. My paper initiated a very spirited and creative dialogue between the women of the department, and between a few of the men and the women, which reverberated in the corridors for months afterwards, quite transforming the former seminarian (though hardly seminal) slumber. This provided the necessary basis for genuine solidarity and commitment which made possible a very successful, dynamic and exciting—though small—annual weekend conference at Ottawa of the Canadian Society for Women in Philosophy (S.W.I.P.) in the Fall of the same year. And it led to the public presentation of more feminist papers at two subsequent Philosophia meetings.

Secondly, the department did explicitly seek a female to fill one (though only one!) of the two full-time tenure-track positions which became available in the next year. They did not, however, invite me for an interview: my bridges have been clearly burned! Nor did they end up hiring a woman. The hiring committee could not agree on which of three possible candidates (none of whom presented herself as a feminist, by the way) was the most desirable for the position. They prevaricated so long, in fact, that the Faculty of Arts closed the positions. So the University of Ottawa's philosophy department remains a bastion of male-stream thought still.* In the meantime, and not surprisingly, the "feminist movement" within it seems to have burned itself out. Let us hope it is only recuperating its energies.

FOOTNOTES

1. Check, for example, the response of male academics to my own discussion of "Why Althusser Killed His Wife" in *Canadian Forum*, Sept./Oct. 1981. The suggestion that Althusser's political and philosophical ideas may have had any connection with his "personal" *praxis* is usually received as anathema and with much more personal outrage than the fact that he did indeed murder his wife.

---

* As of December 1982, one woman has been hired in a tenure-track position.

2. Quoted by Carol Gould, from Kant's *Observations on the Beautiful and the Sublime*, in her essay "Philosophy of Liberation and the Liberation of Philosophy" in Gould 1976:18.
3. Fichte, *The Science of Rights*, quoted by Gould (1976:19).
4. Schopenhauer, "On Women" in Gould 1976:19.
5. Rousseau, *Emile*, Everyman, p. 350, quoted in LeDoeuff 1977:5.
6. Hegel, *Philosophy of Right*, para. 166, Zusatz trans. Knox, pp. 263-64, in LeDoeuff 1977:5.
7. Comte, *Système de politique positive*, Tome II, in LeDoeuff 1977:5.
8. LeDoeuff 1977:2. The analysis which follows concerning women's access to philosophy draws heavily on LeDoeuff's ideas in this particular article.
9. See Neal Ascherson's review essay, "Love and Revolution", review of *Comrade and Lover: Rosa Luxemburg's Letters to Leo Jogiches*, edited and translated by Elzbieta Ettinger, *New York Review of Books*, March 6, 1980:

   "...in her difficult and often exasperating relationship with the socialist leader Leo Jogiches, she was confronting a cluster of problems which the modern women's movement has come to identify very clearly.

   "She had to overcome the guru-disciple syndrome. It's a common enough pattern for clever women: a girl who assumes her own intellectual inferiority forms a sexual and mental bond with a man who is her teacher and authority in politics as well as her first important lover. Sooner or later the girl begins to assert her own intellectual independence and value, sometimes — as in this case — soaring far above the "teacher-lover," and grows to resent his assumption of authority. This emancipation can be a shattering and prolonged struggle, which usually involves the breaking, however reluctant, of the sexual bond." (p. 14).

10. "The reason why men (both now and in the past) can go beyond the initial transference, and why the love component of their transference is sublimated or inflected from the very beginning, so that it can return to the theoretical, is that the institutional framework in which the relationship is played out provides the third factor which is always necessary for the breaking of the personal relationship; the women amateurs, however, have been bound to the dual relationship because a dual relationship does not produce the dynamics that enable one to leave it. The result of imprisonment in such a relationship is that philosophising women have not had access to philosophy, but to a particular philosophy, which, it seems to me, is something very different. Their relationship to the philosophical is limited, from outside the theoretical field, by the relationship from which they could not possibly detach themselves..." (LeDoeuff 1977:4).

11. "There is one area where women today have completely free access, that of classic works of the history of philosophy. No-one considers studies by Marie Delcourt, Geneviève Rodis-Lewis, or

Cornelia de Vogel as 'women's books' to be read with indulgence and condescension. Is this because these women impose on themselves 'the austere necessity of a discipline', so finding the 'third factor' on which they depend in order to direct the desire to philosophise towards the theoretical field? How is one to interpret the fact that our elders succeeded in getting themselves respected and recognized for commentaries or editions, whilst none of them produced such texts as *The Phenomenology of Perception* or *The Critique of Dialectical Reason?* That women should be admitted to the commemorative history of philosophy seems to me to be primarily a reflection of what is generally held to constitute a commentary. Who better than a woman to show fidelity, respect, and remembrance? A woman can be trusted to perpetuate the words of the Great Discourse: she will add none of her own." (LeDoeuff 1977:10).

12. These examples are taken from Janice Moulton's "Sexism in Ordinary Language" in Vetterling-Braggin *et al.* 1978:124-138.

13. John King-Farlow, "Akrasia, Self-Mastery and the Master Self," p. 17.

14. Sartre, *Being and Nothingness*, translated by Hazel Barnes (New York: Washington Square Press, 1972), pp. 776-777. Quoted in Margery Collins & Christine Pierce, "Holes and Slime: Sexism in Sartre's Psychoanalysis" in Gould 1976:117.

15. Sartre, *op. cit.*, p. 777, in Gould 1976:118.

16. Sartre, *Nausea*, translated by Lloyd Alexander (New York: New Directions Publishing Corporation, 1964), p. 59. Quoted by Collins & Pierce in Gould 1976:119.

17. Gilbert Ryle, *The Concept of Mind* (London: Barnes & Noble, 1949).

18. P.F. Strawson, *Individuals: An Essay in Descriptive Metaphysics* (London: University Paperbacks, Methuen, 1959).

19. For a detailed and thorough examination of the value created by reproductive labour and an analysis of the philosophical and political tradition's neglect of that value, and appropriation of it in terms of the creation of men's "second nature," see O'Brien 1981.

20. See Mary O'Brien, "Reproducing Marxist Man" in Clark & Lange 1979:99, and O'Brien 1981.

21. For a more detailed exploration of this theme, see Finn 1982.

CHAPTER 10

The Personal is Political: Feminism and the Helping Professions

Helen Levine

Helen Levine teaches in the School of Social Work at Carleton University, Ottawa, where she is concerned with developing a strong feminist presence in and beyond the curriculum. She has been politically active since 1947 in such groups as the Jewish People's Order (Toronto), the Campaign for Nuclear Disarmament, and the Ottawa Committee to End the War in Vietnam. Since the 1960's, she has been primarily active in the women's movement. She wrote a column on feminist counselling in *Upstream*, a feminist magazine, for two years; worked in Ottawa to help establish Interval House, feminist counselling services and a lesbian/therapist study group; and is a founding member of a feminist group for women over 50 years of age, called the Crones. As well as being active locally, she speaks and presents workshops around the country and has published feminist critiques of the helping professions, motherhood and aging.

*"The bullets of psychobable invade the ears of Everywoman,
informing her in a thousand tongues of her Sickness and need
for Help. This invasion continues unchecked because it fixes
women's attention in the wrong direction, fragmenting and
privatizing perception of problems, which can be transcended
only if understood in the context of the sexual caste system."*

(Daly 1978)

Introduction

There is tremendous opposition to even considering
women, a sex, as an oppressed group. The definition intrudes
on every women's and man's existence. The oppression of
women in its various forms is so rampant and so old that it is
seen by men and by some women as normal and natural.

Contemporary feminist thought, building on feminist
movements of the past, describes the world as one historically
defined by men and for men, with women seen primarily as
property, as modern servants within and outside the home,
and as marginal to the fundamental issues of historical
struggle and change.

Women have been taught to define the central and
primary task of our lives as marriage and motherhood. We
have been conditioned to view happiness and contentment
within restrictive and limiting contexts. Often the absence of
severe problems with a mate, rather than the presence of a
rich and challenging life, is seen as the good life for women.
Men somehow manage to be husbands, fathers and workers.
Women are not supposed to aspire to such an integration of life
if it is in any way disruptive to others, in any way impinges
significantly on men and their needs and aspirations, or on the
lives of children. This is partly what patriarchy is all about.

The female prescription for education, work, marriage
and motherhood constitutes a crippling control of girls' and
women's hopes, plans and possibilities. Women have been
directed to be primarily loyal to individual men in their lives,
to blame themselves and/or other women when troubles
emerge. Under such conditions, solidarity among women in
pursuit of change has been profoundly undermined.

Though both sexes are influenced by the ideology of
romantic, heterosexual love, there exists a decisive difference
in the ideology's impact upon women. For men, love enhances
adult life and work. For women, the meaning of love frequently
translates into a serious addiction to nurturing others which
robs us of the self, the centre of our own adult lives. It keeps us

234

"hooked" on the servicing of men and/or children in the name of love, mainly within the patriarchal structures of marriage and motherhood.

Joining Personal and Political

I would like to explain what I mean by the "personal and political," a concept you will find central to this piece. For me, the two are inextricably interwoven, so that the personal *is* political or vice versa.

It is by claiming and redefining the significance of women's struggles at the personal level — both internally and externally — that we can begin to understand our own experience, the common ground we share with other women. It is by addressing the political, that is, collective issues which have to do with men's power over women, work and the State, that we can begin to reshape the very systems and structures that exert decisive influences over every woman's life.

The artificially divided private and public spheres of life in this century are desperately in need of fusion; thus the determination of the contemporary women's liberation movement to weave the personal and political aspects of living into a unified whole. That movement has forged a new and important link for women between personal pain and political oppression. The link asserts that how women and men share their labour, money and decision-making power at the domestic level is at the same time political, and that how men dominate and control the public sphere — the State, industry, technology, the professions and the unions — is also personal; that politics itself must be redefined by women and men to account for paid and unpaid work, domestic responsibilities and social relations in both private and public spheres.

The personal and the political are dialectically involved in all our lives.

The Essential Feminist Framework — A Redefinition of Women's Reality

Across the planet earth, girls and women — a 52 per cent majority which is treated as a minority group — hold second class status and as a sex are subjected to economic, physical, psychological and sexual violence in daily living.

The violence takes myriad forms. It may mean being

235

physically battered, being segregated in low-paid job ghettoes, doing a lifetime of unpaid work in the home, being threatened, molested or raped within and beyond the family, having promotions or opportunities denied on the basis of gender, suffering considerably higher rates of unemployment and attempted suicide than men, living with blighted potential, being unable to walk the streets freely, carrying two jobs (paid and unpaid) instead of one, or seeing women reflected in the powerful media as figures of flesh, fun, fashions, and white washes.

Despite the myths of strong, competent men protecting weak, fragile women, most women have always worked — hard. We serve as unpaid labour in the home, and masses of employed women have been and are still underpaid, overworked, essential service workers in factories, hospitals, kitchens, restaurants, and offices.

"Women's work" provides our economic system with unpaid labour, reproductive labour and a reserve army of cheap labour. The traditional family includes husband as primary bread-winner and head of household, with his wage or salary maintaining and controlling a family unit; wife as financial dependent held responsible for servicing husband and children without pay; and wife also designated as potential "secondary" wage earner to be moved in and out of the work force as required. This economic arrangement serves to contain women as a sex, a caste, in the role of modern domestic servant.

As well as constituting half the membership of other oppressed groups — be we black, poor, immigrant, or native peoples — women as a sex are mainly relegated to low-paid, unpaid, non-decision-making service jobs. A racist/sexist mythology has been systematically constructed and profoundly entrenched about women's natural capacities, inclinations, and "choices" as a means of legitimating the exploitation. The mythology is rooted in a patriarchal system that creates and promotes a false consciousness about the nature and potential of women and men. It undermines our sense of value and significance in the world at the very core, teaches us that full, human, adult entitlements are not for us, and helps to drive women into subservient relations with men.

In the end, the reality of women and work is and has been historically hidden or distorted by the myths, fairy-tales, and superstructure of a male-defined system in whose economic and personal interest it was and is to keep women "in their place."

The other side of the coin is that women have been taught that the essence of being female is conforming, adapting, nurturing others, and looking sexy and young for men. The happiness of gentle self-sacrifice—enabling others to grow and to develop—is the pedestal reserved exclusively for women. We learn from childhood that we are to be primarily wives and mothers, secondary job holders when convenient, and sexual objects and decorations.

Women, like other minorities, internalize the norms, values and prescriptions of this society. Accordingly, we have a hard time growing confident, resourceful, self-focused and independent, or seeing ourselves as having any authority in the world. Trained to be the opposite, we are censured severely, directly and indirectly, if we exhibit what are seen to be masculine traits or behaviour. We are slotted into a particularly deadly responsibility in the traditional nuclear family. Here women are not only required to exchange domestic and sexual services for economic support, but are also generally held responsible for the happiness of mate and children. Family breakdown has consistently been blamed on women. If we work outside the home, we neglect the family. If we stay at home, we are placid and unmotivated. If we are active in community, we are social butterflies. Put men in any of these same slots and positive associations emerge: hard-working; dedicated to children; community-minded. The double standard relates to more than sexuality.

Women fear the dominant culture (men). Generally, we strive to please—to win approval—out of the fear of not being needed or wanted, or of being abandoned once having been chosen; we live with a basic insecurity, a low self-esteem, and a sense of inferiority; we try to be indispensable to family, friends and employers in order to survive economically and emotionally; we are frequently grateful for exploitive employment outside the home, for limited possibilities and low pay on the job; we marry to start life anew only to frequently find ourselves trapped into personal and economic dependency; we experience sometimes devastating rejection and punishment when we demand for ourselves what others have demanded of us, or expect to be nurtured instead of wishing to take care of others; we have, as do all oppressed groups, an underlying bitterness and anger about being rendered second class as a sex, living daily with the psychic and material abuse such a position implies.

One of the major consequences of the severely cir-cumscribed life pattern set for girls and women is that we gradually become split within ourselves. We are, on the one hand, aspiring towards becoming full and significant human beings in the world at large, and on the other, learning to be female. The latter demands that we give up the self, yield our own individual potential in the name of love, reason or normalcy. The main thrust of our lives, we are told, is to care for and about others.

The inevitable conflicts created by such a destructive prescription for women result in severe personal difficulties at one point or another in our lives. It is then that we are frequently perceived by the traditional helping professions as inadequate, abnormal or sick individuals who need to be assessed, diagnosed, treated — in fact, controlled. We are not and have not been seen by those same professions as a major oppressed grouping which is struggling with the poverty, subservience and indignity built into the very structure of our lives.

This is the feminist framework within which I want to consider a profound experience of my own that has relevance to the theory and practice of the helping professions. The point in sharing one woman's experience — any woman's experience — is to get at the commonalities in every woman's life, and to help fundamentally re-order the priorities of personal and political change.

A Personal and Political Experience

Beginning with my own experience, and connecting my struggles with those of other women, is for me central to being a feminist. Despite class and individual differences, despite uniqueness of temperament and personality, the broad outlines of all women's lives are strikingly similar.

I have been on both sides of the desk and the institution, as consumer and as provider of psychiatric services at different times in my life. One traumatic experience in middle age stands out, when I was hospitalized in 1973 for a severe depression. It would take volumes to fully describe my experiences and those of others I grew to know in a psychiatric hospital. Suffice it to say that I learned and grew from bitter experience far more than I ever had as a professional social worker.

The following are excerpts from my diary during a stay in a small female ward in one of the least objectionable of

238

psychiatric institutions in Ontario. Names are fictitious, facts are not. All doctors and senior administrators encountered were male. The hospital was a microcosm of male authority and female subservience (patients and staff) that is endemic to patriarchal institutions, structures and organizations.[1]

The diary

• *In the living room of a psychiatric hospital. Bona fide psychiatric patient. Dr. L. stressed that in his initial interview. Also threw questions at me like darts as if to say "I'm the guy who calls the shots, do as you're told." No visible concern for what I might be experiencing, no apparent sensitivity to the shock of my being transformed into a patient in a mental institution. In characteristic fashion, I rebelled, stopped, refused to reply. A magnificent beginning.*

• *Rules and regulations are all typed up, handed to me without explanation, make me wince. They rifle your purse and suitcase, allow you $5.00 per week for "tuck" and magnanimously introduce you to "privileges". You* earn *the privilege, for example, of going outdoors on hospital grounds. No, you may not play badminton in the gym since you only have group privileges (ward). Yes, you may go for a walk in a group if chaperoned. You are bit by bit demeaned, dehumanized and made to feel your fifth-class citizenship. As adult patient you are told what to do in minute detail. The "privilege system" is particularly obnoxious and humiliating, makes you feel like a criminal, a child, an object.*

• *Dr. L.'s orders for medication are unbelievable. Anti-depressant (Tofranil)—100 mgs. per day. Librium—5 mgs. four times a day. Sleeping pill (Noderol?) plus two muscular relaxants with it. Iron—my haemoglobin was 85. All in one day, in one person unaccustomed to drug intake. The name— chemotherapy. Chemo perhaps; therapy—my foot.*

• *I am dizzy and dazed as always from medication. My hands shake, my vision is blurred. Most everyone else looks and sounds the same, from medication, shock treatment or both. Reminds me of last summer's visit as social work observer to the operant conditioning ward of Douglas Hospital in Montreal. Not so devastatingly bleak this place, but the same grim flavour.*

• *R. came to visit tonight, my first visitor in this hellish institution. Tears to my eyes, a lump in the throat as I ponder*

239

the meanings of her visit. To have your own child come to see you in a psychiatric hospital. To experience you as one of many "mad" women in this frightening milieu. To have her see you helpless, dazed, repetitive from the giant doses of medication you accept against your will in the desperate hope that something, anything, will improve.

● *All ages in the ward. From 15-year-old E. to aged Mrs. W. This ward is considered to be the best to have landed in. People are said not to be so sick here, the atmosphere pleasant, compatible. My God, it's like appreciating the fact that your husband doesn't beat you.*

● *Poor Mrs. W. —she is old, sick, depressed and deteriorating. The nurses respond with a critique of her behaviour. "One mustn't be permitted to slip into dependency, to regress". So in the name of reality therapy, treatment or prevention of dependency, they leave her to wait, flounder, cry and suffer—alone.*

● *I have encountered only one nurse in this setting thus far who has any human conception of psychiatric nursing. It was she who knew enough to spend some time talking with me instead of handing out pills, orders, etc.*

● *A minor but hurtful early encounter with a nurse young enough to be my daughter. T. phoned and I asked the nurse for information re visiting, said it was long distance, would she check for me? Her response—complete indifference and no information. I told her afterwards that she might have been more helpful, more interested. She replied with a snappy retort, a bit of ugly, snide humour designed to put me in my "place" as mental patient.*

● *So many incidents to recap. The night I called home to say I was discharging myself and going to Montreal to stay with friends. Sobbing on the phone next to the nursing station, no privacy. Tidbits of comments from staff about Mrs. Levine being so hysterical and demanding, her poor husband, etc. Better to risk Montreal than to have my spirit shattered. Better to be a free wreck than an imprisoned soul.*

● *My husband phoned Dr. L. the next morning. Dr. L. responded (to a man?) by calling me in for a long session that was totally different in tone from the others. How could they make the situation more tolerable for me? He promised to check daily re side-effects of medication—personally. Diagnosis?—*

endogenous depression, meaning the kind that needs physical intervention, as opposed to reactive (loss, trauma, etc.), that requires therapy. Oh well, who in hell cares what the label is, if only the wretched depression lifts. Dr. L. offers me relative "freedom" in the hospital and the city with the proviso that the staff know I'm off in one direction or another.

• *There are at least four of us on this ward—all clearly middle class—who challenge orders and react openly and negatively to authoritarian approaches. It's a class thing, the business of dealing with staff. We four are given more leeway and more options because we demand them. The others tend to take orders unquestioningly—they know they're more vulnerable.*

• *The ward meeting of patients and nurses was an eye-opener. Nurses presented their gripes in the form of instructions, one of which was an objection to patients putting their feet on coffee tables. Guess who at that very moment had feet on table! I didn't move them. I felt uncertain, there had been enough difficulty in those first few days. But the feet stayed, almost automatically, whilst a few comments were made about such "universal truths" as lady-like behaviour. So much for the vital issues in helping patients recoup shattered lives.*

• *Patients said almost nothing at the ward meeting except for announcements of activities. And then it ended. I had been intrigued by the idea of this group, its possibilities. I know there have been all kinds of complaints and concerns and so afterwards asked G. why there were no comments, no grievances aired. The reply—fear, FEAR, **FEAR**. Patients are worried about the grapevine from most of the nurses to the doctors, their "dossiers", the repercussions that might arise if real problems were aired. So everyone keeps mum. It's power politics and the women are clear re who holds the power.*

• *Hmm! Lady-like behaviour! Reminds me of how the nurses refer to all of us as "ladies". It's a tainted word in this place. Has a contemptuous ring, an institutional smell. Ladies this and ladies that—a condescension that permeates doctors, nurses and administrators. Some noble exceptions among staff but a general atmosphere that puts patients in their place and drips with contempt.*

• *Talked with P. for a long time today—she had enjoyed R.'s guitar playing when she visited. P. is very depressed, not eating, mostly lies curled up on her bed under a blanket. A sad, wan face, a thin, frail body, in and out of hospital for the past few years. Would gladly end her life, past caring what happens. Husband an executive of a large company so P. feels she has to control her angry, negative feelings for his sake. Yet needs to let go. Put husband through college, now her turn to study but she can't concentrate. Has been told there is too much "child" in her, not enough "adult".*

- *C. and I laughing our heads off. She has a marvellous sense of humour, what a blessing in this humiliating and painful situation. We do yoga together at nights in her room. She looks like a zany blonde who hasn't an idea in her head. Yet she's one of the most interesting women I've met, observant, curious, self-educated.*

- *Much talk of the Ontario hospital today at lunch. D. is just finishing a series of 20 shock treatments, may get another 20 and her doctor has alluded to Ontario hospital a few times recently. Is this a threat? Is he preparing her? M. is depressed thinking she may end up there too. The air is loaded with fear.*

- *G. left today to go back to husband and five kids. Was given a list of six different types of medication to take daily. Feels very shaky, has been here before. I suggested she let him care for the five kids and have the next breakdown.*

- *"My husband and daughter seem to be getting along well... he has a lighter touch than I. An enormous burden slipped from my shoulders when I saw they were coping, with my husband taking over for the first time in a meaningful way. I feel less guilt. What a shift in emphasis from that ridiculously intense mothering role, being held solely responsible for whatever difficulties befall the children".*

- *A strange, awesome experience being with such a mixture of different kinds of human beings, most of whom I might never know in ordinary life. J., creative, restless, with her own special wisdom (committed by her husband, thought she was going out to tea that day). N., now much better, almost beaten to death by an alcoholic husband, has nightmares constantly. K., terrified of shock, had it once before—they are trying to pressure her into "consenting".*

- *Many patients go home weekends. Not so with me. I just can't be adjunct or homemaker any longer—that's out, and I will feel I should be if I am home. S. thinks I'm crazy, I have such a nice husband. B. agrees. How simple it all sounds, how complicated it all is.*

242

- *Women's liberation is badly needed here. The male doctors are in complete control and consciously or unconsciously deal with women's problems oppressively. The nurses are like colonials, doing all the real work and being ordered around by the doctors, then taking out their inevitable frustrations on patients.*

- *New patient, A., confides she is a nurse, asks me not to tell anyone. I tell her I had the same problem earlier on. It's tough to let go of that ridiculous professional image, to admit one's full membership in the human race without pretence.*

- *Took a fitness class today, it was great. Psychiatric settings should stress the physical instead of drugging everyone into oblivion. The doctors are really criminal drug pushers, except they don't get arrested like street people. Once patients are on medication and shock around here, they're beyond using exercise, the outdoors. It's all ass-backwards.*

- *I am boiling! So much distrust, so much snooping and not levelling with patients. J.'s husband turned her private writings from home over to the doctor today—as evidence! Husband complained she was so busy writing she didn't have his supper ready when he came home from work. Then the "expert" male doctor questions "his" female patient as to this seemingly inappropriate behaviour. My anger mounts by the minute—there must be a lot of rage buried deep in women in this god-damn patriarchal society.*

- *Saw O'Neill's "Long Day's Journey into Night" on T.V. I identified with the drug-addicted mother, smitten with guilt and anguish, repetitively going back to her early sorrows after marriage.*

- *A funny incident. I yawned, loudly. Three nurses run to my room. A hilarious moment, worthy of the Marx Brothers. Then I recall the night I was so sick and tortured and no one came or cared. Such is the irony of life in a psychiatric hospital.*

- *Poor Mrs. S., at 82, is getting more shock treatment. A bloody crime. Now that she is really feeble and depressed, the nurses are getting tougher. It's bloody dangerous to get worse in here. They like you less and control you more.*

- *K. had her first shock treatment today. She had refused consent, her husband finally gave his, and Doctor V.*

243

announced he would drag her down with orderlies if she didn't get with it. So much for patient consent, be it for shock, drugs or anything else.

  • I usually hide away when I cry. The snoopy staff, under medical direction, of course, record absolutely everything in this refined gestapo-like setting. They see psychiatric nursing as observing and recording every piece of behaviour and handing observations on to the doctors. Such stupidity. Patient as object, doctor as God, nurse as investigator. The good feeling I have today is that I don't give a damn what they record, that's ME.

  • Last night I brought out my song books and J. and I sang all the old nostalgic tunes. We even got Mrs. S., who wanders about dazed and fearful most of the time, to join in. Sure enough, she knew many of the words to songs like **Maggie** and **Endearing Young Charms**. Soon a group of patients congregated and we had a bit of fun. My God, it would be so easy for staff to create a better mood on the ward by just being human. Too bad they expend so much energy trying to appear mentally and morally superior.

  • S. told me all about her sex life. G. demands sex every night and even mid-afternoons, when possible. Gets furious if refused and reminds her she is being supported by him. Sounds as though he uses her like a machine. S.'s doctor seems to identify with the husband, asks how she would feel if G. were not interested in her sexually! Most doctors here are culture-bound M.C.P.'s.

  • I'd never put up with Doctor V. who rarely sees his patients. J. caught him in the hall recently to report the wretched side-effects of the latest needle he had prescribed. He insists on continuing, said "I wouldn't do anything to hurt you", and walked away.

  • A doctor here has published a book. In it, he says "equality in marriage is destructive, as in any 'management.'" He is for the equality of women outside of marriage, in society at large. This is precisely why women have to join the personal and political.

  • Lent my doctor **Women and Madness** by Phyllis Chesler. One of the male administrators peeked at the title and said, nauseatingly, "they sure go together". "Of course", said I, "in this rotten patriarchal system". J. was so impressed she insisted I put it in my diary.

  • I had made a decision about living away from home and a kind of terror descended on me re the decision and the aloneness. Despite the overwhelming fear, there is no going back.

244

Postscript. I stayed away from home for several months after leaving hospital. The marriage continued under changed arrangements. My husband and I lived together elsewhere part of the time while our house stood empty.

I think that after years of servicing the nuclear family, the house had come to symbolize my oppression as woman and my powerlessness and subservience as wife and mother. Though not the only factors in my breakdown, I somehow realized that my survival depended on not returning to the same set of circumstances, on a drastic re-ordering of the private sphere.

I resigned from shopping, cooking and primary parental responsibility. It meant a fundamental restructuring of daily living and unpaid work. We had grasped the fact that my survival and our survival together depended on change, not adjustment.

The re-ordering of domestic work was not a temporary phase, nor could it have been. It remains intact many years later. It has left me free, for the first time in my adult married life, to concentrate on my own interests and aspirations, to participate seriously in the public sphere.

A Feminist Commentary

As consumer, in and out of hospital, I was "helped," as were others, to see my problems as individual, pathological, personal and blameworthy. I was not helped — except by other patients, some friends and the women's movement — to see myself as only one of millions of women with similar life stresses and strains that cried out for political as well as personal solutions.

My experiences, particularly in hospital, taught me to distrust contemporary professionalism and institutions. Sometimes the most human and thus most effective staff were non-professional, everyday people such as nurses' aides and cleaning staff. Their humanity and simplicity seemed to have been better preserved than that of many professionals whose lives were primarily invested in careers and status. It was the former, for the most part, who could talk of their own lives as well as yours, who dealt humanely and respectfully with people's pain.

I now know that women are drugged, in and out of hospital, to keep us silent and subdued. I know that more and more women are resorting to alcohol and drugs in a desperation

245

born out of coping with and adjusting to unequal, subservient everyday lives. I know the deadly guilt, anxiety, and stress that are frequently borne by women in the wife-and-mother role. I know the pretence women try desperately to maintain about the joys of motherhood, the joys of sex, the joys of nurturing others, and the joys of self-denial and service. The social control of women works well for the patriarchy.

Looking back as a feminist, I realize that from childhood on, I, like other females, was systematically trained to believe that my success or failure in life would revolve centrally around marriage, motherhood, and the care and nurturance of others. I followed the sexist prescription—from my own free choice, I thought—and have since lived and struggled with the inherent personal and political contradictions embedded in it.

Had I not been saddled with central responsibility for the unpaid work and responsibility of the domestic sphere, and with yielding the core of my separate, adult life to others, I might well have developed parts of my life and potential that counted very much to me. My husband was worker, husband, father, with the centre of his life and interests intact. Why not me, and millions of other women helping to create and shape the world at many levels with our talents, wisdom and experience?

It was predictable that my mate, given his fit in a male-constructed world, would gain in confidence and competence throughout the years. And that I would lose. It was not for lack of trying (and seldom is). I worked outside the home part-time for many years. I was involved politically during most of my adult life. But whether at home, in the paid workplace or in political movements, I was locked into subordinate, service, adjunctive positions. Men led; I and other women followed, often questioning our own competence, our capacity for decision-making and leadership; always deferring, for one reason or another, to men.

During our daughters' teen years, conflicts raged between mother and daughters, not with father. He was busy with his important job and his important interests. He was, like most men, said to be preoccupied with "larger" issues. After all, wasn't it natural and normal for a mother to deal with personal and family struggles, to set unwelcome limits, to become the easy scapegoat, in the end to blame herself profoundly for the trials and errors of living and loving?

246

Two years after the diary entries in hospital, I wrote:

I would still be trapped and lost in a profound sense, if I had not, with the support of other women, struggled bitterly for my own personal, intellectual and occupational needs within the family. I now have an intense sense of urgency about my work, a whole area of life that I missed out on earlier as woman. It can never be made up and I am limited by a 52-year-old physical and emotional capacity to invest myself in my own goals.

The wisdom of age tells me nothing in life is absolutely equal. But for the rest of my active years in family and community I want primary consideration in my choice of pursuits and I need the personal support system my husband can provide—as I once did—to help make that possible. The women's movement has been an important countervailing support system for me in a culture heavily weighted in favour of men. It has helped me to struggle for a sense of centrality and importance, both personally and politically. Without that movement and the support it offers, I would not have understood that my behaviour and feelings are common to most women, rather than unique to me.

I have survived, by a hair's breadth thus far, the ups and downs of one woman's life. The struggle to maintain one's fight, one's confidence, and one's global perceptions is a daily one for any second class, powerless minority in this society. I consider my anger, my rebellion, my impatience, and my determination, to be precious, hard-won achievements, though I have been taught to be the opposite all of my life as woman. I am no longer willing to collude in the oppression of myself and other women—half the world—in the name of any profession or any movement for social change that does not actively, visibly and effectively promote the full and unequivocal citizenship of women.[2]

The Helping Professions—A Critique

The essence of contemporary professionalism is linked with the claim to power and authority vested in the professional by virtue of her/his specialized knowledge and training. The helping professions—psychiatry, psychology and social work—have historically located the key source of most personal pain and trouble within the individual and/or between members of a family. Accordingly, the emphasis in practice, regardless of intention, is focused upon individual pathology, faulty communication, deficits of personality, family dysfunction, and ultimately upon adjustment at the personal level.

A feminist critique of conventional counselling and therapy includes the serious charge that its theoretical underpinnings and its modes of practice have left us a legacy of scapegoating women. The theory, for example, of maternal deprivation reflects the emphasis both on psychologizing life experience and on inventing slick, sophisticated, and, in essence, cruel devices for holding women responsible for the outcome of personal and family life.

Be it family breakdown, delinquency or sexuality, the helping professions, reflecting patriarchy, manage to zero in on female rather than male culpability. As a result, women's search for help in clinics, hospitals, and agencies has frequently been disastrous. By and large, women have found that helpers stress adjustment rather than change; individual, not collective solutions; personal pathology instead of social conditions; weakness rather than strength; the psyche, unrelated to the economic and political conditions of women's lives; and the authority of male "experts," male management and male decision-makers, in and beyond the home.

Feminists hold these professionals responsible for negatively defining, categorizing and labelling women's struggles and behaviour—out of political context—whilst frequently finding good reasons, legitimate causes, for men's and children's difficulties. Even regarding questions of violence such as wife-battering, rape and sexual assault, the question is most often put in terms of what women do or do not provoke; what women should or should not do, or should or should not have done. Violence against women is the most clear-cut example of common criminal assault (by men) resulting in an examination of the victim's (women's) behaviour as cause.

Prior to the contemporary women's movement, psychiatry, psychology and social work did not judge these issues worthy of attention, either theoretically or in practice. It was contemporary feminists who exposed rape and wife-battering; who connected and made visible the personal and political implications of such male behaviour in and beyond the family; who set up women's centres, rape crisis services, and transition houses for battered women and their children, usually without benefit of the money, buildings, staff, or status enjoyed by the helping professions.

It is becoming more and more obvious to more and more people that the mental health theories we use in our work, on a day-to-day basis, contain a great deal of folklore in the guise of scientific knowledge. Many of our mental health theories reinforce cultural assumptions about women — that woman's prime, if not only role, is to be wife and mother; that woman's place is to nurture man; that women, in order to be considered mentally healthy, should be submissive, dependent, compliant, sensitive, emotional, unassertive. Healthy women are expected to be content with, or actually seek out, a life of self-sacrifice, in which the needs of others are seen as more important than their own.[3]

Modern feminism and its by now considerable literature has documented the impotence at best, and the destructiveness at worst, of dealing with traditional concerns of marriage, the family, and mental health without a clear and active framework of the substance of women's lives. In addition to the soul-destroying impact of being held subordinate as a sex is the self-evident fact, seldom noted, that women cross-cut all other unequal/oppressed groups in our society — the poor, the elderly, the unemployed, welfare recipients, etc..

"Sex-Role Stereotypes and Clinical Judgements of Mental Health" is a classic study that exposed the double standard of mental health for women and men (Broverman and Broverman 1970). It investigated the responses of both female and male clinicians regarding characteristics said to be found in a healthy woman, a healthy man and a healthy adult. Results indicated that clinicians' definitions of a healthy man were equated with those of a healthy adult. Their definitions of a healthy woman were not. The implications of this study for women who seek treatment are profound, given the common clinical assumption that the normal behaviour of women and adult do not coincide.

Men's stress and distress are generally linked with occupational hazards — too much pressure or responsibility on the job or unemployment — or absence of adequate nurturance and support at home. For women, stress and distress are typically defined as mental health problems. Our turmoil is not linked to the occupational hazards of child-care and domestic labour, to poverty, unemployment or the double work-load, to the mysogyny that assaults us daily at multiple levels. We are not expected to even claim a support system at home — we are supposed to provide it. Women's distress is said to be primarily "in the head."

Underneath the double standard of mental health for women and men has often lurked blame, punishment, and social control for the former. Women with troubles are typically defined as sick, neurotic, negative, frigid, immature,

249

hostile, not so bright, or otherwise deficient. Our pain is both trivialized and pathologized. By contrast, troubled men are typically seen to be struggling with the real world of work and responsibility, with more legitimate, more profound human dilemmas.

To compound the picture, women have been conditioned to blame ourselves and one another for our unhappiness, to view our discontent as a sickness and to seek professional help and/or treatment. Contemporary women are no longer called witches and burned as in the Middle Ages, but are instead helped to self-destruct.[4] This self-destruct training is an insidious tool used to contain women's rage and despair, to invalidate our experience of the world. It produces guilt, anxiety and depression — a sense of impotence that keeps us docile and fearful, unable to act on our own behalf. The helping professions, in practice as in theory, collude with and reinforce the self-destruct mechanism in women. Rather than connecting internal turmoil with external forms of structural oppression, they individualize, privatize and stigmatize women's despair.

Chesler makes the point that marriage and therapy are two parallel institutions deemed acceptable for women.[5] Both involve men as authorities, women as relatively helpless, dependent, subservient patients, and talk as the purported solution to the problem.

Trained to submit to authority, women become deeply entrenched in the patient role when we reach out for help to the male therapists, general practitioners, gynaecologists, etc., who control the health care system. Conditioned to perceive ourselves as without expert knowledge in matters relating to our own bodies and minds, women characteristically defer to male experts who take over medically "for our own good."

Destructive though the prescriptions for female "normalcy" are, women try to fulfill them in order to survive. The price paid by many of us — in depression, suicide, addiction and madness — is barbaric. Even the price makes its own political point. Women frequently express the fear of "going crazy," "losing my sanity," because we know, consciously or unconsciously, that this is how our unhappiness is defined and dealt with by society and the mental health establishment. This consciousness of the consequences of allowing despair and desperation to surface and seriously interfere with our daily functioning constitutes an invaluable deterrent. It helps keep many women in their place, grateful for what they have, instead of risking the uphill struggle for equality and dignity in both public and private spheres of life.

Psychiatric treatment itself reinforces the pattern of women being denied control and autonomy over key aspects of our lives. The female patient, in or out of hospital, is not helped to actively and aggressively take hold of her own life. To *act*. She is more frequently given immobilizing medication and shock therapy that will act upon her, that will reinforce her dependency, that will further rob her of minimal autonomy. There is a vital connection between women being treated as wayward incompetents in the daily routine of psychiatric hospitals, and the control wrested from patients generally by drugs, electric shock, psychosurgery and incarceration. It is important to note that female patients receive more than double the amount of all such forms of "treatment" compared to men.

> I have been mentally ill. Hell, I've been psychotic, schizophrenic, manic-depressive—you name it. I have credentials as long as my arm certifying that I am an abnormal female, desperately in need of help to adjust to society and function in it "normally." The credentials aren't recent—the latest are now four years old. But if I were to return to a psychiatrist he would be pleased to update the diagnosis and pronounce me, if not outright insane, at least seriously ill.
>
> I have done the whole trip—psychoanalysis, tranquilizers, suicide attempts, mental institutions. And the only surprising thing about it is that I emerged from it all still sane.
>
> One day, after a particularly frustrating session, I asked the shrink, "What is the point of all this?" He answered, in tones of the greatest seriousness, "We want to make you into a normal twenty-one-year-old girl." I should have been warned![6]

Some Specific Illustrations

Drugs. "I use these drugs for one purpose and one purpose only—to protect my family from my irritability."[7] This woman had five teen-aged children and had been on tranquillizers for 10 years.

The issue emerging from this statement is why a woman's health is permitted to be sacrificed in the name of the institutions of marriage and motherhood. Are women entitled to have full adult lives as persons, including the full spectrum of human emotion and the right to their own needs, irritability and anger? Why do we train women, as nurturers of men and children, to sacrifice their needs and feelings on the altar of the family?

Women and anger. When women go another route in relation to coping with their lives — via anger, desperation and rebellion — the following is an example of the danger lurking from within psychiatry in relation to defining the problems women present.

> Specific common denominators in the *angry woman syndrome* set it apart from any established present-day classification. These symptoms are periodic outbursts of unprovoked anger, marital maladjustment, serious suicide attempts, proneness to abuse of alcohol and drugs, a morbidly oriented critical attitude to people and a contrary obsessive need to excel in all endeavours, with an intense need for neatness and punctuality. This constant striving for perfection is their undoing.
>
> ...their language during the shouting would make a truck driver blush... Most of the women come from a disturbed family background in which the mother is the dominant personality and is sexually promiscuous, with excessive intake of alcohol. The father usually seeks the daughter out for emotional release which initiates a strong incestual tie...
>
> They resent treatment and blame their husbands for the problems that are presented.[8]

This diatribe against women, in the name of professional theory and practice, is a chilling example of how women are clinically blamed for their anger, desperation and fight, unrelated to the reality of their daily existence. Were Rickles and his ilk to be slotted into female roles of service and subordination, would their anger and curses constitute a "syndrome" or courage and strength? Or is the classification to be reserved for one sex?

The following material on maternal deprivation and incest has been excerpted mainly from "The Power Politics of Motherhood: A Feminist Critique of Theory and Practice," written jointly by Alma Estable and myself.*

Maternal deprivation. The helping professions rely heavily on maternal deprivation as cause in diagnosing personal suffering and unhappiness. Therapists have been and are still intensely preoccupied with "what his mother did to him, what her mother withheld from her", and how the current mother/patient is fulfilling her required nurturant role in relatioin to men, children and others in need.

It is predominantly male "authorities" who have presented women, in the name of theory and reason, with sexist prescriptions for their life work as mothers. Male

---

* Available from The Centre for Social Welfare Studies, Carleton University, Ottawa, Ontario. Price is $2.50 plus .50 for mailing costs.

authors, theoreticians and philosophers abound as experts in the fields of parenting, child-care and the family, despite the fact that this is the single arena in which women have been considered to be "naturals" and irreplaceable. Is it surprising or accidental, then, that women/mothers have been held responsible by the helping professions for conditions as diverse and as ludicrous as mental retardation, delinquency, depression, incest, and violence?

Nathan Epstein, father of family therapy in Canada, described (and prescribed) the normal family in the following way in the 1960's.[9] (Though variations on the theme have followed this earlier work, fundamentally sexist assumptions remain very much embedded in current theories of the family.)

The Father's Role

— *He is a successful breadwinner.*
— *In middle class families, he makes the decisions about money.*
— *He has the ultimate responsibility for important decisions, e.g., place of residence, major expenses, vacations.*
— *He occupies the ultimate authority position in the family. This does not preclude democratic discussion or taking his wife into his confidence.*
— *He enjoys and performs well in his marital sexual activity.*
— *He participates to some degree in caring for and in relationship to the children.*

The Mother's Role

— *She performs efficiently and happily as homemaker and mother.*
— *She enjoys marital, sexual relations and functions satisfactorily in this role.*

Under the guise of expert and sophisticated definitions of normalcy developed primarily by men, women have been kept tied firmly to the institutions of marriage and motherhood as the centre of their lives.

Joseph Rheingold, psychoanalyst, comes to these conclusions:

...woman is nurturance... anatomy decrees the life of a woman... When women grow up without dread of th '~ biological functions and without

253

subversion by feminist doctrines and, therefore, enter upon motherhood
with a sense of fulfillment and altruistic sentiment we shall attain the
goal of a good life and a secure world in which to live.[10]

and

The syndrome of decay, the evil tendency in man is basically rooted in
the mother-child relationship.[11]

Though Epstein focuses on women's contained (and cheerful!) life within home and family, and Rheingold blames mothers for the fate of the world, they both allocate basic responsibility for nurturance of others and sacrifice of the self to women. Psychiatric literature on the family and mental illness highlights mothering as key cause of emotional disturbances, and "the mother is continually the focus of an inescapable indictment " (Smith 1978:283).

What has happened to mothers is that we have been left out of the universal definition of human need. While men are seen to require and deserve financial independence, personal achievement, physical maintenance and nurturance, mothers are subtly excluded from these entitlements. Hiding behind the mystique of motherlove and family, society forces women to accept a less than human life contract.

Feminists note that women serve as scapegoats in the family and provide a convenient and politically vulnerable target for attack. Deemed inferior as a sex, it takes merely one more step to render us inferior and blameworthy as mothers.

Incest. When incest occurs, professional theory and practice routinely point to the mother as having been guilty of a form of desertion within the family—having withdrawn passively or actively from vital aspects of her role, sexually and otherwise. The implication is that "normal" mothers subordinate their own needs, preferences and wishes to those of husband and children. In dealing with the sexual assault committed by husband and father, it is common practice among helping professionals to concentrate on the "inadequate" performance of wife and mother.

The females in the family are considered pivotal. The message is that if mothers/wives were doing their motherwork of meeting the personal and sexual needs of men and fathers, incest would not occur. And if daughters were not inappropriately seductive, fathers would not "fall prey" to sexual assault.

From the Toronto *Globe and Mail*, October 21, 1980—
"A ten-year-old girl who was sexually molested by her foster

father remains in the foster home." The social worker explained why this was so:

> ...the agency was more concerned about the child's behaviour which, in part, prompted the assaults. "We felt she was not attacked seriously or threatened." She described the girl as "sexually provocative" and said the agency wanted to find out why the girl would turn to such techniques to get attention and affection from an adult.

Sandra Butler has summed up the professional trap set for mothers in families where incest occurs.

> Two words which consistently intrude upon all theory and analysis concerning mothers in families in which incestuous assault occurs are "abandoning" and "colluding." These are the names of their crimes, the reasons they are held responsible for the actions of others. If a mother is "passive" she fails by not having provided her child with the strength to resist incestuous overtures. If she is "aggressive," she fails by having caused her husband to feel emasculated and therefore in need of turning to someone else for his emotional and sexual needs.
>
> (Butler 1978:113-114)

Both the literature and practice in relation to father-daughter incest provide vivid examples of how professionals attempt to monitor and control the behaviour of mothers and daughters, and at the same time collude in obscuring the criminal responsibility of fathers.

The conventional definition of the incest problem is familial, with the father emerging as the member of the family who is forced to choose "inappropriate" ways to express his sexual frustration or his unmet needs.

From the *Ottawa Citizen*, April 11, 1978:

> A local psychiatrist... believes incest should be seen for what it is—quite literally a family affair. There are always at least three people involved, the mother, the father and the daughter... usually it is done without *violence*... Mother is particularly uninterested in sexual contact with her husband.

Once the definition of the problem is family focused, it follows that intervention is also familial. In the process of offering "treatment" based upon such a definition of the problem, the objectives of patriarchal ideology are upheld. Girls and women are effectively reminded that they carry responsibility for the behaviour of boys and men; no matter what the cost to females, the nuclear unit is maintained wherever possible; the emphasis is on family dysfunction rather than violence against girls and women.

> The adults who sexually abuse children are overwhelmingly male (97%). The children they abuse are overwhelmingly female (92%). We are talking about a crime which is committed almost exclusively by adult men against girl children... As feminists, we recognize that what we are confronting is the same male power which allows men to rape and batter us...
>
> (Hamblin and Bowen 1981:6)

The professional approach to incest indicates how fathers, husbands, men are viewed as relatively marginal actors in a form of male violence perpetrated against their own female children. So it is that issues of male violence such as incest are assessed mainly in the light of what mothers and daughters have or have not done.

Feminist Counselling

The origins

Consciousness-raising in small groups was one of the key catalysts of the contemporary women's liberation movements. Many women literally and figuratively exploded with the confusion and despair at the centre of their lives. Our personal experience had hitherto been deemed individual, private and subjective, necessarily contained within the sanctity of the nuclear family. Feminists were (and are) criticized for "navel gazing" when we made initial attempts to share our reality, to discover common ground among women, to name our oppression in our own way. In fact, we were beginning to refuse orthodox definitions of politics imposed by men, and to search for our own. The women's movement had begun to join personal and political, to develop a new analysis of the vital connections between women's subservience in family, paid labour force and society.

We returned to the roots of female experience to construct a new way of validating, defining and explaining women's lives. We examined the condition of women from within our own reality.

> In learning to speak our experience and situation, we insist upon the right to begin where we are, to stand as subjects of our sentences, and to hear one another as the authoritative speakers of our experience.[12]

and

> Through consciousness-raising, women grasp the collective reality of women's condition from within the perspective of that experience, not from outside it.

(MacKinnon 1982:536)

Amidst the rebirth of modern feminist thought and the emphasis on consciousness-raising, women shared a great deal of personal information and personal pain with one another. Much of the sharing had to do with "the problem that has no name" (Friedan 1963:Ch. 1). It included the experiences women had had and were having at the hands of psychiatry in

256

particular, but also psychology and social work — the helping professions. It revealed how women's daily struggles to survive had led them to seek help from the very sources that were defining their struggles as sickness and pathology. Feminist literature — fiction and non-fiction — was rapidly documenting the sexual politics of modern health care.

It was out of an analysis of the theories and presumptions of the helping professions, in the midst of a new grasp of the real substance of women's lives, that there began a search for some viable alternative to the predominantly sexist, chemical, adjustment-oriented services offered to women when we needed help. Out of the women's movement came the realization that services for women were largely designed and controlled by men; that embedded in their methods of treatment was a double standard of mental health for women and men, and that the double standard was, directly or indirectly, reinforcing the very oppression from which women were suffering.

Via consciousness-raising and via a new grasp of "the personal is political" emerged both a devastating critique of the health care system and, eventually, new kinds of services for women. These were based on radically different ways of thinking and radically different ways of working. They reflected the recognition by the women's movement that the institutions of marriage and motherhood — in prospect, reality or absence — have to do with women's subordination and inequality; that the personal sphere is frequently women's point of entry towards change at many levels; that we suffer both internally and externally, individually and collectively, the destructive impact of a sexist society.

The base

Feminist counselling is a helping process that means working with women, individually or in groups, around their situation as related to the society that has shaped them. It has to do with an approach, a feminist way of defining women's struggles and facilitating change. It is no mysterious, professional technique. The focus is on women helping women in a non-hierarchical, reciprocal and supportive way.

Feminist counselling focuses on the link between feminism as an ideology (a way of understanding the world and helping to change it) and women's personal, everyday experience. It rests on a critical analysis of the sexism embedded in the theory and practice of the helping professions.

257

It is the antithesis of the various therapies and technologies which have left us a legacy of the cult of the individual, of the decisive role of the psyche and personality in shaping human behaviour.

This kind of work challenges the common premise in the provision of conventional services that "more of the same is better," and states decisively that more of the same would be more of a disaster. It deals with sexism at the heart of its rationale, with the clear implication that services planned, designed, and frequently delivered by men in positions of authority as "experts," have done incalculable harm to women.

Personal stress and distress are seen as a barometer, a kind of fever rating connected to the unequal and unhealthy structures, prescriptions and power relationships in women's lives. There is a rejection of the artificial split between internal feelings and external conditions of living and working, between human behaviour and structural context. A feminist approach to working with women involves weaving together personal and political issues as causes of and potential solutions to women's struggles. Women's troubles are placed within, not outside their structural context. A woman is seen both as individual and as one woman reflecting the collectivity of women.

By defining personal problems from a political perspective, feminist counsellors are able to move in new directions in helping. For example, when women are immobilized with depression, they may well be on strike against killing roles and expectations. When women end up in psychiatrists' offices or dependent on drugs, it may be that they are political refugees from narrow and suffocating lives. When women on public assistance are listlessly apathetic or exploding with anger, their responses are most likely rooted in their powerlessness and poverty, and the daily control of their lives by the State. This approach reflects the linking of the personal and the political in the feminist counselling process.

Feminist counselling, then, looks at the political implications of women's struggles and behaviour, at women's limited control over their own space and lives in family and paid workplace, and at the consequent price paid by most of us at one point or another in a life span.

The traditional family is seen as an institution which has been a particularly effective vehicle in the oppression and containment of women. It is also an institution that the helping professions frequently strive to uphold, no matter what the cost to women in the process. Studies on depression among women suggest that an intensive commitment to marriage and motherhood as primary tasks in contemporary life is potentially crazy-making. And given the double standard of sexuality and aging, a task with little job security.

Feminist counselling recognizes women's entitlement to full, adult involvement in the world. Thus there is a recognition of the importance of significantly increased public participation and leadership for women, and significantly decreased domestic and child-care responsibilities. Though men verbally glorify women's roles in the home, they seldom wish to exchange. Being Somebody's wife or Somebody's girlfriend or Somebody's mother eventually negates a woman's ego and her potential contribution to society at large.

Psychological despair and/or relationship crises frequently trigger women's search for help. Having been contained within the private sphere, this is often the focus of our struggles. However, there is a central assumption in feminist counselling that "women's work" and "women's place" in society are key factors in producing much distress among us. Thus the sexual division of paid and unpaid labour in and beyond the home, its impact upon self-esteem and interpersonal relationships, is a key connection to be made. It is understood that chronic responses of guilt, self-blame and depression in women have more to do with the general subordination of women than with childhood, personality development or patterns of communication.

Feminist counsellors are concerned with the unequal power relations between the sexes as the source of much unhappiness among women. Thus such issues as control of money, major decision-making, sexual relations, primary or exclusive responsibility for domestic labour, child-care and "others," form part of the framework within which personal problems are explored.

This approach refuses to blame the victim or to define women's personal struggles as individual pathology, via the medical model. As feminists, we personally have been helped by the women's movement to consciously address these issues in our own lives. As providers of service, we make no separation between the outline of our own lives and of those who come to us for help. We use the commonality between us as a way of understanding, sharing and helping.

Feminist counselling carries within its mandate a healing process, an educational process, and a political process based on a feminist understanding of society. It is an integrated form of help at best, with consciousness-raising at the core of the work.

It is based on the premise that, as women, we have a vested interest in and the potential power to change what is, for ourselves and for other women; that women need to actively rediscover and reclaim the strength and power and talent that lie dormant and hidden within us; that women can best help ourselves and each other in the healing process, and in fighting back, together; that it is time for men of good will to listen and learn from women, to offer money, resources, and concrete action in favour of women. Theoretical sympathy from men, apart from shared money, labour and power, is seen to be irrelevant.

Feminist counselling helps women to validate their behaviour and experience in their own way. It encourages women to recognize their human entitlement to different ways of living and loving, acting and reacting. The emphasis is on change, not adjustment, on a dynamic, rather than a static conception of human behaviour, and on connecting internal turmoil with external context.

Feminist counselling is, in part, a means of lifting the unjust burden of blame, guilt, and individual responsibility from the shoulders of individual women who have been scapegoated at many levels in society. Accordingly, it is geared to releasing the energies and abilities of women to change their lives, individually and collectively.

Before all else, it is an understanding of the framework of women's lives, a grasp of the institutions and the structures that shape and direct them, of the false consciousness that both women and men have about women's choices, needs and entitlements that is essential for feminist counsellors.

Consciousness-raising is at the heart of this approach. A critical analysis of women in society, shared in some way, at some level, and at all stages of the process, is a vital component of the work. It does not exclude, trivialize or diagnose personal pain or confusion. It works with the pain and the possibilities, respectfully, reciprocally, and within context.

Feminist counsellors do not underestimate the power and the vested interests of the dominant sex. It is because of this recognition that the emphasis on changing ideas, attitudes, and values is seen as significant only in conjunction with concrete action and structural change at both personal and economic levels. The decisive questions have to do with how power, status, work, child-care and money are shared among women and men, in both pivate and public spheres.

It is inequality in favour of women, not equality, that is required in feminist counselling, based on a recognition of the double ghetto of women's lives in family and paid workplace. Women need and have a right to special measures, to more than equal ways and means of beginning to reconstruct lives that have been kept stunted and limited in the service of others.

The answers to women's struggles do not lie in therapeutic blueprints. They most often lie in a redefinition of the problem itself.

Some key considerations

- *An underlying assumption of feminist counselling is that women have the potential strength to forge changes in their lives, especially together with other women. There is a rich appreciation of the joy, the sense of purpose, the self-esteem, and the confidence that comes of tackling keenly felt issues with others who share your experience. A new "vision of the possible" emerges from that solidarity.*

- *One key strategy is helping women to re-assess the value of relationships with other women. Traditionally, women have dreamed of and sought happiness and fulfillment with one man. A feminist counsellor knows how insecure and vulnerable that leaves most women. In encouraging women to validate and like themselves as persons, to appreciate their own significance, she at the same time helps women to enjoy, respect, and seek out other women as primary friends and companions. A support network of women friends is seen as crucial in helping women to fully enjoy life in its many variations and to reduce emotional dependence on men.*

- *A feminist counsellor uses her own life experience — her sorrows and joys, her traumas and learning — if relevant to the consumer's life situation. The sharing helps to demystify the counsellor as omnipotent professional and to truly universalize, in a visible and concrete way, the struggle of human beings to survive and to change.*

- *Feminist counsellors present themselves as imperfect human beings like the rest of us, not professional experts in a one-up, one-down relationship. It is a peer kind of relationship, with the focus necessarily concentrated on the consumer. It is understood that without conscious reciprocal learning between counsellor and consumer, there can be no authentic respect and trust in the counselling relationship.*

- *Both in feminist counselling and in consciousness-raising groups, there is a validation of women's life experience — as they tell it, as they feel it, as they react to it. The validation is a significant experience for most women because it implies respect, dignity, and trust. It is not a question of absolute truth in human relationships and human experience. It is rather a rich experience for women who are not accustomed to being accorded respect and dignity, privately and publicly, in a patriarchal society.*

- *There is the recognitioin that, as with other oppressed groups, a key to regaining and retaining dignity, energy, and self-esteem is the anger that propels us to fight back, and to join together in acting to change our lives.*

- *Women are encouraged to acknowledge and to claim their anger and aggression. It is understood that women have been conditioned to smile, to wait, to endure, to keep up at least a mask of contentment so as not to make life difficult for those around us. Feminist counsellors encourage women to claim the full spectrum of human emotion, no matter the labels attached. Particular conditions call for particular emotions — appropriately.*

- *Feminist counselling is concerned with political and personal questions arising from lesbian relationships. It is understood that lesbian women have to cope with a particularly virulent form of misogyny, that the helping professions have most frequently perceived lesbian women as "sick", and that lesbian women often need help in coping with the common struggles and problems of being women in this society, of being couples, of "coming out", of being different. Feminist counsellors have the added advantage here of harbouring few illusions about what heterosexuality means for women in a sexist society.*

- *It is recognized that women are especially deprived of nurturance. Traditionally, we do the nurturing, the giving, the understanding, the child-care, the worrying, that is all part of the sex role stereotype. Instead of helping a woman to accept the primary nurturant role, the counsellor focuses on her central and essential needs and rights as person. The consumer is not seen as adjunct to family, but as separate person, in relationship to the world at large, sharing and only sharing responsibility for nurturance with significant others in her life.*

- *Feminist counsellors understand the impact on women's lives of being expected to care for and nurture the young, the old, the sick, and the handicapped. It is understood that such assumptions must be smashed, that caring for others*

262

must be turned into shared tasks. Women are encouraged to actively assert their limits and their needs in relation to others, to refuse to be "superwomen."

* *The addiction of girls and women to the ideology of romantic love, and our consequent fear of aloneness and abandonment, is seen as a very serious form of "chemical" dependency designed to maintain us as the property of man.*

* *Consumers are encouraged to shop around for a counsellor before making a decision. In particular, the consumer needs information regarding the counsellor's views of women in society and whether female unhappiness and conflict is seen as "sickness." "Shopping" is a means of the consumer asserting control and decision-making in relation to seeking help, and sets the stage from the beginning for an egalitarian type of working relationship. She/he needs to be free to ask the counsellor about herself and her ways of working.*

* *A feminist counsellor is aware that girls and women have been trained to be "good" and "careful", meaning we are made particularly wary and fearful of making mistakes, large and small, and being penalized for them. This is a major source of disabling guilt. Women are instead encouraged to see life as continuing trial and error, past and present. There is conscious support for consumers trying out new ways of being, acting, and deciding; encouragement for women to claim the right to fail, to be wrong, to move on.*

* *Girls and women are encouraged to seriously examine the structure of their mothers' and foremothers' lives. Given misogyny, most girls and women are taught to judge their mother's performance and experience very harshly, and in the process to set up opposite and impossible expectations for themselves. The mother/daughter connection is recognized as one that is damaged by patriarchy, yet potentially very rich.*

* *It is understood that marriage and/or motherhood, as one part of life, are authentic choices for some women. That other options are equally appropriate, and, in this society, need support and reinforcement. The decision by a woman not to marry, to be a single mother, to remain child-free, to be lesbian, celibate, or sexual in ways other than the State and its institutions have defined, needs additional validation and support from a feminist counsellor. There is the assumption that there are ways for women to love and to live other than marriage and the nuclear family.*

* *Feminist counsellors assume that privatizing the condition of women's lives can only serve to perpetuate the* status

263

quo *for women. Thus, there is emphasis on politicizing rather than personalizing such hitherto seemingly individual issues as wife-battering, unemployment, depression, sexual assault, guilt, chemical addiction, and madness.*

• *It is considered most helpful for women to work in groups, though not exclusively. Women learn from sharing lives they have been taught to keep private. The emphasis is on mutual aid and the commonality of experience, on the deprivatizing of morality in order to put an end to the isolation of women from each other and to make the underside of our lives visible.*

• *Feminist counselling attaches value to action, decision-making, and risk-taking. It is recognized that women have been taught to talk and react rather than to act, to be rather than to do, to feel rather than to decide—this in marriage as well as in traditional therapy or counselling. Women are encouraged to act upon the problems facing them, individually and collectively.*

Does feminist counselling mean imposing an ideology on others? This is a very important question. My response is that if there is not a clear and fundamental working respect for consumers, for their particular pace, preferences and priorities, then this approach is not working. All providers of service have a bias, implicitly or explicitly. The feminist counsellor has a responsibility to make her own bias explicit, to share her view of women's place in the world *when* it seems relevant, *when* it pertains to the consumer's life struggles, or to aspects of her own that may be helpful regarding the issues at hand. Consumers of feminist counselling may or may not move into or out of the women's movement, into or out of marriage. These are decisions to be made with full knowledge of possible costs and benefits and with the advantage in feminist counselling of not having oppressive societal norms reinforced about what women should or should not be. Women, all of us, take distinctive and sometimes unusual paths towards change.

Girls and women need to begin to take back control, piece by piece, bit by bit, over their own lives. It is a continuing process, and a potentially radical one. However, the important lesson to be learned in feminist counselling is that this process cannot be undertaken in isolation from other women, personally or politically.

Conclusion

One of the key contributions of the contemporary women's movement to modern political thought has been the joining of personal and political in theory and practice. Feminism is the only revolutionary movement centrally concerned with the enactment of power politics in daily relations between women and men, in family, paid workplace, and society. There can be no authentic feminist practice without this dimension.

As Geraldine Finn writes regarding "Why Althusser Killed His Wife": "His philosophical and intellectual practice cannot be separated from his personal and emotional practice: they are rooted in the same soil..." (Finn 1981:28).

The helping professions mirror a patriarchal society that has maintained women as men's property in one form or another. Feminist counselling as a way of women helping women is a small, yet significant link in moving towards change. It exemplifies, at a micro level, the efforts of feminists to validate rather than deny women's way of experiencing the world; to work together on women's oppression in its immediate reality; to help translate private, personal pain into public, political issues. In connecting internal turmoil with external structures of oppression, it becomes one tool, one resource for us in taking control of our lives, individually and collectively.

There is a periodic debate within the women's movement about whether feminist counselling or consciousness-raising contributes to reform or revolution. Do they keep us focused on the internal, the personal, the individual, as opposed to material conditions, the political, the collective? The debate is an important one because it makes us aware of the potential splits in our thinking and acting that can prevent us from moving beyond orthodox definitions of "correct" politics.

Feminism refuses the dichotomies between personal and political, subjective and objective, process and product. It refuses the validity of revolutionary movements that have to do primarily with the exchange of power among men (Morgan 1978:127). It represents the struggle toward fundamental changes that integrate the spheres of personal relations and public responsibility. It demands that women take their place as equal participants in both arenas.

Feminism has meant a fundamental shift in my way of feeling, thinking, analyzing and participating in politics and in life. For me, it is no longer a question of confronting violence, poverty, racism, or inequality in general. I have learned that the "general" conveniently masks the "particular," and accordingly renders women's oppression invisible, marginal or secondary. Thus, for example, the particular question of planetary violence against women—physically, economically, sexually and psychologically — is neglected as a central, political priority in all but feminist politics.

Political activists will have to look at themselves inside their own homes, communities and workplaces, will have to act upon the critical women's questions under their very noses, before their classic concerns for the world can be respected by feminists. Feminists are no longer in awe of or intimidated by a definition of politics that supports, by omission or commission, the oppression of women. Without pinpointing the politics of patriarchy as a fundamental issue of theory and practice, there can be no basic re-ordering of women's and men's lives. Yet "...patriarchy as a political ideology and as a practice... is consistently denied, negated or trivialized by the academic and intellectual élite" (Finn 1981:28).

Organized feminism has historically yielded the primacy of its own objectives in favour of "the greater good" and subsequently been buried and forgotten for long periods of time.

> ...there is an enormous pressure, a pressure I think on everybody, but certainly specifically on feminists, to yet once again shelve feminist issues, or what are seen as "merely" women's issues rather than... human issues, and save the planet from nuclear holocaust.
>
> (Rich 1981)

Here Adrienne Rich suggests that feminists must take their own politics very seriously, making sure we are not once again subsumed — as in the past — by whatever is deemed primary by others.

Women are well aware of the value of life and of the horrors of nuclear devastation. We are not, after all, strangers to the threat of, or the reality of personal violence and annihilation. We know it only too well, too intimately in all of its ugliest, sexist manifestations. We want neither patriarchal madness nor nuclear madness. They are cut from the same cloth.

FOOTNOTES

This paper is, with some revisions and additions, based on an amalgamation of the following two articles by the author: Helen Levine, "On Women and On One Woman" in Anne MacLennan (ed.), *Women: Their Use of Alcohol and Other Legal Drugs* (Toronto: Addiction Research Foundation of Ontario, 1976); and Helen Levine, "New Directions for Girls and Women: A Look at the Condition of Women in Society and Feminist Counselling" in Thomas H. Brown (ed.), *Counselling: Challenge of the 80's*, Vol. 11, Planning Committee for the 1979 National Conference of the Canadian Guidance and Counselling Association, St. John's, Nfld., 1980.

This paper also includes significant excerpts from Helen Levine & Alma Estable, "The Power Politics of Motherhood: A Feminist Critique of Theory and Practice," Occasional Paper, Centre for Social Welfare Studies, Carleton University, 1981.

1. Male physicians and administrators dominate the hospital establishment generally. They have high salaries and status and maintain a professional distance from the heavy ongoing pressures and work involved in daily patient care. It is the nurses, the nursing aides, the kitchen workers and cleaning staff who bear the brunt of low pay, low status, hard work, and subservience. Health workers are mainly women; health professionals with power and status, mainly men.
2. Helen Levine, "On Women and On One Woman" in MacLennan 1976.
3. Susan Stephenson, "Special Issues of Women in Therapy" in Dowsling & MacLennan 1978:9.
4. Thomas Szasz, *The Manufacture of Madness* (New York: Harper & Row, 1970).
5. Phyllis Chesler, "Patient and Patriarch: Women in the Psychotherapeutic Relationship" in Gornick & Moran 1971:373.
6. Barbara Findlay, "Shrink! Shrank! Shriek!" in Smith & Davids 1975:59.
7. Ruth Cooperstock, "Women and Psychotropic Drug Use" in Dowsling & MacLennan 1978:47.
8. Nathan K. Rickles, "The Angry Women Syndrome" in *The Archives of General Psychiatry*, Vol. 24, January 1971, pp. 21-94.
9. N.B. Epstein, J.J. Sigal & V. Rakoff, "Family Categories Schema." Unpublished Paper, Dept. of Psychiatry, Jewish General Hospital, Montréal, 1962, p. 9.
10. Joseph Rheingold, *The Fear of Being a Woman* (New York: Grune & Stratton, 1964), p. 714.
11. Joseph Rheingold, *op. cit.*
12. Dorothy E. Smith, "Women and Psychiatry" in Smith & Davids 1975:15.

PART TWO

Politics:
Theory and Practice

CHAPTER 11

Ideological Hegemony in Political Discourse: Women's Specificity and Equality

Angela R. Miles

Angela Miles has a Ph.D. in political science from the University of Toronto and teaches adult education at the Ontario Institute for Studies in Education. She was a member of the Feminist Party of Canada and has been involved in women's studies activities and organizations as well as in such groups as Women Against Violence Against Women and the Canadian Research Institute for the Advancement of Women. She has a research interest in popular female culture in general and romance novels in particular, but her main work is concerned with the theory and practice of feminism as an international politics, feminism's place in history, its current roots in post-industrial socio-economic developments, and its relationship to class politics.

Two recent books that largely share the political perspectives of this article are Nancy Hartsock's *Money, Sex and Power: Toward a Feminist Historical Materialism* (1983) and Charlotte Bunch's collection of her own essays, articles, and speeches, *Passionate Politics: Feminist Theory in Action* (1987). My own monograph, *Feminist Radicalism in the 1980's* (1985), also deals with related political questions.

One of the most crucial political questions facing feminists today is "What is feminism and what is its relationship to women's struggle in general?" or, put another way, "How can we identify the most progressive aspects of women's struggle and, as feminists, develop and strengthen those aspects to become the defining characteristics and organizing principles of the general women's movement?"

In order to begin to address this question systematically, we need to develop a political analysis of feminism which can identify its essential value framework and the nature of the future it represents. Such an analysis, in order to go beyond mere description, would have to consider feminist activism and values in terms of both their fit with the political possibilities of this historical period and their general justice and desirability. This would require a historical and materialist analysis which treats women activists and their movement as both products and producers of social change.

I cannot deal here with both moments of the dialectical relationship between our movement's social context and its ideas. Elsewhere, I have examined the shifting relationship between reproduction and production in advanced industrial society which underlies women's increasing activism and the particular shape it is taking (1979, Chapters 1-4). Here, I want to concentrate, instead, on the developing value basis of feminism in this period. I will argue that feminism's progressive power lies essentially in its ability to affirm *both* women's specificity *and* equality in a transcendent and revolutionary synthesis of these two apparently contradictory conditions. If women's politics *as women* attempts to bypass, ignore or deny women's specificity, its expression of women's interests will necessarily remain merely the expression of sectional interest. In this case it will be incapable of challenging current male ideological hegemony which is enforced and protected by both right-wing and liberal definitions of political discourse. Paradoxically, it is only if we manage to build a new politics on the basis of our specificity as women that the militant expression of our sectional interest can represent a major new definition of this discourse and a new departure for humanity as a whole.

In the beginning of this phase of the women's movement, feminism's expression of women's interests primarily took the form of refusing the dominant stereotype of women and insisting that women were capable of being the same as men. Feminists as diverse as Simone de Beauvoir, Shulamith Firestone and Juliet Mitchell, for instance, all accepted the blatantly ideological relegation of reproduction and reproductive work to semi-human status. In 1967, Juliet Mitchell wrote:

> My thesis is that women are confined within the family which is a segmentary, monolithic unit, today largely separated off from production and hence from social human activity. The reason why this confinement is made possible, is the need for women to fulfill three roles; they must provide sexual gratification for their partners and give birth to children and rear them. All three roles man (sic) shares with other mammals. This confirms de Beauvoir's contention that women are relegated to the species while men—through work—transcend it.

(Mitchell 1967:82)

This view of women's concerns as essentially less human than men's requires that the way forward be seen in terms of leaving these concerns behind. And indeed, Mitchell, de Beauvoir (1953) and Firestone (1970) (who saw hope only in test tube babies) all formulated their feminism in these terms. Much of the brave, courageous and creative feminist writing of this early period reads in some of its aspects like an apology for women. Despite its militant tones, its message includes the assertion that: "We know we are not as decisive and independent and strong and rational as men are, but we can be as good as them if we are given the chance. We are indecisive, dependent, irrational and weak only because we have been stunted by an oppressive system. We would not be fixated on trivial matters like social relationships, personal life, childbearing and rearing if we were not excluded from the important areas of life." This early feminism tended to accept the male-defined evaluation of the world and of women. It consisted largely in the insistence that women's lack of participation in important areas of life stemmed not from women's innate inability, but from our exclusion by men.

The simple androcentric acceptance that men's activities are more human and important than women's, however, soon began to be breached in all areas of feminist thought and activity. Opposing gynocentric constructions of reality began sporadically but persistently to affirm women's specific culture and values, in a challenge to dominant notions of what is valuable in life. For instance, in 1970 Barbara Burris wrote:

> All the female culture traits are defined as negatives by the dominant world culture. We do not believe them to be so (except those that keep us subservient, such as passivity, self-sacrifice, etc.).
>
> We are proud of the female culture of emotion, intuition, love, personal relationships, etc., as the most essential human characteristic. It is our male colonizers—it is the male culture—who have defined essential humanity out of their identity and who are "culturally deprived."

(Burris 1973)

273

Burris was not alone, as feminists in all areas moved decisively beyond merely attempting to add information about women to essentially androcentric bodies of knowledge, to a position where they questioned the very structure of existing disciplines and their core tenets.[1] Elizabeth Minnich indicated the magnitude of the shift when she said: "We set out to make the maps we had a little larger, a little more complete and suddenly we found ourselves needing not flat maps but a globe."[2]

The alternative standards of judging and evaluating the world and humanity that were emerging in feminist scholarship were evident also in feminist political writing. The articulation of new, specifically feminist values, made it possible for feminists to move beyond questioning men's definition of women to question also their definition of humanity:

> Consider the revolutionary: a hard, implacable, dedicated machine that fights and kills and dies for the cause... Are [these] the characteristics... we consider most valuable in human relationships? I don't think so. And I think if we adopt them, we begin to deny, not the basic "femininity" which detractors of women's liberation are so fearful that we might lose, but our basic humanity.
>
> (Likely 1972:159)

This comment, written by Jan Likely in 1971, is an early example of the ways that feminism began to move beyond the demand for women to be "let in" to the existing male-defined world and politics, to challenge that world itself and its definitions not only of femininity but also of humanity.

Alain Touraine, in his analysis of social movements, has identified three essential aspects of their practice and world view, which he calls Identity, Opposition and Totality.[3] Identity is the recognition of a shared condition by the participants; Opposition is the group's oppositional stance and its claiming of a position of struggle; Totality is the alternative rationality of the movement—the particular set of values and way of seeing that challenges the dominant world view. It is the last of these three characteristics that shifts a group from pressure politics with reference primarily to its own members to a politics which can address society and social transformation as a whole.

All feminist activism shares the characteristics of Identity and Opposition. But only a feminism that recognizes and affirms women's specificity can develop the alternative rationality required for the principle of Totality and the move beyond sectional pressure to a universal challenge to society.

274

In many parts of the women's movement, recognition of the specificity of women remains ambivalent, in uneasy co-existence with the equally necessary and apparently contradictory insistence on the equality of male and female in a shared humanity. However, there are many feminists today who recognize and affirm women's specificity without ambivalence.[4] They have been able to articulate an alternative set of values based on the revaluation of the devalued characteristics, concerns and abilities associated with women and reproduction[5] and marginalized in male-dominated society. In the rest of this article, I will attempt to show in more detail how this affirmation of female-associated values makes possible the emergence of an over-arching feminist perspective which can encompass both women's specificity and equality in a "re-visioning" of the world that challenges the very terms of male-defined political discourse rather than simply claiming women's place within it.

Traditional progressive values such as equality, dignity and freedom are central to women's struggle, but to limit the conceptualization of our politics to these existing parameters is to deny its deeper revolutionary implications. Feminist politics must extend earlier progressive values in ways that reflect the transforming presence of women on the political stage. We are not simply entering politics as it has existed. When fully half of the human race has been excluded from the practice and definition of politics, our entry necessarily transforms its very shape and definition. Women's entry into politics *as women* is, in fact, the emergence of the long subordinate, devalued and marginalized sphere of private life and reproduction into the public and political world. It is, potentially, the transformation of politics, and is an event of world historical significance.

The *liberatory* affirmation of the traditionally devalued female aspects of life, on which I argue this transformation must be built, is, of course, an extremely difficult task. For it requires a dynamic, critical and creative perspective which includes transformation in the very moment of affirmation. It also requires that feminists find a way (and build the necessary power) to create a politics that can encompass and affirm our specific being and history as women, even as it challenges the oppression that has been grounded in that specificity. We are playing with fire when we accept our special historical identity with reproduction and caring, sharing, nurturing human values as an essential component of our specific

275

political voice. For our specificity as women has in the past been inseparable from our oppression as women.

Yet we have no choice in historical terms if we are to succeed in redefining humanity's long struggle for a freer and more fully human life. This redefinition requires the inclusion of the despised and denied feminine half of existence in the concept of what it is to be free and human. This is the only way to broaden and deepen progressive struggle to challenge the limiting divisions which currently shape our existence—divisions, for instance, between reproduction and production, private and public life, leisure and work, and male and female. Domination is built on and institutionalized in this fragmentation of human life. This fragmentation extends beyond even the alienation of people's productive powers to the alienation and division of aspects of their being into separate and opposed male and female halves of humanity.

To claim women's humanity only insofar as women can show themselves to be like (as good as) men is to challenge men's definition of women but not their definition of humanity. With the insistence that the cares and concerns and values traditionally associated with women, and indeed women themselves, are human, women's demand for access to male areas is transformed. It is no longer merely a claim to be human in limited male terms. It becomes instead part of the wider struggle to transform people as individuals, and the masculine concept of humanity common to the whole spectrum of male politics, society, culture and scholarship. For women, this includes the task of demanding access to, and developing skills in male-monopolized areas. But because man has been identical with humanity in male-dominated society, and female-identified activity has been devalued and marginalized, the overall direction of political struggle must be primarily to feminize the world and man and the concept of humanity. This is to provide concrete content for values and goals, such as "non-alienated man," which have remained abstractions in male-dominated radical politics. It is also to bring together the psychological and the social, the individual and the collective, the personal and the political, in a far more effective and sustained way than male radicals have been able to do.

This is why the realization of women's revolutionary potential requires that feminism be built from a recognition rather than a denial of women's specificity. At the same time, in a much more immediate way, the developing right-wing attack on feminism requires us to do this. Feminism/antifeminism is now the axis along which the major value questions of the day are being fought. "Women's issues" such as marriage, the family, equal rights, women's involvement in the paid labour force, day-care, abortion, sexual orientation, payment for housework, children's rights, and violence in public and personal life, are currently the most heatedly contested and the most ideologically arousing debates in cultural, social and personal as well as political areas.

The right-wing attempt to structure political debate around the theme of "What is womanhood and its meaning?" is a political ploy to move the discussion to ground where tradition and emotion and people's needs and fears are far more elemental than in the narrow political sphere which has historically been far removed from people's everyday lives. Nevertheless, it is not a red herring or a diversion from the real questions. It is, rather, a response to feminism's opening up of this new territory to political debate. Our understanding of gender domination made the personal political, and brought politics home with a vengeance. The challenge of the right-wing on that very ground is now forcing us to go further in our political development, and to deepen the values and vision we are affirming in our struggle as women.

The right-wing affirms reproduction and private life and the values associated with women in these spheres in order to defend a system built on the fragmentation of life and the division between and within people. This forces us to recognize that the definition and meaning of womanhood is now a key political question. It makes it essential for feminism to break patriarchal ideological hegemony by establishing, for the first time, an authentic and autonomous women's voice in defining womanhood, and necessarily also, men and humanity. To shirk the question of woman's specificity is to avoid the central ground of struggle altogether. It would be an attempt to build a politics without the substance to engage the "enemy" on the new political ground that we ourselves have opened up.

The claims of anti-abortion forces to speak for the "right to life"; of the apologists of an institution of domination, such as marriage is today, to speak for love and trust, care and commitment; or of corporal punishment and anti-day-care advocates to speak in the interests of the child, must be challenged in the name of the values they espouse. Life, love, and trust must be reclaimed by new and free women. And we must explore the new and fuller shape these values will take when they are not enmeshed in gender and class domination.

They will perhaps be so transformed as to be hardly recognizable in their current stunted and distorted shapes. But we can never fight the battle to build the power to name and create a new world by simply ignoring or rejecting or scoffing at values such as these. And women who, powerless as they are, have been the guardians of these values, will never recognize their voice and interests in a feminism which does so. To deny these values as the shaping force of our politics is to deny women — what their lives have stood for and what their lives have meant. It is to doom the women's movement to impotence.

The concept of service is a good example of the political ground on which feminists must challenge patriarchal ideological hegemony. Women have always served others and have been told that their glory and fulfillment is to be found in the denial of themselves in that service; that they find themselves through losing themselves. It is this self-denial in service that is stressed by reactionary definitions of women and becomes a key element of an ideology which disarms and silences women, enchaining them in a world built by them for others.

Yet it is not enough simply to reject the value of service as we reveal its oppressive content. Women's service has not been only forced servitude to their masters, it has been also the caring and nurturing of each other and our children. It has been the building and maintenance of the social connections and commitment that embody what is human in our society. It extends far beyond what is forced from women as subordinates to become in many cases freely chosen expressions of love and support which are not the self-denial but the expression of women's selves in the world. At the same time as it has oiled the wheels of an oppressive system and eased the lot of our rulers, women's service has kept alive an alternative, and in part subversive, set of values and ways of living life.

Recently, a very dear friend of mine was ill for a long time. I have seen how her women friends and neighbours have cared for her, extending themselves over a long period to take up the tasks of her daily reproduction and spiritual sustenance *as a matter of course*. I have also seen how this flexible give-and-take among women, determined by need rather than measured exchange, is under strain today. The social change coming so hard and fast upon us — with increasing social mobility and uprootedness, women's entry into the paid labour force in large numbers and the breakdown of marriages — is increasing our need for support. At the same time, it is straining our resources to provide it for each other. Now that women are adding a paid job to their already full-time unpaid work of managing individual and social reproduction, the space for such extension of self in mutual and caring service has been much restricted. This is a tremendous loss for the quality of our lives as women as well as for the quality of life generally. For we have expressed ourselves in giving support to each other and we have benefitted from receiving that support.

It is important not to glorify or mystify women's activities and the values they represent. As they are currently structured, they undoubtedly form part of the texture of our oppression. Non-reciprocal service to men in an unequal power situation which allows no other avenues of expression for women, clearly is not freely chosen as an expression of self. It is exploitive, and, in its essence, a denial of self. Its forms and structures must be attacked along with the anti-human and anti-woman mythology that holds that the glory and fulfillment of women lies in subordination and self-denial. But the power of these ideas among women cannot be dismissed as simply successful brainwashing, for it lies also in their association with the values of love and caring which are important to women, which women know are essential to human life and which women will not participate in denying or disparaging.

We must attack the forms of women's oppression which limit these values and restrict them to the marginal private realm, and which leave the functioning of the world of production and politics to instrumental quantitative anti-human sets of standards. In the name of free women, we must assert the importance of women's concerns, and build a struggle to have them generally recognized and made central in all areas of life. We must continue to insist on our right to participate fully in public life, but must at the same time challenge its very shape and underlying logic. Our participation must be seen to involve necessarily the transformation of both production and politics to serve the needs of people's reproduction as self-actualizing human beings. It must not be the abandonment of women's concern with people and with reproduction, but its extension to become the organizing principle of all of society.

The pressure on feminists to abandon that concern comes not only from its identification with subservience by the right-wing, but also from the liberal (and often Left) ideological collaboration with the Right in confounding collective women's liberation with the individual "liberated woman." The liberated woman abhorred by the Right and applauded in her various forms by liberals and radicals comes to displace the feminist in a shared alchemy. Women managers in corporations and women activists in male-dominated radical organizations are applauded by both liberals and radicals to the degree that they succeed in becoming one of their boys. The "liberation" of a liberated woman is measured by the distance she has travelled from other women.

Feminism's commitment to the collective liberation of all women, and our recognition that none of us can be free until we are all free, is reinterpreted as a message of individual one-up*man*ship. It becomes a liberation separate from and against other women, and a freedom from the old values of caring, sharing, cooperation and solidarity. Liberated women like this are so few as to be almost a creation of *Cosmopolitan* magazine, and yet they have become the popular image of a feminist. They are, in fact, isolated women, victims of their belief that they can win as individuals if they cut themselves off from other women and enter male arenas on male terms. They think they can reverse the stakes of the game without transforming its competitive and anti-human nature entirely and without altering the power imbalance between men and women. They cannot do this, of course, and they suffer in their attempt—and in the self-contempt which their rejection of other women exhibits. Nevertheless, their much publicized rejection of the values that women have represented is used as an attack on women. And their much vaunted lack of solidarity with women can be an actual threat; for instance, when their uncritical acceptance of men's sexual revolution allows them to be used against men's wives as examples of (and actual) "non-dependent," "understanding," "cooperative" alternative partners. This is used by the media to aggravate women's distance from a feminism that is made to appear to ignore, if not to actively disparage and threaten, the areas of life traditionally associated with women.

This male-defined liberal and radical individualist attack on and denial of women's work and values in the name of the liberated woman can sometimes push women into the arms of the opposing, but equally male-defined, glorification of women's work as subservience. The autonomous women's position which feminism must express has, so far, been submerged in this battle being waged in the name of two different male versions of women.

Only a perspective which refuses these two "alternatives" in the female-defined affirmation of women's specificity can allow us to identify and attack our subordination as women without denying or trivializing ourselves as women. This makes it possible for us to effectively counter right-wing attacks on women made in the name of women, and to develop an alternative to the radicalism that leaves women and women's work invisible. It allows us to express the politically conscious sisterhood of women's liberation as a transforming continuation of the age-old tradition of support and service among women. It will enable us to engage in ideological struggle with male radicalism and liberalism and male reaction more effectively than we have been able to up to now.

Political debate and the political arena are currently defined by the reactionary and radical poles of a spectrum of views that exclude women's autonomous voice (though not women's issues). Feminism remains essentially off-stage. The power of its presence in the wings has influenced the shape of the major political questions today (and the nature of defensive and obfuscatory male debate around these questions), much as the presence of an unseen planet influences the orbit patterns of others. Indeed, it would be hard to understand the content of today's politics without taking into account women's rebellion and growing power. But feminism does not yet have the power to influence the terms of the debate directly. It is, indeed, still heard as intervention in an established dialogue with male-defined parameters. It must be part of feminism's project to challenge the very definitions and content of this dialogue by establishing itself as one pole of the debate. We must build the power, not only to be heard around "women's issues" from time to time, but to wrest ideological control from men through redefining politics and the world.[6]

It is essential in this struggle to affirm not only the values but also the work associated with women and with reproduction. As long as we fail to challenge the liberal devaluation of what have historically been women's work and skills and characteristics, women will not see their voice or interests in us. Space will be left for those who portray feminist sisterhood as a threat to women and acknowledge women's importance only in order to perpetuate our subservience. A public position which actively disparages the work that women do in the home, by implying that women with no paid job are not working and are parasites, attacks women rather than the structures which have institutionalized this work to ensure the economic dependence of women who do

281

it. Housework is full-time and essential work. Women who do a paid job as well are doing two jobs rather than one. It is important for us to recognize this, and combat the new tendency for government and the media and the employers to ignore the necessary work involved in the domestic sphere. When liberals and radicals speak of the need for women to enter politics and production, and to take their place in all areas of society, without addressing the question of the organization of domestic labour (except perhaps for a passing mention of day-care and maternity leave), they may not be overtly disparaging this work, but they are implicitly accepting society's ideological devaluation of its extent and importance.

This down-playing of women's labour and reproduction is a view which reflects the interests of employers, and men in general, who wish to control and benefit, respectively, from women's cheap labour and additional wage without shifting the burden of housework. Unfortunately, this implicit attack on houseworkers (and lack of sympathy with all women, both those inside and outside the paid labour force, in their capacity as houseworkers) is often presented as a feminist position. The reluctance of some feminists to acknowledge women's specificity leaves us vulnerable to this misinterpretation and to the suspicions of women who fear (often without articulating it) that feminists are simply male fellow travellers, who envisage the new woman and new world in man's image.

In fact, the simple abandonment of reproductive concerns and work by women in order to join the existing "real" world of production and public life is not only unappealing to women; it is impossible. The Left/liberal vision of liberated women simply moving into their "rightful place" in the world as it is, or as it has been transformed by public ownership of the means of production, is a myth. It is a dangerous myth that can damage the development of women's solidarity and power, not only by presenting a goal and set of values that are threatening and unattractive to most women, but also by hiding the depth of the changes that feminism must be about.

Any significant increase in women's participation and power in politics and production will require a concomitant change in the organization of the domestic sphere. Work there will not simply disappear. Even if it is shared equally by men, women's presence in the paid labour force without major social restructuring will mean a significant additional work-load for both men and women. As it is, the burden is *not* shared, and the additional load has fallen almost entirely on the shoulders of women. We have, to be sure, marginally reduced our economic dependence because we now have access to half a wage for the two jobs we do. But this is not liberation and will never seem so to women.

If women are to recognize their interests in feminist positions, we must attack the privatization of domestic labour, its invisible and unremunerated nature and the fact that it is largely women's work. Challenge to the oppressive divisions between public and private life, between leisure and work, and between reproduction and production, is an integral part of feminism's resistance to the subordination and marginalization of reproductive activities and values in male-dominated industrial society. More and more feminists are affirming these values and concerns as the central organizing principles of a new, more integrated, less fragmented and less hierarchical society:

> We refuse to remain on the margins of society, and we refuse to enter that society on its own terms... The human values that women were assigned to preserve [must] become the organizing principle of society. The vision that is implicit in feminism [is] a society organized around human needs... There are no human alternatives. The Market, with its financial abstractions, deformed science, and the obsession with dead things... must be pushed back to the margin. And the "womanly" values of community and caring must rise to the center as the only human principle.
>
> (Ehrenreich and English 1979:342)

As a political perspective rooted in women's specificity begins to emerge within feminism, we can see how its emphasis on the simultaneous integrative transformation of the fragmented public and private realms of life opens the way for deep connections among women, across divisions of class and culture. It is this that provides the basis for the clear expression of feminist sisterhood as the affirmation of women together, rather than the threat to women that its enemies (liberal, radical and right-wing) paint it to be.

Women's relationship to paid work varies enormously within and between national economies. Yet within Canada and worldwide (with the exception of a small group of women attached to very wealthy men) *all* women share a responsibility for and experience of reproductive labour. We forget this when we speak as though the adult female population were divided between housewives and "working women." This common phraseology, which parts of the movement have adopted uncritically on occasion, is mystifying in two ways. It hides both the fact that housework and motherhood are *work* and the fact that the "working woman" also does housework

283

and has children. It implies and creates artificial barriers among women by ignoring the ground of commonality on which we can hope to build a specifically woman-defined politics.

Emphasis on the paid work force alone also magnifies barriers between women internationally by focusing on an aspect of women's condition which is unique to developed industrial societies, to the exclusion of the reproductive aspect shared by women of all societies. And yet the reproductive aspect of their lives looms largest even for women in North America. A recent United Nations survey estimated that women worldwide do between 66% and 75% of the work of the world, earn 10% of the income, and own 1% of the property.

The only way we can understand this shared condition is to recognize the key role of unpaid and dependent reproductive labour in defining the situation of women.

The revolutionary Chinese slogan that "Women hold up *half* the sky" was intended to combat the devaluation and invisibility of women's work and to undermine the myth that women are economic parasites. Its intention was to claim for women their rightful place as social contributors. And yet it drastically under-estimates the amount of sky that women actually do hold up. It, too, perpetuates a mystifying male construction of reality. The absolute necessity, and the truly revolutionary implications, of focusing on women's specific experience of and responsibility for reproduction are clear when we see the conservative nature of this "revolutionary" slogan.

The practical realities of women's work and interests, then, as well as the fulfillment of the more abstract liberating potential of women's activism, require that our politics be built from a recognition rather than a denial of women's specific work and values. This recognition is a far cry from its glorification. It acknowledges women's traditional association with reproduction and its values in the very moment of denying the necessity or inevitability of that special relationship, and refusing the oppression that it has institutionalized. It brings the specific perspective of women to the age-old struggle of "Man" against domination, and in doing so posits a revolutionary affirmation and transformation of both radicalism and women's traditional values and self-definition. In affirming women's specificity, feminism articulates new and more universal truths — truths which end narrow, single-sex definitions of the world, and in the process, feminize and humanize politics.

FOOTNOTES

1. The articles in Chapters 1 to 8 of this book are examples of the radical, transforming feminist critiques that have emerged in all the disciplines.
2. "Discussion" *The Scholar and the Feminist IV: Connecting Theory, Practice and Values,* a Conference sponsored by Barnard College Women's Center, April 23, 1977.
3. See *The Post-Industrial Society: Tomorrow's Social History: Classes, Conflicts and Culture in the Programmed Society* (New York: Random House, 1971).
4. Elsewhere, I have called this tendency of feminism *integrative feminism.* See the Introduction to this book and, for a more detailed development of the concept, Miles 1981:481-495.
5. Reproduction is used here in its broadest possible sense to refer to all of the activity involved in the bearing, rearing and maintaining of people throughout their lives.
6. This redefinition/re-visioning of the world is already far advanced in feminist theory. We lack the power to simply translate our new understanding to the political realm where male hegemony remains largely intact. Nevertheless, feminism's struggle for redefinition is evident in as yet isolated but important interventions which will provide the building blocks for future more general challenges to the male definition of political dialogue. Male hegemony of definition is breached, for instance, when (even momentarily), in courts, social work agencies and censorship boards and school text books and radio and T.V. talk shows:
   - rape becomes a political act rather than an individual pathology;
   - pornography becomes an attack on women rather than an exercise in freedom;
   - clitoridectomy becomes a political and health issue rather than a richness of cultural diversity;
   - wife-beating becomes male violence against women rather than a "family dispute";
   - marriage becomes an institution for the ownership rather than the protection of women;
   - housework becomes work rather than the natural expression of feminity;
   - prostitutes become sexual victims rather than "fallen women" or harassers of men.

CHAPTER 12

Feminist Perspectives on Development: A Discussion Paper

Inter-Agency Working Group on Women and Development of the Canadian Council for International Cooperation

This chapter is based on a document developed collectively by members of the Canadian Council for International Cooperation's (CCIC) Inter-Agency Working Group on Women and Development (IAWG-WD). The views expressed do not necessarily reflect those of the Canadian Council for International Cooperation and its members. For further information contact IAWG-WD, CCIC, 200 Isabella St., Suite 300, Ottawa, Ontario K1S 1V7.

"Feminism offers us a wholistic perspective on all issues related to human life—one that strives for the broadest and deepest development of individuals and their societies through freedom from the systems of domination that characterize our world: rich over poor, men over women, North over South."

287

Introduction

This paper was prepared by CCIC's Inter-Agency Working Group on Women and Development. We hope it will serve as a tool to stimulate reflection and discussion on feminist perspectives of development throughout the NGO community.

CCIC established the Women and Development Working Group in 1982 and created the position of Women and Development Coordinator in 1984 to act as a focal point in coordinating and promoting work on women and development.

By January 1986, it had become clear that before the group's priorities and plans could be set, there was a need to more clearly articulate and then adopt a common approach to women and development. The Working Group needed a basis of unity to guide and orient its work.

We believe that our "feminist" perspective on development provides that common base. It incorporates our shared values and represents a vision of the world we work toward, for women and all humanity. We espouse a feminism that seeks not to integrate women into existing structures of domination, exploitation, and inequality, but strives to challenge them fundamentally.

This paper offers a definition of a "feminist philosophy," shows how it can deepen our understanding of development, and explores its implications for NGO work, particularly as it relates to women. It looks specifically at how the overseas development work, political action, and development education undertaken by NGOs can be informed by these principles.

The paper that follows is part of a documented ongoing dialogue among Canadian NGO women on issues of primary concern. It has been a tool for discussion and learning, especially for those of us whose peer group is scattered across this vast country. Its production reflects the conditions of our work together—based on separate regional, historical, personal, and organizational realities and contexts. It also reflects our firm conviction that, as Canadian women involved in global development, we share among ourselves and with women everywhere a commonality of experience with sexism and of hopes for a world characterized by its absence.

Over the past year, the working group has begun to build consensus on a philosophy of feminist development. This statement is part of that ongoing process. We who have contributed to this small bit of the debate within the international women's movement are, in some ways, a special group. The particular conditions of our lives and work give us access to information, to travel, to contact with women engaged in similar work across Canada and around the world; and the time for reflection and analysis. From this position, we attempt to draw the links, build the analysis, and plan for action through which we can more effectively work toward equality, development, and peace.

This is a thought paper. Each of us who has worked on it owes a debt to others who have gone before and done the ground work. The voices of many other women echo through this paper. Its development has helped us better understand each other: our similarities and differences, our agreements and disagreements. We hope it will stimulate others to continue the process. The quotes join our voices with those of women elsewhere. They help us situate ourselves in the context of a global movement of women asking similar questions and moving, each in her own way, toward defining a new vision of development and the means for achieving it.

Each of us is personally affected by the women-and-development issues that concern us. That experience leads us to feminist analysis. Our global perspective reinforces that analysis and encourages us to understand our experience of injustice within a broader political context.

Why a Discussion of Feminist Perspectives?

For women to become a vital force in their societies, change will have to be based on a new theory of development which embraces feminism. Feminism poses some challenges to development theory and praxis that must be addressed if any effective and inclusive work about bringing about a new order is to be done. It questions the artificial barriers between the political, social, and economic aspects of society and how individuals relate to these orders. Feminism asserts that the personal is political and personal change is a prerequisite to societal change... It insists that the experience of women be recognized and validated in all work related to change.

**Anita Anand (U.S.), "Rethinking Women and Development,"
1980, a much reprinted article**

[The Nairobi Forum] was a triumph of Third World thinking and a refusal to limit feminism to the situation of the North. They insisted that feminism include analysis of race, class and country position within the global economy. Feminism offers the only politics which can transform our world into a more humane place and deal with global issues like equality, development and peace—because it asks the right questions: about power; about the links between the personal and the political; and because it cuts through race and class.

Feminism implies consciousness of *all* the sources of oppression: race, class, homophobia, *and* it resists them all. Feminism is a call for action. This is because of a growing feminist consciousness among Third World women; because of global crisis; and because the achievements of the Decade in the areas where gains were made showed up the limitations of national improvements.

Peggy Antrobus (Barbados) at Post-Nairobi Conference, Toronto, from a report on the conference by Liz Willick, 1986

It is time for us to start looking at the women's question from the bottom up. If today we want to further expand the horizons of our freedom, we must look towards the toiling women... The struggle to put an end to all forms of exploitation based on class, caste, religion, race, can be successful only when women join this struggle for a new society—in which one of the most fundamental inequalities, that based on sex, has no place.

Today we no longer say: "Give us more jobs, more rights, consider us your 'equals' or even allow us to compete with you better." But rather: *Let us re-examine the whole question, all the questions. Let us take nothing for granted. Let us not only re-define ourselves, our role, our image—but also the kind of society we want to live in.*

M. Kishwar & R. Vanita (eds.), *In Search of Answers: Indian Women's Voice from Manushi* (Zed Books, 1984)

In 1982, developed countries spent 17 times more on military expenditures than on foreign economic aid. In other words, at the start of the Third Development Decade they were devoting 4.5 percent of their GNP to the military and 0.3 percent to foreign assistance... In 1987, the world is spending $100 billion/year on arms. That is the exact amount the third world is in debt... This diversion of resources toward destructive rather than productive ends breeds violence at the domestic, local, national and international levels...

G. Sen & C. Grown, *Development Crisis and Alternative Visions: Third World Women's Perspectives,* (DAWN, 1985)

[U.N. figures tell us that] women are half of the world's people, but they put in two thirds of the working hours, receive one tenth of the wages, and own only one one-hundredth of the property. They are the Third World's chief beast of burden. They are about 500 million of the world's 800 million illiterates, yet they are the first educators of all coming generations; as well as the daily guardians of their health and nutrition. They are the largest group of landless labourers, the poorest of the poor, and the most powerless of the oppressed.

For 30 years, development programs have largely yielded somewhat disappointing results. This should hardly be surprising. Any effort that systematically ignores half the people involved is nonsense—and is doomed to fail. The full participation of women in development directly involves half of the available human resources, holds the greatest potential for breakthroughs in many sectors and offers the key to unlocking the development dilemma. It is painfully obvious that women have been—and still are being—left out of development.

We must make a full role for women a top priority in Canada's aid program, but it's not easy. There is immense inertia and resistance... The question of women in development... is, at the same time, an issue of human rights, economic efficiency, cultural values and social progress... I count on your help...

Monique Vézina, Minister for External Relations, at CUSO 1984 Annual General Meeting, in: "Evaluation for Planning for Women in Development," Botswana, 1985

Discrimination against women is a profound and subtle sickness that has lodged itself deep in the subconscious of both men and women as well as in the structures of our societies. This makes it one of the hardest sources of inequality to fight—because it grips women from within and without.

Women's analysis of their situations and their courage, both to wrestle with their own internalized view of themselves as weak and powerless, and to start standing up for their rights—often against men they love—has cost them, at best, confusion and heartache; at worst, isolation, imprisonment and death. But it has also created a women's movement that has put sexual equality firmly on the world's agenda...

Debbie Taylor (ed.), *Women: A World Report* (New Internationalist/Methuen, 1985)

Toward a Feminist Philosophy of Development

As part of the network of CCIC's Inter-Agency Working Group on Women and Development (IAWG-WD, or the WG), each of us is actively involved in some aspect of global development work. As women, we cannot divorce our work from the knowledge that all development issues and processes affect women differently.

That difference is rooted in the many faces of sexism: in the interplay of thought and action that makes women's status secondary at all levels of the world's social, political, and economic systems; and that makes much of women's work invisible and not valued.

We know, very clearly, that not all of us are comfortable with the word "feminist." It appears, however, that the international women's movement, in its debates on the relationships between women and development, more and more commonly claims it as its own. By exploring the concept—its meaning and its value to us—we can more clearly understand our own principles as development workers and as women; and in the process develop a common language that expresses our understanding and experience.

At its simplest, feminist development means equality of participation and control for women every step of the way, building a theory and practice of development that is in the interests of the majority of the world's women.

For poor Third World women, peace and struggle against violence cannot be divorced from the struggle for basic needs, economic justice, national liberation, and a development oriented toward these goals. *Peace cannot be separated from development just as equality cannot, because the conditions that breed violence, war, and inequality are themselves often the results of development strategies harmful or irrelevant to the poor and to women.*

G. Sen & C. Grown, *op. cit.*

> If human survival is now the world's most pressing problem, and if women are crucial to that survival, then the empowerment of women is essential for the emergence of new, creative, and co-operative solutions to the crisis.
>
> As part of this process of empowerment, we need to reaffirm and clarify our understanding of feminism... The time has come to articulate the position that feminism cannot be monolithic in its issues, goals, and strategies, since it constitutes the political expression of the concerns and needs of women from different regions, classes, nationalities, and ethnic backgrounds. There is and must be a diversity of feminisms, responsive to the different needs and concerns of different women, and *defined by them for themselves*. This diversity builds on a common *opposition to gender oppression and hierarchy*, which, however, is only the first step in articulating and acting upon a political agenda...
>
> **G. Sen & C. Grown,** *op. cit.*

Feminism offers us a wholistic perspective on all issues related to human life—one that strives for the broadest and deepest development of individuals and their societies through freedom from the systems of domination that characterize our world: rich over poor, men over women, North over South.*

We define feminism as a positive and creative challenge to global systems of domination, exploitation, and inequality. As such, it can unite women from North and South: across race, religion, and national boundaries in a common struggle. We understand that this does not necessarily imply a basis of unity for *all* women. We are not attempting to integrate women into systems organized for the benefit of men, capital, or the powerful corporate interests of the industrialized world.

We have agreed on some essential (and feminist) components of our understanding, our work, and our hopes:

We know that:

- Women constitute the majority of the poor, the unemployed, the underemployed, and the economically and socially disadvantaged in every country.

---

* We recognize that there are many objections to the use of terms such as "First World-Third World," "Underdeveloped-developing-developed," and "North-South." However, we had difficulty using just one set of terms throughout. Please use these terms interchangeably.

- Women's unpaid and underpaid work is crucial economically and socially, although largely unrecognized, undervalued, and ignored by statistics.
- Women's work is vital to the survival and reproduction of human beings. In such areas as food production and processing, provision of fuel, water, health and child care, sanitation—the entire range of basic human survival needs—women's labour is dominant. Development that has as its goals equality, development, and peace must be based on an understanding of women's role as primary workers and producers in these areas.
- Women have borne the brunt of environmental degradation, which is reaching catastrophic proportions globally.

We recognize that:

- Women suffer from oppression in all societies because they are women; the oppression varies in form and degree and is shaped and may be multiplied by their class, race, culture, religion, age, nationality, and many other factors.
- Poor women of the South face a triple oppression and a triple struggle—as citizens of economically poor countries, as part of the marginalized majority within their countries, and as women.
- Many women in Canada face the same struggles as Third World women: in particular, Native women, immigrant women, disabled women, and women who are members of visible and/or marginalized minorities.
- Women's priorities will vary with the particular needs of their situation.

Practical Approaches to Feminist Development

In this part of our discussion paper, we explore some ideas for putting our principles into practice, keeping our experience within Canadian NGOs firmly in mind. Our list is certainly not exhaustive, but it can provide some practical possibilities for focusing our work in research, education, organizing and organizations, and action. We have divided the discussion into three interlocking areas: practical approaches to Overseas Development Work (including male bias, criteria, staff, process, and internal implications); to NGOs and Political Action; and to Development Education.

OVERSEAS DEVELOPMENT WORK

It is now becoming clear that the acute food shortage in Africa, while dramatically and tragically exacerbated by drought and war, may be due in large part to the way women have been systematically excluded from access to land and from control of modern agriculture in that region.

The processes are subtle but are beginning to prove devastating. And the devastation is greatest in Africa because this is the region where women do a greater proportion of the agricultural work... than in any other continent.

In Africa, the pressures that bear down on rural women all over the world are magnified and mount up, one upon another, to force Africa's women onto their knees, taking Africa's food production down with them.

Debbie Taylor, *op. cit.*

In the final analysis, the oppression of women is a universal phenomenon... It is possible not only to introduce feminism into the development process, but even more critical to render development more feminist. It is clear that the subordination of women emerges out of dialectical relationships between culture, the economy, and politics. Because of this fundamental reality, we cannot separate feminism from development or vice versa.

Marie-Angélique Savané (Senegal), "Feminizing Development,"
Development, **1984**

The declaration of the United Nations Decade for Women owes much to pioneering research work by a few women and to the growth of the international women's movement. The decade provided unprecedented space and resources for concentrated research documenting the work that women do and the effect of imposed development priorities and projects on their lives and work.

We believe that:

• Women should and must be included as equal partners in all social, economic, and political decision-making processes.

- The struggle against the oppression of women cannot be compromised or relegated to the future while or until struggles against other forms of oppression are resolved. Through understanding the various forms of oppression that women experience—and their inter-relatedness—we will be better able to develop, participate in, and support effective action to improve women's lives.

- Feminist development is in the interests of the majority of the world's people; not only of its women.

- A feminist vision must include but not end with equality for women. Economic, political, class, and social structures designed to reserve power for a small minority will not accommodate such equality. We realize that some women are part of the world's ruling elites and are favoured by the status quo. When we speak of development with women, our focus is on the dispossessed, the disadvantaged, the economically and politically powerless—the vast majority.

We support:

- The basic right of women to self-determination and self-fulfillment, including access to choices and the power to choose with regard to their own lives and bodies, including control over their own sexuality and fertility.

- The struggles of women around the world for their rights as paid workers, for recognition of unpaid work and a decent standard of living.

- The right of women to be free of domestic, local, and global violence.

*   *   *

This new body of research and analysis of women worldwide provides many examples of how development has directly contributed to deterioration in the status, independence, and earning power of women. Further, because women carry the major responsibility for the well-being of families and communities, the quality of life for many of the world's poor has deteriorated in direct relationship to the increasing impoverishment of women; and in contradiction to the stated aims of most development projects.

By and large, men have almost total control of development planning and processes of international, national, and local issues. The notion that unpaid work is irrelevant or non-work is deeply imbedded, even in women themselves. Women's labour is not counted, their role is not respected, their voices are neither sought nor heard. To far too many development planners and project officers, women are invisible.

What Does Male Bias Mean for Development With Women?

What does male bias in development planning mean for development with women? Here are some examples drawn from Barbara Rogers' book, *The Domestication of Women*. Her context is Africa and her focus is on U.N. Agency projects. The book was published in 1980 and documents attitudes one would hope had ended with the Decade. We know they haven't.

> The assumptions that development planners make about women in society are almost never stated, but are all the more powerful for that reason. It is thought "natural" that a woman's place is in the home and that she has a very specific set of tasks which are thought to be universal because they are based on biological imperatives of sex. The most important role for women, defining their entire life, is portrayed as the bearing and bringing up of children. A man, on the other hand, is seen as the "natural" head of the family, its representative in the outside world and therefore the person with whom the planners will deal. Since it is assumed that men control families ("the master in his own home"), any new resources intended for everyone should be channelled through them...
>
> A few examples with male planners in the field may be used to illustrate the process.

> *An FAO country representative:*
>
> I've just been filling in a questionnaire from headquarters about women. But you know there's hardly anything to say, because we don't have the sort of projects that would involve them. We have nothing against them, in fact we'd like to have more for them; but you see all our projects here are concerned with cattle. Of course we get criticised because the cattle are owned by the richer people.
>
> Rogers:
> Is it perhaps more than just a coincidence that all the money is going into cattle and almost nothing for crops, when cattle are men's responsibility and crops are women's?
>
> FAO:
> I never really saw it like that. But I suppose there is a connection.

297

Onchoceriasis Control Programme (World Health Organization and others):

Rogers:
Why do all your statistics on the incidence of river-blindness only refer to men? Don't women get it? Aren't you concerned whether they do or not?

Repeated several times, with different replies:

There isn't any difference. Women and men get the disease at exactly the same rate as far as I know.

In our village visits, we find it's really a men's disease. Sure, we'll find three or four blind women in each place, but its usually trachoma, not oncho. We might treat them, but only to get the villagers' cooperation for our oncho programme.

There's no common pattern. My sociological data show that it depends entirely on the seasonal work patterns, who works close to the river for the longest periods. In some villages more women have oncho than men. There are so many factors: for example, I find that if there's a small well in a village and the women don't have to go to the river for water, they're less exposed to the fly.

The documents only mention men having the disease? I don't believe it. Let me look it up... Well, how amazing! You're right! D'you know I've worked on this for years, read that document dozens of times and never noticed that it is only about the men. And now I come to think of it, our film only shows pictures of men. But surely the women get it too. I wonder why it was done like that...

Director of a co-operative employment project:

I've tried to introduce vegetable production here too. I got this man to try it, spent hours with him suggesting new techniques, working with him, persuading him to experiment with different methods. Yes, it looks very impressive, and he gets a good income out of it. But I'm very disappointed that it has not been taken up by anyone else in the village, which was my original idea.

Rogers:
Didn't any of the women show any interest?

Director:
Perhaps if I'd tried it with the women in the first place the idea would have got a lot further by now. You know, I just never thought of that, can't think why. Now it's too late.

* * *

Women's input *within* development agencies can help, but finding the appropriate mix of what is needed and what

298

is possible means supporting the local women who will be involved to provide that input.

The WG office at CCIC has a variety of both theoretical background papers and examples of criteria that various agencies have used. These are available as back-up to further general work in this area and for people who may want to develop specific guidelines appropriate to their particular agency's work.

We have observed that the Decade and the resources it made available for work with and about women made the policies and criteria of WID projects popular catch-phrases that do not necessarily imply either understanding or commitment to a vision of development and the future to which women would want to subscribe.

Over the past decade, we have seen many exciting initiatives for women and development springing up on the local level. But progress in national and international development institutions has been slower. In general, development institutions have responded to our demands for a more central role by tacking women's components onto existing programs.

We have had to push hard for a different kind of development process, one that does not treat us as mere appendages. We have insisted that a development program that contributes to women's emancipation means creating conditions for us to state our own priorities, take initiatives and run our own programs. And it means development organizations must look inside their own institutions to see how well women are represented and how much *power* they have to shape policy...

Women in Development: A Resource Guide for Organization and Action (Rome: ISIS International, 1983)

In arguing for special consideration for women's rights through projects, campaigns and organizational structures, we are regularly reminded of the dangers of "ghettoizing." Of course, it is a concern, but not a great one. By the fact of their subordinated position, their marginalization in so-called general analyses, and the diminution of the value of the work they do, women are already in a ghetto. An alternative ghetto in which their needs have priority, their right of self-determination is acknowledged and their work is recognized can only be an improvement. If this "ghetto effect" is accepted... it can be seen as one step in the equalization process for women. Given that the inputs and organization of such ghettos are successful in their outcome, they will naturally outgrow themselves and be replaced as women and men assume equality in social, political and economic life.

From an undated, untitled exerpt from a policy paper by the "Women's Working Party" of War on Want (England)

Criteria for Development With Women

It is important to remember that project criteria are tied to the particular overall development objectives of the agency sponsoring the project. Quite evidently, development agencies may not have feminist perspectives and goals. No one set of criteria can serve the great diversity of agencies. Nor is there one set that, if adhered to, could meet the diverse needs of every recipient group.

However, if development is to work in the interest of the majority, it is essential that agencies have guidelines to ensure that women's views, roles, status, and labour are taken into account. Projects *must* have local input if they are to challenge and change rather than reinforce structures and processes that are oppressive to women. Ways must be found for women to participate in identifying, controlling, planning, implementing, and evaluating projects. Projects must ensure access for women to leadership, training, credit, and control over project resources.

Development Workers and Development With Women

In 1985, the International Coalition for Development Action (ICDA) released the results of its survey on "The Role and Status of Women in Development NGOs in the North." The survey involved 127 responses from fourteen countries. Some of the results were:

- Women on staff in non-secretarial/clerical positions: 56% of agencies had at least 50% women; 27% between 25 and 49%; 17% less than 25%.

- Women on boards, committees, and AGM: 40% had half or more representation of women; 36% between 25 and 49%; 24% less than 25%.

The report concludes:

> The majority of development NGOs have realized the importance of making women more central to development. 56% of respondents rated women in development as a high priority area of concern. However, most NGOs have not moved beyond this stage of recognition and taken concrete action to increase women's participation at all levels and to introduce a women's perspective in their work.
> Significantly, even a high proportion of women on staff and decision-making bodies does not guarantee a woman's perspective in the organization's work. This raises the question about the relative power wielded by women and men within the organizations.
>
> **B. Shah & A. Clarke (Belgium), "Survey: The Role and Status of Women in Development NGOs," 1985**

We must build an awareness within our agencies that sexist biases and attitudes are as unacceptable and as negative a factor in development workers as are racist biases and attitudes. We recognize that cultural, gender-based attitudes of discrimination are as deeply rooted as racist ones and will be no easier to eliminate. We recognize as well that women are not necessarily exempt from those biases.

Development workers who are unable to see or recognize the importance of women's work in their own context are unlikely to be able to work effectively with women overseas. Development workers who do not have a clear understanding that women everywhere are disadvantaged, and that this cripples all efforts for improvements in the lives of poor people generally, will be unable to distinguish between processes that offer real support to the empowerment of women and those that are merely tokens of the popularization of "women's issues."

At all agency levels, we stress the need for consciousness-raising on women's roles and for work toward an approach to development that we have called feminist; and towards equality of women within our NGOs.

Overseas, it is particularly important to increase the number of women project officers and other field workers. Gender biases mean that women workers will more readily have access to local women's domestic settings and organizations; will more easily build the trust necessary for an honest expression of women's perceptions, opinions, and needs.

For NGOs which have overseas staff, the whole question of male-female ratios is a touchy issue. [Some agencies have refused to hire female staff for some regions] where women work at a distinct disadvantage for cultural reasons... Some nationals from the countries in question feel that this is a Western prejudice and state that women from NGO staff are both welcome and respected. Concern has also been expressed by some NGO personnel that female field staff will not remain for much more than four or five years, as their spouses have difficulties obtaining work permits overseas. Open discussion is needed so that NGO staff can determine if there are practical solutions to the problems and to ensure that they are not simply being used as an excuse not to hire women...

Closely related to this discussion is the nature of the working relationship project officers have with members of the opposite sex overseas. One female project officer feels that she has to establish herself as an "honorary man" in order to be accepted and to do an effective job. For the male project officers a problem arises in that women simply will not talk to men about some issues. One male project officer observed that it is far more difficult for a man to gain "honorary woman" status. The idea of working in teams was suggested as a possible solution to some of these problems...

Dana Peebles, "Pre-Study on the Impact of NGO Projects on Women," CCIC, 1982

Agencies must be generous with the time allowed field staff to get to know the people with whom they work. Third World women have argued eloquently for patient support to existing organizations, for avoiding the creation of foreign modes of organization and action, for support for indigenous organizing processes as a prerequisite to the definition of appropriate level projects.

Overseas workers who understand sexism at home are better equipped to understand it as they learn the culture within which they work. This is essential to identifying and supporting the organizations and methods that most effectively improve and support the status of women and the opportunities available to them.

Development Work and Feminist Process

We do not claim to know all the answers to the problems, nor that there are unique solutions to them. In fact, we would assert that the solutions have to be worked out at the local level by the groups themselves. It is also important to recognize the cultural specificity of research methods and, especially, action. These depend on the social and cultural characteristics of regions and groups, though in general, women's groups appear more likely to be nonviolent and concerned about hierarchy and democratic processes. We need a great deal more self-understanding and dialogue about our own methods, problems and successes in building organizations and managing power during the Decade, so that we can move ahead. Respect for the many voices of our movement, for their cross-fertilizing potential, for the power of dialogue, for the humility to learn from the experiences of others are crucial to our vision...

G. Sen & C. Grown, *op. cit.*

Throughout the world, the women's movement has developed a style of work characterized as feminist. While work-styles vary with context, feminist process tends to avoid methods and structures that are seen as promoting and perpetuating the oppression of women.

Feminist process, therefore, tends to avoid power relationships based on ownership or wealth or hierarchical structures. Women's organizing experience has taught us much about shared leadership, consensus decision-making, individual and group support mechanisms, ways of supporting participation from all levels of experience and knowledge. Women's particular experience with building, from personal experience, a broader understanding of social, economic, and political

303

processes can provide models for the empowerment of people generally.

Generally, feminist process reflects the importance women place on mutual understanding and the respect they hold for one another's experience and perspectives. *There are, of course, always exceptions* (this statement applies to all other generalizations about women!). Our experience, after all, is primarily within the various organizations and processes to which we seek alternatives.

We see development as a joint process whereby people work together to overcome oppressive international systems of all sorts: rather than as "aid" from "developed" to "underdeveloped." "Projects" defined in the North and delivered in the South do not necessarily lend themselves to building common goals and a sense of mutual undertaking. We must develop alternative models. There are many examples within and outside the women's movement by which organizations in North and South tackle parallel problems together. Efforts in this direction are to be found especially in liberation solidarity movements, and work designated as "networking," "linkage," and "grassroots organizing."

Effective overseas work is hampered by the failings of our own systems, which have not been created to promote equality and mutuality. We must see our work with people in the South as building a better world for all of us. We must learn from our partners in the South and seek an active exchange of skills, insights, and support. Examples of how feedback from the South has changed our organizations and work in the North can be found in the histories of our own agencies. New priorities on work with local women's groups is one example. Another is the shift from individual child to community sponsorship programmes.

Taking women seriously as partners in development, sharing abilities and insights on internationally important projects and goals implies involvement in feminist process, whether labelled as such or not. It has serious implications for the structure and operation of our own organizations. Feminist process is an alternative to traditional, hierarchical, and male-dominated processes. Even with general agreement on its goals of equality, development, and peace, feminist methods and their practical implications for existing organizations and power structures can place us, in the short term at least, in opposition to traditional practitioners who in practice do not treat development as an egalitarian two-way process.

I remember talking to an angry and eloquent Kenyan who said that if we are serious about working with poor rural women, we must support their right to organize on their own terms and in their own ways without expecting immediately measurable results in a material sense. "Don't pay your people to come here and teach us how to write budgets and proposals," she said. "Send us people who can understand *us*; and then go back and translate our needs into your bureaucratic forms— or else change your bureaucracies to suit *our* needs instead of your own."

From personal notes from the Nairobi Forum by Liz Willick (Sask.), 1985

Implications for NGOs Internally

There are many implications of this discussion of feminist principles and their application. New problems and contradictions will arise, as they always have, from each action we take in building alternatives. Social change is never an easy task. It almost always requires that risks be taken by individuals and their organizations.

As part of the process of moving toward global equality for women, we must urge our NGOs to develop principles and policies with regard to work with and for women if they have not already done so. We must then work towards the application of those principles to internal as well as overseas methods and processes. For example:

- Working conditions within an agency should reflect development goals and practice in working toward women's equality through equal pay for work of equal value, affirmative action in hiring, and protection from sexual harassment.

- We advocate participatory decision-making processes within project development in the South, and this should also be practised within our NGOs.

- Alternatives to existing hierarchical structures should be supported, tested, and implemented, including methods for conflict resolution, hiring practices, job descriptions, two-way evaluations, communications, planning, chairing and meeting processes, two-way accountability at all levels. Increasing the participation of women, especially at policy levels, and recognising their work and potential, should be a goal in developing such alternatives. Education and consciousness-raising will be required throughout the organization; with volunteers, staff, management, and Board.

While half the project officers interviewed were women, in all but three of the agencies, the executive directors and most of the other executive-level staff were male. Support staff is almost entirely female. To quote one male project officer, "in this hive all the drones are women, and all the queen bees are men." An observation made about the situation both here and overseas by several project officers is that "the women do the work and the men make the decisions." A number of project officers strongly questioned the dynamics involved in agencies which are essentially change agents promoting social justice overseas and which practice inequality at home.

Dana Peebles, *op. cit.*

NGOs AND POLITICAL ACTION

A development process that shrinks and poisons the pie available to poor people, and then leaves women scrambling for a larger relative share, is not in women's interests. We reject the belief that it is possible to obtain sustainable improvements in women's economic and social position under conditions of growing relative inequality, if not absolute poverty, for both women and men. Equality for women is impossible within the existing economic, political and cultural processes that reserve resources, power and control for small sections of people. But neither is development possible without greater equity for and participation by women.

G. Sen & C. Grown, *op. cit.*

Feminist issues are political issues, and political issues can always be viewed from a feminist perspective. In political action, equality should be as ever-present a goal as it is in the planning and delivering of development programmes.

NGOs are involved in a variety of ways with directly lobbying governments or mobilizing the public to do so. A commitment to feminist principles in overseas work and in internal operations should logically be extended to work in the political sphere as well. Here are some possibilities we have considered for NGO political action:

- Urge government to consider the role of women in bilateral aid projects, and their effect on women. This is especially important in supporting rather than detracting from the work of women in food production, with consideration for existing roles in rural development and agricultural and community production and structures.

- Urge governments to defend the health of women by working against campaigns for administering inappropriate, unnecessary, and dangerous drugs and contraceptives; and for women's right to make their own choices in reproductive matters.

- Work against the exploitation of women's and girls' labour, especially with regard to Western corporate practices in micro-technology industries and free-trade zones.

- Protest the exploitation of women and girls as hostesses and prostitutes.

- Advocate recognition of the links, in overseas and development education work, between women within and outside Canada to reduce funder-related restrictions on programme content (e.g., Secretary of State Women's Program funds in Canada only; CIDA's Public Participation Program funds internationally-focused programmes).

- Urge the federal government to stop dangerous escalation of the superpower arms race and to redirect funding to social needs in this country and to development assistance.

- NGOs should familiarize themselves with government commitments on equality internally (CIDA WID Policy) and externally (government signing of U.N. Decade Conventions) and maintain constant pressure for implementation of statements of principle and policy (or for the development of changes to such statements where appropriate).

We believe that Canada's Official Development Assistance should be focused on securing self-sufficiency for the poorest of the poor in LDCs. Canada should concentrate on meeting the basic needs of food, fuel, water, and health for poor women. We suggest that Canada can reach these ends only by establishing new priorities:

- Policies must reflect the self-defined needs of poor Third World women;
- ODA funding must be restructured such that tied aid is drastically reduced;
- Funding for both internal and international development assistance should be increased by transferring monies from military expenditures to development assistance.

Women in Development Working Group (Kitchener-Waterloo), "Official Development Assistance and Its Impact on Women," 1986

DEVELOPMENT EDUCATION

Most Canadian development NGOs are involved in "dev ed" of some kind. What it is and how it is done varies widely— from high-tech fund-raising campaigns, to using Latin American popular theatre techniques to understand how international food production and distribution systems affect farm families in rural Canadian communities.

If development involves an international partnership working toward global justice, equality, and peace, then development education must work toward common understanding of global processes and systems that stand in the way of those goals.

Much development-education theory and practice in Canada focuses on building understanding and support among people from North and South—among those whose lives are negatively affected by global systems of power and control. This kind of dev ed sees change in the interests of the majority of the world's people as its goal. Good dev ed often has the characteristics of feminist process.

Defining Good/Feminist Dev Ed

To us, good development education must incorporate alternative, participatory methods and content. Empowering people to act on their own behalf consistent with goals of global equality and justice implies recognition of the importance of people's experience. Traditional approaches, in which an "expert" who has studied but not necessarily lived a situation in question defines for people both problems and solutions, are not adequate.

In our discussions, we have identified some characteristics of good (and feminist) development education:

- The content begins with, and is defined by, the experience of the participants; and encourages reflection and analysis leading to understanding of how that experience is shaped by the world around us.

- Dev ed recognizes that form or method and content are closely linked. It uses active, co-operative, flexible methods that encourage the greatest possible participation among those involved. Such methods are specific to the participant group and are meaningful, non-demeaning, positive, sharing, and supportive.

- From describing the group's reality (reflection) and looking at the factors that have shaped that reality (analysis), development education encourages the identification of action to affect the situation under discussion. Reflection on and analysis of the action and its results leads to further insights, more understanding, and, possibly, further action.

- We recognize the complexity and interrelatedness of the issues and problems we attempt to address. Development education does not, and cannot, offer "quick-fix" solutions. It *can* offer a creative, ongoing learning process that incorporates concrete work in building relationships that reflect the kind of world towards which we work.

- Development education seeks to identify common realities between Canadian and Third World people; to identify the Northern processes by which people in the South and the North are negatively affected; and to identify actions Canadians can take that are supportive of and/or in solidarity with people struggling for justice elsewhere.

Development Education With Women

The developing theory and practice of this kind of dev ed in Canada parallels in many ways what we have called feminist methodology or process. Increasingly, WID-focused programmes have been part of the content and practice. It is no surprise, however, that, as in so many other areas, "women's programmes" are often seen as "an issue area" about and for women.

Culturally-defined gender roles restrictive to women are reinforced by all sorts of relationships and processes and are internalized by women. There is growing awareness of: the need to support and value women's work; how women's gender roles negatively affect their participation in development processes; and how development processes negatively affect women. This awareness, however, has not led to appropriate action by government and NGO operations or the public at large.

- It is therefore important that the impetus of the Decade for Women be maintained and that special programmes continue to research, document, and educate.

  Women's lives are intertwined with every development issue. We must learn to explicitly identify women's roles and relationships in every area we tackle. Women's secondary status and the invisible value of their work makes this essential to redressing the imbalances of sexist inequality.

- Whether our issue be agriculture, international debt, or child care, programmes should look at differential effects on women and attempt to include their perspective on analysis, needs and solutions.

  We have argued that all dev ed programmes explicitly consider and support women's involvement in both content and process. We know, however, that women are restricted by their secondary status. They are less likely to participate fully in mixed groups or to articulate, in the presence of men, their experience with sexism. Women's lack of confidence and experience with public speaking, and their own perceptions of the world, means that men can easily dominate any discussion.

- We therefore see a particular need for education programmes not only about women, but with and for women.

  At the same time, women's lives are inextricably tied to men's—within our families and our communities as well as through all the larger economic, political, and class struc-

310

tures. We must work with the men closest to us to build a common understanding and support and a vision of the potential of men and women working together in equality. Our education work can help us identify and work with male allies.

- Dev ed programmes should always be linked to existing concerns of the participants and should respect their experience. In mixed groups, this may imply special attention to methods that support the equal participation of the women involved.

We must also identify and counter those who have a vested interest in maintaining the subjugation of women and who oppose our efforts to focus attention and resources on women.

Conclusion

Our intent in writing this paper was to clarify the position of the women involved and to provide a guide for those in the development community. It has explored the philosophy of feminist development and the practical approaches to overseas development work. We hope it will be a useful resource for understanding, analyzing, and implementing strategies within organizations, overseas projects, and development education. We look forward to working with a wider group since our struggle is integral to all issues related to human life.

This paper is an important step in our development. We are ready to move again to action... strengthened and energized by a common commitment to equality, development, and peace. We celebrate the contributions and process of the women involved and hope that the reader's vision for the world's people, not only women, has been expanded.

CHAPTER 13

Classism, Racism, and Academic Elitism Run Headlong into Low-Rent Criticism

Anne Cameron

I do not intend to write a bio in the third person, as if I was not even present in or involved in my own life! I know it is the "accepted" thing to do... that suggests to me it's time to stop doing it, time to stop accepting the dehumanization of the writer, because that dehumanization feeds into the cult-of-personality which turns writers into "stars" and separates them from the rest of the world. I've been writing most of my life, and will doubtless continue for the rest of my life. I am told I am "radical" because of my views, and that puzzles me very much. I mean *They* are trying to talk about a survivable nuclear war... how could any protest be radical when weighed alongside the distinct possibility we'll all be turned to radioactive dust? I feel anything we do in protest is little more than mild rebuke.

I believe we must study and learn from the mistakes of the past or we'll merely repeat those mistakes. I try in my writing to challenge, to question, to dare, to defy, to find, identify, and try to weed out fear, which has been used as a weapon against us. I know that whether we recognize it or not, the smell of our nightmares is the smell of the fires that burned fourteen million women as "witches." We know that patriarchy killed fourteen million feminists; we suspect they'd really like to do it again.

313

First there was the Great Egg, and inside it, the promise of all Life. That promise of life began to stir, to swell, to grow, and the shell holding the promise began to stretch. The shell cracked, and from inside the egg, the water of life began to flow, a single river of hope and commitment.

The River of Life brought with it the seeds of grass and tree, of flower and vine, of fruit and vegetable, of all those things which grow on or in the earth and reach for the sky. When these wonders were growing, spreading across the surface of the egg, the fish and fowl emerged, and took their places in the streams and the lakes, in the branches of the trees and in the skies above them. Then the animals came from within the egg, and moved along the river of life, emerging from the water and taking their place in the creation of all things. Every animal, every bird, every fish and every mammal who lives in the water, every snake and turtle, every one of the bugs and insects, every marvel of creation had its place and took it.

The Creator, The Voice Which Must Be Obeyed, made First Woman. Her body was made of the dirt of the earth, this very earth on which we stand, this land, our home, and that was no accident. Her bones and teeth were made of the shells of the creatures of the sea, and the minerals in the rocks, and this was no accident. Her hair was made of the grass and moss, the same grass, the same moss that still grows all around us, and this was no accident. The light in her eyes, the light of life and knowing, was the light of the sun, the moon, the stars, and this was no accident.

First Mother did not come from somewhere else. She did not come from the sky, she did not come from another star, she did not travel here from another planet, she was created here, on this our home, of this very soil, and her blood is the water of the sea, salty and life sustaining.

First Mother did not yet have the gift of speech, but she had the gift of understanding and empathy. And she had within her body the gift of life. From her, from her body, from her body made of the soil and minerals of the earth and the water and salts of the sea, came children, many children, and they were all sisters and brothers, they all had the same mother, First Mother. And as with flowers, these children did not all come in the same colour; the first were black as the night sky, the second brown as the earth, represented by the sacred colour red, the third were saffron, yellow like the autumn grass, the last white with eyes of many hues.

And in the beginning it pleased them, and amused them that they were not identical. In time these children grew to be adults, and had children of their own, but like their Mother, they did not yet have the gift of speech. They all followed the Dream, the Dream of harmony, of love, of responsibility and commitment, of honour and respect, and they gave thanks for the bounty of the earth they shared.

And the Voice Which Must Be Obeyed gave them the gift of speech. They were at the fire, at night, with First Mother, who was by now many times a grandmother and great-grandmother, giving their Thanks, and sparks which come from the cedar as it burns danced in the night darkness, upward, taking with them the prayers of the Children of the Rainbow family. The Creator blessed the prayer and accepted it, sent the sparks back downward, as blessing, and the throats of the Rainbow Family swelled with sound, language burst forth from them, floating on lip-kissed breath, rising with emotion and words were formed, and the first of the words were those words which mean Mother.

The River of Life divided that night and formed four rivers which flowed off in four directions and the Rainbow Family divided, to follow the rivers. The black-skinned cousins moved along one river, to find a homeland and fill their given corner of the earth, the yellow-skinned cousins moved along a second river, the white-skinned cousins along a third, and the cousins with brown/red skin stayed here and spread over this land, their homeland. Each of the family of cousins took with them the knowledge of the Great Egg, the knowledge of First Mother, the knowledge of the Dream and the knowledge that the Earth, which formed the body of First Mother, was Mother of the First Mother and thus Grandmother to us all.

And they all promised that if ever the day came when Mother Earth needed their protection, they would return to aid her, would re-form the Rainbow family, would stand together as one people again, and give of their strength to protect Grandmother Earth, Mother Earth, mother of First Mother, Mother of Us All.

And First Mother knew that her time had come, her purpose was fulfilled, her tasks finished. She left her shell of meat and bones and became something other than what she had been. She became part of the totality of creation, and each time the sun touches our skin, that is her touch, each time the rain moistens the earth, she is with us, when the breeze ruffles our hair, that is her hand, touching us as a mother touches her child, and when we sleep, she watches over us. Her meat and bones went back to the earth, returning to the Mother-Of-All, as will our meat and bones when our days here are finished, and yet she is with us all the time whether we remember her or not.

Some of us, of the far-roaming Rainbow Children have lost our Dream, some of us had the Dream wrenched from us, some of us had the Dream stolen from us, but the Dream is alive. Some of us have fragments of the dream, some of us have pieces others of us have lost. Together we can re-form and re-learn the Dream. We can use the precious gift of speech, which came to us from the sparks of the fire, to warm the hearts of all our cousins, all our children, and with love and responsibility, we can heal ourselves of the sorrows and of the mistakes we have all made, we can once again know ourselves and our parents, our grandparents, First Mother, and we can protect the Old Grandmother, this earth on which we live and to which we will all one day return.

* * *

The 1960s and 1970s have been termed by some a period of social revolution and by others a period of sexual revolution. Both of these supposed revolutions seem to have changed small parts of the externals, but done little or nothing to make any Real change for most women. There are more of us than ever in the work force, but that only means there are more of us than ever being paid less, for doing certain jobs, than men get paid. Most of these women put in their eight hours at work, then go home and put in another three hours cooking, cleaning, caring for kids, doing laundry, etc. The men put in their eight hours at work, then go home and put in less than fifteen minutes, including time spent relating to their children.

Men talk about making meaningful change. I have yet to see anything done by men to cause any kind of real change at all, let alone meaningful change. Talk is cheap and the boys do a lot of talking. They just don't seem to do much thinking, and they don't seem to do any real self-examination which might lead to the taking of their personal responsibilities. Sit in a room with half a dozen supposedly idealistic men and one of the first things they will start talking about is economics. Money this, money that, and the system must be changed. "When everything is free, I am free," one well-intentioned

316

middle-aged man told me recently. I happen to know the guy is a skilled carpenter who hasn't held a job in four years and is living on a combination of welfare and what his wife makes at a part-time job. From where I sit, while he is sitting on his duff thinking up new ways for everything to be free, she's at a job which pays much less per hour than he could make; then she comes home to three hours with the kids and the cooking and housework. I listened to this guy for about half an hour, even though absolutely everything about economics and money bores me to tears because I don't **believe** it exists, then I asked him what his new society would do about spousal abuse, incest, and sexual abuse of children. He hadn't even thought about any of that. He'd figured out a system of government, he'd figured out a system of exchange of goods and services, he hadn't figured out how to keep the brothers he kept referring to from raping three- and four-year-old girls.

Another man wanted to discuss the ecology and the work I've been doing on environmental and native land claims issues. He had a quote from Buddhist teaching, another quote from Tao, he had quotes from Gary Snyder, he had quotes from Aldo Leopold. When I asked him why he was willing to go so far afield to find arguments to support the idea that we really shouldn't destroy this planet when the solution lay on the shelves of the local bookstore, he stared at me. "Feminism," I said, "is based on an analysis which exposes the link between hatred of nature and hatred of female and if you don't come to terms with and get rid of your own hatred of women, you have no hope of saving the planet." I could have gone into the backyard and talked down the borehole to the water, 150 ft. below the surface of the Mother. But I know this guy, I've heard his jokes about women drivers and mothers-in-law, and I know he can talk about "brotherhood" without practising it, he can talk about "freedom" without being able to imagine it, and his idea of "peace" is an absence of war. I asked him once what good it would do women to dedicate our lives to the peace movement when most of us don't have any kind of peace in the homes we share with men. I could have asked my dog: she would have had more with which to deal with the question.

Time and again we've seen men form groups supposedly working for change; everything from Fabian Socialism, through Marxism, to Anarchy, and time and time again the external trappings are different but the heart of things remains the same and the misogynism continues and the power-tripping

317

flows. And the more time the guys spend sitting around growing their beards and talking, the less they will listen to what increasing numbers of women are trying to tell them.

Shere Hite's latest book (1987) brings the message from women that we are not happy in our relationships with men, we find men inadequate even in their love, we want something more, something we are beginning to believe they may not be capable of giving. It has male critics and media personalities shouting objections and flatly denying her research. I believe her. I believe what the boys are doing to Shere Hite and her book is what the Greek kings did if they didn't like the message; they offed the poor slob who delivered the message. Women are increasingly discontent.

How many times have we seen middle-aged "new" men, their growing bald spot covered by a cap of some kind, walking with a naïve eighteen- or nineteen-year-old who is six or seven months pregnant? There are a lot of those guys in the anti-nuke and environmental movement. Talking of the new way to do this and the new way to do that and how wonderful it's going to be to participate in the birth and rearing of the expected child. What they never talk about are the two or three or four ex-wives, each with two or three or four kids who get no support of any kind from the "new" man. Many of these men join the "green" party, which now claims to have "post-patriarchal" focus. So what happened to "feminist"? Why do they have to be "post-patriarchal"? I suggest it is because in the bottom of their hearts they know they are not ready to examine their misogyny, they know they are not and never will be feminist. They're afraid to even look at the word, let alone the analysis; because if they do they will become uncomfortable with the inability to deny they are very privileged.

There are jokes galore about the "war between the sexes," and most of the jokes are told by men. I suppose they are funny jokes if you happen to be a foot soldier in the army which controls the rules. Feminists are not laughing at those jokes, so, of course, that means we have no sense of humour. It doesn't mean the jokes aren't funny; why, the guys are laughing at them...

And yet I often wonder, when did this war start, who declared it, and why can't we stop it? We were all of us children of the same mother, once. What happened?

And I often think the book *Peter Pan* came very close to the truth and those children with outdoor plumbing decided they would never really grow up, while those of us with indoor plumbing dared aspire to maturity.

Of course, the movement is not perfect, nothing in nature is perfect, and we are, above all, connected to nature. There is a split being encouraged in the women's community, a split the male-dominated media would really like to make larger and larger because the greatest weapon the patriarchy has is "divide and conquer." That split worries me. It is the split between the "lower" or working-class woman and the "upper" or academic woman.

I am not an academic. I have grade twelve education from the province of British Columbia. When Simon Fraser University was first opening some twenty years ago, they advertised they would accept students who did not have the academic credits to get into the University of British Columbia but who had demonstrated they were "mature" students who would be able to learn. I applied as a mature student. I was married, with three kids, and was living in suburbia just about ready to go out of my mind with boredom. Simon Fraser sent me a letter saying I did not qualify to attend as a student. Years later, no more academically qualified than I had ever been, I was invited to teach. I have since taught on more than one occasion, but I still do not qualify as a student or as an "academic."

There are books I have started to read and put down because the manguage in them tied my brain in such knots I just felt stuck. Manguage is the kind of silliness Aldo Leopold spouts to the boys who are "in" to ecology. Stuff like "An ethic, ecologically, is a limitation on freedom of action in the struggle for existence." And, sadly, too many academic women are still talking, writing, and thinking in Manguage. They have had to use that Manguage for years just to get through the sausage factory and get the academic qualifications, without which the boys give you no respect at all, and with which a woman gets very little respect anyway.

Words and I are not strangers. Words and I have been on intimate and loving terms since I was less than two years old. Words have nourished me, nurtured me, and helped me feed my children. Words have kept me sane in a world where sanity is threatened daily. So if I, lover of words, user of words, cannot read these dense and complex books written by academic women who use Manguage, what chance have women who have been denied education, verbal skill, or a large vocabulary?

319

Which means academic women wind up writing for academic women and working-class women look elsewhere for what we want and need. With lack of communication comes separation, and that leads to misunderstanding, which seems, inevitably, to lead to distrust and dislike.

I have too often seen advertisements for two- or three-day seminars (why not ovulars?) whereby academic women from across the nation are coming together in a feminist conference. And one academic woman is going to present a paper on Poverty. Another has a paper to present on Working-Class Consciousness. Yet another is going to discuss Welfare Mother Reality, and there is always a paper being given on Immigrant Women. And I know it hurts the feelings of academic women to be told that they don't know five times the square root of sweet ditz-all about any of that! They should stop presenting those papers. Stop playing that same game which for years saw male academics presenting papers to each other about women, telling each other what they thought we wanted, thought, experienced and needed.

No woman who comes from a middle-class childhood that allowed her to go to university while her father picked up the main part of the tab and who is now making fifty or sixty thousand dollars a year, with tenure, at a university, should be giving a paper about poverty. And it is a damned insult to all of us who live below the poverty line year after year that our reality be interpreted for us by someone who is an outsider. It's a continuation of what the boys did to us for years. It's exactly what led to a situation wherein male psychiatrists decided there was no such thing as sexual abuse of little girls, why their own figures showed that girls had fantasies. (Besides which, of course, if it did happen it was because the child had exhibited provocative behaviour and the poor adult man couldn't help himself.)

Any time I hear a woman say she has "chosen downward mobility" I know I am listening to a woman born far enough up the social ladder that there was a "down" for her to consider. Most of us were born so far down there was only "up" to travel.

Time and time again, working-class women, women of colour, immigrant women, and native women try to instigate a discussion of "classism" in the feminist movement and time and time again the academic women sidestep the issue by insisting on talking about Marxism. You have to understand, there are thousands of us out here who know the work of

Marx... Groucho, Harpo and Zeppo. While others had the time and money to study Sociology, the rest of us were slinging hash, typing, driving truck, working as farm labourers, and trying to organize unions. We don't want to listen to yet another dead-end discussion on whether or not Marxism is unable to confront its own misogynism. We have no interest in Marxism. We've heard about it and know it won't work for us.

Time and again we try to analyze and work on ridding ourselves of the racism internalized in every one of us. And find racism so tangled in classism that the tangle just gets worse. And time and again we back off, and go home baffled by the on-going Manguage that sees some of us introduced as "master storytellers."

Time and again we try to discuss our perspective of wife-battering; and get told in polysyllabic language that even violence is an attempt to communicate. It is no such thing, it is an attempt to control. The restricted availability of publications for non-academic working-class women's developing analysis, the imposition of "upper"-class academic editorial interference, and the trivialization of issues affecting working-class women, immigrant women, indigenous women, and welfare moms is as effective a means of control as the bashing, punching, and beating. Many times it hurts more because it is being done to us by women we had hoped to consider our sisters and allies, women so conditioned by a system controlled by the patriarchy that they have not yet even begun to consider they have absorbed more patriarchal programming than they realize. The patriarchal media makes much of the split, driving wedges into it, making it wider, and on both sides of the split, women become entrenched.

The patriarchy benefits from the entrenchment; if we aren't talking to each other, we aren't working with each other, and "divide and conquer" clicks in again. We need anthologies with articles by working-class women, articles uncensored and unedited by academics, articles that reflect working-class reality, not the academic perception of something they would like to think is working-class reality. If misunderstandings are exposed for all the world to see, how wonderful. The feminist movement must always insist there is public accountability and public clearing so that we not only achieve consensus, but appear to have achieved it. We need articles by Shirley Carr to present the reality of unionized working women, and articles that tell what it is like to be a

321

working woman who has no union. We need articles by Chief Ruby Dunstan of the Lytton band and Ada Yovanovitch of the Haida nation. We need to hear from Anna Balan of the Ukrainian women's movement in Canada, and articles by Louise Rose putting forward the position of black feminists in Canada. We need to hear directly from Canadian women of Japanese origin, Chinese origin, and we need to hear directly from refugee women. It is both racism and classism to continue to present views that exclude the points of view, analysis, and reality of minority women, and the only ones who benefit from that racism and classism are the ones who have always benefited most from our oppression and lack of political cohesion.

We feel strongly that academic women are unwittingly helping the patriarchy put the blocks to the feminist movement. Many of us think it is absolutely ridiculous that the representatives sent to "international women's conferences" are chosen from the elite. We know, and it is proved to us again and again, every day of our lives, that the "upper"-class women do not understand the "lower"-class reality. We know that "lower" class in this country is still comparatively well off when judged alongside the sisters from third- and fourth-world countries. If the elite of the more globally fortunate cannot understand the reality of women in their own country, how, name of the Mother, can they begin to understand, empathise with, and give credence to the reality of women from desperately impoverished countries? And what right have they got to attend such a conference and then dominate it because of their overbearing expertise, their verbal skills, and their ease and confidence when speaking in public?

We are all the children of the same Mother, and the split forced on us by the patrist dominant ideology can be repaired only by making sure the internalized and unrecognized influences of the patriarchy are rooted from our movement. The dictum from on high, the pontificating from the ozone layer has to stop. Why should less than four per cent of the population impress their view and analysis on the rest of us?

The boys have always bought off their competition by allowing token members of the minorities to be seen on the fringes of the Network. We have seen this too often to allow that same tokenism to happen in the movement we call our own. We will not be as polite in our protest as some would prefer us to be, our language will contain no euphemism, no group-speak, no party-line, no baffle-gab. We may even step

322

on some well-shod toes and hurt some tender feelings. But one way or another we will make our reality and our analyses known. We are, after all, the majority of the women in this country. We quite positively refuse to be ignored, discounted, or trivialized. The Old Boy's Network couldn't shut us up, and the Old Girl's Network won't do it, either.

Our daughters are going to university in increasing numbers, and are not buying into the old class divisions. Our daughters can see that the rhetoric and verbiage of Europe does not fit the situation in North America. Our daughters can see that the analysis developed somewhere else has little relevance here, and our daughters are helping to find the analysis we need to shrug off the old foolishness and throw away the old burdens. Instead of buying into an academia which grew out of and has always willingly supported the patriarchy, the young women are examining every academic discipline from a feminist awareness, challenging "truths" that turn out to be not the least bit true, turning the most accepted concepts and precepts on their ears and unearthing what the system has tried so hard to keep from us; a knowledge of our own historic struggle, our own historic worth, our own historic presence. Our daughters are educated, our daughters are educators, that doesn't mean they are living in the ivory tower of academia, nor does it mean they joined the old folks' network. If the young women challenge the old girl's network as much as they challenge the old boy's network, that can only be of benefit to the majority of the women in this country, those of us never represented by either network. The patriarchy will try to present this as yet another problem for the women's movement. It is no problem, it is part of our hard-won solution, and the patriarchy has been interpreting too much for us for too long.

Denying the existence of a problem will not make the problem vanish. Refusing to deal with class and race division in the women's movement will not erase classism and racism. Denying the over-representation of highly educated upper-middle-class white women and the under-representation of all the rest of us in the women's movement will not remove the divisions or the resentments. Allowing the patrist media to present and interpret our internal problems will only make them more difficult to understand, more difficult to solve. There is a problem. We will define it and speak to it and we will no longer be ignored or trivialized or made to feel we do not have the right to speak.

If we have to put in eight hours at a crappy job, ride home on crowded, inadequate public transportation because we cannot afford the expensive luxury of a car, pick up our kids from cruddy daycare, take them home, then spend another three hours doing unpaid and unrecognized housework, we'll do that; and when we can pry some time for ourselves, we'll attend meetings, force the unions to represent us more properly, fight for decent daycare, express our opinions on abortion choice, try to reform our churches, criticize and support and inspire the peace and environmental movements, and pressure our own movement to recognize the elitism and do something to weed it out and discard it.

We, too, are the children of First Mother. We, too, are her daughters. We will not allow academic misrepresentation of our reality, we will not allow our lives and our place in our own movement to be negated.

You might not like our analyses, you might not like our straightforward language, you might not like our blunt manner or our less-than-genteel approach, but sooner or later, one day or another, you will have to hear us. When you do, you will understand what we are saying.

Bibliography of Anne Cameron's Published Work

Poetry

Earth Witch (Madeira Park, B.C.: Harbour Publishing, 1982)
The Annie Poems (Madeira Park, B.C.: Harbour Publishing, 1987)

Fiction

Daughters of Copper Woman (Vancouver: Press Gang, 1981)
The Journey (Spinsters/Aunt Lute, Avon Books, 1986)
Dzelarhons: Mythology of the North West Coast (Madeira Park, B.C.: Harbour Publishing, 1986)
Child of Her People (Spinsters/Aunt Lute, forthcoming)
Stubby Amberchuk and the Holy Grail (Madeira Park, B.C.: Harbour Publishing, 1987)
Women, Kids, and Huckleberry Wine (Madeira Park, B.C.: Harbour Publishing, 1988)

Legend and Myth (all published by Harbour Publishing, Madeira Park, B.C.)

How the Raven Freed the Moon (illustrated by Tara Miller, 1985)

How the Loon Lost Her Voice (illustrated by Tara Miller, 1985)

Orca's Song (illustrated by Nelle Olsen, 1987)
Raven Returns the Water (illustrated by Nelle Olsen, 1987)
Lazy Boy (illustrated by Nelle Olsen, 1988)
Spider Woman (illustrated by Nelle Olsen, 1988)

CHAPTER 14

Feminist Praxis

Mary O'Brien

Mary O'Brien is an immigrant Canadian of Scottish origins with a long history of activity in the British Labour Party, and, more recently, in feminist politics in Canada. She was, for 25 years, a nursing practitioner, educator and administrator. In 1976, she earned a Ph. D. in political theory and has taught since 1977 in the active feminist studies focus at the Ontario Institute for Studies in Education. In her work in feminist theory, she seeks to integrate feminist concern with the social relations of reproduction and Marxist analysis of class relations. She is a busy speaker in both political and academic circles where she raises questions of political practice and the development of a materialist analysis of women's oppression. She matches a firm conviction that feminism is currently the progressive force in history with a keen appreciation of the practical difficulties of tactical planning. She has two other ambitions: to cultivate a new rose and to write one passable poem. A collection of her work entitled *Reproducing the World* will soon be published by Westview Press.

Feminism and Revolution*

The fastest way to evade and trivialize the question of the revolutionary potential of feminism is to play the definitional game: "It all depends on what you mean by feminism"—or, for that matter, by "revolution." Having then subscribed implicitly to the notion that meaning inheres in words rather than in happenings, it is a relatively easy task to go on to define the terms in such a way that almost any proposition can be "proved", including the contentions that feminism is "really" *not* revolutionary or that there is "in fact" no such thing as feminism. However, the crass things which can be done with definitional games do not get us off the hook of having to try to say clearly what we mean. For example, it can be argued that feminism is revolutionary because feminism attacks the integrity of the family, that the family is traditionally and actually an irreplaceable foundation brick in the structure of all known societies, and that the removal of this particular brick would bring the whole edifice tumbling down, and thus entail a revolution in social structure. As a matter of fact, what I am going to argue is not all that different from this. What is very different is the way in which I want to argue it. The importance of the family is a gospel of reactionary groups, yet the family and the private realm increasingly engage the attention of active feminists as the social organizations which must be examined in a critical way, and which can only be examined in a critical way from a standpoint within the social realities of feminist experience.

Such a project must go beyond the recovery of women's history and the description of contemporary situations, yet the past and present of feminism constitute the framework of theory and practice. Feminism is revolutionary because it is historical, but also because this is a history of struggle. The perception of history as a process with a revolutionary dynamic was grasped with great clarity and creative intensity by Marx, yet Marx's analysis of history as class struggle does not elucidate the dynamics of the reproductive realm with anything like the clarity which he brings to the understanding of the dynamics of the productive realm. Starting from the history of the lived lives and relations of real people, Marx found in these relations the reality of division by socio-economic class growing

---

* For a fuller exposition of these ideas, see *The Politics of Reproduction* by Mary O'Brien, published by Routledge & Kegan Paul, London, 1981.

out of the historical divisions of labour. Class struggle is revolutionary because it is historical, and history is revolutionary because it is the history of class struggle. This is not just one of these tedious verbal trick circles: actual class struggle and revolutionary activity break through the merely abstract enclosures of circles. Yet there is nothing in this view of history which says that *feminism* is revolutionary, or that the social relations of reproduction generate their own contradictions. Indeed, if it could be demonstrated theoretically that genderic struggle is an integral part of class struggle, then there would be no problem for Marxist feminists. This approach may have been Marx's own, and was certainly that of Engels, and still appeals strongly to large sections of the Left, particularly of the vanguard type. However, "pure" theory is not enough for Marxists, and the available evidence from both simple and complex societies falls far short of demonstrating that gender relations can be subsumed in class relations. In practical terms, it would be nice if it could be shown that only the bourgeoisie beat their wives, or that existing socialist societies have been able to make really substantial inroads on the ideology and practice of male supremacy. The truth is that *male supremacist praxis is transhistorical*, and increasing numbers of women are skeptical of the notion that the inevitable motion of class dialectic will ultimately liberate them.

This does not mean that feminists should abandon class struggle, nor regretfully dismiss Marx as a great guy but a hopeless patriarch. What it does mean is that the ways in which productive and reproductive social formations relate to each other must be opened up to a more rigorous and refined critique. Marx once said, in speaking of his own development of historical materialism, that the route he took was through a critique of Hegel, but it was a critique which necessarily had to be made from *inside* Hegel's systematic philosophy of history. I believe that the critique of male supremacy which can uncover the revolutionary structure of women's history and create a living feminist praxis must be conducted from within Marxism. Some Marxists find the implications of this disturbing, for it is, in a necessary way, "revisionist," yet women must reject the comforts of an orthodoxy which does not reflect the actual conditions of their lives. Female experience affirms that class oppression and sex oppression are related in many ways, but they are not the same. Class oppression and exploitation are the realities within which wage labourers come to reject the false definition of human freedom which bourgeois ideology and practice attempts to lay on them. Women's consciousness and women's oppression is this class experience, but it is also more than this, for in *all* male-dominated societies the oppression and exploitation of women by men crosses class barriers.

Feminism is the history of resistance to male exploitation, and is therefore not a history which can be understood fully in terms of the theory of class struggle. The fact that class struggle and generic struggle are related has meant that, in the more cataclysmic historical moments of class struggle, women have been there, more so than we can know if we read only men's accounts of these events. There is, however, a different struggle and a real struggle which is the true history of feminism. To be sure, this struggle has not produced the dramatic social upheavals which class struggle has precipitated. This fact has lent fuel to the smug notion that women are not, in fact, oppressed by men, but are oppressed by Nature, their own dear mother. But the "invisibility" of women's real resistance to oppression cannot be ascribed, particularly by historical materialism, to the ideological strength of male supremacy, or to biological determinism. It must be understood in terms of visible social structure. If the visible social structure of male oppression is not class struggle, it is incumbent upon feminists to say what it is. I submit that the structure in question is the structure in which the social relations of reproduction have developed historically, and that this is the structure by which private life and the personal have been separated from public life and the political. The opposition of public and private is to the social relations of reproduction what the opposition of economic classes is to the social relations of production.

The significance of the events which this formulation attempts to grasp has not, of course, gone unnoticed. It is the basis of Marx and Engels' view of the need to socialize domestic labour, thus breaking down the privatization and devaluation of women's work. Much recent discussion on the Left has zeroed in on this question of domestic labour, but there appears to linger in domestic labour and its products the same sort of elusiveness which Marx found in the bourgeois version of a commodity. A commodity, Marx noted, seems a straightforward and even trivial thing, yet "analysis shows that it is, in reality, a very queer thing, abounding in

metaphysical subtleties and theological niceties" (*Capital,*
Part I, 1, i. 3.14). Domestic labour and its products have
proven to be resistant to analysis in terms of value or of
productive and non-productive labour. There is no dispute
that domestic labour constitutes a useful bonus to capitalism:
there is a certain reluctance to include in the discussion the
fact that it also constitutes a very real value to its immediate
appropriators, men of all economic classes. Further, there is
no analysis at all of the actual process of reproductive labour
as the material ground of both species continuity and the
separation of public and private life.

Contemporary feminism started off with an uncritical
acceptance of the low value of reproductive labour assigned to
it by "male-stream" thought. In terms of theory, this position,
which was the early position of de Beauvoir, perhaps reached
its apotheosis and its negation in the popular work of Shulamith
Firestone. With impeccable logic, Firestone argued that as
the historical oppression of women was grounded in female
reproductive function, the emancipation of women depended
upon our escape from our biological destiny. This theory is
unsound, for its premise that women's oppression stands in
causal relationship with biological function cannot be
demonstrated empirically. It is also incapable of providing a
rallying point for a widely based women's praxis, for many
women resist the notion that their maternal experience has no
value. But the inadequacies of early feminist theory have not
prevented the growth of the movement, not out of theory but
out of change in the material conditions of women's lives. The
conditions of early theory were the conditions of male
reproductive experience, which has not been subjected to
radical change. Female reproductive consciousness is radically
transformed by the development of contraceptive technology,
a transformation which has not yet been subjected to sustained
theoretical critique from a materialist perspective. The truth
is that contraceptive technology is qualitatively different from
all other technologies in that it makes its major impact on the
social relations of reproduction, and that it does this in a
radical way which has nothing to do with the attractive
marketability of "the pill," the joys of liberated sexuality, nor
even the serious and sombre political considerations involved
in the dizzy dreams of controlled genocide which no doubt
colour bourgeois visions of absolute power. Contraceptive
technology is a world historical event because it actually
transforms the process of reproduction. Just as the development

of capitalism not only changed productive relations but exposed to the light of day the inner workings of the true sub-structure of these relations, so the transformations wrought in reproductive relations by recent changes in contraceptive technology expose the material grounds of generic oppression and open them up to a heretofore impossible critical analysis. This sort of enterprise is one which Marx could no more have undertaken than could Malthus, for the fact that the sub-structure of reproductive relations is the *process of reproduction itself* was simply not visible at a time in history in which that process appears to be mired eternally in the realm of determinism, contingency and brute biology. This is now no longer the case. The process of reproduction is not simply the route from ovulation to birth, but the total sociobiological process from copulation through birth to the nurture and care of dependent children. Reproduction in this sense has always been a unity of thinking and doing, and the fact that the woman engaged in the strenuous process of reproductive labour cannot help what she is doing does not mean that she does not *know* what she is doing and what she has still to do. Women's place in the reproduction of the species involves her body and her mind. So does men's. It is precisely here that the dialectics of reproduction differ from the dialectics of production. Both produce particular forms of consciousness, but the forms of productive consciousness are related to the standpoint of class. The forms of reproductive consciousness are related to gender. Men and women are joined together by class consciousness, but they are separated by reproductive consciousness.

We must note, further, that although reproductive consciousness is generically differentiated, it is not therefore an individual, atomized, purely subjective consciousness. Women do not need to bear children to partake in female reproductive consciousness, for such consciousness is a socially and culturally transmitted collective consciousness. Women have a particular form of reproductive consciousness, not because they are mothers, but because they are women. Likewise, it is not necessary to *be* a father to partake of patriarchal consciousness: indeed male reproductive consciousness has managed to develop patriarchal forms in the teeth of the radical uncertainty of paternity.

There are several aspects of reproductive process which can be released by dialectical analysis from the strait-jackets of conventional wisdom. Take, for example, the proposition that women have a "special relationship" with nature, which, in its extreme form, says that women are *identified* with nature. The fact that this view is a hardy staple of male-stream thought, and has been used historically to draw conclusions which are hardly in women's best interests, should not obscure the fact that it has a significant element of truth. What is wrong with the hand-me-down view is that it suggests that women are *immediately* related to nature when in actual fact women's relationship with nature is *mediated*, and the mode of mediation is reproductive labour. The separation of all people from the natural world is mediated in the process of productive labour, but the relation of women to the biological world of species continuity is mediated by reproductive labour. This is not, of course, the case with men: the process of reproduction entails a *separation* of men from nature in the necessary alienation of the male seed in copulation. Furthermore, this alienation is more than alienation from the natural world, for it also involves a real separation from genetic time. Male experience of time is the experience of species discontinuity, a discontinuity which is, in the female experience, mediated in the reproduction of successive generations.

The profound significance for materialist dialectical science of the fact that man's reproductive consciousness is an alienated consciousness has not been examined with sufficient thoroughness. In Marx's perception of human consciousness, consciousness resists alienation in terms of both thinking and doing. Have men, then, resisted their experienced alienation from biological continuity? The historical record shows quite clearly that they have, in both ideological and practical ways. The most common and most profound mode of resistance which they have employed is the familiar one of appropriation. Men have erected a huge social edifice to facilitate and justify that appropriation of women's children which we call patriarchy. The sealing off of the private realm, the institutions of marriage and the establishment of a "right" to the children of a particular woman are the social acts of a class of appropriators, striving to resist alienation and to make real the idea of a paternity. Not the least of the contradictions of reproductive consciousness lies in the fact that paternity is essentially an idea while maternity is experienced fact.

Paternal rights of appropriation without labour are shared by men of all classes; they are actual social relations, and are a significant building block in the ancient notion of a Brotherhood of Man. How can all men be brothers when they are so experientially remote from one another in diverse and significant ways? Yet this notion of brotherhood is a historically pervasive one which cannot be understood as some kind of simple humanistic opiate or a noble lie cynically generated by a historical succession of ruling classes. It has a material ground in the dialectics of reproductive process, in which men are, by virtue of the alienation of their seed, forced into cooperative efforts to resist this universal male mode of alienation. The brotherhood notion is an essential and materially grounded plank in the ideological platform of male supremacy, which, like reproductive consciousness, transcends class.

The question of the ordering of strategic priorities between the related but opposing needs of class and generic struggle is not one that can be worked out neatly in theory and imposed on political practice. Its resolution must be lived, including the fundamental question of whether the necessary transformation of the social relations of reproduction must be a violent one. The working out is not exclusively a women's problem but a human problem, however women are the progressive social force in the struggle. Men can and do join in, though they must recognize that their participation carries with it the same kind of uncomfortable ambivalence as that experienced by the bourgeois intellectual who opts to join the proleteriat in their historic mission.

Karl Marx, in one of his more celebrated pronouncements, once suggested that in the humane diversity of a classless society, men could be fishermen in the morning, farmers in the afternoon and critical critics in the evening. I wonder how many women have, as I did when I first heard the passage, wondered who was minding the kids. This question is no longer a suppressed disloyalty to the hegemony of the class struggle. It is an up-front problematic in the struggle to abolish generic inequality, now that the material base has been transformed by the fact that motherhood is now a choice as fatherhood has always been.

The bringing to light of the dialectics of reproduction is reflected in the recent history of the Women's Movement. Proclaimed dead, it lives and flourishes. Proclaimed frivolous, it invades ever more deeply the citadels of male intellectual dominance. Proclaimed dependent and derivative, it continues to emancipate itself from the mindcuffs of male-stream thought and the petty potency of private realm imperialism. Accused of shrillness, it nurtures beneath its disagreements a joy in the discovery of sisterhood so profound that it is expressed in silence. Attacked from the Right as life destructive, it joyfully celebrates life's femaleness. Assailed from the Left as a bourgeois deviation, it maintains a thoughtful and activist probe into the deeper realities of the relation of generic struggle and class struggle. In doing these things, feminism moves erratically but irresistibly towards the feminist praxis which understands its past, lives its present for itself, and prepares to make its future.

Feminist Theory
and Feminist Practice

There is one quite important sense in which feminist scholarship is an act of *definition* or, more accurately, redefinition. Definition is, of course, the fruit of analysis, a procedure of *naming*. At the same time, it is, as it has always been, an attempt to *organize* the world. Both of these aspects of definition, however, are aspects which feminists regard with deep suspicion, for language and theory as we know them are shot through with self-serving masculist assumptions. For feminist scholarship and feminist experience, redefinition must therefore, also and always, be critique. However we formulate our analyses, they are critical analyses. When we say, for example, that the family, far from being a haven in a heartless world, is, in fact, the breeding ground not only of children but of the violence which patriarchal thought believes to be the quintessence of power over nature and history, then we are grounding our definition in female experience. We are, nonetheless, constrained to express our critique in the language of the oppressor.[1] We are also entering a fractious world of conceptualization in which the definition of fact is an argumentative metaphysic, and modes of analysis are developed to deal with phenomena, including women, perceived from the stand-

335

point of patriarchy. Nevertheless, while a more appropriate linguistic and analytical complex will in due course arise, the process by which this happens has not been uncovered by patriarchal scholarship and we are constrained by the necessity to criticize patriarchal history while we redefine the definition of definition itself.[2]

Thus, if one argues, as I propose to do, that feminist politics are socialist politics, I enter into debates upon the meaning of socialism, and, if I want to enter that debate on the bases of material rather than ideal perceptions and on historical rather than ideological phenomena, I enter at once into the controversies of socialist development: specifically, into the controversies surrounding Karl Marx as a critical and creative socialist and Marxism as an identifiable historical development of profound political significance. Many feminists have responded enthusiastically to Marx's dictum that the point is not to describe the world, the point is to change it, a phrase which tends to conceal its own definitional aspect.[3] We also respond to the notion of praxis, the unification of theory and practice as a method of changing the world. We have, however, reservations about Marx's theory, and even more about Marxist praxis.[4] Feminist socialist theoretical work tries to transform the former in a way which represents the actual historical experience of women. Women in the Left, on the other hand, have tended to a strategic reliance on a reductionist trivialization of the theory of class struggle, which gives to that theory a theological status and a universality which does not transcend but simply ignores the condition of women.[5] Tactically, this has resulted in an attempt to "infiltrate, sidetrack, recruit or co-opt" feminists (Lamoureux 1981). This admission comes from Josée Lamoureux of In Struggle, and Lamoureux recognizes, as some diehards do not, that this tactic was as visible and offensive to feminists as the patriarchical presuppositions which created it.

Central, then, to feminist struggle is the need to analyze and define from a particular perspective, from the standpoint of women. This phrase is central to Dorothy Smith's feminist sociology, and a very fecund perception is embodied within it.[6] As the standpoint of women has its location, as has that of men, in the realm of necessity, much feminist sociology takes as its theme the waged but also the unwaged labour of women. Much effort has been expended in trying to fit women's dualist work into the process by which capitalism appropriates surplus value.[7] Another scholarly strategy has centred on the question of ideology, and how sex-role definitions are

336

established by what are sometimes called superstructural phenomena—the State, education and the family, law, theology, and literature, for example. Feminist scholarship has learned that the division of labour involved in these enterprises—a division defined according to academic tradition—is constraining, while an arbitrary hegemony given to economic social formations tends to obliterate the equally "necessary" social relations of reproduction. It is clear that feminism must eventually transcend both the academic divisions of labour and the one-sidedness of Marxist theory, and must do this within the dialectical process which we call history. At the same time, it is also clear that such an outcome will not ensue from analysis alone, but from political praxis.

It follows from these arguments, I think, that the first stage of political transformation involves a struggle within socialism. The alternatives are reform, which can at best leave capitalist and State socialist polities slightly kinder in their exercise of violence; on the other hand, and appealing to many feminists, are doctrines which favour the abolition of politics and the State in favour of individual responsibility and communal social organization. To be sure, there are several identifiable strains within feminism which have anarchical connotations: the insistence that the personal is political is one of these, and the rejection of hierarchical modes of organization is another. Carol Ehrlich argues that the basic tasks for feminism are well defined: "Destroy Capitalism, End Patriarchy, Smash Heterosexism" (Ehrlich 1977:29). All other strategies are at best partial, though Ehrlich admits that the prescription for a revolution of individualists acting collectively does present some difficulties. The problem of the autonomous individual presents too many unexamined and unadmitted problems to feminist socialists to be dismissed as bourgeois idealism. The lack of concern for individuals in communist countries is not simply a transitional problem, just as the lack of an analysis of the actualities of birth is not just a theoretical lacuna in Marxism. Individuals are, after all, products of labour—women's labour—and as such they must, by definition, have value. The fact that infants do not always fit into the categories of use, exchange, and surplus value only means that they can be said to have no value if we assume that the women's labour which produces them differs from all other forms of labour in having no value.[8] Such a proposition can be entertained only within a *patriarchal* ideology of value. It cannot survive in an analysis of history from women's standpoint, nor

337

can it be dismissed to some realm categorized as affective and, therefore, in an evaluative way, "immaterial."

The feminist concern for the politicization of the personal is a concern which has roots in a perception of individualism which is directly opposed to the bourgeois mode of individualism which C.B. Macpherson has called "possessive individualism." Liberal individualism in the classic mode redefines the separation of public and private life and, as Marx understood so clearly, redefines it specifically in terms of property relations. In doing this historically, liberalism was compelled to destroy hereditary monarchy, not because it was a powerful symbol of the hegemony of fathers, but rather because it represented, in theory, practice, and symbolic mode, an autocratic view of property relations. All property was in the last analysis the property of the father/monarch, held in trust for his people. Ideologically, of course, his paternalism was supposed to protect his subjects from the exploitation inherent in such property relations, but kings proved to be better symbols of fatherhood than they were impartial administrators of the common wealth. The fact that most bourgeois societies have abolished kings but retain the notion and reality of a "head of State," while communist states have a predilection for personality cults of leadership, may well reflect the needs of patriarchal ideologies rather than the administrative needs of political or economic power relations.

Feminists have, therefore, a monumental task to do in the uncovering of the patriarchal givens of socialist theory, a task which embraces political as well as economic phenomena, and individual as well as class considerations. Marxism has an almost reflex antagonism to the notion of individualism, which is understandable in a society in which an individual is defined as a greedy competitor vested with rights to violence in affirming his productive and reproductive freedoms. For those men unequipped to seize the reins of public violence, to fire their political principles from the mouths of guns, the option of private violence remains open. The separation of public and private, which is an *a priori* assumption of patriarchal political praxis, is far more than a convenient way of organizing the structures of society to deal with a group of activities deemed as essential to the human condition. It is a mode of organization which deals with the existential needs of males, whose self-understanding, whose "theory of human nature," is one in which all social organization is structured to defend the hegemony of patriarchy. Feminist socialism is committed in a way in which Marxist socialism is not to the abolition of this theoretical and actual division of public and private life.

Such a position does not mean, of course, the end of privacy, any more than the abolition of private property means we as individuals cannot "own," e.g., the tools of our trade, the products of our labours or the place where we live. What individuals cannot own under socialism is the control of the means of production, and, under feminist socialism, control of the means of reproduction. In our society, the former is owned by the bourgeois class and the latter by men in general. The struggle within socialism is therefore a struggle to ensure that this dialectical structure is understood as an essential part of socialist praxis. The question is: which of these struggles should have strategic priority? On the whole, socialists have their theoretical act together on the question of control of means of *production*, though there is not a great deal of strategic coherence. In fact, there never will be so long as socialism remains a partial political theory which refuses to recognize the inability of class fixations to comprehend the oppression of women. The current onslaught of the Right is one which, however perversely, *understands* a necessary relation of family and polity and thus sets up the illusion of dealing with political questions in a way which at least addresses the experiential realities of people's lives. The indifference of socialism to the social relations of reproduction has left a gap which conservative praxis rushes in to fill with the timeless propaganda of mysogynous devotion to the conservation of the private realm as the locus of species continuity, moral values, and the maintenance of the privation of women. We may regret but we should not be surprised by the appeal of the Radical Right to women, for the Right is astute enough to speak to women of their experienced concerns. It does not do for socialist feminists to protest that it is wrong to define women in terms of their reproduction when, in the first place, women's experience confirms this, and when, in the second place, no political priority is given to *changing the material conditions of women's lives*, which is what a materialist strategy demands. Delphy is correct in arguing that patriarchy is, in fact, the Main Enemy, for it is not only the oppressor of women but the Achilles heel of socialist praxis: men in general defend their privileges. It is for these reasons that the initial struggle must be within socialism.

The blurring of the edges between the public and private realms has occurred partly because economic realities do pervade both realms. Socialism is historically the response to the initial breech in the wall separating public and private brought about by bourgeois revolution, only to be reinstated by bourgeois ideology, which is full of weary "private" enterprisers seeking refuge from the trials of the marketplace in the bosom of the family. The sheer hypocrisy of this cannot survive the ravages of high-tech production and the universalization of a money economy which drives women out to work. The Right, of course, proclaims that this destruction of the integrity of the private realm is the fruit of women's unseemly lust to work in sweatshops and their rejection of their traditional role as mothers. The Right appeals to women who either are able to evade the sweatshop by making "good" matrimonial choices, or have paid household help, or perceive motherhood as a sacred duty. It is possible for such women to *enjoy* motherhood, whether this be false consciousness or not, and clearly many of them do. The Right has simply out-distanced the Left at this moment of capitalist crisis by understanding the need to mobilize women; and they will continue to do so until the Left is able to come to terms with the proposition that the personal, as represented in the private domain, can be politicized only in terms of a theoretical comprehension of the realities of femininity and the development of strategy based on this.

There are three obvious and many minor impediments to such a development in socialist struggle. The first of these concerns the adequacy of the bi-polar structural model of sub-structure and super-structure. This is currently under fierce attack by socialist feminists.[9] The point is not whether Marx actually postulated such a model: I have shown elsewhere that he is, in fact, less than dogmatic about it, and had some difficulty in locating the social relations of reproduction. In any case, it is quite clear that feminism is currently dealing with this problem, and in doing so is challenging orthodoxy in a serious way. The struggle is not, of course, a fight over the model, but a struggle over the implications of a transformed model which insists that sex struggle transcends class struggle and that capitalism and patriarchy must go down together or not at all. The Left seems to be paralyzed in the face of this revolt and has attempted the tactic of containment in emphasizing the abortion issue to the exclusion of, for example, a fight for equal pay for work of equal value, or preferring to establish day-care as a tactical priority without recognizing it as an interim measure in the pursuit of a cross-gender socialization of domestic labour and child-care. The Left will not concede that the other side of the absorption of women into productive labour is the absorption of men into domestic labour: the men of the Left like their patriarchal freedoms as much as they hate the bondage of wage labour. Until they see the relation of the two, class struggle will soldier on with all the fizzle of day-old beer (O'Brien 1981:25-26).

The other impediments are more serious precisely because they have not yet generated the intra-socialist struggle which can clarify them. There can be little doubt that the dialectical logic of the contradictions both within and between the social processes of production and reproduction constitute the central problematic for a socialist feminology. The clarification of the material base of reproduction has, however, been made more difficult by what can only be described as a chronic dread of biological reductionism. While this may owe something to Marx's own dismissal of the biology of reproduction in the Third Manuscript,[10] it completely ignores the biological basis of the labour process itself. It is a little strange for materialists, such as Delphy, to dismiss biological realities as "ideal," for biological reality is, surely, the sub-structure of Marx's dialectical materialism. Marx's is a theory of necessity, and the sub-structural priority of economic relations derives its hegemony from the proposition that people *must* eat to "reproduce" themselves on a day-to-day basis. Hunger is, in fact, as primitive, no more and no less, as sexuality, and both partake of the classic dialectical confrontation of universal and particular in that both are involved with "reproduction" of individuals and species. The hegemony which Marxism awards to productive relations is rarely defended, presumably because it is judged self-evident. It is, in fact, profoundly sexist. Where it is defended—in *The German Ideology*, for example—the argument is that the necessity to eat is at the same time the necessity to produce, and that in production man (sic) changes the world and himself. He is thus constrained to enter into productive relations with other men, thus, as it were, starting up the process of making history. Reproductive relations, on the other hand, never do manage to make history in this interpretation, for they do not transcend their natural situation in the mindless bog of crude biology. This is pure patriarchal distortion; the act of biological reproduction is *essentially* social and human, and forms of the social relations of reproduction have as important an impact on the social relations of

341

production as *vice versa*. For example, the social identification of the private realm as the fit place for women's work simply does not grow out of the realities which inform productive consciousness: they grow out of the realities of reproductive consciousness and male definitions of women's labour as low in value creation, a fact which has not prevented males of any class enjoying the appropriated values of women's forced domestic labour.

These considerations also emerge in relation to consideration of values. Women like Annie Leclerc, so bitterly attacked by Delphy (Delphy 1977:35-36), have used the "biological difference" argument beloved of partiarchy to stress the psycho-social differences between the sexes, and in this way have rendered the biological argument in an idealist formulation. Yet such women do insist—as opposed to de Beauvoir's classic formulation of the notion that only men create values and the Left's insistence that only a ruling class makes values—that women, in fact, create values out of their own experience. Leaving aside the denigration and empirical fuzziness involved in the proposition that neither women nor people of the working class make values, one may at least be permitted to wonder at the source of the moral passion which informs Marx's own work. More importantly, the question of values is vital to feminist politics in regard to the question of violence. There can be no doubt that class and gender hegemony rest firmly on a base of *culturally legitimated violence*. To be sure, there are obvious gender advantages in creating the ideology of the passive woman, just as there are ruling class advantages in perpetuating the notion of masculinity as violent, insofar as fighting men are an essential component of power structures. The Left, ultimately dedicated to the destruction of class itself by means of revolutionary violence, has a vested interest, too, in keeping up the spirits of fighting men, and will even cautiously countenance a few women on the barricades. The relation of power and violence is a clear one, and insofar as feminist strategy is predicated on the notion of "seizing power," attempts must be made to undo feminine distaste for physical violence. Such distaste is clearly quite old: it is a very long time since Hesiod railed against women for destroying the splendours of the Golden Age of Heroes by an inane insistence that they did not want their sons to be dead heroes.

The question is: does female resistance to violent solutions derive from the norm of passivity invented and enforced by the ruling sex, or does it derive from actual female

342

experience in the reproduction of the race? The way in which feminists answer this question is crucial to the development of feminist strategy. Rowbotham has noted that, historically, the female revolutionary tactic most commonly found in historical enquiry is the bread riot. Women have shown as much reluctance to having their children starve to death as to having them die in battle. Men, on the other hand, show a dread of women adopting a strategy of withholding of sexual "favours." This latter, of course, denigrates female sensuality and is the product of male imagination rather than the historical record. Nonetheless, with the possible exception of feminist anarchists, feminism has not yet seriously faced up to the issue of whether the violence of class and gender hegemony can yield to anything other than violent revolution.

The fact appears to be that none of the political strategies inherited from "male-stream" thought and action appear to be effective in the case of feminist struggles. There are, no doubt, women in many places who are participating in the creation of armament caches for revolutionary activities, but, so far as we know, such activities are not predicated on feminist principles. What we clearly have to do is *create* new modes of political action, and perhaps re-examine some which have been only partially effective in the past—perhaps we should dust off the somewhat ecstatic literature of the General Strike again, or strip Gandhi's notion of passive resistance of its preoccupation with chastity and have another look at it. More importantly, we should attempt to formulate new strategies of emancipation predicated on developing feminist theory. The way to do this, I would submit, is in on-going struggle within the socialist movement and continuous practical efforts to reshape and redefine forms of the social relations of reproduction. We are, in fact, doing these things, but it is surely the responsibility of feminist scholarship to analyze why and how we are doing them, to subject these activities to constructive critical analyses, and to actively participate in the political struggle. The fact is, as Selma James puts it, "The formal organizational expression of a general class struggle does not yet anywhere exist," and it is to the credit of the wages for housework movement that it *did*, in fact, develop creative strategies. These were nipped in the bud as much by Leftist vanguards, defending the "integrity" of the working class to which they themselves actually stand in contradiction, as much as by ruling class counter-revolutionary activity.

343

The historical reality of struggle within the Left may be messy, factional and not immediately and overtly effective, yet what is happening is that feminism as a progressive historical force is working itself out in the only place in which it can ultimately be effective: that is, on the stage of world historical dialectic.

FOOTNOTES

1. Dorothy Smith, "Using the Oppressor's Language", Shirley & Vigier 1979:10-18. See also Spender 1981.
2. Daly 1978 is perhaps the most radical contribution here.
3. Karl Marx, "Theses on Feurbach" in Karl Marx & Friedrich Engels, *Selected Works*, Vol. I (Moscow: Progress Press, 1969), p. 15.
4. See, for example, Miles 1978:25.
5. Rosa Luxemburg is perhaps the most obvious example, although it should be noted that Luxemburg's refusal to consider the oppression of women as a separate issue was in part due to her resistance to attempts by the SPD to neutralize her by pushing her into what was perceived as a harmless tributary of economic struggle, namely, the women's movement. See Waters 1970:5.
6. Dorothy Smith, "A Sociology for Women" in Sherman 1979.
7. A recent contribution and bibliography can be found in Fox 1980.
8. Delphy argues that domestic labour produces no value because it is not exchanged: it is therefore to be analyzed in the context of social relations rather than property relations. This is useful, although it still implies economist hegemony. See Delphy 1977:15,31.
9. Miles 1978:26; Delphy 1977:18-19; O'Brien 1981, Ch. 1.
10. Karl Marx, "Private Property and Communism" in T.B. Bottomore (ed.), *Karl Marx — Early Writings* (New York, Toronto, London: McGraw-Hill, 1963), pp. 152-167. See also Mary O'Brien, "Reproducing Marxist Man" in Clark & Lange 1979:99-111.

CHAPTER 15

Four the Moment

Delvina Bernard, Kim Bernard, Debby Jones, Andrea Currie

Record/cassette distributed by JAM Productions, 2650 Fuller Terrace, Halifax, Nova Scotia B3K 3V7. The map on page 347 is from the cover of the album.

"Four The Moment" is a four-woman a cappella group that fuses Atlantic Canadian and African musical traditions to bring the rhythms of gospel, blues, folk, soul, and reggae to songs of political struggle in Canada and abroad. With three Black members and one White member, the songs they write, set to music, and perform explore what it means to be Black and a woman in Nova Scotia. Their songs protest racial, class, colonial, and sexual oppression around the world as well as environmental and nuclear threats to survival; and they affirm the traditions and the visions and the struggles of the oppressed and of their/our movements.

Delvina Bernard and Jackie Barkley sang together in 1981 at a rally protesting the news that the Ku Klux Klan had plans to establish a Halifax office. They were an instant hit. Delvina's sister Kim and a cousin joined them next to sing at a women's benefit and then for a benefit for the Latin American Information Group. And so the group was born. Its repertoire grew as its audience broadened. By 1982 the diversity and quality of their music and the enormous enthusiasm of fans all across Nova Scotia had drawn the attention of the Canadian Broadcasting Corporation; the provincial and national exposure that followed has brought them a following across the country.

They still combine their music with other full-time work and study, still perform at benefits, rallies, and marches as well as concerts, and still plan only six months ahead. But they have played at Expo '86, at the Olympics Arts Festival, and at the National Arts Centre in Ottawa; they now perform for national as well as local and regional conferences and folk festivals; they have concerts in Toronto as well as in Halifax; and they have just released their first album, "We're Still Standing."

We have reproduced the words of some of these songs in the following pages. It is impossible, without the music, to fully feel the power of the personal and political statements and questions, the analysis and emotion, the anger and love, the despair and hope, the pain and joy, the protest and vision that these songs, grounded in the Black and female and Nova Scotian experience, express for us all.

346

Black Settlement in Nova Scotia

MAP COURTESY 0F PUBLIC ARCHIVES OF CANADA. STATISTICS COURTESY OF ROCKY JONES & BLACK CULTURAL SOCIETY OF NOVA SCOTIA

Immigrations

Approx. 3000 Black Loyalists from New York to Shelburne and Halifax, 1783.
Approx. 600 Maroons, Jamaica to Halifax, 1796.
Approx. 1000 Black Refugees, Delaware and Chesapeake to Halifax, 1813-1815.
Approx. 900 Black Refugees, Delaware and Chesapeake to Halifax, via Bermuda, 1813-1815.

Emigrations

Approx. 1200 Black Loyalists, Halifax to Sierra Leone, 1792.
Approx. 500-600 Maroons, Halifax to Sierra Leone, 1800.
95 Black Refugees, Halifax to Trinidad, 1821.

I Love You Woman

Delvina Bernard © 1984 CAPAC

chorus
We're here, standing at the shoreline
made it through some hard times
Black mother, Black daughter
made it through some hard times
Black mother, Black daughter

I see reflections of a past staring at me
of hard work, and women kneeling to pray
from the dusk, to the dawn
each day hard, each day long
giving me, my claim
I love you woman

repeat chorus

I see waters of east shores wearing you grey.....
of tides white.....but never wearing you down
with your will, by your might
you have kept, gifts of old
giving me, my strength
I love you woman

repeat chorus

From the weakest one, to the strongest one
if we can say, who's weak and who's strong
the wisdom you've given, our blending as women
to conquer that troubled road
from your heart, by your life
you have said, be we bold
giving me, my name
I love you woman

I'm a woman Black, and a woman first
cause I know what I have to meet
fire and thunder.....waters of courage
are the gifts you've given to me
we stand as women
for the cause that needs assistance
against the wrong that needs resistance

Africville

George E. Clarke*/Delvina Bernard © CAPAC

at negro point down by the blue Bedford basin
where catfish jumped and ships went sailin'
we lived...we loved...we worked...we ploughed.
and raised our children black and proud.

we built our Africville and we made it home
Church on Sunday for a hundred years long
no matter rats, cops, the dump next door—
we could've stayed for a hundred years more.

chorus

Africville will never die,
Africville....

the paper said: "these people got to move,
for their own good, and our good, too";
city planners said: "these people can't stay here,
we need their land, for a container pier."

chorus

Africville will never die....

they forced us out with trucks and threats
pushed down homes while old folks wept
maybe they saw bad water in the wells
but we could see sunrise like nowhere else.

chorus

Africville will never die...
...Africville will....

Bulldozers can't break pride
history ain't stopped by lies
Africville will never die
Africville will...
...Africville has made us wise.

* George Clarke is a Black Nova Scotia poet whose powerful Nova Scotia themes have been an inspiration to the group. A collection of his poetry, *Saltwater Spirituals and Deeper Blues*, was published by Pottersfield Press in Halifax in 1983.

Lydia Jackson

Delvina Bernard/George E. Clarke © 1983 CAPAC

Lydia Jackson dark as stars
slaved and served, slaved and starved
in this rough land, cold and hard
water and rock were her guard
water and rock were her guard

she worked in the morning, and laboured at night
she knew day break, and she knew star light
and she knew too, that things weren't right
to be a slave cause not white
to be a slave cause not white

Lydia Jackson slave madonna
had a master Dr. Bullman
a son of Nova Scotia, gave a son to Lydia
gave a son to our Lydia
gave a son to our Lydia

And when she came to him, with the news
he knew just what to do
he beat her, 'till she was black and blue
and their poor son, he died when due

Lydia Jackson, longed for home
heaven seemed, the ocean's moan
the promised land, Sierra Leone

Now our lady of faith, run away
oh Mary don't you weep
oh Mary don't you weep today
Nova Scotia's such a hard place to stay

Lydia Jackson, dark as stars....
Nova Scotia had little to choose
Sierra Leone wasn't too far
and water and rock were her guard
Lydia
Lydia
Lydia look away to Africa

Inkululeko Iyeza*

Delvina Bernard © 1986 CAPAC

It's amazing Lord, how salvation always comes
so late for most, but too soon for some

by and by, the burdens that we bear
will take wings in flight, as we lay down to rest
twenty-six days and twenty-six nights, heaven hurled
down fire
thunder clapped, as scorn rained down, on Pretoria
children called out Steven's name......inkululeko iyeza
cold black blood bickered in my brain.....inkululeko iyeza

Chorus

It's amazing Lord, how salvation always comes
so late for most, but too soon for some
by and by, Lord the burdens that we bear
will take wings in flight, as we lay down to rest

Cuffs on flesh, and flesh on stone, Black freedom kept in
chains
butchers hide, behind apartheid laws, to cover evil schemes
no denying they were lying....
judge and jury harmonizing....inkululeko iyeza

repeat chorus

inkululeko iyeza
inkululeko iyeza
inkululeko iyeza
inkululeko iyeza

* Freedom is coming
(Steven Biko's lament)

351

Freedom Has Beckoned

Delvina Bernard © 1985 CAPAC

chorus

I won't let the world turn my head around
I won't let the world turn my head around
I won't let the world turn my head around
cause freedom has beckoned me to come

I won't stop until the weak become the strong
I won't stop until the weak become the strong
I won't stop until the weak become the strong
cause freedom has beckoned me to come

And we won't be free
until the humble women speak
and we won't be free
until the humble women speak

repeat chorus

I won't stop until Black people stand as one
I won't stop until Black people stand as one
I won't stop until Black people stand as one
cause freedom has beckoned me to come

And we won't be free
until South Africa is free!
and we won't be free
until South Africa is free!

repeat chorus

I won't stop until the Pentagon has fallen
I won't stop until the Pentagon has fallen
I won't stop until the Pentagon has fallen
like Jericho its walls come tumbling down

And we won't be free
until the trumpet sounds for peace
and we won't be free
until the trumpet sounds for peace

repeat chorus

CHAPTER 16

Thoughts on Women and Power

Yolande Cohen

Translated by Francine Sylvestre-Wallace

Yolande Cohen teaches contemporary social history at l'Université du Québec à Montréal. Her activism as a student in France during the turbulent 1960s continues with her involvement in liberation politics and women's struggles in Québec today. Her research and writing is concerned with the lived experience of women's daily lives and their relationship to politics and power. Her current research and writing focus on the development of feminine professions, such as nursing, and voluntary associations, such as Les Cercles de Fermières in Québec during the first half of this century. She edited a collection of essays on international experiences of women in politics, *Femmes et Contre-Pouvoirs*, published in English translation as *Women and Counter-power* by Black Rose Books (1989). She is also author of *Les Jeunes, le socialisme et la guerre* (1988) and, with Y. Levy and M. Berdugo Cohen, *Juifs Marocains à Montréal* (1987).

Francine Sylvestre-Wallace worked under extreme time pressure, a marvelous expression of sisterhood in action, to make it possible for us to publish this article, a longer, more developed version of which appears in French in *Femmes et Politique*, edited by Yolande Cohen and published by Le Jour, Montréal.

The women's movement is currently in a critical phase. The intense activity of women in the 1970's contributed to major changes in the attitudes of individuals. But maintaining the rights acquired during that celebrated decade in the face of the present economic crisis and an apparent rejection of feminist hopes by women seeking to re-establish harmony between men and women by supporting attacks on women's rights and the gay community, and by espousing more conservative ideas, is a constant struggle.

I will attempt here to tackle the question of what keeps feminism a significant subversive force in this new context. I will argue that women's capacity for procreation, and the values this implies, underlie a profound political ambivalence that is at the same time our strength and our weakness. I will examine the process through which, in the 19th and 20th centuries, the family came to represent a privileged area of activity and strength for women, and the effect of this development on women's autonomy. In doing so, I shall contest the popular notion of women as entirely oppressed individuals. I do not question the reality of our oppression — it is obvious that subordinate job ghettoes, inferior wages, degrading working conditions and a double work-load is the common lot of most of us — but I shall attempt, rather, to re-affirm women's place in history as social actors every bit as alienated, and every bit as conscious as men.

It is not enough to state simply that women have been economically and politically disadvantaged when we know that the division of labour has given us a certain sphere of influence. The causes of this division of labour and the particular assignment of roles is still a controversial question that I will not attempt to resolve here.[1] I shall, instead, examine the social and cultural sphere to see how women have developed networks of solidarity and means of social influence from the places where they felt comfortable. This will permit me to deal with areas of female activity that are not often recognized as political. On this basis, I will question the tendency of some feminists, encouraged by the powers-that-be, to reduce feminism to a struggle *for* equality *against* oppression. I will outline a broader, more complex and diverse sense of feminism's significance.

The 1970's: Ripe for the Birth of the Women's Movement

The anti-establishment movement of the years 1960-1970 liberated new and explosive energies which radically transformed the values which legitimize our society. Soldiers refused to fight for just any national cause;[2] students no longer felt particularly attracted to their studies—especially not to the learning which forced their social integration; the labour movement demanded more, and noisily at that; and women were no longer willing to stay home, nor to work for low wages, nor to produce more and more children. The well-oiled system of social reproduction seemed to have broken down.

We heard cries of "It doesn't make sense," "anarchy," and "egotism" (the "me generation") because the central question in all of this was the individual. Revolution no longer sought to abolish systems, States and societies; it aimed first to realize the total self-actualization of the individual in the "here and now."[3]

This reversal of politics meant that everything had to be re-invented. "L'Imagination au pouvoir" (Imagination to Power) became the cherished slogan of my generation. The old models of social transformation by means of taking over political power were forgotten and replaced by the warm, friendly, spontaneous cooperation of individuals working to create different ways of life and different conditions for living. By stressing culture and community and social activism, the counter-movements of the 1970's opened up new areas of confrontation and contributed to the discrediting of politics. Parties and unions of the Right and the Left were disrupted. Wildcat strikes, happenings, spontaneous movements and actions replaced organization and discipline. Needs were articulated at the grass-roots level in a total rejection of all hierarchy and bureaucratic manipulation. In all of these chaotic reversals, power was contested in all its ramifications. We never sought to replace one form of power with another.

Was this the rebellion of spoiled children ruined in a post-war society in full expansion?[4] A temporary generation gap?[5] A failure of an archaic Imperial University? A sexual revolution? The qualifying terms were numerous, and their multiplicity isolated these movements, masking the overall effects of that 10-year period on Western society. Governments did not fall—on the contrary, they have been reinforced and have moved further to the Right. Strong regimes and strong men are in demand after a period of chaos; institutions and parties neither faded away nor were blown up. Yet I believe that my generation was at the heart of major events that have indelibly marked our history.

Today's young people and students not only refuse to adopt the models of their elders, they do not even imagine themselves replacing them in what are now devalued positions. Adult society is instead tempted to value the behaviour of the young and to identify with them.[6] In sociological terms, the transmission of values, and so the mode of renewal of the social body, no longer follows models elaborated by the adult group; adult models co-exist with those of teenage peer-groups. It is this same social renewal which is questioned at another level by the women's movement. Because women hold the power to reproduce, we act (potentially at least) directly on demographic flows and therefore on the survival of our society. The common contestation of the male and adult power structure by these two sectors of the population seems to me sufficiently important to warrant an analysis of its causes and effects — not in order to see these groups as the new[7] motors of history, nor to make them the new saviours of humanity, but to define their part in the making of our history. It is in this specific context that I turn to an analysis of the women's movement.

Women and Politics

By refusing in their slogans to replace one form of power with another, women have situated themselves outside the realm of political power. Our way of re-appropriating politics was to bring it to our own ground. When other groups were crying "everything is political," we were saying "the private is political." At the same time, more than any other group, women have been excluded from the political world, and their practice will necessarily mirror that intrinsic marginality. Some feminists see women's particular political forms only as a result of their oppression and exclusion from politics. I argue that women excluded from political power have a multitude of powers by which they express themselves, giving new sense to the private and the political. Women's attitude to political power is more one of an overall strategy to keep themselves away from it than one of an oppressed group. They do not have political power and they do not want it; they

356

have developed networks of solidarity in communal settings which give them a certain type of power. It would be a mistake for us to try to channel this diverse practice into the narrowly political, for at a time when social groups are searching for new alternatives to devalued political power, "feminine practices" appear to have the potential to create a new basis for the legitimation of society. This helps explain why women were projected so unexpectedly to the vanguard of the current social movement.

I will now go on to more fully explore the nature of politics and women's relationship to it.

From what, exactly, are we excluded?

Women's exclusion from politics is certainly noteworthy. In all States—liberal and totalitarian, past and present—women's presence is minimal, if not totally absent.[8] But we must not overlook our own profound inability to see ourselves in politics, and to define our role once there. Our exclusion has been internalized in a no less pernicious and stubborn way. I will illustrate this point with a reference to my experience in teaching two courses on Women and Politics.

In one of these courses, given at the University of Québec at Montréal, 60 students prepared papers on topics chosen and defined for themselves. Not one of these papers dealt with the political roles of women; there was nothing on the right to vote or on government office, for example. Instead, the class kept returning to a discussion of women's movements (whether to include men, whether to be independent of traditional organizations). Another of our themes focused on a critique of the recommendations made by the Council on the Status of Women. The only activity in this regard which involved us all intensely was the collection of accounts of women's lives which I will discuss below.

What emerged from the exciting experience of this course was our inability to deal with problems in terms of traditional politics. We remained estranged from the political sphere. At most, we could contest it; we never really penetrated it. It remained entirely, if not exclusively, an alien domain, clearly masculine.

My second experience was a Master's seminar at Laval University, where, in small groups of 13 people, we attempted to uncover women's views of politics. We made a collective decision to approach the question using themes that appeared to us to be central — the body, the family, and work. In fact, we decided to interpret reality by inversing dominant relations and studying them from the perspective of women. The future of the family and sexual oppression are unquestionably important topics to tackle, but they certainly cannot replace an analysis centred on the why and how of male domination in politics, the State, and global society.

Since I am critical of the university environment in general, I am tempted to explain our failure to deal with "politics" in these two cases by arguing that it is simply impossible to identify and analyze political problems in a university context. However, the problem appears to me to be much more complex than that, for women outside the university share this inability to deal with "politics."

The following account of a research project will explain further.

Perhaps we are excluded only from "Politics"

I recently directed a research project which dealt with women's perception of Québec history. We used an autobiographical methodology whereby accounts of life stories were collected and analyzed in order to determine the effects of social and individual change on the social fabric.[9] The stories of the 20 or so women interviewed for this study revealed a total inability to understand or fit into the world of "politics," which is *a priori* an exclusively male domain, perceived by women, if at all, only in the limited forms of the vote and newspaper and television news.

Québec women did not obtain the right to vote until 1940 and hence women over 60 years of age are not accustomed to the practice of voting. We found that when casting their ballots for the first time, these women tried not to render their husbands' votes void and therefore asked their husbands for whom they were voting, or they voted as their families (i.e., fathers) had always done, or they abstained. Rarely were women's electoral convictions clearly affirmed; if they were, it was with reference to contradicting or complementing the men's convictions. Regular voting was found to be most common in the age group 35-60, while women between the ages of 18 and 35 showed an almost total lack of interest in voting. Although we cannot draw any firm conclusions from these few examples, it is important to examine the questions which they raise.

358

How is it that almost 100 students and myself, representing a variety of age levels and socio-professional environments, had so much difficulty defining our role in political life? Why is it that even women with access to public life rarely accede to public power? What is women's relationship to monsters such as power, authority, politics, and violence?[10] How do we manage to attain a *modus vivendi* in everyday life when we are largely excluded from political power?

One response to these questions by the women's movement is to demand equal juridical, social and political access. The American struggle for the Equal Rights Amendment and similar struggles throughout the Western world aim to redress the most obvious oppression of women. This movement toward the equality or interchangeability of roles is of fundamental benefit to us all, but it is far from meeting the demands that women are making on society as a whole.

What if we refused to play their political game?

A recent study of female personnel at a university in the northeastern United States examines the attitudes of women in positions of power and throws some light on the question of equality and interchangeability. Sharon S. Mayes[11] first notes the confused attitudes of subordinates when faced with the still unusual phenomenon of a woman in a superior position. She goes on to show that women in these positions tend not to make changes, but, rather, they shape themselves to the positions they occupy.

More important for my concerns here, the author observes that women who have entered the spheres of power appear to have done so at the expense of their families and to the detriment of their sexuality. They are seen as career women. Mayes explains the fact that women hold only one per cent of the positions of power in the university by their general unwillingness to give up the values attached to the family, that women in large majority would rather abstain from exercising public authority than question values they hold to be fundamental. For these women, public power means losing what they see as their identity as women and losing the power which they hold in society via the family. We could go further and suggest they also fear the loss of their sexuality, since our body mediates our relationship to the world.

359

Mayes' study raises important issues about power in a very concrete way. Must any power position involve the oppression of others, and must whoever assumes such a position accept this fact? If so, what interest would we have in struggling for such power? If we are struggling simply to occupy the place left by men, what is left of feminism's subversive social project?

At this level, it becomes essential to reflect on the past, for we cannot explain the history of humanity if we totally ignore women's influence. The simple model of oppression — repression and alienation — is not sufficient to explain things. Put another way, it is no longer enough to simply denounce the family as the primary area of our oppression and hope for it to explode. Giving birth and the consequent confinement in the family has a very important place in the life of all women — whether they free themselves by refusing this role or whether they take pleasure in it. This persistent condition is at the heart of women's ambiguous attitudes to public power, and we must take account of it.

Women and the Family

It seems to me that the history of women in the family has many lessons to offer.[12] Far from being absent from decision-making, women have had important influence, and the modern Western State has sought constantly to reconcile us and to win our support.

Jacques Donzelot has described the 19th century spread of ruling class control in his book, *The Policing of Families*.[13] In the process of intensifying State control, women were assigned the role of guardians of the values of the newly recognized and validated spheres of childbirth and child-rearing. They became the pillars of the bourgeois monogamous family so central to the type of socialization necessary in that enterprising period. In the family, the modern State discovered an agent capable of mediating its power — the same family, ironically, that was also to provide the basis for individual freedom against the State.

The continuing need to legitimize its existence and its power pushed the State to find ways to annex the family. The process of legislation leading to ever tighter State control of the family has been documented by social historians.[14] In taking supreme authority over the family, the State becomes patriarchal:

The visible authority of the father is given to the State and so disappears from the confines of the family, leaving the women with total control over educative, juridical and existential functions.[15]

In fact, the State's reinforcement of the division of labour within the family gives new value to the private and domestic authority of the woman: the public sphere to the man and the private to the woman — each ruler in one domain to the greater benefit of social harmony and the justification of the liberal State. It is not surprising that this situation appeared to women to be advantageous, if still limited. The common lot of women was suddenly being recognized socially.[16]

This helps explain the important charitable work in which women engaged throughout the 19th and early 20th centuries, and the strong reform movement in the Anglo-Saxon world developed under the guidance of women conscious of their new control over morals and culture.[17] Although the movement was shaped by petit-bourgeois ideologies, its impact extended to the lives of working class women, who were also rulers of the home and guarantors of moral standards.

These new functions of women were accompanied by a clear consciousness on the part of some feminists that social valorization must go hand-in-hand with political and economic equality. In the U.S., the feminist movement, particularly the suffrage movement, was to be the principal element in the general movement for reform and liberalization of the State.[18]

The process was somewhat different in Europe, where the intense polarization of classes left little room for the creation of an autonomous feminist movement. The demand for the right to vote, and especially for equality in the work force, seemed minor, while social legislation dealing with women's and children's work came within the sphere of more global working class demands. At the same time, the reduction of hours worked by women and children and the ban on night work well suited the State's need to ensure an intact work force, so that in Europe, too, women found themselves guardians of the private sphere. However, with specialization and the intrusion of the State into the areas of health, education and public welfare, the private domain was losing some of its autonomy. These developments saw the rise of the new female "professions" of teaching, nursing and domestic work[19] as women began to be paid for work they had always done in private for their families. But while the State conceded this paid work to women, it was devalued work, and at the same time women lost some of their influence within the family. This double process does not present a major problem for women so long as their self-image survives the socialization of their roles and they can see their entry into the labour market as an extension of their private activity.

But what will they do with their freedom?

The conflict between career and family reached a peak in the 20th century when women's work in factories and the services was frowned upon. The "decadence" of boyish-looking women, widows with short skirts and shameless office girls, received front-page attention and was regretted in even the most progressive newspapers. For the bosses and the ruling class, women were an inexhaustible supply of cheap labour, posing an assortment of problems for unions and labour parties as women were labelled "job stealers" and "scabs."

European society attempted in various ways to contain the disruptive reactions to these changing conditions. Fascist Italy and Nazi Germany are interesting extreme examples of one type of political response. In opposition to the growing decadence and moral freedom, the totalitarian State promoted the ideal image of the Woman-Mother capable of regenerating the nation and giving it back its grandeur and power. This was, of course, a massive propaganda exercise, but it was more than that. This ideal image tapped women's feeling that what they knew how to do best was not recognized as productive or valuable, that they had lost their reason for being. Women's entry onto the public scene had been accompanied by a loss of authority in the family, and now the State offered women recognition in exchange for their support. For the first time in the history of modern industrial society, the natural role of women was given value, and this campaign, false as it was in many ways, attracted thousands of women to such groups as the Nazi Women's League and Country Women's Associations.

In fact, the three K's (which translate as Children, Church and Kitchen) symbolized a largely mythical role.[20] Recent studies have found that there was no baby boom, no increase in religiosity, and no withdrawal of women from the workplace back into the home.[21] Although three million women were awarded medals by the Fuehrer in 1932 for having given birth to four or more children, the majority of women in this period were largely integrated into industrial and agricultural production.[22] The totalitarian order managed better than the bourgeois democratic regimes to utilize feminine capabilities for its own ends, and the fact that its "adventure" culminated in a demoniacal genocide must not overshadow these other aspects of totalitarian society. We must ask how the German people were duped by the mystification — why women were enticed, or at least silenced, in the face of what we know was Fascism.

I do not intend to attempt an exhaustive answer to such a large question, but I will discuss what I believe to be one of the important factors involved. The extreme instability of liberal society, which parliamentary and democratic mechanisms were unable to influence, saw considerable reshaping of the roles of individuals in the social order. The struggles of social groups, mainly socialist and communist, failed, one after the other, from 1918 to 1928; and the totalitarian alternative offered an end to chaos and a return to greatness. Although women's situation no longer matched the model of the three K's, this slogan represented guarantees of equilibrium. None of Hitler's antagonists — liberals, communists, social or Christian democrats — had paid much attention to finding a place for women in their programmes or practice.[23] The few feminists who were active during the 1920's in Germany were concentrating on increasing the effectiveness of the right to vote, which had been won in 1918, and on winning positions of power for women.

The totalitarian regime built its support on women's ambivalence toward reproduction. Women preferred to believe in a myth rather than face what appeared to be the end of their reason for being. They were enslaved by the model of the three K's. It took a war and the intervention of alien powers to expel Nazism and Fascism.

And so, freedom in contingency?

The modern spread of contraception to larger and larger sectors of the female population has raised questions of reproduction and family which have forced us to change our terms of reference and our models for living. This major phenomenon in our lives and in the history of Western society brings *total* ambivalence. The liberal State cannot any longer let nature take its course (i.e., let individuals in private determine population growth). Borrowing from totalitarian regimes, the State has become the supplier of work and well-being to all individuals, and must equally control our reproduction. The Welfare State, in many ways also a product of the demands of labour, has been established, and while the State guarantees the health and welfare of individuals, it takes control of all our private functions as well. Contraception is one of the most important elements in this contradictory development.[24] It frees women from unwanted and successive pregnancies but it also imposes a plethora of constraints, not the least of which is the drugging of our bodies. So it is not surprising to see the essential demands of the feminist movement crystallize around women's bodies.

A double discourse has developed in this area. On the one hand, the stated aim is to appropriate control of our bodies from the State. On the other hand, the protection of this same State is invoked for alienated and oppressed women who are presumed to be incapable of negotiating this right themselves. This latter position is essentially phrased in terms of the demand for equality. In this duality, the women's liberation movement is closely dependent on the contradictory circumstances which gave rise to it. In response to this contradiction in women's lives, the feminist movement must attempt to define a space which is autonomous and independent from the State.

Women and Power

An examination of the recent Québec phenomenon of the "Yvettes," an episode of mass political activism by women, raises many of the problems we must face and provides a stage for some of my ideas.

Although the Yvette movement has been intensively analyzed elsewhere,[25] a short description is in order. In May 1980, the nationalist government of Québec introduced its Referendum on "sovereignty association" which asked the voters to endorse government intentions to negotiate independence from Canada. During the campaign on the Referendum, the Minister Responsible for the Status of Women in the Parti Québécois government referred to women who opposed sovereignty association as "Yvettes." This was a disparaging reference to housewives, whom she implied were dinosaurs from the past with an obsolete role that was bound to disappear. Seventy thousand women perceived her speech as an insult to their status and immediately mobilized to protest in a series of mass public meetings, although this spontaneous mass activism of women was very soon co-opted by the opposition parties and used as a powerful force against the government campaign for sovereignty association.

Until the 1960's, the life of rural Québec women was dominated first by the Church, and, in the second half of the 20th century, the State. The family was explicitly valued as the key to the survival of the French-Canadian nation. My study of women's magazines of the period[26] shows that women internalized these sentiments in a very personal way and became the essential pillars of a fervent Catholic nationalism. But the reality behind the ideological speeches remains complex. Women actually played a central role in the survival and development of an oppressed and minority nationalism. They did so not only by ensuring the continuation of the nation through procreation and the transmission of culture, but also — and importantly — by building up networks of solidarity (their opposition to conscription, for example) and retaining emotional and economic values in society. These women were very conscious of their active role, and "Politics," with a capital P, did not interest them. They could not see the use of voting once every four years when they could, daily in their homes, "influence the future of their country."[27] Except for the minority of suffragettes, French-Canadian women accepted the sexual division of roles in which they found their social, if not political, value.

The period of post-war affluence saw a decisive restructuring and rationalization of society. The State now took over the role of the clergy and the absent father and working mother. Material consumption and the rational society replaced earlier myths, emotions and social symbols. The new creed of Québec nationalism became economic viability: "If we were to use our immense territory and our natural energies, we could not only survive but win complete independence." We now could express our right to existence in terms of statistics, techniques and competence. Survival of the francophone population, an issue previously in the hands of women and the Church, was being analyzed in new terms. Problems of fertility and social reproduction were replaced by those of the rational constitution of a francophone nation through, for instance, language reform and control of immigration. Suddenly the home and children no longer justify Québec women's existence: work and profitability do.

The women's liberation movement in many ways echoes this new condition of women when it seeks to correct the gross oppression of women by giving them the equality consonant with their economic production. It is clear that the historical base of women's power is narrowing and will soon disappear. Thus the Minister Responsible for the Status of Women argued that the economic equality of Québec women is a condition of their independence and therefore of Québec independence.

But, in a strange way, this speech evoked the opposite response from those concerned. "Yvettes," having been told for years that they are the bastions of French Canada, resent being told that their role is now contemptible, good only for sexist school texts, and that they should struggle for wage and employment equality with men so that the Québec nation can be viable and strong.

For women over 20, who were not born to this egalitarian ideal, the loss was total. With contraception, they lost their most important role as ruler in the home; and with urbanization they lost the benefit of the extended family and community networks—the context of all their support and the only power they could exercise.[28] Not yet benefiting from equality because they are confined to economically and socially devalued "women's work," they have no place in the social fabric of the egalitarian "Utopia" presented by the Minister Responsible for the Status of Women.

When the future of the nation is in question, therefore, women will continue to assert the important role they have historically played. Women will answer: "We are comfortable in our homes and we will stay there. The home is the centre of values over which we have some control." We should not be surprised by a return to the old model at a time when no alternative model has proved successful. Neither is it surprising that traditional politics should have immediately retrieved the "Yvettes" for its own ends, because their existence is testimony to the victory of these politics.

Nevertheless, it is important that we do not simply condemn the movement as reactionary. We must be careful not to throw the baby out with the bath water—the baby in this case being the child-bearing function of women and the social consequences that follow. The feminist movement for equality cannot do without deep reflection on this question.

The preoccupation with the economic status of women has channelled women's energy into an extremely important, but nevertheless reformist, struggle. I have nothing against reforms, particularly when they improve our lot, but I have a feeling that in this instance the movement for equality has reduced us to a sort of mercenary appendage of the State.

Thus, in the absence of a feminist strategy which can encompass the complexity of our existence and the duality of our demands, there is no other direction for women but to revert back to old models. The movement back to these old models is reinforced by threats such as that now being held over our heads about society's inability to ensure its demographic renewal if we do not accept our roles as wives and mothers. From this comes the obvious resurgence of the monogamous family, patriarchal and oppressive, but also stable, religious and moral.

In this context of profound crisis where marginal behaviour is multiplying rapidly without the emergence of a new model, the place of women has still to be defined. We must take the power to create it according to our wishes rather than the wishes of the powers-that-be.

Must We Face the State Alone?

Today's activism is mobilized around individuals' re-appropriation of their rights from a centralizing State. This political activism defines itself in opposition to politics, with an emerging sensitivity which may force the State to alter its method of governing.

If the demand for the Rights of Man occupies a key place in the establishment of a new balance of power between the individual and the State, women's demand for recognition is even more fundamental. The development of a practice which encompasses women's difference, and not just women's equality, and the recognition of women's specificity (including our ambivalence) are necessary if our project is to be one of subversion rather than assimilation. Women have a myriad of powers at the level of daily life, and it is at this level that our constant questioning gives us a formidable political role. The women's movement appears, consciously or otherwise, to understand this and to use it in its practice.

Let me explain. When women demand control of their bodies, and thus of their sexuality, they disturb the established social control of individuals. With demands for the right to abortion and control of their own fertility via contraception, women are breaking barriers between the social body and the human body, because their fertility is, in fact, the demography of societies. All social institutions, including the medical and religious establishments and the State, are obliged to meditate on the female body. It has been pointed out that it is, in fact, sensual pleasure—feminine ecstasy—that is bursting onto the social body.[29] By mixing sexuality, work and reproduction (of both children and surplus-value) women are exploding the carefully erected "natural order" of our society. Disorder opposes itself to Order.

But disorder brings awkward consequences. Imagine people doing what they please with their bodies, and you see work, discipline and Western society go down the drain. Everything will be done to channel and constrain what could become a tidal wave, and one of the most opportune safety valves is the notion of shared power. Although the family was originally given to women as their *one* place of power—a place where their strategies could be acted out and defeated without impact on the political arena, over time this sphere of feminine power has diminished and lost its decision-making role. New forms of innocuous power-sharing have had to be found. Women have been placed in positions where they must adopt male attitudes in order to exercise authority. Even with the best of intentions, women with political power cannot fundamentally change existing relations. The most they can do is denounce them.

Along with power-sharing, and without excluding it, there are many ways we can and must resist the power of the oppressor. If we refuse to have one area of struggle imposed on us, whether the family or the political realm, we oblige the entire social body to define itself in relation to our demands. The list of our demands is impressive and is not yet complete. As they touch every realm of public and private life in this alone they contradict one of the most pernicious forms of domination—the division of life and people into functional categories.

Because we do not have a single political programme which promises emancipation if followed to the letter, we leave the way open for more total subversion. Because we are not limited to politics, we can overturn politics.

In Conclusion

We are at a new level of struggle today. Having said that the private is political and having practised a certain politicization of our daily lives, we are now faced with the question of how our private lives can have a transforming impact on the political sphere. This requires a change of emphasis from our relatively successful attempts in the latter part of the 1970's to achieve positions of power. We have now to feminize society by forcing it to take account of who we are and where we are—and here real problems arise. The feminization of society requires the affirmation of feminine values, which, as we have seen, lie at the root of women's ambivalence and contradictory behaviour. Feminine values are the means of our oppression, the only place we are allowed to be; but they are also potentially subversive because they are so contradictory to the established order outside ourselves. We can give birth to children, nourish them and educate them to serve society, or we can dissociate ourselves from it and maybe change it.

Much as women may laugh at the politics of the patriarchal State, we are forced to negotiate with it for each one of our initiatives. Much as we may want to ignore the State, critique it and go elsewhere, we must inevitably confront it. This is why we must not withdraw into the family, the ecology community, or even the "feminism of difference" that I have outlined. Although these links to the social body have been our alternatives, they are not immune from the contradictions of the rest of society. The privilege they offer to feminist values may give misleading security.

The "Yvettes" tried to protect their power by defending feminine values. But their protest in defense of the family and their role as mother was converted to other ends by a political party. They were mistaken in thinking they could stand in the way of sexual equality and return to an earlier *status quo*. Women cannot go back to the places and roles we had before, and any compromises we make in the attempt to do so will be used against us. We have to recognize that both masculine and feminine values have changed and that the foundations of the family and patriarchal society have been deeply shaken. Attempts to patch them up can only be pathetic.

It is possible that attempts to propose alternatives will also be limited to mere patchwork. This is why it seems to me urgent that we establish our *own* priorities as the basis for a new way of life—forgetting for the moment the contradictions that this way of life will embody. It is useless to hope that radical changes will be achieved by a single revolution. Revolutions, when they happen, merely assimilate earlier social processes into the social body.[30] Contradictions and ambivalence can never be resolved without giving rise to new ones. What counts is that the social change which occurs fully recognize our existence and work to our advantage.

This requires that we impose our values. Women are not a social class, or even a homogeneous group whose place in production can be defined, but are spread throughout society, and our movement is testimony to the potential for change that we embody.

The present eco-feminist movement, still in very early stages in Québec, appears to reflect this potential in a particularly significant way. It does not, and should not, seek to replace or dominate other women's concerns such as battered women, rape, or day-care, but it nevertheless represents a particularly important departure. The movement is not simply a combination of the two 1970's movements focused on ecology and women; nor is it the feminist faction of the ecology movement. It is the product of women's particular importance in the anti-nuclear struggle[31] and their attempts to integrate this into a global struggle for a new society.

Apart from the fear of catastrophic nuclear accidents, the very existence of nuclear plants brings out a residual problem for a male society where technology constantly threatens human life. Women are particularly vulnerable to this threat—their foetuses as well as their life-creating values are all especially liable to destruction.

What is striking is that women are fighting the distortions and death of patriarchal society in the name of protecting the life of nature which they claim to represent. In claiming for women the task of developing an environment and a world where we can live, eco-feminists are not afraid to invoke the much maligned feminine values. In fact, they achieve an essential link in positing our values as the foundation of a new society. By launching an attack against the prime product of Western technology, eco-feminists can isolate a specific target, and, at the same time, build a struggle that touches everyone.[32]

It is tempting, in the absence of a powerful global movement, to hail this small group of activists as the saving vanguard of humanity. But although their politics question the totality of the energy and industrial policies of our society, this movement cannot absolve us from the need for continuing reflection and practice in our own lives. A daily struggle to validate women's way of being and way of seeing is long overdue—a struggle to define the outlines of a subversive politics which challenges all taboos and all prejudices.

This project does not aim to normalize the relationship between the sexes, and thus social relationships, according to predetermined codes and rules (like, for instance, the new sexology with its manuals for sex education). It seeks, rather, a new tranquility of daily life where conflicts are not resolved by the power of one sex over the other and where the confinement of one is not required for the survival of the other.

The affirmation of our individuality is a more radical political act than this placid description suggests. For it challenges the very texture of our social relationships. The family cannot survive the basic need of one of its members for independence, freedom and equality. The old model of patriarchal society crashes down under the pressure of such behaviour. Even if the State quickly responds with more relaxed rules allowing common-law marriage and single-parent families, we must remain vigilant. For, if it is important for us to introduce a defining feminine voice into the politics of social relationships, it is also important that we do not let our wishes become our chains. To keep our creativity without losing it to established institutions is our strength, and maybe even our politics, in this period.

Author's Note:

I would like to thank N.B. Tahon, N. Laurin-Frenette, Andrée Yanacopoulo and J.-M. Piotte for having read my paper and helped me organize it. I am also grateful to the students of our course, History of the Status of Women (Fall 1980, University of Québec at Montréal) for having followed the many circumlocutions of my thought with so much good will, patience and enthusiasm.

FOOTNOTES

1. This topic—the origins of inequality between the sexes—has been well-documented, chiefly by anthropologists (Mead, Rosaldo and Meillassoux, among others).
2. Close to 200,000 soldiers were said to have deserted the American Army during the Vietnam war. Conscientious objection, an individual decision praised in its time by Boris Vian, became in its scope a collective enterprise, leading to a permanent reversal of the situation.
3. As the saying went in 1968 and which Mitterrand cheerfully used for the title of his book.
4. Flacks and Feuer see the post-war affluence as one of the elements which accounted for the student unrest. Richard Flacks, "The Liberated Generation: An Exploration of the Student Protest" in A.M. Orum (ed.), *The Seeds of Politics: Youth and Politics in America* (Prentice Hall, 1972).

5. Eisenstadt, S.N., *From Generation to Generation: Age Groups and Social Structure* (London: Collier Macmillan, 1957).
6. On this topic, see my article on student movements in the 1970's, "Le Mouvement Social," special issue published in 1981.
7. I do not like to use the word "new," a trite and ambiguous term in many ways, but I know no other which so well summarizes this sociological and philosophical tendency pretending to renew social thought and praxis by way of this discovery.
8. This aspect of the topic is largely documented. Given this evidence, most feminist analyses of the oppression of women conclude, as does Helga Novotny, that "Where the Power Is, Women are Not" (Novotny 1980). For Québec, I know of very few particular pieces of research which illustrate this. Christiane Noiseux-Bacave presented a talk entitled "Le Recrutement politique des femmes au Québec" (May 1979). Her methodology was weak, as were her arguments. Francine Fournier's text, "Les Femmes et la vie politique au Québec" in M. Lavigne & Y. Pinard, *Les Femmes dans la société québécoise* (Boréal Express, 1977), summarizes the situation. Some 10 theses have been written in the political sciences on the subject of women in Québec since 1929.
9. This project was the object of a research paper funded for me by the Conseil de Recherche en sciences humaines (Nov. 1980) and of an article summarizing the results, published in "Recherches sociographiques" (March 1981).
10. For an excellent presentation of the problem "Women and Power," the outcome of a conference of the same title, see Kelly 1979; also Carroll 1980.
11. See Mayes 1979.
12. The historiography of the family has known many changes. The last 20 years have seen a revival of interest in the topic, which is tackled differently since Philippe Ariès studied *L'Enfant et la vie familiale sous l'ancien régime*. A special issue of the *Annales ESC* of 1972 (July-October) "Famille et Société" summarizes all these new tendencies. But we are still a long way from defining the specific place occupied by women in the family, not only as mothers, spouses, house-cleaners, housekeepers, etc., but as historical agents in their own right.
13. Jacques Donzelot, *The Policing of Families* (New York: Pantheon, 1979).
14. Michel Foucault initiated this with his *Histoire de la sexualité, la volonté de savoir* (Paris: Gallimard, 1977). Somewhat in opposition to Foucault, Michelle Perrot directed a seminar at Paris VII and also a special issue of the *Mouvement Social*: "Travaux de femmes" (Oct.-Dec. 1978), both contributing greatly to further reflection in this area. See also *Histoire sans qualités*, Collective (Paris: Galilée, 1979).
15. Jacques Donzelot, *op. cit.*, p. 100, pp. 33-35, s.q.. This interpretation by Donzelot appears to be made hastily and is not convincing

enough from a woman's point of view. While re-locating women in history, he constrains them to a very functional history of the family; he continues to contribute to the view which alienates women from their families and the State. He does not depict women as makers of their own history.

16. For a meticulous study which gives us a glimpse of the scope of this interpretation, see Cloward & Fox-Piven 1979.

17. Regarding this issue, see the excellent study by Mary P. Ryan, "The Power of Women's Networks" (Ryan 1979). Using the study of the American Female Reform Society, she concludes two points which I find important: (a) she notes the innovative and formative aspect of the role played by women in the system of American associations; in developing ways to organize and cooperate, adapted to their needs, women introduced a new means of political intervention; and (b) Ryan defines as decisive the intervention of this society of women in the setting up of sexual norms regulating the behaviour of young men and young women. The creation and defense of this very rigid moral code afforded them access to local decision-making. Gossiping became a form of social intervention; a man who was disrespectful toward his wife would earn a "bad reputation" and would even find himself refused all banking credit.

18. W. Leach, *True Love and Perfect Union* (Basic Books, 1980).

19. See Anne Martin-Fugier, *Les Bonnes*, Michelle Perrot, *op. cit.*, and Alain Corbin, *Les filles de noces*.

20. Renate Bridenthal & Claudia Koonz, "Beyond Kinder, Kuche, Kirche: Weimar Women in Politics and Work" in Carroll 1975:301-329.

21. M.A. Macchiochi in *Éléments d'analyse du fascisme* (Paris: Coll. 10/18, 1976) and *Les Femmes et leurs maîtres* (Paris: Ch. Bourgeois, 1978). Statistics even point to a lowering of the birth rate in Italy; the birth rate was 27.5 per 1000 residents in 1927 and was down to 23.5 in 1939.

22. In Italy, women, who were under-qualified and were paid half the salary which men earned, by decree of the Duce, account for an important component of the industrial work force, it must be noted (75.6% of industrial textile manufacturing, 50% of the paper industry, and 49.8% of the leather industry). In Germany, the women's work phenomenon is even clearer, since between the years 1933 and 1945 there was a doubling of the female work force. Note, however, that this participation in the labour market was limited, since all the liberal professions were closed to women.

23. I have not forgotten German socialist women even though I limit their existence to a simple note. Clara Zetkin and Rosa Luxemburg, to name only the most well-known, were at the front of an authentic revolutionary force. The International Conference of Socialist Women, which in March 1915 proclaimed the struggle of women for peace, opposed war even before the

Zimmerwald and Kienthal conferences. But there again, the results of that militancy were in large part channelled into the socialist movement rather than the feminist movement.

24. Historical demography is one of the tools capable of shedding light on these problems. Angus McLaren has managed an important synthesis, "Contraception and the Working Classes: The Social Ideology of the English Birth Control Movement in Its Early Years" in *Comparative Studies in Society and History*, 1976. See also the works of William Langer. In Québec, despite important research done by the Laboratoire de démographie de l'université de Montréal, few interdisciplinary studies have utilized the material, which is so rich in many ways. See *La Fin de la revanche des berceaux* by E. Adamagck and J. Henripin.

25. See Renée Dandurand et Evelyne Tardy, "Le Phénomène des Yvettes à travers quelques quotidiens" in *Femmes et Politique*, ed. Yolande Cohen et Andrée Yanacopoulo, Le Jour, Division de Sogides Ltée., 1981. ("Yvette" is the Québec equivalent of "Jane" in the "Dick and Jane" of school text books.)

26. *La Garde-malade Canadienne-française*, *La Bonne Fermière*, and *La Revue Moderne* were totally perused (1919-1965) in the scope of my research: "Les Femmes dans l'histoire".

27. This argument is made very explicitly, many times, by the editors of *La Revue Moderne* and repeated in other forms by the two other magazines, all equally opposed to the right to vote for women. *La Revue Moderne*, No. 2, 1920, p. 56; No. 6, 1933; No. 6, 1935.

28. It would be precocious and false to infer the total disappearance of that model. Modes of resistance and accommodation to urbanization are numerous and varied; there are still ways to adapt and maintain vigorous forms of solidarity between women. How often do mothers-in-law, mothers, friends, neighbours, etc., baby-sit children? I merely stress here that those familial networks no longer exist; we must create them to suit our needs.

29. Pascal Bruchner & Alain Finkieltrault: *Le Nouveau Désordre amoureux*.

30. On this matter, see a work which is essential to an understanding of the French Revolution: F. Furet & J. Ozouf, *Lire et Écrire* (Paris: Editions Minuit, 1978).

31. A Harris poll conducted in April 1979 after the accident at Three Mile Island indicated that 63% of women (and 30% of men) opposed or were hesitant about the construction of other nuclear plants in the United States, cited by D. Nelkin.

32. Dorothy Nelkin: "Nuclear Power as a Feminist Issue." Communication with the author, October 1980.

CHAPTER 17

My Body in Writing

Madeleine Gagnon

Translated and with an Introduction by Wendy Johnston

Madeleine Gagnon is a well-known novelist, poet, literary critic, and subversive. She held a professorship in the Département d'Etudes littéraires of l'Université du Québec à Montréal from 1969 to 1982 and was writer in residence there from 1985 to 1987. She is presently visiting professor at l'Université de Montréal. In her academic and intellectual work, she specializes in literary and psychoanalytic theory, rhetoric, and semiology, with special emphasis on contemporary Québec literature and the writing of women. Of Gagnon's own writing, Monique Roy has said, "She writes in order to break the hold of fear, of codes, of censures, of taboos... She tries to locate power, name it, and strip it bare." She has participated in liberation struggles through written contributions to such journals as *Chroniques*, *Parti-Pris*, *Socialism Québécois*, *Sorcières*, and *Les Cahiers de la Femme*, and through active involvement in the women's and trade-union movements.

This chapter is made up of translated fragments from Madeleine Gagnon's essay "Mon corps dans l'écriture" which appeared in *La Venue à l'écriture* (The Birth of Writing), Editions 10/18, Paris, France.

Introduction
by Wendy Johnston

A renaissance is happening in feminist writing in Québec. Pauline Julien, Madeleine Gagnon, Denise Boucher, Louky Bersianik, among others, are saying and singing things that we have felt and thought, but could never say. They speak of multiple revolutions, tenderness, love, revalorizing the feminine, demanding our equality and claiming our difference. And they speak from a profound generosity and love of our multiplicity and of our resemblance. Theirs is a deeply radical and woman-centred re-visioning of the world, the affirmation of a project which can transcend the dualisms and the contradictions of our unfree world, in the making of a fuller and freer world. In this they mirror, if more poetically, themes expressed in the other writing in this volume.

They say we have to re-invent everything (Annie Leclerc), the world, ourselves, the way people think, words, concepts, grammar, everything, even (and especially) love.

> When women decide to fight against exploitation, they destroy not only a few "prejudices", they upset all the systems that reflect the dominant values: economic, social, moral, sexual. They question all existing theories, all modes of thought, all languages insofar as they have been monopolized by men. Women challenge the very foundation of our social and cultural order whose organization has been ordained by the patriarchal system.
> Luce Irigaray, *Ce sexe qui n'en est pas un*
> (Paris: Editions Minuit)
> [My translation]

These feminists assert our difference as women. As Christiane Rochefort, a French feminist, says: "We do, finally, feel different... Because of our socio-historical condition." I (and, I think, many of us) had for many years tried to deny that difference. Our socialization as women has been oppressive, it is true, because we have been excluded, silenced, and made into the the "second" sex. But our very exclusion has also given us, paradoxically, the potential to re-invent everything, the possibility to look at everything in a new way.

Instead of denying our difference(s), repressing our desires and fantasies, ignoring our bodies and trying to integrate ourselves into the male myth and its values, we should assume our difference, as women, as fighters, as lovers, assume our diversity and our multiplicity in the framework of common struggles. Recently, a male friend "accused" me, in one breath, of being "irrational, emotional and analytical."

The paradox evaded him, but I appreciated it. My "irrationality" is a rejection of male, bourgeois reason, and the emergence of another way of thinking that is not inferior just because it does not conform to the dominant values. My "emotionality" is an affirmation of too long denied or repressed feelings. And my "analytical" approach a tool I use to try and understand, particularly those "magical" (read "too complicated") things like relationships and people. A few years ago, such an "accusation" would have sent me scurrying back to the socially accepted framework of "rationality" and "objectivity," thus denying my multiplicity and difference. This time, I laughed.

This difference is undefinable. To define it, like a dictionary entry, would smother and destroy it. Definitions generally deny difference(s). To define a Québécois, a woman, a black... imprisons diversity, creates myths and images that don't reflect reality. Christiane Rochefort calls this difference "the look of the living," Madeleine Gagnon has her "night-ocean," others refer to the unconscious, the black continent. We all have to discover our own differences, "There is no model for the one who seeks what she has never seen" (*Retailles*, Madeleine Gagnon & Denise Boucher).

To want this difference is a revolutionary desire, for it is in direct contradiction to the approach of the male, racist, bourgeois thought, which functions according to the economy of sameness. This mirror-image approach is the basis of all knowledge as categorized by men, whether it be philosophy, sociology or theories of human relationships. Difference(s) are classified into oppositions, into dichotomies, into hierarchies of values, where diversity dies. Women's difference finds itself in the dichotomy of the masculine/feminine myth, in which the feminine myth is classified as inferior. Emotions, for example, are considered inferior to the intellect, passivity (even the most active) is the polar opposite of aggressivity, and its inferior. The sexual difference is transformed into a sexual opposition. Any difference that does not reflect and enlarge the male myth has to be conquered and controlled. Multiplicity must be defined, categorized and classified, thus eliminating its life.

Equally revolutionary is the desire of these women for resemblance, the resemblance of bodies, of struggles, but not a resemblance that levels differences. Their resemblance does not, like the male economy of sameness, become a force of domination and conformity.

Des luttes et des rires (Struggles and Laughter) is the name of a new Québécois feminist journal. "C'est par amour que nous changeons d'histoire" (It is out of love that we are changing history(ies)) is a line from a song on Pauline Julien's album, "Femmes de Paroles." "Ecstasy and Tenderness: A Feminist Reclaiming of Love" is the title of an article by Gloria Feman Orenstein. It's been a long time since I thought or wrote those words together: struggles, laughter, history, love, ecstasy and tenderness. It's about time. It's about time we put these words back together, put love and tenderness back into our struggles. It's time we re-invented love, instead of, through default, allowing it to be defined by people and systems based on death and hate. As Madeleine Gagnon puts it: "Love is no more bourgeois than hunger."

This integration of desire, love, tenderness and fantasies into the struggle is reflected in the birth of feminist writing both in Québec and in France. Madeleine Gagnon's "My Body in Writing" collates political discourse, dreams, fantasies, her body and her feelings into one text. Similarly, in Annie Leclerc's *Parole de femme* (Woman's Talk), you will find a feminist critique of philosophy alongside Annie's feelings and thoughts about childbirth, her menstrual period and her breasts.

This re-invention also shakes up the *status quo* of language. They use male, linear, grammatically and syntactically "correct" language when they find it useful. But when their feelings and ideas become constrained by too many rules, they overthrow syntax and grammar, write in circles, play on and with words and concepts with "no respect for the rules." They speak and write a multiplicity of languages and make no effort to establish one as the "norm." Sedition!

It's dfficult to express the undefinable, to imagine the unimaginable. But that's what they do. It's what all feminists must do. As a translator, I feel that my efforts (with others) to translate the Québécois multiplicity of languages into the English multiplicity can only help to make our diversity overflow and enlarge.

My Body in Writing

by Madeleine Gagnon

My body is words. Some erased by others that stay, and others emerging when writing seizes me. I want to record this polymorphous history here to the very limit of erasing, returning and repeating. Like millions of women, I want to write my body into struggle, because something tells me —and it is not my male science—that a great part of history, never thought out or written by us, has been embedded in the memory of the female body. I will participate in the struggles around me against capitalist exploitation, against national domination, against racism, but I want to tell about, to explore the silences of my mothers, my aunts, my sisters and myself.

* * *

I want to love in my women's language. Explain in my own way, in my man's tongue, since I possess two languages and the first has yet to be affirmed. I am male in my history and in my body and in my male science. I recognize in myself the man I love. In their science, I have lived the extreme subtlety of the difference, the refinement of the logocentric axis. I now experience the resemblance. I am double sex, double history, multiple love. I am male because I recognize myself as female. The more I become the brillant night, the new day, the more I love the phallic light at my side. I love it vibrating inside me, I want him to come with me on this radiant quest of our bodies' affinity. Whole centuries have been based on the difference —of class, of colour, of sex —now I want to learn the solidarity of our consonance. If we make a revolution, let it be together, brothers and sisters, against our masters. They are strong and powerful, but we are many. We are two inside each one of us. It is because we are double that struggle is possible. I cannot liberate my sex without yours, since we are inextricably linked by a history that has objectified our bodies, a history of fragmenting ideologies where, until now, the phallus has been the dominant fragment. I have to bring my own particles, even the tiniest atom. I will join you my love, in the chain of discourse. I am even there before you, having too long submitted to your restraints, I am born many and many-faceted before the bell sounds all the defeats because around the world they thought they had tried everything, the solutions of knowledge and of action, but they couldn't imagine that half the world would join the other half in a struggle that is unimaginable because it is based on affinity and not on difference, that the struggle is written in the first breath, the first tenderness, the first taboos of us all, and that, without levelling out all the differences and contradictions, the struggle will embrace them from the angle of sameness, of the parallel, of the identical, of solidarity.

* * *

We have never been masters of others or of ourselves. We do not have to confront ourselves in order to free ourselves. We do not have to look at ourselves, to construct this other me, erect in front of us, in order to understand ourselves. We only have to let the body flow, from inside, erase like we used to do on the slateboard, erase what weighs us down, what prevents us from writing; keep what fits and what pleases us. But a man confronts himself constantly. He measures himself and stumbles against his upright sex. For him, every slip is a tragedy, every erasure, death. Tragedy of his strength, his force, his sex. He is constantly double—himself and phallus. From the deepest memory of time, he constructs the binary relation without giving birth to it. He sets up the mirror, projects the fantasy. He becomes his own representative and his own reference. He becomes master of himself, having found within him an other, his diminished second, his slave. So he becomes. Master of others.

* * *

If, for every revolution, there is always the same problem for the vanguard, whose ideology is generally bourgeois and petit bourgeois (Lenin), the problem is two-fold with respect to woman, because she finds herself on ground that has already been cleared away, thought through and analyzed by men. She uses language that has already been constructed, largely without reference to woman, to her body or to the unconscious inscriptions of her desire: built outside her sexuality.

Even though I agree with a large part of Engels' analysis (*The Origin of the Family*), I do not believe that the division of society into classes was the determining cause of the domination of males over females (through the sharing of tasks and the social division of labour). I think it happened in exactly the opposite way: because one of the sexes was repressed and its real value hidden behind the work of the male; because, from the very beginning, exchange was written into sexuality itself; because in this exchange our bodies definitely became merchandise to be consumed (for the male's copulation, for the possession of his goods, for his poetic hallucinations, for his philosophic discourses, etc.); because the *desire* of men (and undoubtedly of women, too) is based on barter-exchange rather than on pleasure and sharing, the rest of the social organization flowed from this desire, fixed, in its dominant or inversed form in each person: the history of men is not only determined by buying and selling relationships, but is essentially based on the inequality of this exchange: domination, possession, rivalry, competition, envy, jealousy: power. All the world's colonized people are a duplicate, a reproduction of the male/female couple. There would not have been black, yellow or red slaves if, from the very beginning, women had been equal on all levels to men. The proletariat wouldn't exist either.

A gratuitous hypothesis? No more so than all the others. Why has male domination of women cut across all the "great civilizations," whether black, white, red or yellow? Why has this domination cut across all known modes of production? Up until now, no science has given adequate answers and we can outline a series of reasons that take a recognition acknowledgment of the inscription of desire in ourselves as a starting point. It is true that historical materialism was the first to address this problem and gave not only certain elements of analysis, but also the beginning of a solution (the socialist countries and especially China). Throughout history, male domination of the female has gradually become primarily a class problem: in the socially unequal distribution of tasks where the majority of women on an international scale can be considered as super-exploited proletarians. But the economic (and political) inequalities are woven into the complex material of sexual inequalities whose effects are felt, regardless of the mode of production.

* * *

To return to language. We should not hesitate to use this foundation of our struggle, although it has already been molded by men We should use it, first of all, to convince, but also—and this applies equally to bourgeois culture in a proletarian revolution—because we cannot destroy a whole history, unless we repress ourselves and close ourselves into an ineffectual schizophrenia, which would, however, be our choice. This political gesture [of schizophrenia, Translator] was the choice (conscious or unconscious) of many of our sisters in the past, because they did not feel the kind of solidarity that we are now experiencing; they could only wage their solitary struggle alone. As for us, we are beginning to speak, to speak in multiple tongues; those of male speech that we can still use: let's take hold of this language, make it non-alienating; recognize its phallic marks and add ourselves, a process that will make the language overflow everywhere; let's add the double sex that is missing; make our mark; then we have our own way of speaking and writing to invent in proportion to the awakening of our sex, because if it was repressed by males, in a certain sense it was also camouflaged by us. But underneath this camouflage, we were not destroyed—if this had happened, we wouldn't know how to speak or act—we still have to decipher our inscriptions. It doesn't matter if it comes out crazy, hysterical, broken-up, upset, sad or angry, as long as it surfaces; we might seem confused at first—not like Plato, nor Jesus Christ, nor Hegel, nor Kant, nor Marx, nor Freud, this is of little importance to us—some day, when everyone has spoken, we will classify all these writings, we're not in a hurry, history has made us patient and, what's more, we have nothing to lose. Humanity has everything to gain from a sexuality that has been put back into its central place.

Even scientific discourse will be transformed by our efforts. Knowledge itself is divided, compartmentalized, atomized, bartered in the image of the sexes. It serves the needs of the marketplace: like merchandise or different products, marked for sale, the whole system of knowledge guarantees its own self-perpetuation. But essentially, knowledge is divided into three categories: technical-scientific; theoretical-scientific; fiction. Within the framework of the first category one finds technology and the "world of work"; at the centre of the second is the "real" learned university knowledge; within the sphere of the third, delirium or insanity. These are fixed categories and you cannot switch from one to another. The second category sees itself as special since it analyzes the other two, which gives the majority of the "great" intellectuals the impression of being protected and

382

free, regardless of the particular conjuncture or the mode of production. The knowledge around which our world seems to be organized is structured by a speech devoid of sex, lacking in pulsation or fantasy. It is knowledge stripped of desire. This is where I think that we can intervene as women and this is where we are making our mark: to return desire to the centre of language. If women — and even the most "knowledgeable" — make use more and more of what we call fiction, for lack of a better word, it is because up until now it was the only form of writing (and of speech) that could integrate the pulsations, fantasies and desires we all feel. And if, at the extremes of fiction, the delirious tongues of madmen and women frighten us, it is undoubtedly because what they are telling us — as Michel Foucault and Roger Gentis have often pointed out — is a profound threat to our very conception of knowledge, because madness refuses to disassociate sexuality from knowledge.

We have to fearlessly try to counteract these barriers of knowledge wherever they exist, even inside the same text. Pass from theory to what we call fiction, using all kinds of writing — male or female — as well as many different forms of language (bourgeois, proletarian, colonized, etc.) in order to create a truly communist writing that can advance communism: we will never reach this classless world as long as we don't accept our bisexuality and its sharing, in love by both sexes. What forms will this love take? We will never know if we decide, once again, not to say them when we begin, unpredictably, to experience them.

* * *

I want to propose love as the only strategy for the struggle, courage as the only strategy for love, and, as the loom on which to weave our courage, exploration, openness, total receptivity, not passivity but secret explosions each time that I get ready to discover this body that tells of craters, of shadows, of hills... of familiar movements and others that surface without warning. Bloodless in my distant past and in my near future. Bloodless, outside my body, I exist at the limits of my blood, I exist, I leave, exult and don't want to leave out any of the substance of fantasy. And if, times, the syntax erupts and revolts against acquired linearity, I will follow the movements, the disintegration, the inflections of myself into a vocabulary that is not alien to me, but denounced by the cops of law and

383

order. Male or female cops, males above all, for whom the language of the oppressed is a threat in its sudden freshness and its youthful violence, joyously erupting, tracing its secret contours with unexpected plunges and obsessive convulsions.

* * *

To love ourselves means first of all to demand our place as subject in history. Infiltrate or rather affirm ourselves in the chain of speech. Act, speak, with all the consequences implied for our ideas of madness and normality. We bring a certainty to our work: the double of logos or its binary visions, the narcissism or mirror of the representation is sexual. We know that the great phallic signifier refers only to a deficiency, whereas this lack is the other, the alien, even the mother, because she does not hold or determine the laws that he endures and perpetuates. She is mother-object in the formation of fantasy—or object fragments. He is organization—structure—in the formation of symbols—or language. She is pieces. He is order. She is absence. He abstract. Let us demand our right to theory and its practice. The right to be wrong, to come back and to explain. We aren't used to it. The right to revolution, to overflowing tenderness, to a new love. The right to desire that joins science and history. Repressed of History, this "black continent" from which we flow with our multiple cries that surge, uncontrolled... We have no choice. The right to speak and write. The right of bodies let us go back and see our written history. Raise the corner of the mysterious veil. Unfold, undouble ourselves. Decentre ourselves. Underneath the bear fur is lace. Is satin. Let us rummage through all our patchwork. Reconstitute the archives. Writing writing itself. Words playing with themselves. We are weaving history, no more intrigues. Poetry will be for everyone the day that all women plunge into it. We will never be the sex of others. All of us together will be other and ourselves. Different and similar. Fights and loves. Struggles and tendernesses. Women demand this for everyone. They reach to the heart of the double, of the lining of logocentrism. They add many meanings to the phallic meaning. One, two, three other meanings. They do not simplify. They multiply. They reach the Other of the phallus in its own law. The law of the father. The law of order. The name of the father. They attack the organization of language to the point of seeming mad. They laugh. They demand the right to the symbolic. Repressed of history, they have understood the

384

organization of taboos because they themselves served in this exchange. They are no longer the unhistory or they don't want to perish there. No longer images. The mirror. The fantasy of the other.

Let us speak. We are not crazy. It is another kind of logic being born. With their nails they claw across the generations. Clawing the walls of their houses. Of their asylums. They are sometimes paralyzed by hysteria. They are walled in, sometimes broken by schizophrenia. Now, overflowing everywhere, they speak of new loves and of struggles, how to read, to live madness. They attack the abstract order of taboos. They speak of the concrete meanings that structure this organization: these are parts of the moving body. Crumbling clauses. For thousands of years. At first they do this in an untrammeled and crazy way. Then they enjoy and understand. They make the paradigms into other paradigms of itself.

* * *

There are those, and unfortunately I know them, who scream that the liberation of the hysterics has nothing to do with the revolution. There are those who yell in my ears and I want to throw up, they yell leave the schizophrenics aside, it is not revolutionary. There are those who clamour, who sloganeer, that the struggle of bodies, that the struggle of the sexes, that the struggle of languages is secondary to a central struggle, the right line that will magically outline the meaning of all the other lines. To see the revolution stretched out like a tight-rope that only certain wisemen can walk? To see the proletarian struggle as the one and only reference point for everything that moves? Our revolutions will well up from everywhere. Warm, sticky, marching, mixed together, knotted and stretched. My brain is not linear; my sex is circular, it folds and unfolds and describes convoluted circles; my eyes are round; my ears so complicated as to defy all description; my tongue is twisted; my tongues of writing alien and familiar, my tongues of speech more than contradictory; my arms are crossed and uncrossed, arms that take, embrace; my hands that caress, play on the shadows or weave straight and proud on invisible touches or can strangle and convulse all those who are guilty; my womb has already lived four lives, one death and love; my multiple loves, my love, my unfinished stories and all these proletarians of the world who might fall back into

385

infinite abyss or could climb out, their backs bent by so many cliffs and learn to love. To be convulsed by love because we have been without it for so long. My loves, given and received among so many victories. My body stretches out and I enjoy myself in all the spirals of our childhood games. We do not have to re-invent love. It is there, it gives itself. I do not need to see the final result because the path there satisfies me. I do not fear the eventual end, I enjoy a bit of it at every moment. For me there are no deaths when you live and love the multiple struggles.

Afterword

Upon re-reading this text and its translation five years later, I still agree with the latter, while questioning the former in many ways. Of course, in order to answer the questions that come up, to think them over carefully, a whole new text would be necessary; for I cannot see how it would be possible for me to re-trace the route of my original text in all its ramifications without going through another process of re-thinking the question of body and writing. This would have to be done within a framework that would remain true to the spirit of the earlier text, yet would allow me to go back on particular statements, thus performing certain separations. In other words, I would have to *retract* certain terms (in Pasolini's and Barthes' sense of the word) without rejecting the core. I can say, however, that a number of these questions have been *in process* in my writing since then, and are being thought out in my current writing.

Nevertheless, I do have two comments to make. The first one has to do with the authoritarian and trimphant tone of certain observations and judgments: authoritarian when attacking, denouncing or *diagnosing* the effects of sexual oppression and domination; triumphant when advocating possible solutions or, even worse, when proclaiming that these have been *found*: displaying the radiant happiness of certainty. It is true that I was certainly not the only artist among the intellectuals of the old Left to become involved in moralizing about specific *solutions* in connection with every *cause*, but that is still no excuse. I now believe that ethical problems, which are hard to get away from, must be thought about for each innovation, for each creative act. In addition, I have now come to believe that chance occurrences are of much greater importance than has so far been acknowledged in the history of thought. To renounce all absolute determinism in this way necessarily entails confusion and giddiness, as well as a strange happiness and alarming thoughts: a thought which does not frighten remains an impenetrable dream. The mystery of the sphinx consists in what is dreamt, and cannot easily be *represented* in straightforward thought. Fiction operates in the true subjective and therefore lies close to the truth.

My second comment pertains to what I will simply call style. It now seems to me that certain textual collages are shortcuts in thought, even trick imagery, whose purpose —and this I did not realize at the time — is to artificially conceal the gaps, to fill the cracks and crevices of thought or language. I believe this "technique" fits in with what I expressed earlier; the need to make one's thought whole and complete, even if it means having to resort to patchwork; such thought does not yet accept the consequences of uncertainty. But this process of ripping things apart, if I may call it that, be it at the lexical, syntactic, or conceptual level, turns out to be so difficult in practice that sometimes this rhetorical subterfuge, with its accompanying fictional procedures, appears to be necessary for a time, in a stage of transition.

As a matter of fact, *My Body in Writing* is a *transitional* text: now I consider it to be a *reflective pause* in the process of my work; for my writing was then, and still is, dependent on the outside world, the "social scene," to use a sophisticated term, in which I exist and live, and which I have taken upon myself to describe, in my own way.

Bibliography of Madeleine Gagnon's Books

Les Morts-vivants, Editions HMH, 1969 (The Living Dead: short stories)

Pour les femmes et tous les autres, l'Aurore, 1974 (For Women and Other Selves: poems)

Portraits du voyage, l'Aurore, 1974 with Jean-Marc Piotte and Patrick Straram (Portraits of the Voyage: narration)

Poélitique, Les Herbes rouges No. 26, March 1975 (Poelitics: Poems)

La Venue à l'écriture (with Hélène Cixous and Annie Leclerc) Union Générale d'Éditions, Coll. 10/18 "Feminism Futur", 1977 (The Birth of Writing)

Retailles (with Denise Boucher) l'Étincelle, 1977 (Patchwork: a political lament)

Autre, Les Herbes rouges, No. 65-66, 1978 (Cavern)

Lueur, Éditions VLB (Glimmer: archaeological novel)

Au cœur de la lettre, Éditions VLB (poems in China ink)

Autographie 1 Fictions 1970-80 (Éditions VLB, 1982)

Pensées du poème. Poésie (Éditions VLB, 1983)

La Lettre infinie. Récit (Éditions VLB, 1984)

Les Fleurs du Catalpa (Éditions VLB, 1986)

L'Infante immémoriale. Poésie (La Table Rase, 1986)

Au pays des gouttes (Éditions Paulines, 1986)

Les Samedis fantastiques (Éditions Paulines, 1986)

Translations into English

"Mouth Full of Words/Des mots de corps plein la bouche" tr. Josée M. Leblond, in *A Room of One's Own* IV, 1 & 2, 1978

"I am writing/J'écris", tr. Linda Hutcheon and Wendy Johnston in *Les stratégies du réel/The Story So Far*, anthology edited by Nicole Brossard, the Coach House Press, 1979

"Body I," tr. Isabelle de Courtivron in *New French Feminisms*, edited by Isabelle de Courtivron and Elaine Marx, Univ. of Massachusetts Press, 1980

CHAPTER 18

From Radical to Integral[1]

Nicole Brossard

Translated by Marlene Wildeman

Nicole Brossard was born in 1943 in Montréal, where she lives today. Poet, novelist, and essayist, she has published more than twenty books since 1965, a number of which have been translated into English. She is co-founder of the literary magazine *La Barre du Jour* (1965) and of the feminist newspaper *Les Têtes de Pioche* (1976-79). She co-directed the National Film Board film *Some American Feminists* (1976) and is one of the three feminist subjects of the 1986 NFB film *Firewords*. She was president of the Third International Feminist Book Fair (Montréal 1988), has spoken at many international conferences, and has been published in numerous American and European magazines. She is twice winner of the Governor General's Award for poetry. Her most recent novel is *Le Désert mauve*.

This article was presented at the conference "L'émergence d'une culture féminine" at l'Université de Montréal in 1982 and appears in a collection of Nicole Brossard's work entitled *The Aerial Letter*, translated by Marlene Wildeman, (Women's Press, 1988). Another English translation of this article, by Lise Weil, appeared in *Trivia* (No. 5, Fall 1984).

if patriarchy can take what exists and make it not, surely we can take what exists and make it be. But for this we have to want her in our own words, this very real integral woman we are, this idea of us, which like a vital certitude, would be our natural inclination to make sense of what we are.

To attest to the emergence of, or to critically examine a female culture in the context of millennia and the present patriarchal civilization, is a project I can only envision around a single expression: *to make sense*. For as soon as we speak of culture, we necessarily speak of codes, signs, exchanges, communication, and recognition. Likewise, we must speak of a system of values which, on the one hand, determines what makes sense or non-sense and which, on the other, normalizes sense so that eccentricity, marginality, and transgression can be readily identified as such, in order to control them if need be. In other words, I would like here to touch upon the question of sense and non-sense, where perceptions, desires, reality, fiction, and ideology meet, cancel each other out, or transform one another. For nothing is ever lost of what makes sense or non-sense; it could all culminate in a straitjacket or it could be put to good use in creative work. In other words, once again I will have to make text of my body, focused on the patriarchal system and its tenacious will to endure in us, keeping us on the out/side of the magic of words. By the magic of words, I mean that which proceeds to elaborate thought and its emotion, that which transforms, which motivates being, the being I am or she who I could be, or, further still, she who I desire to be to the point of becoming her in an unalienable present, to the point of being what happens to me, that is, what I am.

I

Life in the One-Way Sense

Between Simone de Beauvoir's expression "One is not born a woman, one becomes one" and Jacques'[2] "Woman does not exist," the semantic effect of the word *woman* allows us to think that, one way or the other, to speak of *woman* is something that is appropriate only in a so-called fictional environment or, to return to the etymological sense of the word *fiction*, in a realm of pretence and deceit. If the content of these two affirmations seems to be in agreement, "woman is a fiction," those who produced them certainly are not. While Simone de Beauvoir's statement is the product of a search ending in the painful recognition of the non-existence of woman as being, Jacques' statement is the repetition of a proven political formula; men's good fortune proves it.

Woman, in the one-way sense, would thus be a word having only a patriarchal root. For there, at the root of words, lies what we believe exists.

A) Having an Accent

Rooted in foreign semantic earth, we have made a substance (Man) our own without understanding that the root is "what grows in the opposite direction from the stalk." *Root* also means "the irreducible element of a word, obtained by the elimination of all *inflections* and *grammatical markers* and which constitutes a *base for meaning*." Which amounts to saying in the analogy I have chosen to establish that the man-root exists as base for meaning *only* insofar as all the elements of our social, perceptual, intellectual, and sexual development are eliminated from discourse. Moreover, man is root only if the grammatical markers of our existence are suppressed—and here I am, of course, thinking of the silent 'e' in French, as well as all the 'feminitudes' systematically dispossessed by the masculine, or worse yet, neutralized to the masculine.

The greatest achievement of patriarchy is to have caused, through the force of code, law, and then by habit, a situation wherein each woman takes patriarchal semantic substance as her own. This has not, however, altered the fact that whether well assimilated, poorly assimilated, or not assimilated at all, this foreign language, which inhabits us so familiarly, is spoken by all of us women with *an accent*. Furthermore, it is by this accent that we are able to recognize one another without, for all that, necessarily understanding each other. It is therefore not with words that we will recognize each other in the first instance, for we are still incapable of taking ourselves at our word, in other words, seriously.

No, it is by our *accent*, that is, in our divergence from the norm, a spirant divergence marked by *an increase in intensity* when using certain words with certain sounds, for this accent is expressive. Among us, there is still not enough *rapprochement*, the result of a collective practice of semantic divergence. At the accent stage, there are not yet any feminists. Rather, there are women here and there, isolated, ill-instructed by men, that is, ill-literate, either strong and courageous or weak and weary.

What I have just said would have made no sense (in terms of direction and movement) if women's recognition of one another by the intensity of their accent were not followed up by diligent association with one another. Associating with other women increases the intensity in each one of us, as if each woman were making ready to unveil the volume that lives within her, that circumsribes her.

B) The Intensity

Now with intensity I will root myself in the place that resembles me. Intensity is how I will initiate myself to other women. The roots are aerial. The light which nourishes them nourishes, at the same time, the tender shoots (the culture) and the root. The root is integral and aerial, the light coherent.

Can intensity give rise to semantic divergence? Will it enable the heart of our thinking to one day be written out in full? Does it give courage? Is intensity intention?

Intensity is like a strength with which we exceed the norm, the ordinary. When we say, "I have outdone my thoughts," or "words have outdone my thinking," what do we mean to say, we who have been steeped in patriarchal fiction, accustomed to keeping quiet about our perceptions, our intuitions, our most vital certitudes? *Outdo*: "To leave in back of or behind oneself while going faster" / "to go beyond what is possible or imaginable." But how does one succeed in getting ahead of one's thinking with foreign words?

What characterizes people who have an accent is that they distort sounds, and consequently each time they speak a foreign language they may create misunderstandings, ambiguities, even non-sense. As well, they may very well accentuate, that is, emphasize, what in principle is out of place, what theoretically is not done.

It doesn't take much for *god* to become *dog*, and it takes nothing, in French, for "she is as named" to be heard as "she is like a man."[3] The magic of words is also this way with which, and this 'what' with which we can transform reality or the sense we give to it.

C) Differences

Now, the magic of words is given to intense women, but regardless of how intense women are, differences between them have previously—have they not?—been identified. Differences related to having correctly assimilated the foreign language (making good use of the dictionary, grammar, and syntax), poorly assimilated the foreign language (using words incorrectly), or not having assimilated the foreign language (lacking vocabulary, not subordinating her words, and not establishing contact with the aid of expressive collage).

These differences are not without consequence for the sense we give to words. Thus, for example, we might imagine three formulations on which to base the definition of the word *woman*: a woman is a man, a woman is a woman, a woman is what I am. Three ways, then, of intervening in the word *woman*: synonymous (N.B.: a synonym "serves to avoid a repetition"), tautological (N.B.: a tautology is a "flaw in form"), and polysemic (because the *I am* spoken by each woman has a different meaning). This is also a matter of conjugating the verb *to be* in several different tenses. But at this stage, whatever expression we choose in order to define ourselves, and by the very fact of defining the word *woman*, each one of us is radically convinced that the expression she uses makes sense of *her life* and consequently of *life in general*. Yes, each expression indeed makes sense but it is strange that while each formulation marks a different approach to women's self-perception, all three converge in the same sense: one-way sense.

A Woman is a Man

As much as this expression rings false to the ear and to what we might understand by it, I believe that if we internalize it as true, it is because it has been subliminally transmitted to us as our only chance to participate in the social ritual (i.e. discourse, knowledge, politics, etc.). The will to participate would explain our feeling that we have the right and even the duty to claim—in the name of Man—justice, freedom, fraternity, equality. This would also explain why so many women prefer to engage in political struggle as Québécois, or as workers,[4] rather than to take political action as feminists.

A Woman is What I Am

This is another definition of self-as-woman, which implies that it is in the name of humanity (that is, in the name of the Man lying dormant in us) that we can lay claim to autonomy, subjectivity, individualism, and creativity. "A woman is what I am" also explains why so many creative women have refused, and still refuse, to identify themselves with women. Do not many women poets, artists, filmmakers, psychologists, sociologists, etc., say (in fine masculine form) that art and science have no gender?

Thus we have at the outset two formulas which root women in Man and which assure him a solidarity worthy of his name.

A Woman is a Woman

If this expression is a flaw in form, which refers us back to biology, or, for want of something better, allows us to lay claim to a difference which has been only too systematized in inverse proportion to our energies, what humanity can we find here? What woman would want to take the risk of being a woman, a fiction she did not originate? In the environment which encircles her, woman does not exist, meaning she does not figure into sense. Outside the environment which encircles her, she appears as non-sense. This is, then, tantamount to saying that whoever aspires to humanity could not know how to identify with women, much less take up their common cause. Now it happens that some women have set about claiming the opposite. We call them radical feminists and their humanity is found precisely there, in the conquest they make, word by word, body to body, of the being, *woman*.

Therefore, were it not for a radical feminist consciousness intersecting the word *woman*, each of the three expressions would result in a reinforcement of patriarchal one-way sense.

In investing the word *woman* with feminist consciousness, those women who are radical feminists have put their finger on the button which gives access to the magic of words.

394

II
The Explosion of Sense

A) Excited Sense

The general excitement of women confronted with excited sense excites the thought of emotion and the emotion of intensity. In the excitement, one cries "Preserve our roots," another "Let's tear them all up," while another says nothing but trembles throughout her entire being. Sense oscillates. Each woman who participates in this excitement is at the height of her being. The vertigo is great. The root, aerial.

Thus, intense, diverse, and gathered together, women exchange their views by means of words which are foreign to their perception, to their experience, and in this itself have difficulty agreeing on the meaning to give to words and, consequently, to their lives and their projects. In the course of these *exchanges*, certain words become devoid of meaning, some take form, others produce unexpected effects, while still others are used with extreme precision. This is revolution, in the sense that it is heady turmoil, but it is also—for each word—a revolution around its axis: we examine the root from all angles, from every point of view. It is a general excitement.

The etymology of *excite* begins with "excitare," which means "to set in motion." The word *excite* also means "to provoke (something)" and "to incite." What is going to count and be recounted at this stage of general excitement is, above all, the polyvalent value with which words will become imbued. Polyvalence, because situated where we women are coming from—multiple and different—we make ambiguous use of several words, and this ambiguous usage, born of our ambivalence with regard to sense, amounts to our collectively diverging temporarily from the usual meaning of words. "One-way thinking" oscillates under a continuous onslaught of words going off in all directions. It is this unfurling of polyvalent and multi-directional words which is going to make way for:

1. Exploding one-way sense
   shattering the concept of man as universal
   interrupting the circle of femininity

2. Producing a void, a mental space which, little by little, will become invested with our subjectivities,

thus constituting an imaginary territory, where our energies will begin to be able to take form.

This stage of exploding sense is, in some ways, crucial: in fact it is at this stage that everything could either culminate in a straitjacket or be put to use in creative work. This is where one becomes or does not become a radical feminist; this is where we move back into patriarchal parameters— ready to permit ourselves a few transgressions (for women, this always costs)—or where we abandon them for unknown and unlimited spaces; this is where we leave behind our fragmented women's garb so that we can become *integral women*; this is where we quit the circle in order to enter into the spiral, that is, where the power of our energy takes form, is cultivated, is transmitted, is renewed. This is where we say good-bye, patriarchal woman, valiant shadow in the light of high noon. This is where I take the imaginary earth out from under your imagined feet. The root is aerial. The light coherent. I take it all away, for I know all there is of us: the whole. It is here where sense begins to be made. The origin is not the mother, but the sense I make of words, and originally I am a woman.

III
I Make Sense of Life

at the point of becoming in an inalienable present, at the point of being what I am, life. I speak in I to assure the permanence of us. If I do not assume what in me says we, the essence of what I am would live for only a lifetime, mine, and that is too short for us.

We have seen previously that, caught between the sense we give to reality and the non-sense patriarchal reality constitutes for us, we are most often forced to adapt our lives to simultaneous translation of the foreign tongue. This posture is uncomfortable. Our balance precarious. The environment hostile. How, then, *to make sense collectively*? For this is what is at stake, I think, when we discuss female culture. How to ensure the exchanges between us, how to circulate our thoughts, our bodies, our emotions—in short, our subjectivity—in such a way as to be able to conjugate it in objectivity? It takes at least a minimal agreement on the meaning we give to words to be able to contemplate the emergence of a culture which reflects us. I call this minimal agreement the territory of our imaginary, from which we can take flight.

While in the first instance, the activation of our differences confronting one-way patriarchal sense resulted in the explosion of sense and its void, from this point forward we have to envisage our differences as stemming from a primary sense that has come from us. In other words, the differences issuing from patriarchal sense have given rise to *a movement*, while the differences issuing from us as the original centre will give rise to *the emergence of female culture*.

A) The Territory of the Imaginary

This territory would thus be constituted by female subjectivity traversed by a feminist consciousness. What I am naming feminist consciousness is none other than our humanity. The illusion of our humanity is everywhere, and undoubtedly this is why very few women until today have taken the trouble to look for, much less achieve, their humanity. One day humanity was lifted from us (and this is no metaphor). I remind you that for centuries we had no soul and that, in Canada, we became persons only in 1929. About our humanity, we know little more than our life-experience in the patriarchal system. Our memory is short, our heroines rare and camouflaged by censure, our senses impaired by our conditioning for self-sacrifice. They say that the unconscious is without words. What will humanity's unconscious have to say when we finally speak our humanity? It remains to be seen and heard. And remember, the territory of our imaginary is hidden in mythology, knowledge, and art. It all belongs to us. And left to us is the task of sorting out what belongs to humanity and what belongs to the conceited, megalomaniac, violent subjectivity of man. Where our humanity begins, everything begins: there where the first spire of the spiral of female culture begins, spiral of female culture where each spire would be a constituent part of a civilization spiral—for which nothing has prepared us if not the shattering of the circle provoking the very first spire.

B) Energy

The emergence of female culture depends on the energy we have/will have at our disposal, but above all it depends on the energy we will generate, the solidarity in our common will to change the world. At the present time, we generate acts, words, and thought, which still make do with the linear/binary patriarchal mentality. I speak of energy because the spiraling emergence of female culture is directly related to the mental image we make, and will continue to make, of ourselves as a source of energy for other women, and of the form which our energized interactions will take in the social, political, and intimate spheres.

Personally, I don't think female culture will be either viable over the long term in a linear/binary thought system (by that I mean that it engenders other spires), or able to overcome the atrocities of a dialectic knowledge founded on patriarchal reason.

Rather, the vitality of female culture seems to me related to a system of thought and perceptions which would bring together simultaneously, in three-dimensional forms, the objects of our thought, which until now we have been forced to see only on the surface, without really knowing their volume. It is from the volume of our thought that *integral women* rises up.

C) Integral Women

The integral woman is radical. My senses origynate in her. She shares in their integrity. Time, space, belong to her; she is female symbol for all of us, "symbola," a reconnaissance sign of recognition. Figure, image, metaphor, with the meaning she gives to words, she always makes and in/core/porates sense. The light is coherent. When I saw you right in the middle of a sentence, it occurred to me I was naturally inclined toward you, as real as the idea I have of us, as real as the energy which speaks me emerging from our life stories.

AERIAL VISION

The SPIRAL's sequences in its energy and movement towards a female culture

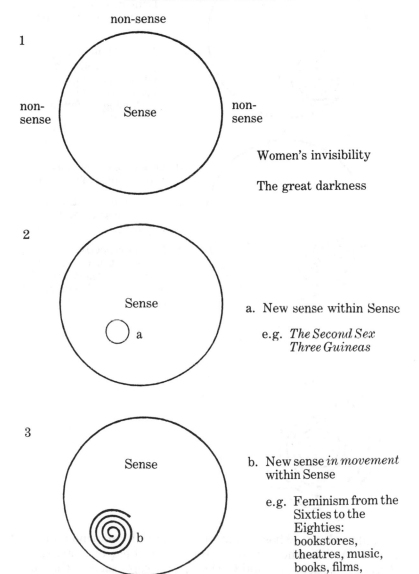

1

non-sense

non-sense · Sense · non-sense

Women's invisibility

The great darkness

2

Sense

a

a. New sense within Sense

e.g. *The Second Sex*
Three Guineas

3

Sense

b

b. New sense *in movement* within Sense

e.g. Feminism from the Sixties to the Eighties: bookstores, theatres, music, books, films, demonstrations, etc.

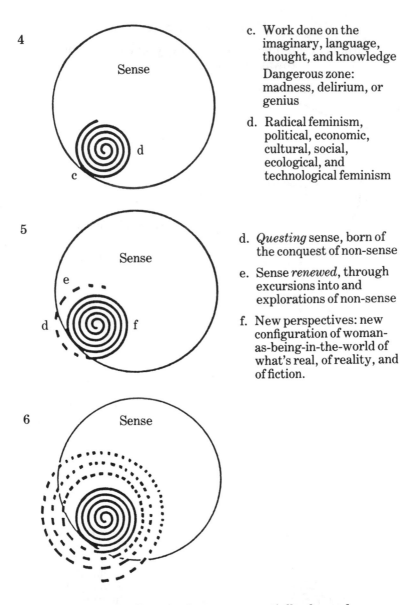

4

Sense

c. Work done on the imaginary, language, thought, and knowledge

Dangerous zone: madness, delirium, or genius

d. Radical feminism, political, economic, cultural, social, ecological, and technological feminism

5

Sense

d. *Questing* sense, born of the conquest of non-sense

e. Sense *renewed*, through excursions into and explorations of non-sense

f. New perspectives: new configuration of woman-as-being-in-the-world of what's real, of reality, and of fiction.

6

Sense

Female culture, whose existence essentially depends on our incursions into the territory until today held by non-sense. Without sequences 5 and 6, the spiral, repressed in the borderlines of sense, would end up closing in on itself.

FOOTNOTES

1. Brossard brings about a collective presence in "l'intégrales," a singular noun populated by the plural collective subjectivity of all integral radical feminists, that is, those who have become complete or whole.
2. Jacques Lacan, a French psychoanalyst and theoretician.
3. "Elle est comme on nomme" and "Elle est comme un homme."
4. As distinct from "Québécoises" and "women who work."

Bibliography of Nicole Brossard's Books Available in English Translation

A Book, translated by Larry Shouldice (Toronto: Coach House Press, 1976)

Turn of a Pang, translated by Patricia Claxton (Toronto: Coach House Press, 1976)

The Story So Far, translated by Patricia Claxton and others (Toronto: Coach House Press, 1979)

Daydream Mechanics, translated by Larry Shouldice (Toronto: Coach House Press, 1980)

These Our Mothers, or the Disintegrating Chapter, translated by Barbara Godard (Toronto: Coach House Press, 1983)

French Kiss, translated by Patricia Claxton (Toronto: Coach House Press, 1986)

Lovhers (Montréal: Guernica Press, 1986)

The Aerial Letter, translated by Marlene Wildeman (Toronto: Women's Press, 1988)

FOOTNOTES

CHAPTER 19

Fighting the Good Fight: Separation or Integration?

Patricia Hughes

Patricia Hughes is an active feminist who has been a director of the Canadian Abortion Rights Action League, a federal candidate for the New Democratic Party, and an active member of the Feminist Party of Canada. With a Ph.D. in political theory from the University of Toronto and an LL.B from Osgoode Hall Law School, she publishes and speaks in the areas of liberal and feminist theory and Canadian politics and law. While with the Ministry of the Attorney General of Ontario, she helped develop an analysis of the Canadian Charter of Rights and Freedoms and pay-equity legislation. She is currently a Vice-Chair of the Ontario Labour Relations Board.

403

Goodness knows feminists have plenty of concerns to occupy our time and our minds without worrying about the fate of men in the feminist movement. Yet it is an issue that is not easily dismissed, for both moral and strategic reasons. I shall argue that the role of men should correspond to the nature of the group involved; in some cases, participation by men will be antithetical to the very purpose of the group's existence, while in other cases exclusion of men will be a denial of the association's tenets.

Oppressed peoples have always known the compulsion of outsiders, victims by definition of segregation; they have experienced integration only in a restricted sense, subject to the grace of the oppressing group. As they then struggle to defeat their oppressors and to exalt themselves as independent political human beings, they must grapple with the relations between themselves and their oppressors. Most significantly, they must be the ones who define that relationship: they must decide whether to redefine separation so that it benefits themselves, or to seek to bring members of the tyrannical group into some kind of harmonious and integrated relationship.

Women's growth as political beings has necessarily included consideration of this dilemma. We have never been fully participating members of society: the parameters of our lives have been designated for us and have been such as to ensure that we remain for the most part on the periphery of community life. Previously excluded by law and/or by custom from all but a few occupations and activities, we are still collected in our ghettoes — a segregation based on typewriter and dictaphone, kitchen and den, bedroom and boardroom. For the most part, integration with the male world (which in many ways has been held to be the only legitimate world — a presumption which is the core of the feminist challenge) has occurred through the mechanisms of sex and service (often one and the same). Women and men have lived the most integrated lives possible in a physical sense, but in a political sense they have inhabited different worlds, the one dominant and public and the other subservient and private. The themes of the private world have been diminished, and women with them.

As women unite to defeat our abuse and suffering, we must determine whether the great gulf between those two worlds can be breached. It is up to us and us alone to determine whether we now *choose* to continue to define our lives in

404

separation from men, but this time on our own terms, or to work towards a successful male presence in the politics of women.

We face the damage done by the male sex daily in virtually all aspects of our lives. Yet there are men who claim to support us, who declare themselves our allies, who wish to work beside us as we labour to defeat our oppression — by them and their brothers. We could call this problem "The Man Question," but as I shall indicate below, that simplifies it, and perhaps even trivializes it, for our ultimate concern is with male values and male structures rather than with a human enemy, albeit the values are personified in human beings.

Is feminism to be a winding procession of women marching beside each other, unbroken by any male image? Or is it to be cavalcade of men and women, mingling together as they proceed toward a common vision? I shall argue that there is a role for men but that it is circumscribed by women in the pursuit of goals defined by women. It is not acceptable that men be involved everywhere and for all purposes. We are displacing men as the agents of revolutionary activity; at most, men can be fellow-travellers. Even that limited role has been attacked, however, as incompatible with a women-identified politics. Perhaps my position can be best stated in the following way: while there may be a presumption *against* male participation, in some instances that presumption can be rebutted by factors which outweigh the need for women's distinct political/cultural activity (one such factor is a desire to establish a power base among the electorate).

But before I elaborate on this position, I shall lay out the assumptions upon which my considerations will be based. To speak of "feminism" without relaying the sense in which it is meant is to speak of an empty politics. The following premises or assumptions, then, really denote my own world view which I think of as feminism; they thus indicate the context within which I believe the separatist/integrationist question should be addressed. The discussion of these assumptions must of necessity be sparse but it should be sufficient for the limited purpose of this paper, albeit wanting in other respects. I propose eight postulates which together comprise the content of feminist ideology:

1. Feminism holds that women's oppression is founded in patriarchy: male-dominated, male-defined assumptions and institutions. It is important to note that in speaking of male values or male institutions, we are speaking of an

405

ideology; it is true that the ideology and the individuals coincide and that all men benefit in some way from their status as males in a patriarchy, but the focus of our feminist ideology should be masculinist ideology or malism. Thus we seek our release and self-affirmation through the act of overthrowing or transcending male political, economic, and legal institutions, male concepts, male values, and male culture, and the mechanisms that perpetuate them — violence against women, pornography, and ridicule; insofar as they embody those institutions, concepts, values, and culture, as a sex, we also oppose men.

2. But feminism is far from being merely destructive of malism, for self-affirmation can truly arise only out of creation, not out of destruction. Feminism entails a vision which contemplates a metamorphosis of society along feminist principles. Since a feminist society could not tolerate any form of oppression, it would be incompatible with feminist theory not to accept that all people are at least implicitly affected by that transformation. It is not realistic to believe that the world of women will be dramatically transformed without its having repercussions for men. Feminism is not simply our existing society in reverse; that is, it is not based on the notion that women will hold power (defined as controlling others and the distribution of goods in society), and that men will not. Such a view contradicts a vision which conceives of power as the ability or capacity to define self, power as the energy to transform. This means that while feminist practice does not *require* men, it must recognize their existence and determine their place in the theory and in the practice because they, too, will be part of feminist society.

3. Yet feminism is unabashedly about women's condition, which it sees as central to the unjust nature of our society as a whole. Feminism's very reason for being is women's condition. It declares women's oppression to be the first and deepest oppression, and the end of that oppression to be the end of alienation from our human attributes. Elsewhere, I have stated that

> The hallmark of feminist theory is *synthesis*, the merging of the public and the private, the objective and the subjective; its differentiating characteristic lies in its statement about the realm of reproduction which best symbolises this synthesis. Feminist theory is based on the hypothesis that the distinguishing element of human nature is the ability to make rational, conscious decisions as well as to act emotionally, not only, but most notably, in the spheres of reproduction and

production... The fact that we can both produce and reproduce rationally identifies us as human beings; until we experience the conditions which let us activate that capacity, we shall not be fully realised human beings.

(Hughes 1979:16)

Reproduction is the epitome of creativity, the ultimate creative act, and it belongs particularly to women; but reproduction also means the growth and development of human beings; there is species reproduction as well as individual reproduction. For feminists, birth, not death, and creation, not destruction, are at the centre of human existence. Feminists intend to change women's condition in a substantial way by transforming that which has been the root of women's oppression, the ability to reproduce, into the foundation of revolutionary activity which will result in life and creation becoming the organizing force of society.

4. Because women and the life principle (that symbolic power to create and recreate which is the subject of the preceding premise) are central to feminist ideology, feminist politics can be defined only by women. Only women can perceive and state the full reality and significance of women's condition, which is also society's condition. Women's oppression has been manifested specifically in the way they have been defined in relation to reproduction; and society's oppression has been manifested in the repression of the life principle. Women's statement and activity will take the form of battles on many fronts, for women perceive their immediate interests to be varied. These "fronts" may appear disparate; in truth, however, they are linked in their common adherence to feminism. Most importantly, the issues around which we collect are chosen by women and the strategies by which they are to be realized are devised by women.

5. An ideology which is defined by women must be realized by women; thus the feminist struggle in its essential elements must be enacted by women. The feminist celebration is woman-centred. Women are the physical force by which the theoretical framework developed by women will find itself in practice. For many of us, our lives are most fully realized in the company of women. Our friendships with women constitute the strength of our existence, at times our retreat, but most often our support in struggle. We delight in a community of women, a community of womanness (Cassell 1977:51).

407

6. And it surely does not need to be said that this concept of "womanness" must be ascertained and verified by women. We may think of society as being recreated through feminism and the species being constantly created; we as women as also being newly formed, experiencing a rebirth, this one through the activity of women: our spiritual birth will come through women as did our physical birth. Thus women's culture is crucial in its transmission of our sense of womanness; it is prominent in its forging of the bonds of sisterhood; it is vital in its assertion of the chararcteristics of feminist society. Feminist culture provides our battle cry, our unity, our action, our victory, our pleasure: all in a way which extends our concept of *woman*, freeing it from the chains of definition by Other.

7. In the feminist process, women have become initiators; we are no longer passive recipients of an Other-directed set of norms, values and behaviours. We are actors, not reactors. And our most salient activity may well be our reclamation of our bodies and identities from the alien male world (Morgan 1978:161). We must treat feminism as a new definition of "the good," one that is originally and innovatively defined and not merely a response to events conducted by others. This does not mean that we will or can ignore events. For example, cutbacks in child-care funding require a response from women, but that response is made within a framework of feminist action; furthermore, we do not wait for action on child-care but initiate it ourselves. We do not use our energies in responding to every event, for then we become controlled by those who control the events. A decision to counter an action or statement must be independently reached and determined by specific facts, by the consequences for and benefits to women. Otherwise, we continue to be little more than puppets on a patriarchal stage.

8. I cannot accept as feminist the replacement of the Other-defined set of values by which women have tended to live by another Other-defined set of values, even if the Other refers to other women. In the context of this paper, I mean that we have to determine our relations with men for ourselves, and to condemn women who choose to associate with men is to replace one tyranny by another. To do so is an abuse of the brilliance of "the personal is political" (Koedt 1973:255). I return to my first premise: it is male values with which we are concerned, and male values, we must admit, can be incorporated in a woman's body. Our commitment to a woman who subscribes to male ideology may be greater and our belief that she may transcend those values firmer than if we were dealing with a man, but we would be naïve to dispute that some women who have not accepted feminism have embraced the male world, a far more significant action than merely embracing a man.

Thus the premises upon which the following discussion of separatism/integration rests: feminism is woman-defined, woman-enacted; women are initiators and actors; and in initiating and enacting, we seek to put into motion the overthrow of patriarchy, male-defined and male-dominated institutions and values, which are the source of women's oppression. Such an ideology contains the implicit assumption that women cannot be free or self-determining simply by playing a larger role in this kind of society; we cannot be self-determining by being like men, by playing men's games in the forum and the marketplace.

Our efforts to establish a woman-defined existence for ourselves are scarcely limited to political action in the usual sense of that term. We live our commitment to that world in our friendships with women and in our recognition that there are some experiences which men seem incapable of appreciating: the fear of walking along our own streets after dark or the sickening in the pit of our stomachs when we see the abuse of women in pornography, for example.

Other contributors to this collection have explored another arena of woman-assertion, that of feminist scholarship, which women have been developing in the face of pressures to bring them back into the "male-stream" through ridicule or by the treatment of such work as secondary or "topical," inadequate for promotion. Similarly, women's politics is said to be narrow, faddish, acted out in ignorance of the "real" or "important" issues. Feminist philosophers, political scientists, anthropologists, psychologists, and others, have attacked their alienation from the disciplines in which they were trained by building a feminist scholarship, woman-identified analyses. Feminist scholars must address the question of how much effort can be given to men when the purpose of feminist scholarship is to bring to women knowledge of their history and of their current existence. And we must ask the same question in the broader political context: given the premises discussed above and the reality of living as women in a male world, is it at all possible that men might have a place in the revolutionary activity of feminism?

409

The following three positions encompass the vast proportion of thought on this question:

1) No distinction should be made between women's and men's participation in the movement.
2) Men should be excluded from all aspects of the movement.
3) Men's role should be determined in accordance with the nature and purposes of the specific group involved.

The advocates of the first position argue that men should be welcomed into the movement and encouraged to take part: those men who profess feminist sympathies should enjoy equality with women. They contend there are two major reaons for their position: first, that men have helped women by supporting women who are active in the movement, by introducing legislation on "women's issues" and by sharing housework, for instance; and second, that we should take the opportunity to educate men, for how can we expect them to change if we ignore them?

Diametrically opposed to this school of thought is the view that men have no place at all in the movement. Since the cause of women's oppression is to be found in patriarchy, then involving men in the movement would be like allowing management's involvement in union activity. Men are just not capable of sufficiently overcoming their status as oppressor to empathize with and share women's condition. They cannot, in a nutshell, be women; as men, they cannot avoid being tainted with the mark of the oppressor. Should the lines ever be drawn in a full struggle, each man who has professed feminism will revert to his kinship with men.

A more fundamental expression of this view states that women's oppression lies specifically in heterosexual relations, which symbolize patriarchy:

> Heterosexuality keeps women separated from each other. Heterosexuality ties each woman to a man. Heterosexuality exhausts women because they struggle with their man—to get him to stop oppressing them—leaving them little energy for anything else.
>
> How can women liberate themselves if they are still tied to that male supremacist world? How can a woman tied to men through heterosexuality keep from betraying her sisters?
>
> (Brown 1976:111)

Even celibacy would not be an assertion of one's rejection of ties with men: "If you cannot find it in yourself to love another woman, and that includes physical love, then how can you truly say you care about women's liberation?" (Brown 1976:110)

The supporters of men's exclusion also cite practical experience as a justification for their position. Men participating in women's activities invariably seek to dominate (I have heard a man explain to a group of women what the experience of giving birth is like—to the bemusement of the women, who could not imagine such folly being serious). This dominance is explained by reference to women's training in deferring to men, a pattern begun outside the movement and continuing within it (or by the fact that women are embarrassed to discuss certain topics in the presence of men). A sub-category of this type of behaviour is exhibited by the man's turning the discussion towards himself so that the group finds itself probing his concerns, fears and aspirations, and his articulation of sentiments favouring women. Finally, women, having developed (desirable) nurturing qualities and other attributes of caring and sensitivity, feel sorry for the sole man amongst women, especially if men are being attacked, and they attempt to ensure that he will be heard, understood, and not hurt.[1]

This second view holds that we should not be expending our energies on men, neither to battle them, nurture them nor educate them. If they care, men must seek their own liberation. This view may extend to the advocacy of a separatist society. Some women have tried to achieve such a goal to the extent possible within a male-dominated society; at the least, then, they want a separatist politics. The separatist solution has been criticized as being a personal one that denies the reality of a malist super-structure.[2] The personal may be an avoidance of the political. It can be argued that the woman who claims that the answer lies in separation, calling the assertion of her sexuality a political act in itself, is as responsible for the continuation of patriarchy as the woman who uncritically devotes her sexuality to men; for both women have fallen into a patriarchal habit—defining themselves in terms of sexuality.

The middle road has fallen out of favour in recent years, confused as it is with avoidance of position. And it is true that the middle position runs the risk of either being trampled should the two sides lunge at each other or of isolation should each of the groups go off in its own direction. Yet the middle is often the only link preventing the complete dissolution of the movement, a mechanism by which the two "extremes" can seek the commonality, at least some of the time. The middle in this case is to allow men's involvement sometimes and in some ways, but not at all times nor in all ways; if the articulation of this position leans to one side or the other, it is toward the second position outlined above.

It is not possible to make a specific determination of which groups should seriously consider not excluding men in membership of some type.[3] Most groups in the women's movement are devoted in one way or another to the development and articulation of women's culture. Yet culture, the importance of which I discussed in assumption 6, above, is itself political. The problem, of course, is that "political" has a traditional meaning (as in political party, although this does not mean that that party is based on traditional premises or concepts and will necessarily follow traditional strategies), and it has a radical meaning (as in "power relations"). Culture is political in this second sense; women's groups are built on a rejection of male-determined power relations and on a celebration of womanness — their purpose is to establish a new form of power relations, a form arising out of cooperation and equality, a task to be effected by women for women without any male intrusion at all. But cultural groups do not normally consider it part of their mandate to deal with the public at large, at least when that means trying to convince the public.

We can say, then, that various types of women's groups can be found along a spectrum ranging from those concerned particularly with women's own growth to those which intend to attract public support. In between, we find groups which attempt to influence public opinion and/or educate or force public awareness of issues, without seeking a public mandate. Interaction with the public is incidental for some groups; they might have a public presence because they lobby or hold demonstrations, but their energies are not directed towards gaining mass support. Political parties, on the other hand, mandate themselves to acquire mass support.[4]

Men have no place in cultural/political groups such as consciousness-raising groups or "cauci" (for example, a woman's caucus of a psychological or political science association or of a particular profession such as law). These groups are designed specifically as support groups, counter to the "main" group with which they have a loose association (the "official" psychological or political science association or the profession of lawyers generally). It is hardly necessary to add that these are far from being women's auxiliaries, which are designed as support groups for men or to perform certain "female" tasks (preparing church suppers, for example); rather they are political groups, part of a network of women's groups and activities. Their support is directed towards women, and their energies are directed towards changing their profession in feminist directions, and/or changing women's place within the profession, and/or developing new forms of relations with the clients of the profession, reconsidering delivery systems, and breaking down hierarchical relationships.

At one end of the spectrum, then, consciousness-raising groups would be an example of groups which would likely never have male participation. The purpose of such groups is to provide an environment in which women can express and explore their oppression; the goal (or one of them, at least) is to develop growth and assertiveness (or anger and the strength to change the world), as women consciously and joyfully identify themselves as women; and the process involves forming bonds with other women and expressing our own particular experiences of oppression. The presence of men would be antithetical to the very meaning of the consciousness-raising group. There are other obvious examples: rape crisis centres, women in transition houses, and so on. In all such groups and associations, the participation of men would destroy the purpose and nature of women working together.

At the opposite end of the continuum is the political party which has pretensions to become part of the broad political scene. The political party may appear to be more accepting of traditional or mainstream approaches than many other feminist groups, but it is nevertheless united with other groups through its content; it will emphasize the types of issues which have become identified with feminists, such as opposition to nuclear power, improved transportation services and alternative housing systems. By the criteria outlined above, however, it is much harder to argue that the party should be separatist. Its purpose is to elect candidates (and to educate, of course; if its purpose is only to educate, the case cannot be made nearly as easily against male exclusion); its goal is to bring about change through the electoral process. Both purpose and goal require that men not be excluded, from a practical standpoint; and its processes — internal decision-making — do not necessitate male exclusion as do the processes of the consciousness-raising group.

A political party dedicated to the objectives of a feminist political party, based on feminism as outlined in assumption 2, cannot be exclusionary: this is, as has been so marvellously expressed, the difference between "the politics of possibility

413

and the politics of limitation."[5] The reasons for not excluding men are pragmatic, theoretical and ethical.

It makes sense when forming a political party to think of it as trying to appeal to as many people as possible within the confines of its ideological base. A party cannot expect support if it deliberately excludes half the electorate (that traditional parties have effectively done so is no reason to continue the practice); blatant sexism, even if by the subordinate group, does not lie well beside a platform against exclusion. A feminist party would be justified in refusing membership to a man who belonged to an explicitly anti-woman group, that is, a man who had made a clear choice (his reason for wanting to join the feminist party would only be for subversion). It can probably be argued, of course, that all men belong to an explicitly anti-woman group—that is, male-dominated society—but while that is true, conscious choice is not involved. However, exclusion on the basis of biology is a different matter.[6] We cannot claim ignorance of the implications of such a policy; we have far too many historical examples to which to refer. Discrimination on the grounds of biology has been associated with the worst in our nature, not only with regard to those who have practised it, but also with regard to those who stood by and allowed it to be practised. We might say that it is different when the oppressed do it to the oppressor, and for a moment one is lulled by the apparent justice in that argument. Yet would we be prepared to re-enact other injustices meted out by the various oppressors this world has known?

I return to an earlier point, that our concern is with an oppressive ideology which is manifested by one sex. It is not difficult to agree with Robin Morgan that " 'man-hating' is an honorable and viable *political* act, that the oppressed have a right to class-hatred against the *class* that is oppressing them." She goes on : "although there are exceptions (as in everything), i.e., men who are trying to be traitors to their own male class, most men cheerfully affirm their deadly class privileges and power" (Morgan 1978 : 178). The class is the embodiment of the values ; it is the class (read "sex") that we should oppose. Individuals must be dealt with on an individual basis in the specific context. To exclude them totally assumes that no man is capable of overcoming patriarchy or even of attempting to do so. Men may not be flocking to transcend their own form of oppression as oppressors, nevertheless such stringent lines make little sense when we are dealing with a biological basis of difference. A white skin does not make it impossible to appreciate black or Native suffering, although it

414

may require an empathy of which most of use are not capable ; nor does a penis preclude understanding women's condition, although it will be a rare man who does acquire that level of understanding.

Perhaps men do have a more stringent test to pass, a presumption to overcome : a woman has to prove she is not a feminist, a man that he is, for us to depart from our usual perception of women as sisters and men as oppressors. But should men overcome that presumption, they should be full members of the party-type groups. Even so, they should not be spokespersons for associations of women, begun by women for women. To permit otherwise would deny a most significant aspect of self-assertion by women. Here we reach an antagonism between process and male participation that is reached earlier in other types of groups. Self-definition is the basis for participation in every sort of women's group and the inclusion of men in, for example, a political party is not incompatible with that; symbolically, however, it is vital that women speak for ourselves. For that reason, a male spokesperson is incongruous within the process of feminism.

For the women who are an integral part of the type of association that cannot justifiably exclude men, the acceptance of men's presence may be reluctant indeed. They may well be women who personally have had little to do with men, who have rejected men's intrusion into their private lives and who have endured the presence of men in their public associations; such women have despaired, hated, been angered by and frustrated with men, yet they countenance a male presence in the public sphere of the political party or similar association. They recognize two different realities: the one, their personal life, is a reality over which they may be able to exercise extensive, even if not absolute (alas, even if not sufficent) control; the other, the political party, is one which must interact, once it exists, with the rest of the world. Willing in this context to suffer men, they do not shift their identification from women to men.

None of this is meant to suggest that the inclusion of men would be free of problems; rather, it is to say that as far as certain types of groups are concerned, it is preferable to confront these problems rather than suffer the disadvantages deriving from exclusion. The political association of the kind discussed here holds out to the world an invitation to join our politics; we cannot wait until our invitation is met to decide where our selectivity begins and ends. Once we receive the response we seek, we will not be able to avoid that question; and most certainly we shall be in a less favourable situation to control the answer. Strategically and ethically, the political party that is postulating what it hopes will become a universal politics is on tenuous ground when it attempts to exclude men who sincerely accept its tenets, *just because they are men*. At the same time, we reserve the right to impose restrictions if men cannot adjust to the conditions of membership; we reserve the right to insist on silence if the opportunity to speak is abused.

It should perhaps be made very clear that a non-exclusionary policy for certain types of feminist organizations does not mean that such organizations should seek men out; that is not our responsibility and should not be the focus of our energies. We do not need men's presence for its own sake, for an articulation of the man's point of view. I, for one, get enough of the man's point of view every day of my life, in my studies and workplace, when I read the newspaper or watch the television, when I walk down the street. The man's point of view is in the very air we breathe, the water we drink, the gruesomeness of war. I do not need the man's point of view, thank you. Nor do I see value to a link with men for its own sake. I care not if men are actually there, but I do believe that a feminist politics that is exclusionary in its most public face is not feminism at all — it is a continuation of the man's point of view, a continuation of male exclusionary tactics and politics. It brings to bear on what I believe to be the revolutionary politics of today and of the future, all the sexist, racist, biologically determined politics of the past. I see no advantage, no gain, no delight in being anti-male — although I see much in being anti-patriarchal and even more in being pro-woman.

For women who live as feminists and who therefore must confront every day of their lives the insidious patriarchy of our world, there is a comfort and a joy in knowing that we have a haven — the companionship of our sisters, a space to rest and regroup. It is understandable that there be apprehension that a man will bring even a little of that patriarchy with him if he is allowed entrance to one of our havens. It would be nice to avoid the question — but it would also be out of keeping with our desire to change the world. The problems of the world are not of our making; but that does not mean we are free of their effects, nor for most of us does it mean we retreat to live in isolation. We know that there are issues we must confront because it is only by confrontation

416

that we defeat them. We have to remember that the world is not as we would have it be: but we do not say, "ignore it: it is not something we want to have to worry about, it is far easier not to"; on the contrary, we tackle it, knowing it will not always be pleasant. So it is with the question of men's participation: we may not want to work with men particularly, or at all, but the structure of our politics may make it unavoidable.

I have argued that as a woman-centred politics, feminist politics will tend in most of its aspects towards separatism, but that under certain conditions the acceptance of a male presence will be necessary, and I have suggested that a political party will be one type of feminist organization faced with those conditions. I have advanced practical and moral reasons for this integration, but when it comes to final argument, I should say this: the political party is our most public vehicle of our values and our vision; it seeks to advance our cause and our demands for justice throughout the entire society. It cannot, I suggest, carry its message with integrity if it does not found its appeal at least in the type of justice that we as women demand for ourselves and our sisters.

FOOTNOTES

1. I do not believe that the presence of men need have the debilitating effect its opponents say it will. Women have the capacity to deal with the problems which no doubt will arise; the women who are still developing this ability will have the support of other women.
2. Laurel Galana, "Toward a Womanvision" in Covina & Galana 1975:189.
3. "Not excluding men" is a more comfortable phrase than its obverse, "including men," because this position is not intended to be construed as making a special effort to include men.
4. I do not consider whether this is a valid strategy; I merely observe that it is one which carries with it this issue.
5. This phrase was used by Debbie Magidson during discussion by the Feminist Party of Canada on this point.
6. It is important to realize that there is a distinction between the presence of men being antithetical to the purposes of a group so that men are excluded on that basis and their presence not being antithetical but just not wanted so that exclusion is on biological grounds.

Conclusion

Geraldine Finn

Feminism, as these essays have shown, does not speak with one voice. It does not describe a body of knowledge, a set of opinions, nor even a single strategy for social change. It describes most essentially a *movement* and a commitment; of and to women — women's values, goals and understanding; of and to women's liberation from the historic rule of men. That rule has penetrated our hearts and our minds as much as it has penetrated our bodies, and our struggle against it must, therefore, be waged at the theoretical level and the practical level at once. We have to liberate ourselves from men's control of our thoughts and our feelings, i.e., from the ideology and rationalizations of male oppression, as well as from the more overt and more readily recognized manifestations of male oppression in the material realities of our daily lives. And the one depends on the other. Radical social change requires both thought and action: action informed by reflection, reflection transformed by action... and so forth. That is why we cannot and will not define feminism once and for all. For what feminism is and does and thinks is a function of what is; and feminism, if it is to succeed in its revolutionary goals and aspirations, must (and does) change in response to the social reality it is itself in the process of transforming. What does not change is feminism's commitment to women, women's knowledge and values and women's liberation.

The essays in this collection contribute to the feminist revolution specifically in their attempt to reclaim women's hearts and minds from male domination, through a disciplined and informed critique of the traditional rationalizations of "male-stream" thought and social practice. The motivation of our respective and collective criticisms is not *merely* theoretical; it is not the production of an alternative ideology, for example. Our goal is a practical and political one: the production of the practical truths and theoretical tools necessary and indispensable for liberation. Traditional truths and tools for the analysis and understanding of the social world and human behaviour were built by men for men on the social and intellectual premise of male dominance. They have not proved very useful to women and women's needs for freedom, self-development or autonomy. We must, therefore, forge new truths and new tools from the partial and distorted ones we have inherited, to serve our interests, our growth and our liberation.

Our purpose in publishing these papers as a collection is therefore twofold: first, to contribute to the building of feminist theory and solidarity across the historically fragmented "disciplinary" boundaries of thought and scholarship which have kept us isolated and alienated thus far — with the shared understanding that revolutionary social change requires the transformation of consciousness as a necessary condition of the radical and lasting transformation of social structures; and secondly, to make these theoretical developments of feminism more available to more people. As the feminist revolution grows in strength, so does the anti-feminist backlash and the corresponding need for feminists to remedy the common distortions and ignorance of their message. Such a distortion not only "leaves the woman who is just beginning to question the gender-based power structure around her... with the lonely and time-consuming necessity of reinventing many wheels..."[1] but frequently misleads that same woman into rejecting feminism as a wild, untenable and irrational dogma of a bunch of hard-nosed, ball-breaking, would-be-men — women who have nothing to say to her, her needs and her values. On the contrary, all of the papers in this collection testify to feminism's commitment to the affirmation and promotion of those same needs and values which women cherish and of which they have always been the traditional guardians. These are the values of life: sharing, caring, nurture, cooperation, and feeling, for example.

We believe that the articles here are representative of some of the most significant recent developments in feminist praxis. But they are not the only or even necessarily the most important theoretical material available. The collection is neither inclusive nor conclusive, the choice of topics reflecting not so much our own estimate of priorities as our personal and particular positions within movement networks. Integrative feminist critiques of the arts, of literature and language, of music and education, and of medicine and biology, are not represented, though important work is being done in these

420

areas which should be made accessible to more people than is presently the case, where disciplines and expertise are fragmented. The collection is also limited by the fact that none of the articles explicitly addresses the issue of socially enforced heterosexuality, nor the corresponding heterosexual privilege which results from it, and the effects of both of these on feminist consciousness and politics. The challenge to "heterosexism" is, nevertheless, implicit in all the papers by virtue of their common refusal of the dichotomies, polarities and dualisms of traditional male-stream thought—of which that between the sexes is recognized by all as the most fundamental and the most damaging. One of the essential strengths of the theoretical framework presented in these pages is that it indicates and can support the developing identification of and challenge to heterosexism in male-stream and much feminist thought.

The papers probably raise more particular issues than they resolve: concerning the specific relationship of feminism to other liberatory politics and forms of protest, for example; of feminism to men and men to feminism; of women's domestic labour to wage-labour; of women's oppression to other forms of social oppression; of women's values to men's values, like freedom, equality, strength, independence... and so forth. These are issues which we will resolve only in practice, however, as we respond case-by-case and day-by-day to the demands of women's needs, and not the requirements of good theory. Solution to these issues cannot be *anticipated* in theory, although our actions and reactions to the situations which provoke them must nevertheless be *informed* by theory, by the feminist knowledge and understanding thus far acquired from previous struggle.

All the contributors agree, however, that feminism is revolutionary and that the feminist revolution will be a total one, leaving no aspect of social life unchanged—even our language will mean differently. We are already seeing this happen as more women claim the word, the right to name, describe and "define" reality. Traditional categories for analyzing social life are acquiring new meanings or being rendered redundant, as women's knowledge of that life confronts men's: categories like class, alienation, oppression, equality, privilege, power, dissent, progress, and humanity, for example, are being quite transformed, along with the classical distinctions between public and private life, personal and political experience and struggle, between productive

421

and reproductive labour, and objective and subjective knowledge. The "private" realm (i.e., the realm of *men's* private lives: of their affective, reproductive and sexual lives — wherever, traditionally, they have associated with women) is where the struggle appears to be located, because that is where women have been contained. But the focus of the struggle, and its effect, is to destroy the realm itself and the artificial barriers between public and private, production and reproduction, and polis and kin, which have been the historical and material bases of our oppression by men, and men's oppression of children and other men as well.

Although our primary commitment is to women and to ending women's oppression, our revolutionary goal nevertheless extends beyond women to men. For men and women are what history has made of them, and if women change, men, too, will change, albeit unwillingly. As Madeleine Gagnon rightly acknowledges, "I cannot liberate my sex without yours since we are inextricably linked by a history that has objectified our bodies."[2] This feminist revolution is not, however, always recognized as such by those impatient for social change, who identify revolution with the seizure of State power and evaluate political theory, organization and strategy in terms of their effectiveness in achieving that goal. We do not believe that such revolutions hold out much hope for women. From our point of view, they can only be, at best, palace-revolutions, changes of government, and not changes of power relations themselves. Such revolutions are incapable of generating the radical social transformations which women desire and require for their liberation, because the men and women who make them will remain men and women created by, for, and within the social relations of patriarchy. We have internalized those oppressive relations and we are constituted by them. Seizing State power will not change that. On the contrary, the kind of organizational structures and strategies required for such an assault — hierarchical, impersonal, disciplined, pragmatic, instrumental, authoritarian, self-sacrificing and inevitably blood-letting, demand the very same kind of human beings we are rebelling against: men and women who will assume or submit to leadership, authority and bureaucratic control, and to the fragmentation of their lives into the personal and the political, their actions into means and ends, themselves into rational and emotional, objective and subjective... and so on. These characteristics will not disappear overnight once such a

422

revolution has been won; indeed they cannot, for they are also required for the successful exercise of State power once it has been seized.

There are, however, "two ways of getting rid of a structure... One is to put a bomb under it... and the other is to dig around and undermine it till it topples."[3] The latter better describes the strategic approach to the destruction of patriarchal social structures espoused by the writers of these articles. The revolution which women are making is a revolution from the ground up.[4] It begins in our own lives, but its goal and direction is the radical transformation of all social relations, i.e., of what it means to be a woman and what it means to be a man. The movement is necessarily fragmented because we must fight for our freedom *on all fronts at once*, at our own pace, in response to our own needs and our own knowledge — for our objective is the acquisition of power over our own lives — and all these conditions are historically and personally variable. There is no lynch-pin to patriarchal power; no Winter Palace which can be assaulted collectively and appropriated once and for all — though all the contributors are united in their recognition of the control of reproduction as one of its fundamental constituents. The mechanisms of male dominance are multiform and interconnected (they have had a long time to grow and consolidate) — the family, the economy, the church, and the educational system, for example. These pivotal points of control have to be *undermined*, not merely assaulted, but dismantled bit-by-bit from the ground up.

The common ground of all the instruments of male power has been women's socially contrived *powerlessness* and corresponding *dependency* on men for their social and material security and survival. These are the objective social and material conditions of patriarchal power and they are conditions which are changing — rapidly, considering the long history during which they have remained relatively unchanged. Women are gaining power, both as individuals and as a collectivity.[5] This increased control of women over their own lives reduces their dependency on men — socially, economically, emotionally and sexually — and thus their powerlessness; and so undermines our allegiance to men, to their strength and to their social status — for we no longer need that allegiance to survive; in fact, it has become a liability.[6] This growth in women's power and independence in turn undermines men's strength and status, and the power which is its condition of possibility. The back-lash we are currently experiencing to the women's movement is evidence of this shifting of the ground of patriarchal power. A governing order resorts to violence only when it is losing power, and it loses power when those over whom it rules withdraw their consent and support, and refuse to collaborate in their own domination — as women are doing now. While violence itself is utterly incapable of creating power, and, in fact, only exacerbates the impotence which motivates it, power, on the other hand, "springs up whenever people act together and act in concert..."[7]. Women in the 1980's are acting together and acting in concert. They are becoming powerful. Men are finding it increasingly difficult to do either, while random acts of violence against themselves as well as others are becoming more and more common. And while we may not be able to destroy their power over us by putting a bomb under them, they most certainly hold that threat over us. The lines are drawn, however, and it is becoming increasingly difficult for the uncommitted to maintain a comfortable position with a foot in both camps. Men's destructive power must be undermined if we, women *and* men, are to survive. The feminist movement is working towards this end. It remains to be seen who will join us in this historical struggle for our lives, as well as for our hearts and our minds.

FOOTNOTES

1. Gloria Steinem in *Quest*, 1981, Xi.
2. This volume, Chapter 12. A similar and related point has been made somewhat more "objectively" by Paulo Freire in his *Pedagogy of the Oppressed:* "As the oppressed, fighting to be human, take away the oppressors' power to dominate and suppress, they restore to the oppressors the humanity they had lost in the exercise of oppression," *Pedagogy*, translated by Myra Ramos (New York: A Continuum Book, The Seabury Press, 1970), p. 42.
3. Grace MacInnis, quoted (without reference) by Dorothy Livesay in "The Woman Writer and The Idea of Progress" in *Canadian Forum*, November 1982, p. 35.

4. This is *not* the same as saying that it is a "grass-roots" movement in the sense traditional to socialism. For a more comprehensive treatment of this dynamic of the feminist movement see Nancy Hartsock "Political Change: Two Perspectives on Power" in *Quest*, 1981.
5. For details of this movement of women in Canada towards self-determination and increasing power over their own lives see *Still Ain't Satisfied: Canadian Feminism Today*, Fitzgerald, *et. al.*, 1982.
6. Consider, for example, the very high incidence of wife-battering and incest in the contemporary family, the poverty of the widowed wife, etc.. See also Lucia Valeska's contribution to *Quest* 1981. "If All Else Fails I am Still a Mother," where she demonstrates how formerly "motherhood was the primary and *only* route to social and economic well-being for women," while nowadays the "expendability of mothers and children is built into the economic system that controls us" (p. 78, 79).
7. Hannah Arendt, *On Violence* (New York and London: Harvest/HBJ Books, Harcourt, Brace, Jovanovich, 1969), p. 52.

Selected Bibliography of Feminist Material

Aas, Berit, 1985, "Mobilizing Women for Action" in Aisla Thomson (ed.), *The Decade for Women* (Toronto: Canadian Congress for Learning Opportunities for Women).

Alexander, Judith, 1979, "Women and Unpaid Work: The Economic Consequences" in *Atlantis*, Spring 1979.

Allen, Christine, 1971, "Can a Woman Be Good in the Same Way as a Man?" in *Dialogue*, X, 1971.

Altschul, Susan, & Christine Carron, 1975, "Chronology of Some Legal Landmarks in the History of Canadian Women" in *McGill Law Journal*, Vol. 21, No. 4, 1975, p. 476.

Anand, Anita, 1984, "Rethinking Women and Development" in CUSO Journal, *Women in Development* (a much reprinted article first published in 1980).

Arditti, Rita, 1980, "Feminism and Science" in Rita Arditti, Pat Brennan, & Steve Cavrak (eds.), *Science and Liberation* (Montréal: Black Rose Books).

Armstrong, Pat, & Hugh Armstrong, 1983, "Beyond Numbers: Problems With Quantitative Data" in M. Kinnear & G. Mason (eds.), *Women and Work*, Proceedings of a Conference on Data Requirements, 9-10 Dec. 1982 (Ottawa and Winnipeg: Social Sciences and Humanities Research Council in association with the Institute for Social and Economic Research).

Armstrong, Pat, & Hugh Armstrong, 1984, *The Double Ghetto*, rev. ed. (Toronto: McClelland & Stewart).

Backhouse, Constance B., 1983, "Involuntary Motherhood: Abortion, Birth Control and the Law in Nineteenth Century Canada" in *Windsor Yearbook of Access to Justice*, Vol. 3, 1983, p. 61.

Backhouse, Constance B., 1985, "'To Open the Way for Others of My Sex': Clara Brett Martin's Career as Canada's First Woman Lawyer" in *Canadian Journal of Women and the Law*, Vol. 1, No. 1, 1985, p. 1.

Beauvoir, Simone de, 1953, *The Second Sex* (New York: Alfred A. Knopf).

Belenky, Mary Field, Blythe McVicker Clinchy, Nancy Rule
    Goldberger, & Jill Mattuck Tarule, 1986, *Women's Ways
    of Knowing: The Development of Self, Voice and Mind*
    (New York: Basic Books).
Benston, Margaret, 1977, "The Political Economy of Women's
    Liberation" in N. Glazer & H.Y. Waehrer (eds.), *Women
    in a Man-Made World* (New York: Rand McNally),
    pp. 216-25.
Blaxall, Martha, & Barbara Reagan, 1976 (eds.), *Women and
    the Workplace* (Chicago: University of Chicago Press).
Boston Lesbian Psychologies Collective, 1987, *Lesbian Psy-
    chologies: Explorations and Challenges* (Urbana: Uni-
    versity of Illinois Press).
Bowles, Gloria, & Renate Duelli Klein, 1983 (eds.), *Theories
    of Women's Studies* (London: Routledge & Kegan Paul).
Boyd, Susan B., & Elizabeth Sheehy, 1987, "Canadian Feminist
    Legal Scholarship: Theory and Practice" in *Canadian
    Journal of Women and the Law*, Vol. 2, No. 1, 1987,
    p. 1.
Boyle, Christine, 1985, "Sexual Assault and the Feminist
    Judge" in *Canadian Journal of Women and the Law*,
    Vol. 1, No. 1, 1985, p. 93.
Boyle, Christine, 1987, *Feminist Reform of the Canadian
    Criminal Code* (Ottawa: NAWL).
Boyle, Christine, *et al.* (eds.), 1986, *Charterwatch: Reflections
    on Equality* (Toronto: Carswell).
Bridenthal, Renate, & Claudia Koonz, 1977 (eds.), *Becoming
    Visible: Women in European History* (Boston: Houghton
    Mifflin).
Brossard, Nicole, 1988, *The Aerial Letter*, trans. by Marlene
    Wildeman (Toronto: Women's Press).
Broverman, Inge, & Donald Broverman, 1970, "Sex-Role
    Stereotypes and Clinical Judgements of Mental Health"
    in *Journal of Consulting and Clinical Psychology*, Vol.
    34, No. 1, 1970, pp. 1-7.
Brown, Leslie, & Linda Christiansen-Ruffman, 1986, "Women's
    Community Work: A Third Part of the Puzzle," revision
    of paper presented at the conference on Women and
    the Invisible Economy, Montréal, 21-23 Feb. 1985, and
    forthcoming in Suzanne Peters & Marilyn Porter, *Now
    You See It, Now You Don't: Women and the Invisible
    Economy* (Montréal: McGill-Queen's University Press).
Brown, Rita Mae, 1976, *A Plain Brown Wrapper* (Oakland:
    Diana Press).

Bunch, Charlotte, 1987, *Passionate Politics: Feminist Theory in Action* (New York: St. Martin's Press).

Burris, Barbara, 1973, "The Fourth World Manifesto" in Koedt, *et al.* (eds.), *Radical Feminism* (New York: Quadrangle Books).

Butler, S., 1978, *The Trauma of Incest* (San Francisco: New Glide Publications).

Canadian Psychological Association, 1977, "Report of the Task Force on the Status of Women in Canadian Psychology" in *Canadian Psychological Review*, Vol. 18, 1977, pp. 3-18.

Canadian Research Institute for the Advancement of Women (CRIAW), 1986, *Women's Involvement in Political Life: A Pilot Study*, prepared for UNESCO Division of Human Rights and Peace and published as CRIAW Paper No. 16/17 (Ottawa: CRIAW, 151 Slater St.).

Caplan, Paula, 1982 (ed.), *Psychology Changing for Women* (Montréal: Eden Press).

Carroll, Berenice, 1975 (ed.), *Liberating Women's History: Theoretical and Critical Essays* (Urbana: University of Illinois Press).

Carroll, Berenice, 1980, "Political Science, Part II: International Politics, Comparative Politics and Feminist Radicals" in *Signs: Journal of Women in Culture and Society*, Vol. V, No. 3, Spring 1980, pp. 449-458.

Cassell, Joan, 1977, *A Group Called Women: Sisterhood and Symbolism in the Feminist Movement* (New York: David McKay).

Charnas, Suzy McKee, 1974, *Walk to the End of the World* (New York: Ballantine).

Charnas, Suzy McKee, 1976, *Motherlives* (New York: Ballantine).

Chicago, Judy, 1979, *The Dinner Party: A Symbol of Our Heritage* (New York: Anchor Books, Doubleday).

Chodorow, Nancy, 1978, *The Reproduction of Mothering: Psychoanalysis and the Sociology of Gender* (Berkeley: University of California Press).

Choices for Science: Symposium Proceedings, 1980 (Cambridge, Mass.: Radcliffe College).

Christ, Carol, & Judith Plaskow, 1979, *Womanspirit Rising: A Feminist Reader in Religion* (New York: Harper & Row).

Christiansen-Ruffman, Linda, 1980, "Women as Persons in Atlantic Canadian Communities" in *Resources for Feminist Research*, Special Publication No. 8, pp. 55-57.

Christiansen-Ruffman, Linda, 1982, "Comment on Lawson and Barton's 'Sex Roles in Social Movements: A Case Study of the Tenant Movement in New York City'" in *Signs: Journal of Women in Culture and Society*, Vol. 8, No. 2, Winter 1982, pp. 382-86.

Christiansen-Ruffman, Linda, 1985, "Participation Theory and the Methodological Construction of Invisible Women: Feminism's Call for Appropriate Methodology" in *Journal of Voluntary Action Research*, Vol. 14, Nos. 2&3, 1985, pp. 94-111.

Christiansen-Ruffman, Linda, *et al.*, 1986, *Sex Bias in Research: Current Awareness and Strategies to Eliminate Bias Within Canadian Social Science*, Report of the Task Force on the Elimination of Sexist Bias in Research (Ottawa: Social Science Federation of Canada—SSFC).

Clark, Lorenne, 1976, "Politics and Law: The Theory and Practice of the Ideology of Male Supremacy; or, It Wasn't God Who Made Honky Tonk Angels" in David Weisstub, 1976 (ed.), *Law and Policy*, p. 35.

Clark, Lorenne, and Debra Lewis, 1977, *Rape: The Price of Coercive Sexuality* (Toronto: Canadian Women's Educational Press).

Clark, Lorenne, & Lynda Lange, 1979 (eds.), *The Sexism of Social and Political Theory: Women and Reproduction from Plato to Nietzsche* (Toronto: University of Toronto Press).

Clarke, E., 1966, *My Mother Who Fathered Me* (London: Allen & Unwin).

Cloward, Richard A., & Frances Fox-Piven, 1979, "Hidden Protest: The Channelling of Female Innovation and Resistance" in *Signs: Journal of Women in Culture and Society*, Vol. IV, No. 4, 1979, pp. 651-669.

Cohen, Marjorie, 1987, *Free Trade and the Future of Women's Work: Manufacturing and Service Industries* (Toronto: Garamond).

Cohen, Marjorie, 1988, *Women's Work, Markets and Economic Develpment in Nineteenth Century Ontario* (Toronto: University of Toronto Press).

Cohen, Yolande, 1987 (ed.), *Femmes et Contre-Pouvoirs* (Montréal: Boréal); translated as *Women and Counterpower* (Montréal: Black Rose, 1989).

Cohen, Yolande, Y. Levy, & M. Berdugo Cohen, 1987, *Juifs Marocains à Montréal* (Montréal: VLB).

Cohen, Yolande, 1988, *Les Jeunes, le socialisme et la guerre* (Paris: L'Hermetteu).

Cohn, Anne Foote, 1979 (ed.), *Women in the U.S. Labor Force* (New York: Praeger).

Cole, J., 1979, *Fair Science: Women in the Scientific Community* (New York: Free Press).

Connelly, M. Patricia, 1978, *Last Hired, First Fired: Women and the Canadian Work Force* (Toronto: Women's Press).

Cook, Gail, 1976 (ed.), *Opportunity for Choice* (Ottawa: Statistics Canada).

Courtivron, Isabelle de, & Elaine Marx, 1980 (eds.), *New French Feminisms* (Amherst: University of Massachusetts Press).

Covina, G., & L. Galana, 1975 (eds.), *The Lesbian Reader* (Oakland: Amazon Press).

Daly, Mary, 1973, *Beyond God the Father: Toward a Philosophy of Women's Liberation* (Boston: Beacon Press).

Daly, Mary, 1978, *Gyn / Ecology: The Meta-Ethics of Radical Feminism* (Boston: Beacon Press).

Daly, Mary, 1984, *Pure Lust* (London: Women's Press).

Daniels, Arlene Kaplan, 1975, in M. Millman & R. Kanter (eds.), *Another Voice: Feminist Perspectives on Social Life and Social Science* (New York: Octagon).

Davis, Dona Lee, 1979, "Social Structure, Sex Roles and Female Associations in a Newfoundland Fishing Village," paper presented at the CESCE meeting, Banff, Feb. 1979.

DAWN, Development Alternatives with Women for a New Era, 1985, *Development, Crises and Alternative Visions: Third World Women's Perspectives* (New Delhi: DAWN and Institute of Social Studies Trust).

Delphy, Christine, 1977, *The Main Enemy* (London: Women's Research & Resources Centre Publications).

Dinnerstein, Dorothy, 1976, *The Mermaid and the Minotaur: Sexual Arrangements and Human Malaise* (New York: Harper & Row).

431

Dowsling, J., & A. MacLennan, 1978 (eds.), *The Chemically Dependent Woman* (Toronto: Addiction Research Foundation of Ontario).

Eagley, A., 1978, "Sex Differences in Influenceability" in *Psychological Bulletin*, 85, 1978.

Eberts, Mary, 1979, "The Rights of Women" in R. St. J. Macdonald & John P. Humphrey, 1979 (eds.), *The Practice of Freedom: Canadian Essays on Human Rights and Fundamental Freedoms* (Toronto: Butterworths), p. 225.

Ehrenreich, Barbara, & Deirdre English, 1979, *For Her Own Good: 150 Years of the Experts' Advice to Women* (New York: Anchor Press, Doubleday).

Ehrlich, Carol, 1977, *Socialism, Anarchism and Feminism* (Baltimore: Research Group One Report, No. 26, 1977).

Eichler, Margrit, 1980, *The Double Standard: A Feminist Look at Feminist Social Science* (New York: St. Martin's Press).

Eichler, Margrit, 1983, *Sexism in Research and Its Policy Implications*, CRIAW Paper No. 6 (Ottawa: Canadian Research Institute for the Advancement of Women, 151 Slater St.).

Eichler, Margrit, 1988, *Non-Sexist Research Methods: A Practical Guide* (Boston: Allen and Unwin).

Eichler, Margrit, & Jeanne LaPointe, 1985, *On the Treatment of the Sexes in Research* (Ottawa: Social Sciences and Humanities Research Council).

Eisenstein, Zillah, 1981, *The Radical Future of Liberal Feminism* (New York: Longman).

Ettinger, Elzbieta, 1980, *Comrade and Lover: Rosa Luxemburg's Letters to Leo Jogiches* (Cambridge, Mass.: M.I.T. Press).

Farcia, Sister, 1976, "Forward Up Daughter," *Rasta Voice*, No. 86:16, 1976.

Finn, Geraldine, 1981, "Why Althusser Killed His Wife" in *Canadian Forum*, Sept./Oct. 1981.

Finn, Geraldine, 1982a, "Women and the Ideology of Science" in *Our Generation*, Vol. 15, No. 1, 1982.

Finn, Geraldine, 1982b, "Reason and Violence: More than a False Antithesis—An Instrument of Patriarchal Power" in *Canadian Journal of Political and Social Theory*, Vol. 6, No. 3, Fall 1982.

Firestone, Shulamith, 1970, *The Dialectic of Sex* (New York: Morrow).

Fisher, Elizabeth, 1979, *Woman's Creation: Sexual Evolution and the Shaping of Society* (New York: McGraw-Hill).

Fitzgerald, Maureen, C. Guberman, & M. Wolfe, 1982 (eds.), *Still Ain't Satisfied: Canadian Feminism Today* (Toronto: Women's Press).

Fox, Bonnie, 1980 (ed.), *Hidden in the Household: Women's Domestic Labour Under Capitalism* (Toronto: Canadian Women's Press).

Freize, I., *et al.*, 1978, *Women and Sex Roles* (New York: Norton).

Friedan, Betty, 1963, *The Feminine Mystique* (New York: Dell).

Gearhart, S., 1979, *The Wanderground: Stories of the Hill Women* (Persephone).

Gilligan, Carol, 1977, "In a Different Voice: Women's Conception of Self and of Morality" in *Harvard Educational Review*, 47, 1977, pp. 481-517.

Gilligan, Carol, 1979, "Women's Place in Man's Life Cycle" in *Harvard Educational Review*, 49, 1979, pp. 431-446.

Gilligan, Carol, 1982, *In a Different Voice* (Cambridge: Harvard University Press).

Gornick, Vivian, & Barbara Moran, 1971 (eds.), *Woman in Sexist Society* (New York: Basic Books).

Gould, Carol, & Marx Wartofsky, 1976 (eds.), *Women and Philosophy: Toward a Theory of Liberation* (New York: Capricorn Books, G.P. Putnam's Sons).

Graham, Martin J., 1980, "On Becoming a Male Feminologist" in *Resources for Feminist Research*, Vol. IX, No. 2, July 1980.

Greer, Germaine, 1979, *The Obstacle Race: The Fortunes of Women Painters and Their Work* (London: Secker & Warburg).

Griffin, Susan, 1978, *Woman and Nature* (New York: Harper & Row).

Griffin, Susan, 1981, *Pornography and Silence: Culture's Revenge Against Nature* (New York: Harper & Row).

Grimke, Sarah, & Angelina Grimke, 1848, *American Slavery As It Is* (New York: Arno Press, 1968) (published under the name of Theodore D. Weld).

Grimshaw, Jean, 1986, *Philosophy and Feminist Thinking* (Minneapolis: University of Minnesota Press).

Hamblin, A., & R. Bowen, 1981, "Sexual Abuse of Children" in *Spare Rib* (London, England), No. 106, May 1981.

Hamilton, Roberta, 1978, *The Liberation of Women: A Study of Patriarchy and Capitalism* (London: George Allen and Unwin).

Harding, Sandra, 1986, *The Science Question in Feminism* (Ithaca, N.Y.: Cornell University Press).

Harding, Sandra, 1987 (ed.), *Feminism and Methodology* (Bloomington and Milton Keynes: Indiana University Press and Open University Press).

Harding, Sandra, & Merrill B. Hintikka, 1983, *Discovering Reality: Feminist Perspectives on Epistemology, Metaphysics, Methodology, and the Philosophy of Science* (London and Boston: D. Reidel, Dordrecht).

Hartsock, Nancy, 1983, *Money, Sex and Power: Toward a Feminist Historical Materialism* (New York: Longman).

Hawrylyshyn, Oli, 1978, *Estimating the Value of Household Work in Canada 1971* (Ottawa: Statistics Canada).

Henry, Frances, & P. Wilson, 1975, "The Status of Women in Caribbean Societies" in *Social and Economic Studies*, 24, 1975.

Hite, Shere, 1987, *Women and Love: A Cultural Revolution in Progress* (New York: Knopf).

Hodge, M., 1974, "The Shadow of the Whip" in O. Coombs (ed.), *Is Massa Day Dead?* (New York: Anchor Books, Doubleday).

Hodge, M., 1977, "Young Women and the Development of Stable Family Life in the Caribbean" in *Savacou*, 13, 1977.

Hughes, Patricia, 1979, "Towards the Development of Feminist Theory" in *Atlantis*, 16, Fall 1979.

Ilaloo, Sister, 1981, "Rastawoman as Equal" in *Yard Roots*, I, 1, 1981.

Innis, Mary Quayle, 1966, *The Clear Spirit: Twenty Canadian Women and Their Times* (Toronto: University of Toronto Press).

International Journal of Women's Studies, 1981, Issue on Women and Science, Vol. 4, 1981.

Irigaray, Luce, *Ce Sexe qui n'en n'est pas un* (Paris: Editions Minuit).

ISIS International, 1983, *Women in Development: A Resource Guide for Organization and Action* (Rome: ISIS International).

James, Selma, 1974, "Sex, Race and Working Class Struggle" in *Race Today*, Jan. 1974.

Journal of Education, 1985, Issue on Women's Development and Education.

Kanter, Rosabeth, 1977, *Men and Women of the Corporation* (New York: Basic Books).

Keller, Evelyn Fox, 1979, "The Cognitive Repression in Contemporary Physics" in *American Journal of Physics*, Vol. 47, 1979, pp. 718-721.

Keller, Evelyn Fox, 1980, "Feminist Critique of Science: A Forward or Backward Move?" in *Fundamenta Scientiae*, Vol. 1, 1980.

Keller, Evelyn Fox, 1985, *Reflections on Gender and Science* (New Haven, Conn.: Yale University Press).

Kelly, Joan, 1979, "The Doubled Vision of Feminist Theory: A Postscript to the Women and Power Conference" in *Feminist Studies*, Vol. V, No. 1, Spring 1979, pp. 216-227.

Kelly, Joan, 1984, *Women, History and Theory: The Essays of Joan Kelly* (Chicago and London: University of Chicago Press).

Kishwar, Madhu, & R. Vanita, 1984 (eds.), *In Search of Answers: Indian Women's Voices from Manushi* (London: Zed Books).

Knight, Rolf, 1974, *A Very Ordinary Life* (Vancouver: New Star Press).

Koedt, Anne, *et al.*, 1973, *Radical Feminism* (New York: Quadrangle Books).

Kome, Penny, 1986, *The Taking of Twenty-Eight* (Toronto: Women's Press).

Kramer, Cheris, Barrie Thorne, & Nancy Henley, 1978, "Perspectives on Language and Communication," Review Essay in *Signs: Journal of Women in Culture and Society*, Vol. 3, No. 3, Spring 1978.

Lahey, Kathleen A., 1984, *Feminism, Theory, and Method: Developing Approaches to Legal Theory* (Conference on Feminism and Legal Theory, Osgoode Hall Law School, Toronto).

Lahey, Kathleen A., 1985, "...Until women themselves have told all that they have to tell..." in *Osgoode Hall Law Journal*, Vol. 23, No. 3, 1985, p. 519.

Lahey, Kathleen A. (ed.), 1986, *Women in the Canadian Economy* (Ottawa: CACSW).

Lahey, Kathleen A., 1987a, "Male Technology and 'Lifestyle' Conflicts: The Lesbian Challenge" in *Broadside*.

Lahey, Kathleen A., 1987b, "The Criminal 'Justice' System and Reproductive Technology" in *Resources for Feminist Research*, Vol. 14, No. 4, 1987, p. 27.

Lamoureux, Josée, 1981, "The Women's Struggle and Socialism" in *In Struggle!* pamphlet. Speech for International Women's Day, 1981.

Leacock, Eleanor, 1981, *Myths of Male Dominance* (New York: Monthly Review Press).

LeDoeuff, Michèle, 1977, "Women and Philosophy" in *Radical Philosophy*, 17, Summer 1977.

Lerner, Gerda, 1979, *The Majority Finds Its Past: Placing Women in History* (New York and Oxford: Oxford University Press).

Lerner, Gerda, 1986, *The Creation of Patriarchy* (Oxford: Oxford University Press).

Liddington, Jill, & J. Norris, 1978, No Cause Can Be Won Between Dinner and Tea, Most of Us Who Were Married Had to Work With *One Hand Tied Behind Us: The Rise of the Women's Suffrage Movement* (London: Virago).

Light, Beth, & Alison Prentice, 1980 (eds.), *Pioneer and Gentlewomen of British North America* (Toronto: New Hogtown Press).

Likely, Jan, 1972, "Women and Revolution" in *Women Unite!* Canadian Women's Educational Press, editor & publisher.

Loutfi, Martha, 1980, *Rural Women: Unequal Partners in Development*, United Nations International Labour Organization.

Lowe, Marian, & Ruth Hubbard, 1981 (eds.), *Women's Nature: Rationalizations of Inequality* (New York: Pergamon Press).

Luxton, Meg, 1980, *More Than a Labour of Love: Three Generations of Women's Work in the Home* (Toronto: Women's Press).

Maccoby, Eleanor, & Carolyn Jacklin, 1974, *The Psychology of Sex Differences* (Stanford, Calif.: Stanford University Press).

Mackinnon, C., 1982, "Feminism, Marxism, Method and the State: An Agenda for Theory" in *Signs: Journal of Women in Culture and Society*, Vol. VII, No. 3, Spring 1982.

MacLennan, Anne, 1976 (ed.), *Women: Their Use of Alcohol and Other Legal Drugs* (Toronto: Addiction Research Foundation of Ontario).

Maguire, Patricia, 1987, *Doing Participatory Research: A Feminist Approach* (Amherst, Mass.: University of Massachusetts)

Mathurin, L., 1975, "The Rebel Woman in the British West Indies During Slavery" (Kingston: Institute of Jamaica).

Mathurin, L., 1977, "Reluctant Matriarchs" in *Savacou*, 13, 1977.

Matthaei, Julie, 1982, *An Economic History of Women in America: Women's Work, the Sexual Division of Labour, and the Development of Capitalism* (New York: Schocken Books; Brighton: Harvester Press).

Mayes, Sharon S., 1979, "Women in Positions of Authority: A Case Study of Changing Sex Roles" in *Signs: Journal of Women in Culture and Society*, Vol. IV, No. 3, Spring 1979, pp. 556-568.

McCaffrey, K., "Images of Women in the Literature of Selected Developing Countries," Pacific Consultants Contract afr-C-1197, Work Order 36.

McGlen, Nancy E., & Karen O'Connor, 1983, *Women's Rights: The Struggle for Equality in the Nineteenth and Twentieth Centuries* (New York: Praeger Special Studies).

Merchant, C., 1980, *Death of Nature: Women, Ecology and the Scientific Revolution* (San Francisco: Harper & Row).

Miles, Angela R., 1978, "Feminism and Class Analysis" in *Atlantis*, 111, 2, Spring 1978.

Miles, Angela R., 1979, "The Politics of Feminist Radicalism: A Study of Integrative Feminism," Ph. D. Thesis, University of Toronto.

Miles, Angela, R., 1981, "The Integrative Feminine Principle in North American Feminism: Value Basis of a New Feminism" in *Women's Studies International Quarterly*, IV, 4, 1981.

Miles, Angela, 1984, "Integrative Feminism" in *Fireweed*, Summer/Fall 1984.

Miles, Angela, 1985, *Feminist Radicalism in the 1980's* (Montréal: Culture Texts).

Miles, Angela, & Mary O'Brien, 1979 (eds.), "Political Theory: A Feminist Perspective" in *Resources for Feminist Research*, Vol. 8, No. 1, March 1979, pp. 14-63.

Miller, Barbara, 1982, "Women in the Public Domain in Developing Countries" in *International Supplement to the Women's Studies Quarterly*, Vol. 1, Jan. 1982, pp. 6-9.

Miller, Jean Baker, 1976, *Toward a New Psychology of Women* (Boston: Beacon Press).

Millman, M., & R. Kanter, 1975 (eds.), *Another Voice: Feminist Perspectives on Social Life and Social Science* (New York: Octagon).

Mitchell, Juliet, 1966, "Women: The Longest Revolution" in *New Left Review*, 40, Nov./Dec. 1966, pp. 11-37.

Mitchell, Juliet, 1967, "Reply to Discussion on Juliet Mitchell's *Women: The Longest Revolution*" in *New Left Review*, 41, 1967, pp. 81-83.

Morgan, Robin, 1978, *Going Too Far* (New York: Vantage Books).

Murray, Hilda Chaulk, 1979, *More Than Fifty Percent: Woman's Life in a Newfoundland Outport 1900-1950* (St. John's: Breakwater Books).

Novotny, Helga, 1980, "Where the Power is, Women are Not" in *Feminist Review*, 1980.

Oakley, Anne, 1974a, *The Sociology of Housework* (New York: Pantheon).

Oakley, Anne, 1974b, *Woman's Work* (New York: Pantheon).

O'Brien, Mary, 1976, "The Dialectics of Reproduction" in J. King-Farlow & W. Shea (eds.), *Contemporary Issues in Political Philosophy* (New York: Watson).

O'Brien, Mary, 1981, *The Politics of Reproduction* (London: Routledge & Kegan Paul).

O'Brien, Mary, 1984, "Hegemony and Superstructure: A Feminist Critique of Neo-Marxism" in Jill McCalla

Vickers, *Taking Sex into Account: The Policy Consequences of Sexist Research* (Ottawa: Carleton University Press).

Okin, Susan Moller, 1979, *Women in Western Political Thought* (Princeton, N.J.: Princeton University Press).

Ortner, Sherry, 1974, "Is Female to Male as Nature is to Culture?" in M. Rosaldo & L. Lamphere (eds.), *Woman, Culture and Society* (Stanford, Calif.: Stanford University Press).

Parlee, Mary Brown, 1979, "Review Essay / Psychology" in *Signs: Journal of Women in Culture and Society*, Autumn 1979.

Peebles, Dana, 1982, *Pre-Study on the Impact of NGO Projects on Women*, Canadian Council for International Cooperation (CCIC).

Pierson, Ruth Roach, 1986, *They're Still Women After All: The Second World War and Canadian Womanhood* (London: Croom Helm).

Pierson, Ruth Roach, 1987 (ed.), *Women and Peace: Theoretical, Historical and Practical Perspectives* (London: Croom Helm).

Pierson, Ruth Roach, & Beth Light, forthcoming (eds.), *No Easy Road: Women in Canada 1920s-1960s*, third volume in the Documentary Series in Canadian Women's History (Toronto: New Hogtown Press).

Porter, Marilyn, 1983, "Women and Old Boats: The Sexual Divison of Labour in a Newfoundland Outport" in Eva Garmarnikow, *et al.* (eds.), *The Public and Private* (London: Heineman).

Porter, Marilyn, 1985, "The Tangly Bunch: Outport Women of the Avalon Peninsula" in *Newfoundland Studies*, Vol. 1, No. 1, 1985.

Prentice, Alison, *et al.*, 1988, *Canadian Women: A History* (Toronto: Harcourt Brace Jovanovich)

Quest, 1981, *Building Feminist Theory*, Essays from Quest, a Feminist Quarterly Introduced by Charlotte Bunch, Foreword by Gloria Steinem (New York and London: Longman).

Rasmussen, Linda, *et al.*, 1976 (eds.), *A Harvest Yet to Reap* (Toronto: Women's Educational Press).

Reed, Evelyn, 1975, *Woman's Evolution* (New York and London: Pathfinder Press).

Resources for Feminist Research, 1986, Issue on Women Of/ Under/In/And the Natural Sciences, Vol. 15, No. 3, 1986.

Rich, Adrienne, 1981, "The Taste and Smell of Life" in *Broadside*, Vol. 2, No. 8, June 1981.

Richards, Janet, 1980, *The Sceptical Feminist: A Philosophical Enquiry* (London: Routledge & Kegan Paul).

Riessman, Catherine, 1987, "When Gender is Not Enough: Women Interviewing Women" in *Gender and Society*, Vol. 1, No. 1, June 1987, pp. 172-207.

Rifkin, Janet, 1980, "Toward a Theory of Law and Patriarchy" in *Harvard Women's Law Journal*, Vol. 3, 1980, p. 83.

Roberts, G., & S. Sinclair, 1978, *Women in Jamaica: Patterns of Reproduction and Family* (Millwood, N.Y.: KTO Press).

Roberts, Helen, 1981 (ed.), *Doing Feminist Research* (London: Routledge & Kegan Paul).

Roe, A., 1956, *The Psychology of Occupations* (New York: Wiley).

Rogers, Barbara, 1980, *The Domestication of Women: Discrimination in Developing Societies* (London and New York: Tavistock).

Rohrlich, Ruby, 1987, "Law and Disorder: Impact on Women of the Early Laws in Mesopotamia and Mesoamerica," paper presented at the Third International Interdisciplinary Congress on Women, Dublin, 1987.

Ross, Kathleen Gallagher, 1978 (ed.), *Good Day Care: Fighting For It, Getting It, Keeping It* (Toronto: Women's Press).

Rossi, Alice (ed.), 1972, *Feminist Papers* (New York: Bantam).

Rowbotham, Sheila, *et al.*, 1981, *Beyond the Fragments: Feminism and the Making of Socialism* (London: Alyson Pub.).

Rubin, Lillian, 1979, *Women of a Certain Age: The Midlife Search for Self* (New York: Harper & Row).

Ruether, Rosemary, 1975, *New Woman—New Earth: Sexist Ideologies and Human Liberation* (Seabury Press).

Ryan, Mary, 1979, "The Power of Women's Networks" in *Feminist Studies*, Summer 1979.

Sanday, Peggy Reeves, 1981, *Female Power and Male Dominance: On the Origins of Sexual Inequality* (Cambridge: Cambridge University Press).

Savané, Marie-Angélique, 1984, "Feminizing Development" in *Development*, Journal of the Society for International Development, Vol. 14, 1984.

Scott, Hilda, 1984, *Working Your Way to the Bottom: The Feminization of Poverty* (London: Pandora Press).

Seidenberg, Faith A., 1985, "The Bifurcated Woman: Problems of Women Lawyers in Courtrooms" in *Canadian Journal of Women and the Law*, Vol. 1, No. 1, 1985, p. 219.

Sen, Gita, & C. Grown, 1985, *Development, Crisis, and Alternative Third World Women's Perspectives*, DAWN.

Sherman, J., & E. Beck, 1979 (eds.), *The Prism of Sex* (Madison: University of Wisconsin Press).

Shipley, Carol, 1985, *Evaluation for Planning for Women in Development* (Botswana: CUSO Office of Planning and Evaluation).

Shirley, M., & R. Vigier, 1979 (eds.), *Proceedings: In Search of the Feminist Perspective* (Toronto: Resources for Feminist Research, Special Publication 5, Spring 1979).

Signs, 1985, "On *In a Different Voice*: An Interdisciplinary Forum," *Signs*, Vol. 11, No. 2, 1985, pp. 304-33.

Silman, Janet, 1987 (ed.), *Enough is Enough: Aboriginal Women Speak Out* (Toronto: Women's Press).

Smith, Dorothy, 1978, "A Particular Eclipsing: Women's Exclusion from Man's Culture" in *Women's Studies International Quarterly*, Vol. 1, 1978, pp. 281-96.

Smith, Dorothy, 1979, "A Sociology for Women" in J. Sherman & E. Beck (eds.), *The Prism of Sex* (Madison: University of Wisconsin Press).

Smith, Dorothy, 1987, *The Everyday World as Problematic: A Feminist Sociology* (Toronto: University of Toronto Press).

Smith, Dorothy, & S. Davids, 1975 (eds.), *Women Look at Psychiatry* (Vancouver: Press Gang).

Spender, Dale, 1981, *Man Made Language* (London: Routledge & Kegan Paul).

Spender, Dale, 1981, *Men's Studies Modified: The Impact of Feminism on the Academic Disciplines* (Oxford: Pergamon Press).

Stacey, Margaret, & Marion Price, 1981, *Women, Power and Politics* (London: Tavistock).

Stanley, Liz, & Sue Wise, 1983, *Breaking Out: Feminist Consciousness and Feminist Research* (London: Routledge & Kegan Paul).

441

Stanton, Elizabeth C., Susan B. Anthony, & Matilda J. Gage, 1881, *History of Woman Suffrage* (Rochester, N.Y.: Charles Mann), reprinted in Alice Rossi 1972 (ed.).

Stark-Adamec, Connie, 1980, (ed.), *Sex Roles: Origins, Influences and Implications for Women* (Montréal: Eden Press).

Stark-Adamec, Connie, & Meredith Kimball, 1984, "Science Free of Sexism: A Psychologist's Guide to the Conduct of Nonsexist Research" in *Canadian Psychology*, Vol. 25, 1984.

Stewart, A., & D. Winter, 1977, "The Nature and Cause of Female Suppression" in *Signs: Journal of Women in Culture and Society*, Vol. II, No. 3, Spring 1977.

Strong-Boag, Veronica, 1972 (ed.), *In Times Like These* (Toronto: University of Toronto Press).

Swan, Carole, 1982, "Women in the Canadian Labour Force: The Present Reality" in Naomi Hersom & Dorothy Smith, 1982 (eds.), *Women and the Canadian Labour Force* (Ottawa: SSHRC), p. 29.

Taylor, Debbie, 1985 (ed.), *Women: A World Report* (London: New Internationalist/Methuen).

Tilly, Louise A., & Joan W. Scott, 1978, *Women, Work and Family* (New York: Holt, Rinehart & Winston).

Trofimenkoff, Susan Mann, & Alison Prentice, 1977 (eds.), *The Neglected Majority: Essays in Canadian Women's History* (Toronto: McClelland & Stewart).

Vetterling-Braggin, Mary, Frederick Elliston, & Jane English, 1978 (eds.), *Feminism and Philosophy* (Totowa, N.J.: Littlefield, Adams & Co.).

Vicinus, M., 1972 (ed.), *Suffer and Be Still: Women in the Victorian Age* (Bloomington: University of Indiana Press).

Vickers, Jill McCalla, 1984, *Taking Sex into Account: The Policy Consequences of Sexist Research* (Ottawa: Carleton University Press).

Vickers, Jill, & Margrit Eichler, 1987, "A Dialogue on the Goal of Non-Sexist Research" in *Resources for Feminist Research*, Vol. 16, No. 4, Dec. 1987.

Wallace, Michele, 1979, *Black Macho and the Myth of Superwoman* (New York: Dial Press).

Waters, M., 1970 (ed.), *Rosa Luxemburg Speaks* (New York: Pathfinder Press).

442

Webb, Beatrice, 1971, *My Apprenticeship* (Harmondsworth: Penguin).

Willick, Liz, 1986, A Report on the Post Nairobi Conference, Toronto, Oct. 1986.

Wollstonecraft, Mary, 1790, *A Vindication of the Rights of Women*, reprinted in Alice Rossi 1972 (ed.).

Women in Development Working Group, 1986, "Official Development Assistance and Its Impact on Women," Women in Development Working Group (Kitchener-Waterloo, Ontario).

Women Unite!, 1972, edited and published by Canadian Women's Educational Press.

Women's Studies International Quarterly, 1981, Issue on Women and Science, Vol. 3, 1981.

The Coming of World War III

by Dimitrios Roussopoulos

It will never happen. It can happen. It will happen.
Politicians and military and scientific personnel
working for various nation-states remain firmly
convinced that their nuclear weapons policies are
both logical and righteous while also believing that
there will never be a nuclear war.

A large group of scientists, journalists and academics believe that the possibilities of a nuclear 'accident', a computer error, for example, in which missi-
les are launched by mistake, or the deliberate use of
these weapons, can lead to a nuclear holocaust.

After working with the disamament movement for
more than 20 years, and having just completed a thorough investigation of the intensified arms race and
the emergence of the new disamament movements in
Europe and North America, Dimitrios Roussopoulos
believes a third world war will happen, because not
enough is being done to prevent it. This conclusion
has a number of radical implications for activists in
the peace movement, sympathisers to its aims and
those interested in social change.

Dimitrios Roussopoulos founded the Combined
Universities Campaign for Nuclear Disamament in
1959 and the journal SANITY, monthly newspaper of
the Canadian CND, as well as OUR GENERATION
AGAINST NUCLEAR WAR, a peace research journal. He was also a founding member of the International Confederation for Disarmament. THE
COMING OF WORLD WAR III is the fruit of eight
months of research and travel covering 10 countries.

Paperback ISBN: 0-920057-02-0 $12.95
Hardcover ISBN: 0-920057-03-9 $22.95

WOMEN AND COUNTER-POWER

edited by Yolande Cohen

Essays by scholars and activists compare the experiences of women in various countries: the significance of women's work in voluntary associations (Italy and Canada), in writing (France), under military dictatorship (Argentina), during a war of national liberation (Algeria), in Solidarnosc (Poland). This is a fresh vision of the emancipation of women in sweeping international scope.

Contributors are: Renata Siemienska, Marta Petrucewicz, Judith Astelarra, Gloria Bonder, Marie-Blanche Tahon, Michela De Giorgio, Caroline Andrew, Denise Boucher, Maria Belo, Micheline De Sève, Somer Brodribb, Margaret Gillett, Elisabeth Badinter, and Naomi Black.

Yolande Cohen teaches history at the Université du Québec à Montréal.

This book contributes to the debate on the many aspects of women's participation.
Le Devoir

Each author presents not only the historical importance of the women's struggle, but also its contradictions and ambivalence.
Espace, Population et Société

Realistic and systematic...should be widely read.
Nos Livres

244 pages
Paperback ISBN: 0-921689-10-1 $19.95
Hardcover ISBN: 0-921689-11-X $39.95
Women/Politics/History

WORK AND MADNESS
The Rise of Community Psychiatry

by Diana Ralph

In this meticulously researched and immensely readable book, Diana Ralph takes on the community mental health systems. In a penetrating analysis of the expansion and innovation of mental health practices since the second world war, she argues that these changes have not been simply quantitative but that a qualitative shift has taken place in the definition and treatment of so-called mental health disorders.

These changes cannot be explained by available social theories whether liberal, Marxist or the radical anti-psychiatry approaches. Ralph proposes an alternative "labour theory" which situates the ideological origins of contemporary psychiatric practices within the tradition of industrial psychology and the needs of industrial management for control and regulation of the work force.

Dr. Ralph teaches social work at the University of Regina. She has been involved in a range of progressive issues including trade union and unemployment issues, occupational and environmental health programmes, native people's rights, and women's issues. She has also worked in a large mental health hospital and at counselling and rehabilitation centres.

Paperback ISBN: 0-919619-05-3 $12.95
Hardcover ISBN: 0-919619-07-x $22.95

WOMEN & REVOLUTION

edited by Lydia Sargent

Women and Revolution deals with contemporary
political theory and practice. It is a debate concerning the
importance of patriarchy and sexism in industrialized
societies — are sexual differences and kin relations as
critical to social outcome as economic relations? What is
the dynamic between class and sex? Is one or the other
dominant? How do they interact? What are the implications for efforts at social change?

The principle essay to which all others respond —
either criticizing it, extending, or attempting to improve
it — is "The Unhappy Marriage of Marxism and Feminism" by Heidi Hartmann. Hartmann argues that class
and patriarchy are equally important and that neither a
narrow feminism nor an economistic Marxism will
suffice to help us understand or change modern society —
instead we need a theory that can integrate the two
analyses.

Table of Contents include: Beyond the Unhappy
Marriage: a critique of the Dual Systems Theory by Iris
Young; Socialism, Feminism, and Gay / Lesbian Liberation by Christine Riddiough; The Incompatible Meange
a Trois by Gloria Joseph; The Unhappy Marriage, can it
be saved? by Carol Erlich; The First Division of Labour
by Sandra Harding; Capitalism is an advanced stage of
Patriarchy but Marxism is not Feminism by Azizah al-
Hibri; Trial Separation or Something else? by Lise
Vogel; Cultural Marxism: Nonsynchrony and feminist
practice by Emily Hicks; From Private to Public Patriarchy by Carol Brown; The Marriage of Capitalist and
Patriarchal Ideologies by Katie Stewart; Reform and / or
Revolution — Towards a Unified Women's Movement
by Zillah Eisenstein.

Paperback ISBN: 0-919619-19-8 $ 9.95
Hardcover ISBN: 0-919619-20-1 $19.95
Contains: Canadian Shared Cataloguing in Publication Data

BLACK ROSE BOOKS
has published the following books of related interests

Peter Kropotkin, Memoirs of a Revolutionist, introduction by George Woodcock
Peter Kropotkin, Mutual Aid, introduction by George Woodcock
Peter Kropotkin, The Great French Revolution, introduction by George Woodcock
Peter Kropotkin, The Conquest of Bread, introduction by George Woodcock
  other books by Peter Kropotkin are forthcoming in this series
Marie Fleming, The Geography of Freedom: The Odyssey of Elisée Reclus, introduction by George Woodcock
William R. McKercher, Freedom and Authority
Noam Chomsky, Language and Politics, edited by C.P. Otero
Noam Chomsky, Radical Priorities, edited by C.P. Otero
George Woodcock, Pierre-Joseph Proudhon, a biography
Murray Bookchin, Remaking Society
Murray Bookchin, Toward an Ecological Society
Murray Bookchin, Post-Scarcity Anarchism
Murray Bookchin, The Limits of the City
Murray Bookchin, The Modern Crisis
Edith Thomas, Louise Michel, a biography
Walter Johnson, Trade Unions and the State
John Clark, The Anarchist Moment: Reflections on Culture, Nature and Power
Sam Dolgoff, Bakunin on Anarchism
Sam Dolgoff, The Anarchist Collectives in Spain, 1936-39
Sam Dolgoff, The Cuban Revolution: A critical perspective
Thom Holterman, Law and Anarchism
Etienne de la Boétie, The Politics of Obedience
Stephen Schecter, The Politics of Urban Liberation
Abel Paz, Durruti, the people armed
Juan Gomez Casas, Anarchist Organisation, the history of the F.A.I.
Voline, The Unknown Revolution
Dimitrios Roussopoulos, The Anarchist Papers
Dimitrios Roussopoulos, The Anarchist Papers 2

send for a complete catalogue of books
mailed out free
BLACK ROSE BOOKS
3981 boul. St-Laurent, #444
Montréal H2W 1Y5, Québec, Canada

Printed by
the workers of
Les Éditions Marquis, Montmagny, Québec
for
BLACK ROSE BOOKS